extraordinary uses for ordinary things

extraordinary uses for ordinary things

{ FEATURING **Vinegar**, Baking Soda, **Salt**, Toothpaste, **String**, Plastic Cups, **Mayonnaise**, Nail Polish, **Tape**, and More Than 200 Other Common Household Items }

2,317 WAYS TO SAVE MONEY AND TIME

Reader's Digest

The Reader's Digest Association, Inc.
Pleasantville, New York | Montreal

Project Staff

EDITOR * Don Earnest

DESIGNERS * Richard Kershner
and Michele Laseau

CONTRIBUTING COPY EDITOR *
Jeanette Gingold

CONTRIBUTING INDEXER * Nan Badgett

HUMOR ILLUSTRATION * © Chuck Rekow

HOW-TO ILLUSTRATION * © Bryon Thompson

Reader's Digest Home & Health Publishing

EDITOR IN CHIEF AND PUBLISHING
DIRECTOR * Neil Wertheimer

MANAGING EDITOR * Suzanne G. Beason

ART DIRECTOR * Michele Laseau

PRODUCTION TECHNOLOGY MANAGER *
Douglas A. Croll

MANUFACTURING MANAGER *
John L. Cassidy

MARKETING DIRECTOR * Dawn Nelson

VICE PRESIDENT AND GENERAL MANAGER *
Keira Krausz

Reader's Digest Association, Inc.

PRESIDENT, NORTH AMERICA GLOBAL
EDITOR-IN-CHIEF * Eric W. Schrier

Text prepared especially for Reader's Digest by

NAILHAUS PUBLICATIONS, INC.

PUBLISHING DIRECTOR David Schiff

WRITERS Marilyn Bader, Serena Harding,
Beth Kalet, Kathryn Kasturas,
Michael Kaufman,
Steven Schwartz, Anita Seline,
Angelique B. Sharps, Delilah
Smittle, and Amy Ziffer

First printing in paperback 2007

Copyright ©2005 by The Reader's Digest Association, Inc.

Copyright ©2005 by The Reader's Digest Association (Canada) Ltd.

Copyright ©2005 by The Reader's Digest Association Far East Ltd.

Philippine Copyright ©2005 by The Reader's Digest Association Far
East Ltd.

Library of Congress Cataloging-in-Publication Data
Extraordinary uses for ordinary things / Reader's Digest.-- 1st ed.
   p. cm.
 Includes index.
 ISBN 0-7621-0705-7 (hardcover)
 ISBN 10: 0-7621-0649-2 (paperback)
 ISBN 13: 978-0-7621-0649-3 (paperback)
 1. Home economics. I. Reader's Digest Association.
 TX145.E95 2004
 640--dc22

                              2004020058

We are committed to both the quality of our products and the
service we provide to our customers. We value your comments, so
please feel free to contact us.

The Reader's Digest Association, Inc.
Editor-in-Chief, Home & Health Books
Reader's Digest Road
Pleasantville, NY 10570-7000

Visit our website at **rd.com**

Printed in China

3 5 7 9 10 8 6 4 (hardcover)

9 10 8 (paperback)

Note to Readers
The information in this book has been carefully researched, and all
efforts have been made to ensure accuracy and safety. Neither Nailhaus
Publications, Inc. nor Reader's Digest Association, Inc. assumes any
responsibility for any injuries suffered or damages or losses incurred as
a result of following the instructions in this book. Before taking any
action based on information in this book, study the information carefully and make sure that you understand it fully. Observe all warnings
and Take Care notices. Test any new or unusual repair or cleaning
method before applying it broadly, or on a highly visible area or valuable item. The mention of any brand or product in this book does not
imply an endorsement. All prices and product names mentioned are
subject to change and should be considered general examples rather
than specific recommendations.

{ Yes, Extraordinary }

Welcome to *Extraordinary Uses for Ordinary Things!* Inside you'll find
thousands of ingenious, money-saving tips just like these. Jump in,
raid your pantry, and start saving money today!

CLEAN YOUR DISHWASHER WITH KOOL-AID

Don't buy special powder to get rid of dishwasher iron deposits. Just dump in a packet of
unsweetened Kool-Aid. It's a much cheaper way to make the inside of your dishwasher sparkle.

MAKE FLUFFY PANCAKES WITH CLUB SODA

Substitute club soda for the liquid called for in your favorite pancake or waffle recipe.
You'll be amazed at how light and fluffy the breakfast treats will be.

REMOVE LIPSTICK STAINS WITH HAIR SPRAY

Got lipstick on your shirt? Apply hair spray and let it sit for a few minutes.
When you wipe the spray off, the stain will come off with it.

HAVE A FACIAL WITH CAT LITTER

Make a deep-cleaning mud mask for your face with a couple of handfuls of cat litter.
The clay in the litter detoxifies your skin by absorbing dirt and oil from the pores.

MELT SIDEWALK ICE WITH BAKING SODA

For an effective way to melt ice on steps and walkways, sprinkle them with generous amounts of
baking soda mixed with sand. It won't stain or damage concrete surfaces.

GIVE CUT FLOWERS A LONGER LIFE WITH SODA POP

Pour about a quarter cup of soda pop into the water in that vase of flowers
and the sugar in the drink will make the blossoms last longer.

TABLE OF CONTENTS

Most Useful Items
FOR JUST ABOUT ANYTHING

YOUR COMPLETE A-Z Guide

✳ Denotes a SUPER ITEM: A household item with an amazingly large number of uses.

INDEX 388

DISCOVER WHAT'S HIDING IN
{ Your Cupboard }

Once upon a time, in the days before computers, cable television, drive-through coffee bars, and carpet-sweeping robots, washing windows was a simple affair. Our parents poured a little vinegar or ammonia in a pail of water, grabbed a cloth, and in no time had a clear view of the outside world through gleaming glass. Then they would use the same combination to banish grime and grit from countertops, walls, shelves, fixtures, floors, and a good bit else of the house.

Some things, like window washing, shouldn't ever get more complicated. But somehow, they did. Today, store shelves are laden with a dazzling array of cleaning products, each with a unique use, a special formula, and a multimillion-dollar advertising campaign. Window cleaners alone take up shelves and shelves of space. The bottles are filled with colorful liquids and have labels touting their orange power, berry bouquet, or lemon or apple herbal scent. Ironically, many boast the added power of vinegar or ammonia as their "secret" ingredient.

This is the way of the world today. Every problem, every mess, every hobby, every daily task seems to require special tools, unique products, and extensive know-how. Why use a knife to chop garlic when there are 48 varieties of garlic presses available? Why use a rag for cleaning when you have specialized sponges, wipes, Swiffers, magnetically charged dusters, and HEPA-filter vacuums?

Which brings us to the point of this book: Why *not* just use a solution of vinegar or ammonia like our grandparents did to clean the windows? It works just as well as those fancy products—if not better. And it costs only about a quarter as much, sometimes less.

204 Everyday Items with Over 2,300 Uses

Making do with what you've already got. It's an honorable, smart, money-saving approach to life. And in fact, it can be downright fun. Sure you can buy a fancy lint brush to remove cat hairs from pants, but it's pretty amazing how a penny's worth of tape does the job even better. Yes, you can use strong kitchen chemicals to clean the inside of a vase that held its flower water a bit too long. But isn't it more entertaining—and easier—to use a couple of Alka-Seltzer tablets instead to fizz away the mess?

Welcome to *Extraordinary Uses for Ordinary Things*. On the following pages, we'll show you more than 2,300 ingenious ways to use 204 ordinary household products to restore, replace, repair, or revive practically everything in and around your home or to pamper yourself or entertain your kids. You'll save time and money—and you'll save shelf space because you won't need all those different kinds of specialized commercial preparations. You'll even save on gasoline, because you won't need to speed off to the mall every time you run out of a staple such as air freshener, shampoo, oven cleaner, or wrapping paper.

The household items featured in this book are not costly commercial concoctions. Rather, they are everyday items that you're likely to find in your home—in your kitchen, medicine cabinet, desk, garage, and even your wastebasket. And you'll be amazed by how much you can actually accomplish using just a few of the most versatile of these items, such as baking soda, duct tape, pantyhose, salt, vinegar, and WD-40. In fact, there's a popular maxim among handymen that whittles the list to a pair of basic necessities: "To get through life," the saying goes, "you only need two tools: WD-40 and duct tape. If it doesn't move, but should, reach for the WD-40. If it moves, but shouldn't, grab the duct tape."

Less Toxic and More Earth-Friendly Items

In addition to saving you time and money, there are other, less tangible advantages to using these everyday household products. For one thing, many of the items are safer to use and considerably more environmentally friendly than their off-the-shelf counterparts. Consider, for example, using vinegar and baking soda to clear a clogged bathroom or kitchen drain (page 64). It's usually just as effective as a commercial drain cleaner. The only difference is that the baking-soda-and-vinegar combination is far less caustic on your plumbing. Plus, you don't have to worry about getting it on your skin or in your eyes.

The hints in this book will also help you reduce household waste by giving you hundreds of delightful and surprising suggestions for reusing many of the items that you would otherwise toss in the trash or recycling bin. To name a few, these include lemon rinds and banana peels, used tea bags and coffee grinds, orphaned socks and worn-out pantyhose, plastic bags, empty bottles and jugs, cans, and newspapers.

At the end of the day, you'll experience the distinct pleasure that can only come from learning creative, new ways to use those familiar objects around your house that you always thought you knew so well. Even if you'll never use Alka-Seltzer tablets to lure fish onto your line, or need to plug a hole in your car radiator with black pepper, isn't it great to know you can?

Folk Wisdom for the 21st Century

As we noted earlier, much of the advice you'll find in *Extraordinary Uses for Ordinary Things* is not really new—it's just new to us. After all, "Waste not, want not" isn't merely a quaint adage from a bygone era; it actually defined a way of life for generations. In the days before mass manufacturing and mass marketing transformed us into a throwaway society, most folks knew perfectly well that salt and baking soda (or bicarbonate of soda, as it was commonly referred to in those times) had dozens upon dozens of uses.

Now, as landfills swell, and we realize that the earth's resources aren't really endless, there are signs of a shift back to thrift, so to speak. From recycling programs to energy-efficient appliances to hybrid cars, we're constantly looking for new ways to apply the old, commonsense values of our forebears. Even the International Space Station is an example of thrifty technologies at work today. When the station is completed, nearly every waste product and used item onboard the craft will be recycled for another purpose.

How We Put This Book Together

Of course, our number one priority was to provide you with the most reliable information available. To meet that goal, we conducted countless interviews with experts on everything from acne cures to yard care and scrutinized stacks of research materials. We also performed numerous hands-on tests in our own kitchens, living rooms, bathrooms, and other areas around our homes.

The result, we believe, is the most comprehensive and dependable guide to alternative uses for household products you can find. Like a great stew, we've combined some time-honored, traditional tips (such as using apple cider vinegar to kill weeds in your garden) with new tips given to us by various reliable sources (like recycling used fabric softener sheets to clean PC and TV screens), and a few tips that we came up with on our own (such as using bathtub appliqués to steady a legless PC case).

As in any comprehensive compilation such as this, the practical wisdom contained in this book is as much art as it is science. That is to say, although we employed trial-and-error methods wherever possible to provide you with specific amounts and clear directions for using household products and objects to obtain the desired results, we can't guarantee that these solutions will work in all situations. In other words, your mileage may vary.

Moreover, while we're confident that every one of the 204 products used for all the tips included here is generally safe and effective when used as directed, please pay close attention to our "Take Care" warnings about using, storing, and especially combining certain products, particularly *bleach* and *ammonia*. Under no conditions should you ever mix these two chemicals, or use them in poorly ventilated areas.

What's on the Following Pages

The main part of this book is arranged like an encyclopedia, with the 204 product categories organized in A-Z fashion (running from Adhesive Tape to Zucchini), to provide instant access to information as well as entertaining reading. But before that, in the first part of this book, you'll find a guide to the items that are most useful for certain areas, such as the garden or for cooking.

Scattered throughout, you'll also find hundreds of fascinating asides and anecdotes. Some highlight specific warnings and safety precautions, or offer advice about buying or using certain items. But many are just plain fun—providing quirky historical information about the invention or origins of products. Haven't you always wondered who invented the Band-Aid or how Scotch tape got its name? We've also included dozens of engaging and enlightening activities and simple science experiments you can do with your children or grandchildren (and not a single one requires a visit to the local toy store).

Whether you delight in discovering new ways to use commonplace household items, or if you simply hate to throw things away, we're sure you'll find the ideas in this book entertaining and enlightening. So, pull up a comfortable chair, settle back, and get ready to be dazzled by the incredible number of everyday problems that you'll soon be able to solve with ease. We're confident this is one book you'll return to over and over again for helpful hints, trustworthy advice, and even some good, old-fashioned inspiration.

—*The Editors*

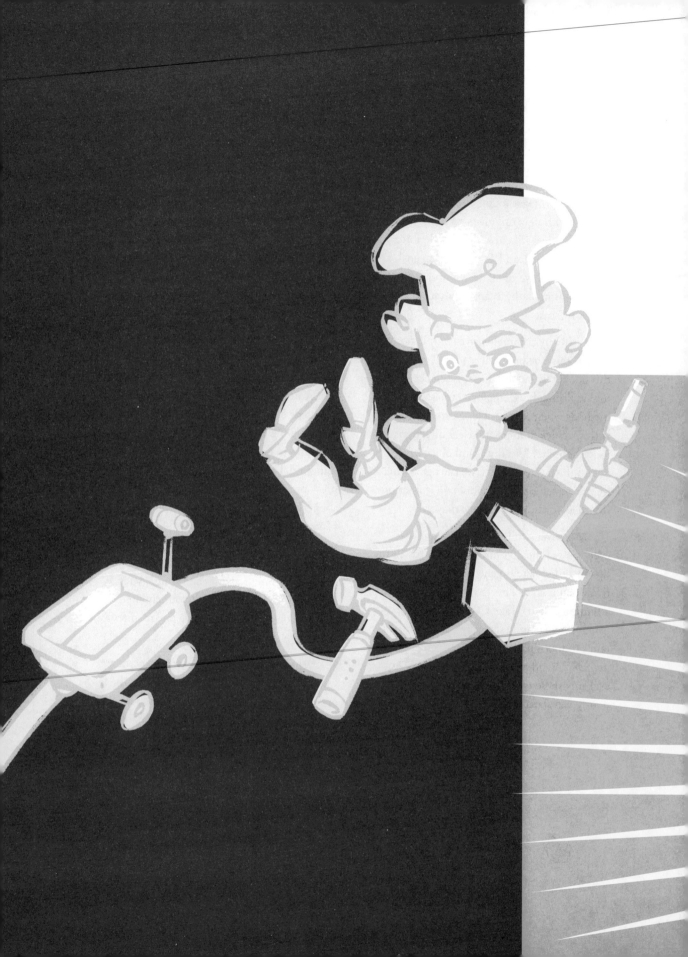

MOST { Useful Items* } FOR JUST ABOUT ANYTHING

* If you have a special interest, such as cooking or health and beauty, you'll soon discover that certain household items are especially useful. There are, for example, close to a dozen uses for plastic bottles in the garden. On these pages, you'll find these helpful items listed for most everyday areas of interest.

TOP

10 Most Useful Items for around the

house

pad a package with a disposable diaper …

p. 152

Carpet scraps

{ PAGE 115 }

Make an exercise mat, car mat, or knee pad. • Muffle appliance noise. • Protect floor under plants. • Cushion kitchen shelves. • Give your car traction. • Protect tools.

Compact discs

{PAGE 138}

Use as holiday ornaments, driveway reflectors, or a circle template. • Catch candle drips. • Make an artistic bowl, decorative sun catcher, or clock.

Duct tape

{PAGE 153}

Remove lint. • Repair toilet seats, screens, vacuum hoses, and frames. • Cover a book, pocket folder, or present. • Make a bandage or bumper sticker. • Catch flies. • Replace a grommet. • Reinforce a book binding. • Hem pants. • Hang Christmas lights. • Make Halloween costumes.

Fabric softener sheets

{PAGE 167}

Freshen air and deodorize cars, dogs, gym bags, suitcases, and sneakers. • Pick up pet hairs. • Repel mosquitoes. • Stop static cling. • Make sheets smell good. • End tangled sewing thread.

Nail polish

{PAGE 217}

Mark hard-to-see items. • Mark thermostat and shower settings and levels in measuring cups and buckets. • Label sports gear and poison containers. • Seal envelopes and labels. • Stop shoe scuffs and keep laces, ribbons, and fabric from unraveling. • Make needle-threading easier. • Keep buckles and jewelry shiny. • Stop a stocking run. • Temporarily repair glasses. • Fix nicks in floors and glass. • Repair lacquered items. • Plug a hole in a cooler. • Fill washtub nicks.

Pantyhose

{PAGE 236}

Find and pick up small objects. • Buff shoes. • Keep hairbrush clean. • Remove nail polish. • Keep spray bottles clog-free. • Organize suitcases. Hang-dry sweaters. • Secure trash bags. • Dust under fridge. • Prevent soil erosion in houseplants.

Paper bags

{PAGE 242}

Pack on trips for souvenirs. • Dust off mops. • Carry laundry. • Cover textbooks. • Create a table decoration. • Use as gift bags and wrapping paper. • Reshape knits after washing. • Use as a pressing cloth. • Bag newspapers for recycling.

Plastic bags

{PAGE 261}

Keep mattresses dry. • Bulk curtains and stuff crafts. • Drain bath toys. • Clean pockets in the laundry. • Make bibs and a high-chair drop cloth. • Line a litter box. • Dispose of a Christmas tree.

Rubber bands

{PAGE 276}

Reshape your broom. • Childproof cabinets. • Keep thread from tangling. • Make a holder for car visor. • Use to grip paper. • Extend a button. • Use as a bookmark. • Cushion a remote control. • Secure bed slats and tighten furniture casters.

Sandwich and freezer bags

{PAGE 292}

Protect pictures and padlocks. • Dispense fabric softener. • Display baby teeth. • Carry baby wipes. • Mold soap. • Starch craft items. • Feed birds. • Make a funnel.

17

TOP

12

Most Useful Items for the

cook

*the secret to perfect
poached eggs is vinegar …*

p. 354

Aluminum foil

{PAGE 39}

Bake a perfect piecrust. • Soften brown sugar. • Decorate a cake and create special-shaped pie pans. • Keep rolls and bread warm. • Make an extra-large salad bowl. • Make a toasted cheese sandwich with an iron.

Apples

{PAGE 53}

Keep a roast chicken moist and cakes fresh. • Ripen green tomatoes. • Fluff up hardened brown sugar. • Absorb excess salt in soups.

Baking soda

{PAGE 62}

Clean fruits and vegetables. • Remove fish smells. • Reduce the acidity of coffee and tomato-based sauces. • Reduce the gas-producing properties of beans. • Make fluffy omelets. • Replace yeast.

Coffee filters

{PAGE 133}

Cover food in microwave. • Filter cork crumbs from wine or food remnants from cooking oil. • Hold a taco, ice cream bar, or ice pop.

Ice cube trays

{PAGE 187}

Freeze eggs, pesto, chopped vegetables and herbs, chicken soup—even leftover wine—for future use.

Lemons
{PAGE 198}

Prevent potatoes from turning brown or rice from sticking. • Keep guacamole green. • Make soggy lettuce crisp. • Freshen the fridge and cutting boards.

Paper towels
{PAGE 248}

Microwave bacon, clean corn, and strain broth. • Keep vegetables crisp and vegetable bin clean. • Prevent soggy bread and rusty pots.

Plastic bags
{PAGE 264}

Cover a cookbook. • Bag hands to answer phone. • Crush graham crackers. • Use as mixing bowl or salad spinner. • Ripen fruit.

Rubber bands
{PAGE 276}

Keep spoons from sliding into bowls. • Secure casserole lids for travel. • Anchor a cutting board. • Get a better grip on twist-off lids and glasses.

Salt
{PAGE 283}

Prevent grease from splattering. • Speed cooking. • Shell hard-boiled eggs or pecans easier. • Test eggs for freshness and poach eggs perfectly. • Wash spinach better. • Keep salad crisp. • Revive wrinkled apples and stop cut fruit from browning. • Use to whip cream, beat eggs, and keep milk fresh. • Prevent mold on cheese.

Sandwich and freezer bags
{PAGE 293}

Store grater with cheese. • Make a pastry bag. • Dispose of cooking oil. • Color cookie dough. • Keep ice cream from forming crystals. • Soften marshmallows, melt chocolate, and save soda. • Grease pans.

Toothpicks
{PAGE 336}

Mark steaks for doneness. • Retrieve garlic cloves from marinade. • Prevent pots from boiling over. • Microwave potatoes faster. • Limit salad dressing. • Fry sausages better.

11

Most Useful Items for health and

beauty

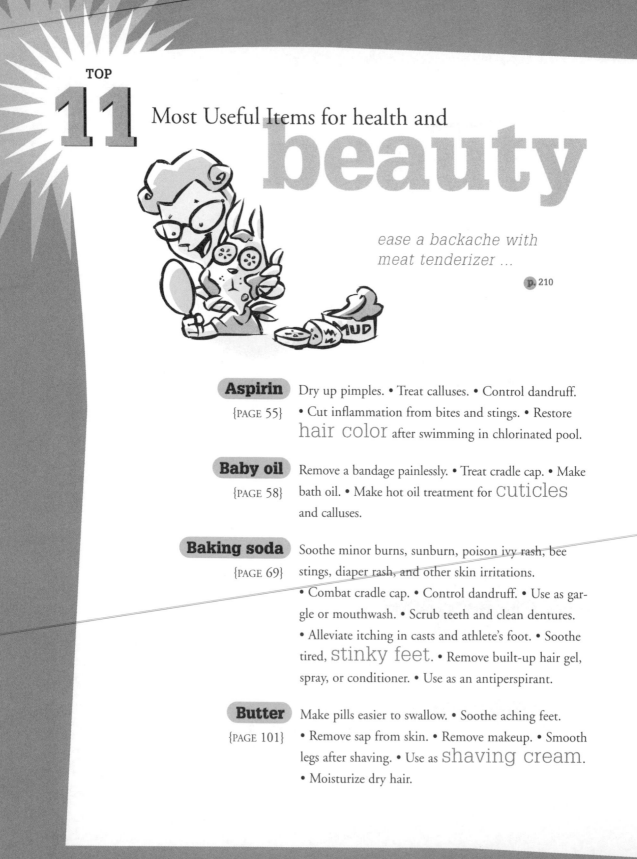

ease a backache with meat tenderizer ...

p. 210

Aspirin Dry up pimples. • Treat calluses. • Control dandruff.
{PAGE 55} • Cut inflammation from bites and stings. • Restore hair color after swimming in chlorinated pool.

Baby oil Remove a bandage painlessly. • Treat cradle cap. • Make
{PAGE 58} bath oil. • Make hot oil treatment for cuticles and calluses.

Baking soda Soothe minor burns, sunburn, poison ivy rash, bee
{PAGE 69} stings, diaper rash, and other skin irritations.
• Combat cradle cap. • Control dandruff. • Use as gargle or mouthwash. • Scrub teeth and clean dentures.
• Alleviate itching in casts and athlete's foot. • Soothe tired, stinky feet. • Remove built-up hair gel, spray, or conditioner. • Use as an antiperspirant.

Butter Make pills easier to swallow. • Soothe aching feet.
{PAGE 101} • Remove sap from skin. • Remove makeup. • Smooth legs after shaving. • Use as shaving cream.
• Moisturize dry hair.

Chest rub

{PAGE 122}

Make calluses disappear. • Sooth aching feet. • Stop insect-bite itch. • Treat toenail fungus. • Repel biting insects.

Lemons

{PAGE 200}

Disinfect cuts and scrapes. • Soothe poison ivy rash. • Relieve rough hands and sore feet. • Remove warts. • Lighten age spots. • Create blond highlights. • Clean and whiten nails. • Cleanse and exfoliate your face. • Treat dandruff. • Soften dry elbows.

Mayonnaise

{PAGE 204}

Relieve sunburn pain. • Remove dead skin. • Condition hair. • Make a facial. • Strengthen fingernails.

Mustard

{PAGE 216}

Soothe aching back pain. • Relax stiff muscles. • Relieve congestion. • Make a facial mask.

Petroleum jelly

{PAGE 254}

Heal windburn. • Help diaper rash. • Protect baby's eyes from shampoo. • Moisturize lips. • Remove makeup. • Moisturize your face. • Create makeup. • Strengthen perfume. • Soften hands. • Do a professional manicure. • Smooth eyebrows.

Tea

{PAGE 327}

Relieve tired eyes. • Soothe bleeding gums. • Cool sunburn. • Relieve baby's pain from injection. • Reduce razor burn. • Condition dry hair and get the gray out. • Tan your skin. • Drain a boil. • Soothe nipples sore from nursing. • Soothe mouth pain.

Vinegar

{PAGE 355}

Control dandruff and condition hair. • Protect blond hair from chlorine. • Apply as antiperspirant. • Soak aching muscles. • Freshen breath. • Ease sunburn and itching. • Banish bruises. • Soothe sore throat. • Clear congestion. • Heal cold sores and athlete's foot. • Pamper skin. • Erase age or sun spots. • Soften cuticles. • Treat jellyfish or bee stings.

10

Most Useful Items for

cleaning

*clean fireplace doors
with ashes …*

p. 54

Ammonia
{PAGE 49}

Clean carpets, upholstery, ovens, fireplace doors, windows, porcelain fixtures, crystal, jewelry, and white shoes. • Remove tarnish and stains. • Fight mildew. • Strip floor wax.

Baking soda
{PAGE 62}

Clean baby bottles, thermoses, cutting boards, appliances, sponges and towels, coffeemakers, teapots, cookware, and fixtures. • Clear clogged drains. • Deodorize garbage pails. • Boost dishwashing liquid or make your own. • Remove stains. • Shine jewelry, stainless steel, chrome, and marble. • Wash wallpaper and remove crayon. • Remove must.

Borax
{PAGE 89}

Clear a clogged drain. • Remove stains. • Clean windows and mirrors. • Remove mildew from fabrics.
• Sanitize your garbage disposal.
• Eliminate urine odor.

Fabric softener sheets
{PAGE 167}

Lift burned-on food. • Freshen drawers. • Remove soap scum. • Repel dust from TV screen. • Freshen hampers and wastebaskets. • Buff chrome. • Keep dust off blinds. • Renew stuffed toys.

Lemons

{PAGE 196}

Get rid of tough stains on marble. • Polish metals. • Clean the microwave. • Deodorize cutting boards, fridge, and garbage disposal.

Rubbing alcohol

{PAGE 278}

Clean fixtures, venetian blinds, windows, and phones. • Remove hair spray from mirrors. • Prevent ring around the collar. • Remove ink stains.

Salt

{PAGE 280}

Clean vases, discolored glass, flowerpots, artificial flowers, percolators, refrigerators, woks, and wicker. • Give brooms long life. • Ease fireplace or flour cleanup. Make metal polish. • Remove wine and grease from carpet, water marks from wood, and lipstick from glasses. • Restore a sponge. • Freshen the garbage disposal. • Remove baked-on food. • Soak up oven spills. • Remove stains from pans and clean cast iron.

Toothpaste

{PAGE 334}

Clean piano keys and sinks. • Polish metal and jewelry. • Deodorize baby bottles. • Remove ink or lipstick from fabric, crayon from walls, and water marks from furniture.

Vinegar

{PAGE 343}

Clean blinds, bricks, tile, paneling, carpets, piano keys, computers, appliances, and cutting boards. • Clean china, crystal, glassware, coffeemakers, and cookware. • Banish kitchen grease. • Deodorize drains and closets. • Polish metal. • Erase ballpoint pen marks. • Remove water rings and wax from furniture. • Revitalize leather. • Clean fixtures and purge bugs.

WD-40

{PAGE 377}

Remove carpet stains and floor scuffs. • Remove tea and tomato stains. • Clean toilet bowls. • Condition leather furniture. • Clean a chalkboard. • Remove marker and crayon from walls.

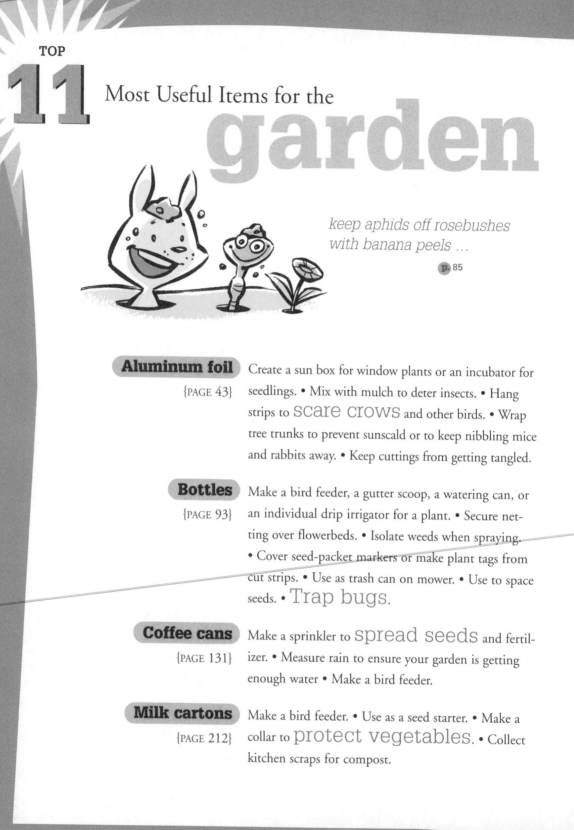

TOP

11

Most Useful Items for the
garden

*keep aphids off rosebushes
with banana peels ...*

p. 85

Aluminum foil
{PAGE 43}

Create a sun box for window plants or an incubator for seedlings. • Mix with mulch to deter insects. • Hang strips to SCare Crows and other birds. • Wrap tree trunks to prevent sunscald or to keep nibbling mice and rabbits away. • Keep cuttings from getting tangled.

Bottles
{PAGE 93}

Make a bird feeder, a gutter scoop, a watering can, or an individual drip irrigator for a plant. • Secure netting over flowerbeds. • Isolate weeds when spraying. • Cover seed-packet markers or make plant tags from cut strips. • Use as trash can on mower. • Use to space seeds. • Trap bugs.

Coffee cans
{PAGE 131}

Make a sprinkler to spread seeds and fertilizer. • Measure rain to ensure your garden is getting enough water • Make a bird feeder.

Milk cartons
{PAGE 212}

Make a bird feeder. • Use as a seed starter. • Make a collar to protect vegetables. • Collect kitchen scraps for compost.

Newspaper
{PAGE 224}

Protect and ripen end-of-season tomatoes. • Use as mulch or add to compost to remove odor. • Block weeds in flower and vegetable beds. • Get rid of earwigs.

Pantyhose
{PAGE 240}

Tie up tomatoes and beans. • Fill with hair clippings to repel deer. • Make a hammock for growing melons. • Store onions and off-season bulbs. • Prevent soil lost in houseplants. • Fill with soap scraps for cleaning hands at garden spigot.

Plastic bags
{PAGE 265}

Protect plants from frost and shoes from mud. • Speed budding of poinsettias and Christmas cactus. • Keep bugs off fruit on trees. • Store outdoor equipment manuals. • Bring a favorite cracked vase back into use. • Make disposable work aprons.

Plastic containers
{PAGE 267}

Make traps for slugs and wasps. • Stop ants from crawling up picnic table legs. • Use to start seedlings.

Salt
{PAGE 287}

Kill snails and slugs. • Inhibit the growth of weeds in walkway cracks. • Extend the life of cut flowers. • Clean flowerpots.

Tea
{PAGE 330}

Spur growth of rosebushes. • Water acid-loving plants. • Nourish houseplants. • Prepare a planter for potting. • Speed the decomposition of compost.

WD-40
{PAGE 379}

Keep animals out of flowerbeds and squirrels off bird feeders. • Keep tool handles from splintering. • Stop snow from sticking on shovel or snow thrower. Prevent wasps from building nests and repel pigeons. • Kill thistle plants.

11

Most Useful Items for

outdoors

lubricate skate wheels with hair conditioner ...

p. 181

Aluminum foil
{PAGE 44}

Improve outdoor lighting. • Keep bees away from beverages. • Make an impromptu picnic platter or improvise a frying pan. • Make a drip pan for your barbecue and clean the grill. • Warm your toes when camping and keep your sleeping bag and matches dry. • Make a fishing lure.

Baking soda
{PAGE 74}

Keep weeds out of concrete cracks. • Clean plastic resin lawn furniture. • Feed your flowering plants. • Maintain proper pool alkalinity. • Scour the barbecue grill.

Bottles
{PAGE 93}

Use a plastic jug to make a scoop or bailer for your boat. • Make a plastic jug into an anchor for your boat and for landlubber jobs. • Make a bird feeder. • Fill a plastic jug with sand or cat litter for winter traction. • Keep your cooler cold.

Bubble pack
{PAGE 98}

Keep soft drinks cold. • Sleep on air while camping. • Cushion bleachers and benches.

Buckets
{PAGE 99}

Boil lobster over the campfire. • Use as a footlocker. • Build a camp washing machine or make a camp shower.

Cat litter
{PAGE 118}

Give your car traction on ice. • Prevent barbecue grease fires. • Keep tents and sleeping bags must-free. • Remove grease spots from driveway.

Cooking spray
{PAGE 140}

Prevent grass from sticking to your mower. • Spray on fishing line for quicker casting. • Prevent snow from sticking to your shovel or your snow-thrower chute.

Duct tape
{PAGE 157}

Seal out ticks. • Create a clothesline. • Stash a secret car key. • Patch a canoe or a pool. • Repair outdoor cushions and replace lawn furniture webbing. • Make bike streamers. • Tighten hockey shin guards and revive your hockey stick. • Preserve skateboarders' shoes. • Repair your ski gloves or a tent. • Waterproof your footwear.

Sandwich and freezer bags
{PAGE 296}

Inflate to make valuables float when boating. • Make a hand cleaner for the beach. • Apply bug spray with ease.

Vinegar
{PAGE 363}

Keep water fresh. • Clean outdoor furniture and decks. • Repel insects. • Trap flying insects. • Get rid of ants. • Clean off bird droppings.

WD-40
{PAGE 381}

Repel pigeons and wasps. • Waterproof shoes. • Remove wax from skis and snowboards. • Remove barnacles from boat and protect it from corrosion. • Untangle your fishing line and lure fish. • Clean and protect golf clubs. • Remove burrs from a horse's mane and protect hooves in winter. • Keep flies off cows.

13

Most Useful Items for

storage

tortis

stash your valuables at the gym in a tennis ball …

p. 331

Baby wipe containers
{PAGE 61}

Organize sewing supplies, recipe cards, coupons, craft supplies, old floppy disks, small tools, photos, receipts, bills, and more. • Store plastic shopping bags. • Store towels and rags.

Bottles
{PAGE 91}

Store sugar. • Store small workshop items. • Use as a boot tree. • Make a bag or string dispenser.

Cans
{PAGE 104}

Compartmentalize your tool pouch with juice cans. • Make a desk organizer. • Create pigeonholes to store silverware, nails, office supplies, and other odds and ends.

Candy tins
{PAGE 107}

Make an emergency sewing kit. • Store broken jewelry. • Make a birthday keepsake. • Prevent jewelry chain tangles. • Organize a sewing box. • Store car fuses. • Keep earrings together. • Store workshop items.

Cardboard boxes
{PAGE 109}

Make magazine holders from detergent boxes. • Make a home-office in-box. • Store hoes, rakes, and other long-handled garden tools. • Protect glassware or lightbulbs. • Store posters and artwork. • Store

Christmas ornaments. • Organize dowels, moldings, furring strips, 2x2s, and metal rods.

Cardboard tubes
{PAGE 112}

Store knitting needles and fabric scraps. • Keep Christmas lights tidy. • Preserve kids' artwork, important documents, and posters. • Keep linens crease-free, pants wrinkle-free, and electrical cords tangle-free. • Protect fluorescent lights. • Store string.

Clothespins
{PAGE 125}

Keep snacks fresh. • Organize workshop, kitchen, bathroom, and closets. • Keep gloves in shape.

Coffee cans
{PAGE 131}

Make a kids' bank. • Hold kitchen scraps. • Carry toilet paper when camping. • Store screws, nuts, and nails. • Organize and store belts. • Collect pocket stuff in the laundry.

Egg cartons
{PAGE 161}

Store and sort coins. • Organize buttons, safety pins, threads, bobbins, and fasteners. • Store golf balls or Christmas ornaments.

Film canisters
{PAGE 169}

Make a stamp dispenser or a sewing kit. • Organize pills. • Store fishing flies. • Carry change for tolls. • Stash jewelry at the gym. • Carry dressings, cooking spices, and condiments. • Carry nail polish remover.

Pantyhose
{PAGE 236}

Store wrapping paper. • Bundle blankets. • Store onions or flower bulbs.

Plastic bags
{PAGE 261}

Store wipes. • Collect used clothes. • Protect clothes. • Store skirts. • Keep purses in shape.

Sandwich and freezer bags
{PAGE 292}

Store breakables. • Save sweaters. • Create a sachet. • Add cedar to a closet. • Make a pencil bag. • De-clutter the bath.

TOP 15

Most Useful Items for

kids

make finger paints from yogurt ...

p. 386

Aluminum pie pans

{PAGE 47}

Use as mold for ice ornaments. • Minimize glitter mess and make trays for craft supplies.

Baking soda

{PAGE 66}

Make watercolor paints or invisible ink. • Produce gas to blow up a balloon. • Clean crayon marks from walls and baby spit-up from clothing. • Combat cradle cap and diaper rash. • Wash chemicals out of new baby clothes.

Bathtub appliqués

{PAGE 81}

Stick to bottom of kiddie pool. • Affix to sippy cups and high-chair seats.

Cardboard boxes

{PAGE 110}

Make a medieval castle, a puppet theater, or a sundial. • Make a garage for toy vehicles. • Store tennis rackets, baseball bats, fishing poles, and other sporting goods. • Use as an impromptu sled. • Play beverage-box ski-ball.

Cardboard tubes

{PAGE 112}

Make a kazoo or a megaphone. • Preserve your kids' artwork. • Build a toy log cabin. • Make no-gunpowder "English" firecrackers.

Compact discs
{PAGE 138}

Make a fun picture frame. • Make wall art for a teen's room. • Create spinning tops.

Corks
{PAGE 141}

Use burnt cork as Halloween face paint. • Create a craft stamp. • Make a cool bead curtain for a kid's room.

Duct tape
{PAGE 155}

Make Halloween costumes, a toy sword, or hand puppets. • Create bicycle streamers.

Jars
{PAGE 190}

Make a savings bank. • Dry kids' mittens. • Bring along baby treats and store baby-food portions. • Collect insects. • Create a miniature biosphere.

Margarine tubs
{PAGE 205}

Make a baby footprint paperweight. • Divvy up ice cream so kids can help themselves. • Bring fast food for baby. • Make a coin bank. • Give kids some lunch-box variety.

Paper bags
{PAGE 242}

Cover textbooks. • Make a kite. • Create a life-size body poster.

Paper plates
{PAGE 248}

Make index cards and Frisbee flash cards. • Make crafts, mobiles, and seasonal decorations.

Pillowcases
{PAGE 258}

Prepare travel pillows for kids. • Make wall hangings for kids' rooms. • Clean stuffed animals.

Sandwich and freezer bags
{PAGE 292}

Display baby teeth. • Make baby wipes. • Dye pasta for crafts. • Make kids' kitchen gloves. • Make a pencil bag. • Keep spare kids' clothes in car for mishaps. • Cure car sickness. • Play football while making pudding.

Tape
{PAGE 326}

Secure a baby's bib. • Create childproofing in a pinch. • Make a multicolor pen. • Make an unpoppable balloon.

TOP

14

Most Useful Items for quick

repairs

*repair your garden hose
with a toothpick ...*

p. 338

Adhesive tape
{PAGE 36}
Remove broken window glass safely. • Hang caulk tubes for storage. • Get a better grip on tools.

Aluminum foil
{PAGE 45}
Make flexible funnel for hard-to-reach places. • Reflect light for photography. • Reattach vinyl floor. • Make an artist's palette. • Prevent paint from skinning over. • Line roller pans and keep paint off doorknobs.

Baking soda
{PAGE 73}
Clean car-battery terminals and remove tar from car. • Use as a walkway de-icer. • Tighten cane chair seats. • Give deck a weathered look. • Clean air conditioner filters • Keep humidifier odor-free.

Basters
{PAGE 78}
Cure musty air conditioner. • Transfer paints and solvents. • Fix leaky refrigerator.

Bottles
{PAGE 78}
Make a neater paint bucket. • Store paints. • Make a workshop organizer. • Use as a level. • Make an anchor for weighting tarps and patio umbrellas.

Bubble pack
{PAGE 78}
Prevent toilet-tank condensation. • Insulate windows. • Cushion work surface and protect tools.

Buckets
{PAGE 99}

Hold paint and supplies when painting on a ladder and use lids to contain paint drips. • Make stilts for painting ceiling. • Organize extension cords. • Soak your saw to clean. • Use as a Christmas tree stand.

Cardboard boxes
{PAGE 111}

Make a temporary roof repair. • Protect fingers while hammering small nails. • Make an oil drip pan. • Identify fluid leaking from your car. • Make a bed tray. • Make an in-box. • Organize workshop. • Keep upholstery tacks straight.

Clothespins
{PAGE 125}

Clamp thin objects. • Make a clipboard. • Grip a nail to protect fingers. • Float paintbrushes in solvent.

Duct tape
{PAGE 155}

Temporarily fix a car taillight or water hose. • Repair siding. • Make a short-term roof shingle. • Create a clothesline. • Stash a secret car key. • Patch a canoe. • Repair a garbage can.

Garden hose
{PAGE 176}

Protect handsaw. • Make a rounded sanding block. • Make a paint-can grip.

Pantyhose
{PAGE 241}

Test a sanding job. • Apply stain in tight corners. • Patch holes in screens. • Strain paint.

Plastic bags
{PAGE 267}

Protect ceiling fan when painting ceiling. • Store paintbrushes. • Contain paint overspray.

Vinegar
{PAGE 369}

Wash concrete off skin. • Remove paint fumes. • Degrease grates, fans, and air-conditioner grilles. • Disinfect filters. • Help paint adhere to concrete. • Remove rust from tools. • Peel off wallpaper. • Slow plaster hardening. • Revive hardened paintbrushes.

YOUR COMPLETE
A-Z Guide*

On the following pages you'll find 204 common household items that altogether have more than 2,300 unexpected uses—uses that are not just surprising and clever but can save you time, money, and effort. Some of the items, such as aluminum foil and vinegar, are labeled Super Items because they have so many extraordinary uses.

A

✱ Adhesive Tape

Remove a splinter Is a splinter too tiny or too deep to remove with tweezers? Avoid the agony of digging it out with a needle. Instead, cover the splinter with adhesive tape. After about three days, pull the tape off and the splinter should come out with it.

Stop ants in their tracks Is an army of ants marching toward the cookie jar on your countertop or some sweet prize in your pantry? Create a "moat" around the object by surrounding it with adhesive tape placed sticky side up.

Make a lint-lifter To lift lint and pet hair off clothing and upholstery, you don't need a special lint remover. Just wrap your hand with adhesive tape, sticky side out.

Reduce your hat size Got a hat that's a bit too big for your head? Wrap adhesive tape around the sweatband—it might take two or three layers depending on the size discrepancy. As a bonus, the adhesive tape will absorb brow sweat on hot days.

Clean a comb To remove the gunk that builds up between the teeth of your comb, press a strip of adhesive tape along the comb's length, and lift it off. Then dip the comb in a solution of alcohol and water, or ammonia and water, to sanitize it. Let dry.

Cover casters Prevent your furniture from leaving marks on your wood or vinyl floor by wrapping the furniture's caster wheels with adhesive tape.

Hang glue and caulk tubes Got an ungainly heap of glue and caulk tubes on your workbench? Cut a strip of adhesive or duct tape several inches long and fold it over the bottom of each tube, leaving a flap at the end. Punch a hole in the flap with a paper hole punch and hang the tube on a nail or hook. You'll free up counter space, and you'll be able to find the right tube fast.

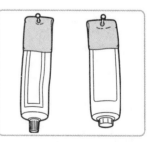

Safely remove broken window glass Removing a window sash to fix a broken pane of glass can be dangerous; there's always the possibility that a sharp shard will fall out and cut you. To prevent this, crisscross both sides of the broken pane with adhesive tape before removing the sash. And don't forget to wear heavy leather gloves when you pull the glass shards out of the frame.

Get a grip on tools Adhesive tape has just the right texture for wrapping tool handles. It gives you a positive, comfortable grip, and it's highly absorbent so that tools won't become slippery if your hand sweats. When you wrap tool handles, overlap each wrap by about half a tape width and use as many layers as needed to get the best grip. Here are some useful applications:

● Screwdriver handles are sometimes too narrow and slippery to grip well when you drive or remove stubborn screws. Wrap layers of adhesive tape around the handle until the tool feels comfortable in your hand—this is especially useful if you have arthritis in your fingers.

● Take a tip from carpenters who wrap wooden hammer handles that can get slippery with sweat. Wrap the whole gripping area of the tool. A few wraps just under the head will also protect the handle from damage caused by misdirected blows.

● Plumbers also keep adhesive tape in their tool kits: When they want to cut a pipe in a spot that's too tight for their hacksaw frame, they make a mini-hacksaw by removing the blade and wrapping one end of the blade to form a handle.

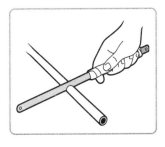

DID *You* KNOW?

In the 1920s, Josephine Dickson, an accident-prone New Jersey housewife, inspired the invention of the Band-Aid bandage. Her husband, Earle, who tended her various burns and wounds, hit upon the idea of sticking small squares of sterile gauze onto adhesive tape, covering it with a layer of crinoline, then rolling it back up so that Josephine could cut off and apply the ready-made bandages herself.

Earle's employer, Johnson & Johnson, soon began producing the first Band-Aids. By the time Earle died in 1961—by then a member of the company's board of directors—Band-Aid sales exceeded $30 million a year.

✳ Alka-Seltzer

Clean your coffeemaker Fill your percolator or the water chamber of your drip coffeemaker with water and plop in four Alka-Seltzer tablets. When the Alka-Seltzer has dissolved, put the coffeemaker through a brew cycle to clean the tubes. Rinse the chamber out two or three times, then run a brew cycle with plain water before making coffee.

Clean a vase That stuck-on residue at the bottom of narrow-neck vases may seem impossible to scrub out, but you can easily bubble it away. Fill the vase halfway with water and drop in two Alka-Seltzer tablets. Wait until the fizzing stops, then rinse the vase clean. The same trick works for cleaning glass thermoses.

Clean glass cookware Say so long to scouring those stubborn stains off your ovenproof glass cookware. Just fill the container with water, add up to six Alka-Seltzer tablets, and let it soak for an hour. The stains should easily scrub away.

Clean your toilet The citric acid in Alka-Seltzer combined with its fizzing action is an effective toilet bowl cleaner. Simply drop a couple of tablets into the bowl and find something else to do for 20 minutes or so. When you return, a few swipes with a toilet brush will leave your bowl gleaming.

Clean jewelry Drop your dull-looking jewelry in a glass of fizzing Alka-Seltzer for a couple of minutes. It will sparkle and shine when you pull it out.

Unclog a drain Drain clogged again? Get almost instant relief: Drop a couple of Alka-Seltzer tablets down the opening, then pour in a cup of vinegar. Wait a few minutes and then run the hot water at full force to clear the clog. This is also a good way to eliminate kitchen drain odors.

Soothe insect bites Mosquito or other insect bite driving you nuts? To ease the itch, drop two Alka-Seltzer tablets in half a glass of water. Dip a cotton ball in the

SCIENCE FAIR

Turn plop, plop, fizz, fizz into whoosh, whoosh, gee whiz with this **Alka-Seltzer rocket.** The rocket gets its thrust from the gas created when you drop a couple of Alka-Seltzer tablets into some water inside a film canister.

The type of film canister is key: Use a **Fuji 35mm plastic canister** that has a lid that fits inside the canister. Canisters with lids that fit around an outside lip won't work. You'll also need a couple of pieces of **construction paper, transparent tape,** and **scissors.**

To form the body of the rocket, wrap a piece of construction paper around the canister with the canister's open end facing out the bottom end of the tube. Then tape the paper in place. Form a quarter-sheet of construction paper into a nose cone. Then trim it even on the bottom and tape it onto the top of the rocket body.

To launch the rocket, fill the canister about halfway with refrigerated water—cold water is vital to a successful liftoff. Plop in two Alka-Seltzer tablets. Quickly pop on the lid, set the rocket on the ground, and stand back. The gas will quickly build up pressure in the canister, causing the canister lid to pop off and the rocket to launch several feet into the air.

glass and apply it to the bite. *Caution:* Don't do this if you are allergic to aspirin, which is a key ingredient in Alka-Seltzer.

Attract fish All avid anglers know fish are attracted to bubbles. If you are using a hollow plastic tube jig on your line, just break off a piece of Alka-Seltzer and slip it into the tube. The jig will produce an enticing stream of bubbles as it sinks.

Aluminum Foil

✳ ALUMINUM FOIL **IN THE KITCHEN**

Bake a perfect piecrust Keep the edges of your homemade pies from burning by covering them with strips of aluminum foil. The foil prevents the edges from getting overdone while the rest of your pie gets perfectly browned.

Create special-shaped cake pans Make a teddy bear birthday cake, a Valentine's Day heart cake, a Christmas tree cake, or whatever shaped cake the occasion may call for. Just form a double thickness of heavy-duty aluminum foil into the desired shape inside a large cake pan.

Soften up brown sugar To restore your hardened brown sugar to its former powdery glory, chip off a piece, wrap it in aluminum foil, and bake it in the oven at 300°F (150° C) for five minutes.

Decorate a cake No pastry bag handy? No problem. Form a piece of heavy-duty aluminum foil into a tube and fill it with free-flowing frosting. Bonus: There's no pastry bag to clean—simply toss out the foil when you're done.

Make an extra-large salad bowl You've invited half the neighborhood over for dinner, but don't have a bowl big enough to toss that much salad. Don't panic. Just line the kitchen sink with aluminum foil and toss away!

Keep rolls and breads warm Want to lock in the oven-fresh warmth of your homemade rolls or breads for a dinner party or picnic? Before you load up your basket, wrap your freshly baked goods in a napkin and place a layer of aluminum foil underneath. The foil will reflect the heat and keep your bread warm for quite some time.

Catch ice-cream cone drips Keep youngsters from making a mess of their clothes or your house by wrapping the bottom of an ice-cream cone (or a wedge of watermelon) with a piece of aluminum foil before handing it to them.

Toast your own cheese sandwich Next time you pack for a trip, include a couple of cheese sandwiches wrapped in aluminum foil. That way if you check into a hotel after the kitchen has closed, you won't have to resort to the cold, overpriced snacks in the mini-bar. Instead, use the hotel-room iron to press both sides of the wrapped sandwich and you'll have a tasty hot snack.

Polish your silver Is your silverware looking a bit dull these days? Try an ion exchange, a molecular reaction in which aluminum acts as a catalyst. All you have to do is line a pan with a sheet of aluminum foil, fill it with cold water, and add two teaspoons of salt. Drop your tarnished silverware into the solution, let it sit for two to three minutes, then rinse off and dry.

Keep silverware untarnished Store freshly cleaned silverware on top of a sheet of aluminum foil to deter tarnishing. For long-term storage of silverware, first tightly cover each piece in cellophane wrap—be sure to squeeze out as much air as possible—then wrap in foil and seal the ends.

Preserve steel-wool pads It's maddening. You use a steel-wool pad once, put it in a dish by the sink, and the next day you find a rusty mess fit only for the trash. To prevent rust and get your money's worth from a pad, wrap it in foil and toss it into the freezer. You can also lengthen the life of your steel-wool soap pads by crumpling up a sheet of foil and placing it under the steel wool in its dish or container. (Don't forget to periodically drain off the water that collects at the bottom.)

Scrub your pots Don't have a scrub pad? Crumple up a handful of aluminum foil and use it to scrub your pots.

Tip **Foil-Eating Acidic Foods**

> Think twice before ripping off a sheet of aluminum foil to wrap up your leftover meat loaf—particularly one that's dripping with tomato sauce. Highly acidic or salty foods such as lemons, grapefruits, ketchup, and pickles accelerate the oxidation of aluminum and can actually "eat" through foil with prolonged exposure. This can also leach aluminum into the food, which can affect its flavor and may pose a health risk. If you want to use foil for that meat loaf, however, cover it first with a layer or two of plastic wrap or wax paper to prevent the sauce from coming into contact with the foil.

Keep the oven clean Are you baking a bubbly lasagna or casserole? Keep messy drips off the bottom of the oven by laying a sheet or two of aluminum foil over the rack below. *Do not* line the bottom of the oven with foil; it could cause a fire.

Improve radiator efficiency Here's a simple way to get more heat out of your old cast-iron radiators without spending one cent more on your gas or oil bill: Make a heat reflector to put behind them. Tape heavy-duty aluminum foil to cardboard with the shiny side of the foil facing out. The radiant heat waves will bounce off the foil into the room instead of being absorbed by the wall behind the radiator. If your radiators have covers, it also helps to attach a piece of foil under the cover's top.

Keep pets off furniture Can't keep Snoopy off your brand-new sofa? Place a piece of aluminum foil on the seat cushions, and after one try at settling down on the noisy surface, your pet will no longer consider it a comfy place to snooze.

Protect a child's mattress As any parent of a potty-trained youngster knows, accidents happen. When they happen in bed, however, you can spare the mattress—even if you don't have a plastic protector available. First, lay several sheets of aluminum foil across the width of the mattress. Then, cover them with a good-sized beach towel. Finally, attach the mattress pad and bottom sheet.

Hide worn spots in mirrors Sometimes a worn spot adds to the charm of an old mirror; sometimes it's a distraction. You can easily disguise small flaws on a mirror's reflective surface by putting a piece of aluminum foil, shiny side facing out, on the back of the glass. To hold the foil in place, attach it to the backing behind the mirror or to the frame with masking tape. Don't tape it to the mirror itself.

Kids' Stuff Mixing **finger paints** is a great way for kids to learn firsthand how colors combine while also expressing their creativity. Unfortunately, their learning experience can be your "Excedrin moment."

To **contain the mess,** cut down the sides of a **wide cardboard box** so that they are about three inches high. Line the inside of the box with **aluminum foil** and let the kids pour in the paint. With any luck, the paint should stay within the confines of the box, keeping splatters off walls and the floor.

Sharpen your scissors What can you do with those clean pieces of leftover foil you have hanging around? Use them to sharpen up your dull scissors! Smooth them out if necessary, and then fold the strips into several layers and start cutting. Seven or eight passes should do the trick. Pretty simple, huh? (See page 43 to find out how you can use the resulting scraps of foil for mulching or keeping birds off your fruit trees.)

Clean jewelry To clean your jewelry, simply line a small bowl with aluminum foil. Fill the bowl with hot water and mix in one tablespoon of bleach-free powdered laundry detergent (not liquid), such as Tide. Put the jewelry in the solution and let it soak for one minute. Rinse well and air-dry. This procedure makes use of the chemical process known as ion exchange, which can also be used to clean silverware (see page 40).

Move furniture with ease To slide big pieces of furniture over a smooth floor, place small pieces of aluminum foil under the legs. Put the dull side of the foil down—the dull side is actually more slippery than the shiny side.

Fix loose batteries Is your flashlight, Walkman, or your kid's toy working intermittently? Check the battery compartment. Those springs that hold the batteries in place can lose their tension after a while, letting the batteries loosen. Fold a small piece of aluminum foil until you have a pad that's thick enough to take up the slack. Place the pad between the battery and the spring.

Don't dye your glasses You want to catch up on your reading during the time it takes to color your hair. But you can't read without your specs, and if you put them on, hair dye can stain them. Solution: Wrap the temples of your glasses with aluminum foil.

Clean out your fireplace Looking for an easy way to clean the ashes out of your fireplace? Place a double layer of heavy-duty aluminum foil across the bottom of the fireplace or under the wood grate. The next day—or once you're sure all the ashes have cooled—simply fold it up and throw it away or, even better, use the ashes as described on pages 54-55.

✳ ALUMINUM FOIL **IN THE LAUNDRY ROOM**

Speed your ironing When you iron clothing, a lot of the iron's heat is sucked up by the board itself—requiring you to make several passes to remove wrinkles. To speed things up, put a piece of aluminum foil under your ironing board cover. The foil will reflect the heat back through the clothing, smoothing wrinkles quicker.

DID *You* KNOW?

Have you ever wondered why aluminum foil has one side that's shinier than the other? The answer has to do with how it's manufactured. According to Alcoa, the maker of Reynolds Wrap, the different shades of silver result during the final rolling process, when two layers of foil pass through the rolling mill simultaneously. The sides that contact the mill's heavy, polished rollers come out shiny, while the inside layers retain a dull, or matte, finish. Of course, the shiny side is better for reflecting light and heat, but when it comes to wrapping foods or lining grills, both sides are equally good.

ALUMINUM FOIL*

42

Attach a patch An iron-on patch is an easy way to fix small holes in clothing—but only if it doesn't get stuck onto your ironing board. To avoid this, put a piece of aluminum foil under the hole. It won't stick to the patch, and you can just slip it out when you're finished.

Clean your iron Is starch building up on your clothes iron and causing it to stick? To get rid of it, run your hot iron over a piece of aluminum foil.

✳ ALUMINUM FOIL **IN THE GARDEN**

Put some bite in your mulch To keep hungry insects and slugs away from your cucumbers and other vegetables, mix strips of aluminum foil in with your garden mulch. As a bonus benefit, the foil will reflect light back up onto your plants.

Protect tree trunks Mice, rabbits, and other animals often feed on the bark of young trees during winter. A cheap and effective deterrent is to wrap the tree trunks with a double layer of heavy-duty aluminum foil in late fall. Be sure to remove the foil in spring.

Tip **Prevent Sunscald on Trees**

> Wrapping young tree trunks with a couple of layers of aluminum foil during the winter can help prevent sunscald, a condition widely known as southwest disease, since it damages the southwest side of some young thin-barked trees—especially fruit trees, ashes, lindens, maples, oaks, and willows. The problem occurs on warm winter days when the sun's rays reactivate some dormant cells underneath the tree's bark. The subsequent drop in nighttime temperatures kills the cells and can injure the tree. In most regions, you can remove the aluminum wrapping in early spring.

Scare crows and other birds Are the birds eating the fruit on your trees? To foil them, dangle strips of aluminum foil from the branches using monofilament fishing line. Even better, hang some foil-wrapped seashells, which will add a bit of noise to further startle your fine-feathered thieves.

Create a sun box for plants A sunny window is a great place for keeping plants that love a lot of light. However, since the light always comes from the same direction, plants tend to bend toward it. To bathe your plants in light from all sides, make a sun box: Remove the top and one side from a cardboard box and line the other three sides and bottom with aluminum foil, shiny side out, taping or gluing it in place. Place plants in the box and set it near a window.

Build a seed incubator To give plants grown from seeds a healthy head start, line a shoe box with aluminum foil, shiny side up, allowing about two inches of foil to extend out over the sides. Poke several drainage holes in the bottom—penetrating the foil—then fill the box slightly more than halfway with potting soil, and plant the seeds. The foil inside the box will absorb heat to keep the seeds warm as they germinate, while the foil outside the box will reflect light onto the young sprouts. Place the box near a sunny window, keep the soil moist, and watch 'em grow!

Grow untangled cuttings Help plant cuttings grow strong and uncluttered by starting them in a container covered with a sheet of aluminum foil. Simply poke a few holes in the foil and insert the cuttings through the holes. There's even an added bonus: The foil slows water evaporation, so you'll need to add water less frequently.

✳ ALUMINUM FOIL **IN THE GREAT OUTDOORS**

Keep bees away from beverages You're about to relax in your backyard with a well-deserved glass of lemonade or soda pop. Suddenly bees start buzzing around your drink—which they view as sweet nectar. Keep them away by tightly covering the top of your glass with aluminum foil. Poke a straw through it, and then enjoy your drink in peace.

Make a barbecue drip pan To keep meat drippings off your barbecue coals, fashion a disposable drip pan out of a couple of layers of heavy-duty aluminum foil. Shape it freehand, or use an inverted baking pan as a mold (remember to remove the pan once your creation is finished). Also, don't forget to make your drip pan slightly larger than the meat on the grill.

Clean your barbecue grill After the last steak is brought in, and while the coals are still red-hot, lay a sheet of aluminum foil over the grill to burn off any remaining foodstuffs. The next time you use your barbecue, crumple up the foil and use it to easily scrub off the burned food before you start cooking.

Improve outdoor lighting Brighten up the electrical lighting in your backyard or campsite by making a foil reflector to put behind the light. Attach the reflector to the fixture with a few strips of electrical tape or duct tape—*do not* apply tape directly to the bulb.

DID *You* KNOW?

"Hand me the tinfoil, will ya?" To this day, it's not uncommon for folks to ask for tinfoil when they want to wrap leftovers. Household foil *was* made only of tin until 1947, when aluminum foil was introduced into the home, eventually replacing tinfoil in the kitchen drawer.

Make an impromptu picnic platter When you need a convenient disposable platter for picnics or church suppers, just cover a piece of cardboard with heavy-duty aluminum foil.

Improvise a frying pan Don't feel like lugging a frying pan along on a camping trip? Form your own by centering a forked stick over two layers of heavy-duty aluminum foil. Wrap the edges of the foil tightly around the forked branches but leave some slack in the foil between the forks. Invert the stick and depress the center to hold food for frying.

Warm your toes when camping Keep your tootsies toasty at night while cold-weather camping. Wrap some stones in aluminum foil and heat them by the campfire while you are toasting marshmallows. At bedtime, wrap the stones in towels and put them in the bottom of your sleeping bag.

Keep your sleeping bag dry Place a piece of heavy-duty aluminum foil under your sleeping bag to insulate against moisture.

Keep matches dry It's a tried-and-true soldier's trick worth remembering: Wrap your kitchen matches in aluminum foil to keep them from getting damp or wet on camping trips.

Lure a fish None of your fancy fishing lures working? You can make one in a jiffy that just might do the trick: Wrap some aluminum foil around a fishhook. Fringe the foil so that it covers the hook and wiggles invitingly when you reel in the line.

✳ ALUMINUM FOIL **FOR THE DO-IT-YOURSELFER**

Make a funnel Can't find a funnel? Double up a length of heavy-duty aluminum foil and roll it into the shape of a cone. This impromptu funnel has an advantage over a permanent funnel—you can bend the aluminum foil to reach awkward holes, like the oil filler hole tucked against the engine of your lawn tractor.

Re-attach a vinyl floor tile Don't become unglued just because a vinyl floor tile does. Simply reposition the tile on the floor, lay a piece of aluminum foil over it, and run a hot clothes iron over it a few times until you can feel the glue melting underneath. Put a pile of books or bricks on top of the tile to weight it down while the glue resets. This technique also works well to smooth out bulges and straighten curled seams in sheet vinyl flooring.

Make an artist's palette Tear off a length of heavy-duty aluminum foil, crimp up the edges, and you've got a ready-to-use palette for mixing paints. If you want to get a little fancier, cut a piece of cardboard into the shape of a palette, complete with thumb hole, and cover it with foil. Or if you already have a wooden palette, cover it with foil before each use and then just strip off the foil instead of cleaning the palette.

Prevent paint from skinning over When you open a half-used can of paint, you'll typically find a skin of dried paint on the surface. Not only is this annoying to remove, but dried bits can wind up in the paint. You can prevent this by using a two-pronged attack when you close a used paint can: First, put a piece of aluminum foil under the can and trace around it. Cut out the circle and drop the aluminum foil disk onto the paint surface. Then take a deep breath, blow into the can, and quickly put the top in place. The carbon dioxide in your breath replaces some of the oxygen in the can, and helps keep the paint from drying.

Line roller pans Cleaning out paint roller pans is a pain, which is why a lot of folks buy disposable plastic pans or liners. But lining a metal roller pan with aluminum foil works just as well—and can be a lot cheaper.

Keep paint off doorknobs When you're painting a door, aluminum foil is great for wrapping doorknobs to keep paint off them. Overlap the foil onto the door when you wrap the knob, then run a sharp utility knife around the base of the knob to trim the foil. That way you can paint right up to the edge of the knob. In addition to wrapping knobs on the doors that you'll paint, wrap all the doorknobs that are along the route to where you will clean your hands and brushes.

Keep a paintbrush wet Going to continue painting tomorrow morning? Don't bother to clean the brush—just squeeze out the excess paint and wrap the brush tightly in aluminum foil (or plastic wrap). Use a rubber band to hold the foil tightly at the base of the handle. For extended wet-brush storage, think paintbrush Popsicle, and toss the wrapped brush in the freezer. But don't forget to defrost the brush for an hour or so before you paint.

Reflect light for photography Professional photographers use reflectors to throw extra light on dark areas of their subject and to even out the overall lighting. To make a reflector, lightly coat a piece of mat board or heavy cardboard with rubber cement and cover it with aluminum foil, shiny side out. You can make one single reflector, as large as you want, but it's better to make three 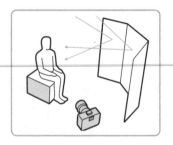 panels and join them together with duct tape so that they stand up by themselves and fold up for handy storage and carrying.

Shine your chrome For sparkling chrome on your appliances, strollers, golf club shafts, and older car bumpers, crumple up a handful of aluminum foil with the shiny side out and apply some elbow grease. If you rub real hard, the foil will even remove rust spots. *Note:* Most "chrome" on new cars is actually plastic—don't rub it with aluminum foil.

✻ Aluminum Pie Pans

Make an instant colander Your pot of linguine is almost done when you realize you forgot to replace your broken colander. No need to panic. Just grab a clean aluminum pie pan and a small nail, and start poking holes. When you're done, bend the pan to fit comfortably over a deep bowl. Rinse your new colander clean, place it over the bowl, and *carefully* pour out your pasta.

Rein in splatters when frying Why risk burning yourself or anyone else with oil splatters from a hot frying pan? A safer way to fry is to poke a few holes in the bottom of an aluminum pie pan and place it upside down over the food in your frying pan. Use a pair of tongs or a fork to lift the pie pan and don't forget to wear a cooking glove.

Create a centerpiece Here's how to make a quick centerpiece for your table: Secure a pillar candle or a few votive candles to an aluminum pie pan by melting some wax from the bottom of the candles onto the pan. Add a thin layer of water or sand, and put in several rose petals or seashells.

Contain the mess from kids' projects Glitter is notorious for turning up in the corners and crevices of your home long after your youngster's masterpiece has been mailed off to Grandma. But you can minimize some messes by using an aluminum pie pan to encase projects involving glitter, beads, spray paint, feathers ...well, you get the picture.

Kids' Stuff Looking for a way to keep the kids busy indoors on a cold, wintry day? How about making an ice ornament that you can hang on a tree outside your house as a **homemade winter decoration?** All you'll need is an **aluminum pie pan,** some **water,** a piece of heavy **string** or a shoelace, and a mix of decorative—preferably biodegradable— materials, such as **dried flowers, dried leaves,** pinecones, seeds, shells, and twigs.

Let the children arrange the materials in the pie pan to their liking. Then fold the string or shoelace in half and place it in the pan. The fold should hang over the edges of the pan, while the two ends meet in the center. Slowly fill the pan with water, stopping just shy of the rim. You may have to place an object on the string to keep it from floating to the top.

If the temperatures outside your home are indeed below freezing, you can simply put the pan on your doorstep to freeze. Otherwise just pop it into your **freezer.** Once the water has frozen solid, slide off the pan and let your children choose the optimal outdoor location to display their artwork in ice.

Make trays for craft supplies Bring some order to your children's—or your own—inventory of crayons, beads, buttons, sequins, pipe cleaners, and such by sorting them in aluminum pie pans. To secure materials when storing the pans, cover each pan with a layer of plastic wrap.

Keep bugs out of pet dishes Use an aluminum pie pan filled with about a half-inch of water to create a metal moat around your pet's food dish. It should keep those marauding ants and roaches at bay.

Train your dog If Rover has a tendency to leap up on the sofa or kitchen counter, leave a few aluminum pie pans along the counter edges or the sofa back when you're not home. The resulting noise will give him a good scare when he jumps and hits them.

Keep squirrels and birds off your fruit trees Are furry and feathered fiends stealing the fruit off your trees? There's nothing better to scare off those pesky intruders than a few dangling aluminum pie pans. String them up in pairs (to make some noise), and you won't have to worry about finding any half-eaten apples or peaches come harvest time.

Make a mini-dustpan If you need a spare dustpan for your workplace or bathroom, an aluminum pie pan can fit the bill quite nicely. Simply cut one in half, and you're ready to go.

Use as a drip catcher under paint can Next time you have something that needs painting, place an aluminum pie pan under the paint can as a ready-made drip catcher. You'll save a lot of time cleaning up, and you can just toss the pan in the trash when you're done. Even better, rinse it off and recycle it for future paint jobs.

Store sanding disks and more Since they're highly resistant to corrosion, aluminum pie pans are especially well suited for storing sanding disks, hacksaw blades, and other hardware accessories in your workshop. Cut a pan in half and attach it (with staples or duct tape around the edges) open side up to a pegboard. Now get organized!

Use as an impromptu ashtray No ashtray on hand when you host a smoker in your home? No sweat. An aluminum pie pan—or even a piece of heavy-duty aluminum foil folded into a square with the sides turned up—should suffice.

Protect fingers during cookouts There's nothing like a cookout in the great outdoors. Whether you're planning a day trip or a longer excursion, be sure to pack a few aluminum pie pans. Put a small hole in the middle of each pan, then push them up the sticks used for roasting hot dogs or marshmallows. The pans deflect the heat of the fire, protecting your hands and your children's hands.

Ammonia

Clean your oven Here's a practically effortless way to clean an electric oven: First, turn the oven on, let it warm to 150°F (65°C), and then turn it off. Place a small bowl containing 1/2 cup ammonia on the top shelf and a large pan of boiling water on the bottom shelf. Close the oven door, and let it sit overnight. The next morning, remove the dish and pan, and let the oven air out awhile. Then wipe it clean using the ammonia and a few drops of dishwashing liquid diluted in a quart of warm water—even old burned-on grease should wipe right off. *Warning: Do not use this cleaning method with a gas oven unless the pilot lights are out and the main gas lines are shut off.*

TAKE CARE Never mix ammonia with bleach or any product containing chlorine. The combination produces toxic fumes that can be deadly. Work in a well-ventilated space and avoid inhaling the vapors. Wear rubber gloves and avoid getting ammonia on your skin or in your eyes. Always store ammonia out of the reach of children.

Clean oven racks Get the cooked-on grime off your oven racks by laying them out on an old towel in a large washtub. You can also use your bathtub, though you might need to clean it afterward. Fill the tub with warm water and add 1/2 cup ammonia. Let the racks soak for at least 15 minutes, then remove, rinse off, and wipe clean.

Make crystal sparkle Has the twinkle gone out of your good crystal? Bring back its lost luster by mixing several drops of ammonia in 2 cups water and applying

 DID *You* KNOW?

During the Middle Ages, ammonia was made in northern Europe by heating the scrapings of deer antlers, and was known as spirits of hartshorn. Before the start of World War I, it was chiefly produced by the dry distillation of nitrogenous vegetable and animal products.

Today most ammonia is made synthetically using the Haber process, in which hydrogen and nitrogen gases are combined under extreme pressures and medium temperatures. The technique was developed by Fritz Haber and Carl Bosch in 1909, and was first used on a large-scale basis by the Germans during World War I, primarily for the production of munitions.

AMMONIA*

with a soft cloth or brush. Rinse it off with clean water, then dry with a soft, dry cloth.

Repel moths Pesky kitchen moths seem to come out of nowhere! Send them back to wherever they came from by washing your drawers, pantry shelves, or cupboards with 1/2 cup ammonia diluted in 1 quart (1 liter) water. Leave drawers and cabinets open to thoroughly air-dry.

✽ AMMONIA **AROUND THE HOUSE**

Eliminate paint odors Your freshly painted home interior sure looks great, but that paint smell is driving you up the wall! There's no need to prolong your suffering, though. Absorb the odor by placing small dishes of ammonia in each room that's been painted. If the smell persists after several days, replenish the dishes. Vinegar or onion slices will also work.

Clean fireplace doors Think you'll need a blowtorch to remove that blackened-on soot from your glass fireplace doors? Before you get out the goggles, try mixing 1 tablespoon ammonia, 2 tablespoons vinegar, and 1 quart (1 liter) warm water in a spray bottle. Spray on some of the solution; let it sit for several seconds, then wipe off with an absorbent cloth. Repeat if necessary—it's worth the extra effort.

Clean gold and silver jewelry Brighten up your gold and silver trinkets by soaking them for 10 minutes in a solution of 1/2 cup clear ammonia mixed in 1 cup warm water. Gently wipe clean with a soft cloth and let dry. Note: Do not do this with jewelry containing pearls, because it could dull or damage their delicate surface.

Remove tarnish from brass or silver How can you put that sunny shine back in your tarnished silver or lacquered brass? Gently scrub it with a soft brush dipped

?? DID *You* KNOW?

AMMONIA*

in a bit of ammonia. Wipe off any remaining liquid with a soft cloth—or preferably chamois.

Remove grease and soap scum To get rid of those ugly grease and soap-scum buildups in your porcelain enamel sink or tub, scrub it with a solution of 1 tablespoon ammonia in 1 gallon (3.7 liters) hot water. Rinse thoroughly when done.

Restore white shoes Brighten up your dingy white shoes or tennis sneakers by rubbing them with a cloth dipped in half-strength ammonia—that is, a solution made of half ammonia and half water.

 Testing Ammonia

> Not sure if it's safe to put ammonia solution, or any other stain remover, on a particular fabric or material? Always test a drop or two on an inconspicuous part of the garment or object first. After applying, rub the area with a white terry-cloth towel to test colorfastness. If any color rubs off on the towel or if there is any noticeable change in the material's appearance, try another approach.

Remove stains from clothing Ammonia is great for cleaning clothes. Here are some ways you can use it to remove a variety of stains. Be sure to dilute ammonia with at least 50 percent water before applying it to silk, wool, or spandex.

- Rub out perspiration, blood, and urine stains on clothing by dabbing the area with a half-strength solution of ammonia and water before laundering.

- Remove most non-oily stains by making a mixture of equal parts ammonia, water, and dishwashing liquid. Put it in an empty spray bottle, shake well, and apply directly to the stain. Let it set for two or three minutes, and then rinse out.

- To erase pencil marks from clothing, use a few drops of undiluted ammonia and then rinse. If that doesn't work, put a little laundry detergent on the stain and rinse again.

- You can even remove washed-in paint stains from clothes by saturating them several times with a half-ammonia, half-turpentine solution, and then tossing them into the wash.

Clean carpets and upholstery Lift out stains from carpeting and upholstery by sponging them with 1 cup clear ammonia in 1/2 gallon (2 liters) warm water. Let dry thoroughly, and repeat if needed.

Brighten up windows Dirty, grimy windows can make any house look dingy. But it's easy to wipe away the dirt, fingerprints, soot, and dust covering your windows. Just wipe them down with a soft cloth dampened with a solution of 1 cup clear ammonia in 3 cups water. Your windows will not only be crystal-clear, but streak-free to boot.

Strip wax from resilient flooring Wax buildup on resilient flooring causes it to yellow in time. Remove old wax layers and freshen up your floor by washing it with a mixture of 1 cup ammonia in 1/2 gallon (2 liters) water. Let the solution sit for three to five minutes, then scrub with a nylon or plastic scouring pad to remove the old wax. Wipe away leftover residue with a clean cloth or sponge, then give the floor a thorough rinsing.

Clean bathroom tiles Make bathroom tiles sparkle again—and kill mildew on them—by sponging them with 1/4 cup ammonia in 1 gallon (3.7 liters) water.

✻ AMMONIA IN THE GARDEN

Use as plant food Give the alkaline-loving flowering plants and vegetables in your garden—such as clematis, lilac, hydrangea, and cucumbers—an occasional special treat with a shower of 1/4 cup ammonia diluted in 1 gallon (3.7 liters) water. They'll especially appreciate the boost in nitrogen.

Stop mosquito bites from itching If you forget to put on your insect repellent and mosquitoes make a meal of you, stop the itching instantly by applying a drop or two of ammonia directly to the bites. Don't use ammonia on a bite you've already scratched open, though; the itch will be replaced by a nasty sting.

Keep stray animals out of your trash Few things can be quite as startling as a raccoon leaping out of your garbage pail just as you're about to make your nightly trash deposit. Keep away those masked scavengers and other strays by spraying the outside and lids of your garbage bins with half-strength ammonia or by spraying the bags inside.

Remove stains from concrete Tired of those annoying discolorations on your concrete work? To get rid of them, scrub with 1 cup ammonia diluted in 1 gallon (3.7 liters) water. Hose it down well when you're done.

Fight mildew Ammonia and bleach are equally effective weapons in the battle against mold and mildew. However, each has its own distinct applications, and under no conditions should the two ever be combined.

Reach for the ammonia for the following chores, but be sure you use it in a well-ventilated area, and don't forget to wear rubber gloves:

● Clean the mildew off unfinished wooden patio furniture and picnic tables with a mixture of 1 cup ammonia, 1/2 cup vinegar, 1/4 cup baking soda, and 1 gallon (3.7 liters) water. Rinse off thoroughly and use an old terry-cloth towel to absorb excess moisture.

● To remove mildew from painted outdoor surfaces, use the same combination of ingredients.

● To remove mildew from wicker furniture, wash it down with a solution of 2 tablespoons ammonia in 1 gallon (3.7 liters) water. Use an old toothbrush to get into hard-to-reach twists and turns. Rinse well and let air-dry.

✳ Apples

Roast a juicy chicken If your roasted chicken tends to emerge from the oven as dry as a snow boot on a summer's day, don't fret. The next time you roast a chicken, stuff an apple inside the bird before placing it in the roasting pan. When it's done cooking, toss the fruit in the trash, and get ready to sit down to a delicious—and juicy—main course.

Keep cakes fresh Want a simple and effective way to extend the shelf life of your homemade or store-bought cakes? Store them with a half an apple. It helps the cake maintain its moisture considerably longer than merely popping it in the fridge.

Ripen green tomatoes How's that? You just became the proud owner of a bunch of green tomatoes? No sweat. You can quickly ripen them up by placing them—along with an already-ripe apple—in a paper bag for a couple of days. For best results, maintain a ratio of about five or six tomatoes per apple.

Fluff up hardened brown sugar Brown sugar has the irritating habit of hardening up when exposed to humidity. Fortunately, it doesn't take much to make this a temporary condition. Simply place an apple wedge in a self-sealing plastic bag with the chunk of hardened brown sugar. Tightly seal the bag and put it in a dry place for a day or two. Your sugar will once again be soft enough to use.

Absorb salt in soups and stews Salting to taste is one thing, but it is possible to overdo it. When you find yourself getting heavy-handed with the saltshaker, simply

?? DID You KNOW?

That old saying "One bad apple spoils the bunch" just might be true. Apples are among a diverse group of fruits—others include apricots, avocados, bananas, blueberries, cantaloupe, and peaches—that produce ethylene gas, a natural ripening agent. So the increased level of ethylene produced by a single rotten apple in a bag can significantly accelerate the aging process of the other apples around it.

Ethylene-producing fruits can help speed the ripening of something (like a green tomato, see hint on this page). But they can also have unwanted effects. Placing a bowl of ripe apples or bananas too close to freshly cut flowers, for instance, can cause them to wilt. And if your refrigerated potatoes seem to be sprouting buds too soon, they may be too close to the apples. Keep them at least one shelf apart.

drop a few apple (or potato) wedges in your pot. After cooking for another 10 minutes or so, remove the wedges—along with the excess salt.

Use as decorative candleholders Add a cozy, country feel to your table setting by creating a natural candleholder. Use an apple corer to carve a hole three-quarters of the way down into a pair of large apples, insert a tall decorative candle into each hole, surround the apples with a few leaves, branches, or flowers, and voilà! You have a lovely centerpiece.

✳ Ashes

Clean fireplace doors You normally wouldn't think of using dirty wood ashes to clean glass fireplace doors, but it works. Mix some ashes with a bit of water, and apply them with a damp cloth, sponge, or paper towel, or simply dip a wet sponge into the ashes. Rub the mixture over the doors' surfaces. Rinse with a wet paper towel or sponge, then dry with a clean cloth. The results will amaze you, but remember—wood ash was a key ingredient in old-fashioned lye soap.

𝒥𝒾𝓅 Selecting Firewood

For a hot-burning and long-lasting fire, you can't do much better than well-seasoned sugar maple. Green or wet wood burns poorly and builds up heaps of creosote (the leading cause of chimney fires) in your chimney; pine is another major producer of creosote. Never burn scraps of pressure-treated wood; it contains chemicals that can be extremely harmful when burned.

Don't be a fanatic about cleaning ashes from your fireplace. Leave a 1- to 2-inch (2.5 to 5 centimeters) layer of ash under the andiron to reflect heat back up to the burning wood and protect your fireplace floor against hot embers. Just be sure not to let the ashes clog up the space under the grate and block the airflow a good fire needs.

Reduce sun glare Pro ball players often wear that black stuff under their eyes to cut down glare from the sun or bright stadium lights. If you're troubled by sun glare while driving or hiking, you may want to try it too. Just put a drop or two of baby oil on your finger, dip it in some wood ashes, and apply under your eyes.

Use as plant food Wood ashes have a high alkaline content and trace amounts of calcium and potassium, which encourage blooms. If your soil tends to be acidic, sprinkle the ashes in spring around alkaline-loving plants such as clematis, hydrangea, lilac, and roses (but avoid acid-lovers like rhododendrons, blueberries, and azaleas). Avoid using ashes from easy-to-ignite, pre-formed logs, which may contain chemicals harmful to plants. And be sparing when adding ashes to your compost pile; they can counteract the benefits of manure and other high-nitrogen materials.

Repel insects Scatter a border of ashes around your garden to deter cutworms, slugs, and snails—it sticks to their bodies and draws moisture out of them. Also sprinkle small amounts of ashes over garden plants to manage infestations of soft-bodied insects. Wear eye protection and gloves; getting ashes in your eyes can be quite painful.

Clean pewter Restore the shine to your pewter by cleaning it with cigarette ashes. Dip a dampened piece of cheesecloth into the ashes and rub it well over the item. It will turn darker at first, but the shine will come out after a good rinsing.

Remove water spots and heat marks from wood furniture Use cigar and or cigarette ashes to remove those white rings left on your wooden furniture by wet glasses or hot cups. Mix the ashes with a few drops of water to make a paste, and rub lightly over the mark to remove it. Then shine it with your favorite furniture polish.

✳ Aspirin

Revive dead car batteries If you get behind the wheel only to discover that your car's battery has given up the ghost—and there's no one around to give you a jump—you may be able to get your vehicle started by dropping two aspirin tablets into the battery itself. The aspirin's acetylsalicylic acid will combine with the battery's sulfuric acid to produce one last charge. Just be sure to drive to your nearest service station.

 DID **You** KNOW?

The bark of the willow tree is rich in salicin, a natural painkiller and fever reducer. In the third century B.C. Hippocrates used it to relieve headaches and pain, and many traditional healers, including Native Americans, used salicin-containing herbs to treat cold and flu symptoms. But it wasn't until 1899 that Felix Hoffmann, a chemist at the German company Bayer, developed a modified derivative, acetylsalicylic acid, better known as aspirin.

Remove perspiration stains Before you give up all hope of ever getting that perspiration stain out of your good white dress shirt, try this: Crush two aspirins and mix the powder in 1/2 cup warm water. Soak the stained part of the garment in the solution for two to three hours.

> **TAKE CARE** About 10 percent of people with severe asthma are also allergic to aspirin—and, in fact, to all products containing salicylic acid, aspirin's key ingredient, including some cold medications, fruits, and food seasonings and additives. That percentage skyrockets to 30 to 40 percent for older asthmatics who also suffer from sinusitis or nasal polyps. Acute sensitivity to aspirin is also seen in a small percentage of the general population without asthma—particularly people with ulcers and other bleeding conditions.
>
> Always consult your doctor before using any medication, and do not apply aspirin externally if you are allergic to taking it in internally.

Restore hair color Swimming in a chlorinated pool can have a noticeable, and often unpleasing, effect on your hair coloring if you have light-colored hair. But you can usually return your hair to its former shade by dissolving six to eight aspirins in a glass of warm water. Rub the solution thoroughly into your hair, and let it set for 10-15 minutes.

Dry up pimples Even those of us who are well past adolescence can get the occasional pimple. Put the kibosh on those annoying blemishes by crushing one aspirin and moistening it with a bit of water. Apply the paste to the pimple, and let it sit for a couple of minutes before washing off with soap and water. It will reduce the redness and soothe the sting. If the pimple persists, repeat the procedure as needed until it's gone.

Treat hard calluses Soften hard calluses on your feet by grinding five or six aspirins into a powder. Make a paste by adding 1/2 teaspoon each of lemon juice and water. Apply the mixture to the affected areas, then wrap your foot in a warm towel and cover it with a plastic bag. After staying off your feet for at least ten minutes, remove the bag and towel, and file down the softened callus with a pumice stone.

Control dandruff Is your dandruff problem getting you down? Keep it in check by crushing two aspirins to a fine powder and adding it to the normal amount of shampoo you use each time you wash your hair. Leave the mixture on your hair for 1-2 minutes, then rinse well and wash again with plain shampoo.

Apply to insect bites and stings Control the inflammation caused by mosquito bites or bee stings by wetting your skin and rubbing an aspirin over the spot. Of course, if you are allergic to bee stings—and have difficulty breathing, develop abdominal pains, or feel nauseated following a bee sting—get medical attention at once.

Help cut flowers last longer It's a tried-and-true way to keep roses and other cut flowers fresh longer: Put a crushed aspirin in the water before adding your flowers. Other household items that you can put in the water to extend the life of your flower arrangements include: a multivitamin, a teaspoon of sugar, a pinch of salt and baking soda, and even a copper penny. Also, don't forget to change the vase water every few days.

Use as garden aid Aspirin is not only a first-aid essential for you, but for your garden as well. Some gardeners grind it up for use as a rooting agent, or mix it with water to treat fungus conditions in the soil. But be careful when using aspirin around plants; too much of it can cause burns or other damage to your greenery. When treating soil, the typical dosage should be a half or a full aspirin tablet in 1 quart (1 liter) water.

Remove egg stains from clothes Did you drop some raw egg on your clothing while cooking or eating? First, scrape off as much of the egg as you can, and then try to sponge out the rest with lukewarm water. Don't use hot water—it will set the egg. If that doesn't completely remove the stain, mix water and cream of tartar into a paste and add a crushed aspirin. Spread the paste on the stain and leave it for 30 minutes. Rinse well in warm water and the egg will be gone.

✳ Baby Oil

Remove a bandage You can eliminate—or at least, significantly lessen—the "ouch" factor, and subsequent tears, when removing a youngster's bandage by first rubbing some baby oil into the adhesive parts on top and around the edges. If you see the bandage working loose, let the child finish the job to help him overcome his fear. Adults who have sensitive or fragile skin may also want to try this.

Make your own bath oil Do you have a favorite perfume or cologne? You can literally bathe in it by making your own scented bath oil. Simply add a few drops of your scent of choice to 1/4 cup baby oil in a small plastic bottle. Shake well, and add it to your bath.

Buff up your golf clubs Don't waste your money on fancy cleaning kits for your chrome-plated carbon steel golf club heads. Just keep a small bottle filled with baby oil in your golf bag along with a chamois cloth or towel. Dab a few drops of oil on the cloth and polish the head of your club after each round of golf.

Slip off a stuck ring Is that ring jammed on your finger again? First lubricate the ring area with a generous amount of baby oil. Then swivel the ring around to spread the oil under it. You should be able to slide the ring off with ease.

Clean your bathtub or shower Remove dirt and built-up soap scum around your bathtub or shower stall by wiping surfaces with 1 teaspoon baby oil on a moist cloth. Use another cloth to wipe away any leftover oil. Finally, spray the area with a disinfectant cleaner to kill any remaining germs. This technique is also great for cleaning soap film and watermarks off glass shower doors.

Shine stainless steel sinks and chrome trim Pamper your dull-looking stainless steel sinks by rubbing them down with a few drops of baby oil on a soft, clean cloth. Rub dry with a towel, and repeat if necessary. This is also a terrific way to remove stains on the chrome trim of your kitchen appliances and bathroom fixtures.

Polish leather bags and shoes Just a few drops of baby oil applied with a soft cloth can add new life to an old leather bag or pair of patent-leather shoes. Don't forget to wipe away any oil remaining on the leather when you're done.

Get scratches off dashboard plastic You can disguise scratches on the plastic lens covering the odometer and other indicators on your car's dashboard by rubbing over them with a bit of baby oil.

Remove latex paint from skin Did you get almost as much paint on your face and hands as you did on the bathroom you just painted? You can quickly get latex paint off your skin by first rubbing it with some baby oil, followed by a good washing with soap and hot water.

Treat cradle cap Cradle cap may be unsightly, but it is a common, usually harmless, phase in many babies' development. To combat it, gently rub in a little baby oil, and lightly comb it through your baby's hair. If your child gets upset, comb it a bit at a time, but do not leave the oil on for more than 24 hours. Then, thoroughly wash the hair to remove all of the oil. Repeat the process in persistent cases. *Note:* If you notice a lot of yellow crusting, or if the cradle cap has spread behind the ears or on the neck, contact your pediatrician instead.

Baby Powder

Give sand the brush-off How many times have you had a family member return from a day at the beach only to discover that a good portion of the beach has been brought back into your living room? Minimize the mess by sprinkling some baby powder over sweaty, sand-covered kids (and adults) before they enter the house. In addition to soaking up excess moisture, the powder makes sand incredibly easy to brush off.

Cool sheets in summer Are those sticky, hot bed sheets giving you the summertime blues when you should be deep in dreamland? Cool things down by sprinkling a bit of baby powder between your sheets before hopping into the sack on warm summer nights.

?? DID *You* KNOW?

When shopping for baby powder, you're invariably faced with three choices: ordinary, cornstarch, or medicated.

Ordinary baby powder is primarily talcum powder, which is not good for infants to breathe. Using talc on baby girls is particularly discour-aged, since studies suggest that it could cause ovarian cancer later in life.

Pediatricians often recommend using a cornstarch-based powder—if one is needed at all—when changing diapers. Cornstarch powder is coarser than talcum powder but does not have the health risks. But it can promote fungal infection and should not be applied in skin folds or to broken skin.

Medicated baby powder has zinc oxide added to either talcum powder or cornstarch. It is generally used to soothe diaper rash and to prevent chafing.

Dry-shampoo your pet Is the pooch's coat in need of a pick-me-up? Vigorously rub a handful or two of baby powder into your pet's fur. Let it settle in for a couple of minutes, and follow up with a thorough brushing. Your dog will both look and *smell* great! You can even occasionally "dry shampoo" your own, or someone else's, hair by following the same technique.

Absorb grease stains on clothing Frying foods can be dangerous business—especially for your clothes. If you get a grease splatter on your clothing, try dabbing the stain with some baby powder on a powder puff. Make sure you rub it in well, and then brush off any excess powder. Repeat until the mark is gone.

Clean your playing cards Here's a simple way to keep your playing cards from sticking together and getting grimy: Loosely place the cards in a plastic bag along with a bit of baby powder. Seal the bag and give it a few good shakes. When you remove your cards, they should feel fresh and smooth to the touch.

Slip on your rubber gloves Don't try jamming and squeezing your fingers into your rubber gloves when the powder layer inside the gloves wears out. Instead, give your fingers a light dusting with baby powder. Your rubber gloves should slide on good as new.

Remove mold from books If some of your books have been stored in a less than ideal environment and have gotten a bit moldy or mildewed, try this: First, let them thoroughly air-dry. Then, sprinkle some baby powder between the pages and stand the books upright for several hours. Afterward, gently brush out the remaining powder from each book. They may not be as good as new, but they should be in a lot better shape than they were.

Dust off your flower bulbs Many savvy gardeners use medicated baby powder to dust flower bulbs before planting them. Simply place 5-6 bulbs and about 3 tablespoons baby powder in a sealed plastic bag and give it a few gentle shakes. The medicated-powder coating helps both reduce the chance of rot and keep away moles, voles, grubs, and other bulb-munching pests.

✳ Baby Wipes

Use for quick, on-the-move cleanups Baby wipes can be used for more than just cleaning babies' bottoms. They're great for wiping your hands after pumping gas, mopping up small spills in the car, and cooling your sweaty brow after a run. In fact, they make ideal travel companions. So, next time you set off on the road, pack a small stack of wipes in a tightly closed self-sealing sandwich bag and put it in the glove compartment of your car or in your purse or knapsack.

Shine your shoes Most moms know that a baby wipe does a pretty good job of brightening Junior's white leather shoes. But did you ever think of using one to put the shine back in *your* leather pumps—especially with that 10 a.m. meeting fast approaching?

Recycle as dust cloths Believe it or not, some brands of baby wipes—Huggies, for instance—can be laundered and reused as dust cloths and cleaning rags for when you straighten up. It probably goes without saying, but only "mildly" soiled wipes should be considered candidates for laundering.

Buff up your bathroom Do you have company coming over and not much time to tidy up the house? Don't break out in a sweat. Try this double-handed trick: Take a baby wipe in one hand and start polishing your bathroom surfaces. Keep a dry washcloth in your other hand to shine things up as you make your rounds.

Remove stains from carpet, clothing, and upholstery Use a baby wipe to blot up coffee spills from your rug or carpet; it absorbs both the liquid *and* the stain. Wipes can also be effectively deployed when attacking various spills and drips on your clothing and upholstered furniture.

Clean your PC keyboard Periodically shaking out your PC's keyboard is a good way to get rid of the dust and debris that gathers underneath and in between the keys. But that's just half the job. Use a baby wipe to remove the dirt, dried spills, and unspecified gunk that builds up on the keys themselves. Make sure to turn off the computer or unplug the keyboard before you wipe the keys.

Soothe your skin Did you get a bit too much sun at the beach? You can temporarily cool a sunburn by gently patting the area with a baby wipe. Baby wipes can also be used to treat cuts and scrapes. Although most wipes don't have any antiseptic properties, there's nothing wrong with using one for an initial cleansing before applying the proper topical treatment.

Remove makeup It's one of the fashion industry's worst-kept secrets: Many models consider a baby wipe to be their best friend when it comes time to remove that stubborn makeup from their faces, particularly black eyeliner. Try it and see for yourself.

✳ Baby Wipes Containers

Organize your stuff Don't toss those empty wipes containers. These sturdy plastic boxes are incredibly useful for storing all sorts of items. And the rectangular ones are stackable to boot! Give the containers a good washing and let them dry thoroughly, then fill them with everything from sewing supplies, recipe cards, coupons, and craft and office supplies to old floppy disks, small tools, photos, receipts, and bills. Label the contents with a marker on masking tape, and you're set!

Make a first-aid kit Every home needs a first-aid kit. But you don't have to buy a ready-made one. Gather up your own choice of essentials (such as bandages, sterile gauze rolls and pads, adhesive tape, scissors, and triple-antibiotic ointment) and use a rectangular baby wipes container to hold it all. Before you add your supplies, give the container a good washing—and rub the inside with alcohol on a cotton ball after it dries.

Use as a decorative yarn or twine dispenser A clean cylindrical wipes container makes a perfect dispenser for a roll of yarn or twine. Simply remove the container's cover, insert the roll, and thread it through the slot in the lid, then reattach the cover. Paint or paper over the container to give it a more decorative look.

Tip **Removing Labels**

> Use a blow-dryer on a high setting to heat up the labels on baby wipes containers to make them easier to pull off. You can get rid of any leftover sticky stuff by applying a little WD-40 oil or orange citrus cleaner.

Store your plastic shopping bags Do you save plastic shopping bags for lining the small wastebaskets (or perhaps for pooper-scooper duty)? If so, bring order to the puffed-up chaos they create by storing the bags in cleaned, rectangular wipes containers. Each container can hold 40 to 50 bags—once you squeeze the air out of them. You can also use an empty 250-count tissue box—the kind with a perforated cutout dispenser—in a similar manner.

Make a piggy bank Well, maybe not a "piggy" bank, per se, but a bank nonetheless, and one that gives you a convenient place to dump your pocket change. Take a clean rectangular container and use a knife to cut a slot—be sure to make it wide enough to easily accommodate a quarter—on the lid. If you're making the bank for a child, you can either decorate it or let her put her own personal "stamp" on it.

Hold workshop towels or rags A used baby wipes container can be a welcome addition in the workshop for storing rags and paper towels—and to keep a steady supply on hand as needed. You can easily keep a full roll of detached paper towels or six or seven good-sized rags in each container.

super item
83 *uses!* Baking Soda

✳ BAKING SODA **IN THE KITCHEN**

Clean your produce You can't be too careful when it comes to food handling and preparation. Wash fruits and vegetables in a pot of cold water with 2-3 table-spoons baking soda; the baking soda will remove some of the impurities tap water leaves behind. Or put a small amount of baking soda on a wet sponge or vegetable brush and scrub your produce. Give everything a thorough rinsing before serving.

Tenderize meat Got a tough cut of meat on your hands? Soften it up by giving it rubdown in baking soda. Let it sit (in the refrigerator, of course) for three to five hours, then rinse it off well before cooking.

Soak out fish smells Get rid of that fishy smell from your store-bought flounder filets and fish steaks by soaking the raw fish for about an hour (inside your refrigerator) in 1 quart (1 liter) water with 2 tablespoons baking soda. Rinse the fish well and pat dry before cooking.

Reduce acids in recipes If you or someone in your family is sensitive to the high-acid content of tomato-based sauces or coffee, you can lower the overall acidity by sprinkling in a pinch of baking soda while cooking (or, in the case of coffee, before brewing). A bit of baking soda can also counteract the taste of vinegar if you happen to pour in a bit too much. Be careful not to overdo it with the soda, though—if you add too much, the vinegar-baking soda combination will start foaming.

Bake better beans Do you love baked beans but not their aftereffects? Adding a pinch of baking soda to baked beans as they're cooking will significantly reduce their gas-producing properties.

Fluff up your omelets Want to know the secret to making fluffier omelets? For every three eggs used, add 1/2 teaspoon baking soda. Shhhh! Don't let it get around.

Tip **Out of Baking Powder?**

> If you are out of baking powder, you can usually substitute 2 parts baking soda mixed with 1 part each cream of tartar and cornstarch. To make the equivalent of 1 teaspoon baking powder, for instance, mix 1/2 teaspoon baking soda with 1/4 teaspoon cream of tartar and 1/4 teaspoon cornstarch. The cornstarch slows the reaction between the acidic cream of tartar and the alkaline baking soda so that, like commercial baking powder, it maintains its leavening power longer.

Use as yeast substitute Need a stand-in for yeast when making dough? If you have some powdered vitamin C (or citric acid) and baking soda on hand, you can use a mixture of the two instead. Just mix in equal parts to equal the quantity of yeast required. What's more, the dough you add it to won't have to rise before baking.

Rid hands of food odors Chopping garlic or cleaning a fish can leave their "essence" on your fingers long after the chore is done. Get those nasty food smells off your hands by simply wetting them and vigorously rubbing with about 2 teaspoons baking soda instead of soap. The smell should wash off with the soda.

63

Clean baby bottles and accessories Here's some great advice for new parents: Keep all your baby bottles, nipples, caps, and brushes "baby fresh" by soaking them overnight in a container filled with hot water and half a box of baking soda. Be sure to give everything a good rinsing afterward, and to dry thoroughly before using. Baby bottles can also be boiled in a full pot of water and 3 tablespoons baking soda for three minutes.

Clean a cutting board Keep your wooden or plastic cutting board clean by occasionally scrubbing it with a paste made from 1 tablespoon each baking soda, salt, and water. Rinse thoroughly with hot water.

Clear a clogged drain Most kitchen drains can be unclogged by pouring in 1 cup baking soda followed by 1 cup hot vinegar (simply heat it up in the microwave for 1 minute). Give it several minutes to work, then add 1 quart (1 liter) boiling water. Repeat if necessary. If you know your drain is clogged with grease, use 1/2 cup each of baking soda and salt followed by 1 cup boiling water. Let the mixture work overnight; then rinse with hot tap water in the morning.

Boost potency of dishwashing liquid Looking for a more powerful dishwashing liquid? Try adding 2 tablespoons baking soda to the usual amount of liquid you use, and watch it cut through grease like a hot knife!

Make your own dishwashing detergent The dishwasher is fully loaded when you discover that you're out of your usual powdered dishwashing detergent. What do you do? Make your own: Combine 2 tablespoons baking soda with 2 tablespoons borax. You may be so pleased with the results you'll switch for good.

Deodorize your dishwasher Eliminate odors inside your automatic dishwasher by sprinkling 1/2 cup baking soda on the bottom of the dishwasher between loads. Or pour in half a box of baking soda and run the empty machine through its rinse cycle.

DID You KNOW?

Baking soda is the main ingredient in many commercial fire extinguishers. And you can use it straight out of the box to extinguish small fires throughout your home. For quick access, keep baking soda in buckets placed strategically around the house.

Keep baking soda near your stove and barbecue so you can toss on a few handfuls to quell a flare-up. In the case of a grease fire, first turn off the heat, if possible, and try to cover the fire with a pan lid. Be careful not to let the hot grease splatter you.

Keep a box or two in your garage and inside your car to quickly extinguish any mechanical or car-interior fires.

Baking soda will also snuff out electrical fires and flames on clothing, wood, upholstery, and carpeting.

Clean your refrigerator To get rid of smells and dried-up spills inside your refrigerator, remove the contents, then sprinkle some baking soda on a damp sponge and scrub the sides, shelves, and compartments. Rinse with a clean, wet sponge. Don't forget to place a fresh box of soda inside when you're done.

Clean your microwave To clean those splatters off the inside of your microwave, put a solution of 2 tablespoons baking soda in 1 cup water in a microwave-safe container and cook on High for 2-3 minutes. Remove the container, then wipe down the microwave's moist interior with a damp paper towel.

Remove coffee and tea stains from china Don't let those annoying coffee and/or tea stains on your good china spoil another special occasion. Remove them by dipping a moist cloth in baking soda to form a stiff paste and gently rubbing your cups and saucers. Rinse clean and dry, then set your table with pride.

Clean a thermos To remove residue on the inside of a thermos, mix 1/4 cup baking soda in 1 quart (1 liter) water. Fill the thermos with the solution—if necessary, give it a going-over with a bottle brush to loosen things up—and let it soak overnight. Rinse clean before using.

Freshen a sponge or towel When a kitchen sponge or dish towel gets that distinctly sour smell, soak it overnight in 2 tablespoons baking soda and a couple of drops of antibacterial dish soap dissolved in 1 pint (450 milliliters) warm water. The following morning, squeeze out the remaining solution and rinse with cold water. It should smell as good as new.

Remove stains and scratches on countertops Is your kitchen countertop covered with stains or small knife cuts? Use a paste of 2 parts baking soda to 1 part water to "rub out" most of them. For stubborn stains, add a drop of chlorine bleach to the paste. Immediately wash the area with hot, soapy water to prevent the bleach from causing fading.

Shine up stainless steel and chrome trim To put the shine back in your stainless steel sink, sprinkle it with baking soda, then give it a rubdown—moving in the direction of the grain—with a moist cloth. To polish dull chrome trim on your appliances, pour a little baking soda onto a damp sponge and rub over the chrome. Let it dry for an hour or so, then wipe down with warm water and dry with a clean cloth.

Get rid of grease stains on stovetops Say good-bye to cooked-on grease stains on your stovetop or backsplash. First wet them with a little water and cover them with a bit of baking soda. Then rub them off with a damp sponge or towel.

Clean an automatic coffeemaker Properly caring for your automatic coffeemaker means never having to worry about bitter or weak coffee. Every two weeks or so, brew a pot of 1 quart (1 liter) water mixed with 1/4 cup baking soda, followed by a pot of clean water. Also, sweeten your coffeemaker's plastic basket by using an old toothbrush to give it an occasional scrubbing with a paste of 2 tablespoons baking soda and 1 tablespoon water. Rinse thoroughly with cold water when done.

Care for your coffeepots and teapots Remove mineral deposits in metal coffeepots and teapots by filling them with a solution of 1 cup vinegar and 4 tablespoons baking soda. Bring the mixture to a boil, then let simmer for five minutes. Or try boiling 5 cups water with 2 tablespoons soda and the juice of half a lemon. Rinse with cold water when done. To get off annoying exterior stains, wash your pots with a plastic scouring pad in a solution of 1/4 cup baking soda in 1 quart (1 liter) warm water. Follow up with a cold-water rinse.

Remove stains from nonstick cookware It may be called nonstick cookware, but a few of those stains seem to be stuck on pretty well. Blast them away by boiling 1 cup water mixed with 2 tablespoons baking soda and 1/2 cup vinegar for 10 minutes. Then wash in hot, soapy water. Rinse well and let dry, then season with a bit of salad oil.

Clean cast-iron cookware Although it's more prone to stains and rust than the nonstick variety, many folks swear by their iron cookware. You can remove even the toughest burned-on food remnants in your iron pots by boiling 1 quart (1 liter) water with 2 tablespoons baking soda for five minutes. Pour off most of the liquid, then lightly scrub it with a plastic scrub pad. Rinse well, dry, and season with a few drops of peanut oil.

Clean burned or scorched pots and pans It usually takes heavy-duty scrubbing to get scorched-on food off the bottom of a pot or pan. But you can make life much easier for yourself by simply boiling a few cups of water (enough to get the pan about 1/4 full) and adding 5 tablespoons baking soda. Turn off the heat, and let the soda settle in for a few hours or overnight. When you're ready, that burned-on gunk will practically slip right off.

Deodorize your garbage pail Does something smell "off" in your kitchen? Most likely, it's emanating from your trash can. But some smells linger even after you dispose of the offending garbage bag. So, be sure to give your kitchen garbage pail an occasional cleaning with a wet paper towel dipped in baking soda (you may want to wear rubber gloves for this). Rinse it out with a damp sponge, and let it dry before inserting a new bag. You can also ward off stinky surprises by sprinkling a little baking soda into the bottom of your pail before inserting the bag.

❋ BAKING SODA **AROUND THE HOUSE**

Remove crayon marks from walls Has Junior redecorated your walls or wallpaper with some original artworks in crayon? Don't lose your cool. Just grab a damp rag, dip it in some baking soda, and lightly scrub the marks. They should come off with a minimal amount of effort.

Wash wallpaper Is your wallpaper looking a bit dingy? Brighten it up by wiping it with a rag or sponge moistened in a solution of 2 tablespoons baking soda in 1 quart (1 liter) water. To remove grease stains from wallpaper, make a paste of 1 tablespoon baking soda and 1 teaspoon water. Rub it on the stain, let it set for 5-10 minutes, then rub off with a damp sponge.

Clean baby spit-ups Infants do tend to spit up—and usually not at opportune moments. Never leave home without a small bottle of baking soda in your diaper bag. If your tyke spits up on his or her (or your) shirt after feeding, simply brush off any solid matter, moisten a washcloth, dip it in a bit of baking soda, and dab the spot. The odor (and the potential stain) will soon be gone.

Deodorize rugs and carpets How's this for a simple way to freshen up your carpets or rugs? Lightly sprinkle them with baking soda, let it settle in for 15 minutes or so, then vacuum up. Nothing to it!

Remove wine and grease stains from carpet What's that? Someone just dropped a slab of butter or a glass of cabernet on your beautiful white carpeting! Before you scream, get a paper towel, and blot up as much of the stain as possible. Then sprinkle a liberal amount of baking soda over the spot. Give the soda at least an hour to absorb the stain, then vacuum up the remaining powder. Now ... exhale!

Kids' Stuff Make **watercolor paints** for your kids using ingredients in your kitchen. In a small bowl, combine 3 tablespoons each of **baking soda, cornstarch,** and **vinegar** with 1 1/2 teaspoons **light corn syrup.** Wait for the fizzing to subside, then separate the mixture into several small containers or jar lids. Add eight drops of **food coloring** to each batch and mix well. Put a different color in each batch or combine colors to make new shades. Kids can either use the paint right away, or wait for them to harden, in which case, they'll need to use a wet brush before painting.

Freshen up musty drawers and closets Put baking soda sachets to work on persistent musty odors in dresser drawers, cabinet hutches, or closets. Just fill the toe of a clean sock or stocking with 3-4 tablespoons soda, put a knot about an inch above the bulge, and either hang it up or place it away in an unobtrusive corner. Use a few sachets in large spaces like closets and attic storage areas. Replace them every other month if needed. This treatment can also be used to rid closets of mothball smells.

Remove musty odor from books If those books you just took out of storage emerge with a musty smell, place each one in a brown paper bag with 2 tablespoons baking soda. No need to shake the bag, just tie it up and let it sit in a dry environment for about one week. When you open the bag, shake any remaining powder off the books, and the smell should be gone.

Polish silver and gold jewelry To remove built-up tarnish from your silver, make a thick paste with 1/4 cup baking soda and 2 tablespoons water. Apply with a damp sponge and gently rub, rinse, and buff dry. To polish gold jewelry, cover with a light coating of baking soda, pour a bit of vinegar over it, and rinse clean. *Note:* Do not use this technique with jewelry containing pearls or gemstones, as it could damage their finish and loosen the glue.

Get yellow stains off piano keys That old upright may still play great, but those yellowed keys definitely hit a sour note. Remove age stains on your ivories by mixing a solution of 1/4 cup baking soda in 1 quart (1 liter) warm water. Apply to each key with a dampened cloth (you can place a thin piece of cardboard between the keys to avoid seepage). Wipe again with a cloth dampened with plain water, and then buff dry with a clean cloth. (You can also clean piano keys with lemon juice and salt.)

Remove stains from fireplace bricks You may need to use a bit of elbow grease, but you can clean the smoke stains off your fireplace bricks by washing them with a solution of 1/2 cup baking soda in 1 quart (1 liter) warm water.

Remove white marks on wood surfaces Get those white marks—caused by hot cups or sweating glasses—off your coffee table or other wooden furniture by making a paste of 1 tablespoon baking soda and 1 teaspoon water. Gently rub the spot in a circular motion until it disappears. Remember not to use too much water.

Remove cigarette odors from furniture To eliminate that lingering smell of cigarette or cigar smoke on your upholstered furniture, simply lightly sprinkle your chairs or sofas with some baking soda. Let it sit for a few hours, then vacuum it off.

Shine up marble-topped furniture Revitalize the marble top on your coffee table or counter by washing it with a soft cloth dipped in a solution of 3 tablespoons baking soda and 1 quart (1 liter) warm water. Let it stand for 15 minutes to a half hour, then rinse with plain water and wipe dry.

Clean bathtubs and sinks Get the gunk off old enameled bathtubs and sinks by applying a paste of 2 parts baking soda and 1 part hydrogen peroxide. Let the paste set for about half an hour. Then give it a good scrubbing and rinse well; the paste will also sweeten your drain as it washes down.

Remove mineral deposits from showerheads Say so long to hard-water deposits on your showerhead. Cover the head with a thick sandwich-size bag filled with 1/4 cup baking soda and 1 cup vinegar. Loosely fasten the bag—you need to let some of the gas escape—with adhesive tape or a large bag tie. Let the solution work its magic for about an hour.

Then remove the bag and turn on your shower to wash off any remaining debris. Not only will the deposits disappear, but your showerhead will be back to its old shining self!

Absorb bathroom odors Keep your bathroom smelling fresh and clean by placing a decorative dish filled with 1/2 cup baking soda either on top of the toilet tank or on the floor behind the bowl. You can also make your own bathroom deodorizers by setting out dishes containing equal parts baking soda and your favorite scented bath salts.

Tidy up your toilet bowl You don't need all those chemicals to get your toilet bowl clean. Just pour half a box of baking soda into your toilet tank once a month. Let it stand overnight, then give it a few flushes in the morning. This actually cleans both the tank and the bowl. You can also pour several tablespoons of baking soda directly into your toilet bowl and scrub it on any stains. Wait a few minutes, then flush away the stains.

✳ BAKING SODA IN THE MEDICINE CABINET

Treat minor burns The next time you grab the wrong end of a frying pan or forget to use a pot holder, quickly pour some baking soda into a container of ice water, soak a cloth or gauze pad in it, and apply it to the burn. Keep applying the solution until the burn no longer feels hot. This treatment will also prevent many burns from blistering.

Cool off sunburn and other skin irritations For quick relief of sunburn pain, soak gauze pads or large cotton balls in a solution of 4 tablespoons baking soda mixed in 1 cup water and apply it to the affected areas. For a bad sunburn on your legs or torso—or to relieve the itching of chicken pox—take a lukewarm bath with a half to a full box of baking soda added to the running water. To ease the sting of razor burns, dab your skin with a cotton ball soaked in a solution of 1 tablespoon baking soda in 1 cup water.

Soothe poison ivy rashes Did you have an unplanned encounter with poison ivy when gardening or camping recently? To take away the itch, make a thick paste from 3 teaspoons baking soda and 1 teaspoon water and apply it to the affected areas. You can also use baking soda to treat oozing blisters caused by the rash. Mix 2 teaspoons baking soda in 1 quart (1 liter) water and use it to saturate a few sterile gauze pads. Cover the blisters with the wet pads for 10 minutes, four times a day. *Note:* Do not apply on or near your eyes.

Make a salve for bee stings Take the pain out of that bee sting—fast. Make a paste of 1 teaspoon baking soda mixed with several drops of cool water, and let it dry on the afflicted area. *Warning*: Many people have severe allergic reactions to bee stings. If you have difficulty breathing or notice a dramatic swelling, get medical attention at once. (You can also treat bee stings with meat tenderizer. See page 210.)

Fight diaper rash Soothe your baby's painful diaper rash by adding a couple of tablespoons of baking soda to a lukewarm—not hot—bath. If the rash persists or worsens after several treatments, however, consult your pediatrician.

Combat cradle cap Cradle cap is a commonplace, and typically harmless, condition in many infants. An old but often effective way to treat it is to make a paste of about 3 teaspoons baking soda and 1 teaspoon water. Apply it to your baby's scalp about an hour before bedtime and rinse it off the following morning. Do not use with shampoo. You may need to apply it several consecutive nights before the cradle cap recedes. (You can also treat cradle cap with baby oil. See page 59.)

Tip Baking Soda Shelf Life

How can you tell if the baking soda you've had stashed away in the back of your pantry is still good? Just pour out a small amount—a little less than a teaspoon—and add a few drops of vinegar or fresh lemon juice. If it doesn't fizz, it's time to replace it. By the way, a sealed box of baking soda has an average shelf life of 18 months, while an opened box lasts 6 months.

Control your dandruff Got a bit of a "flaky" problem? To get dandruff under control, wet your hair and then rub a handful of baking soda vigorously into your scalp. Rinse thoroughly and dry. Do this every time you normally wash your hair, but only use baking soda, no shampoo. Your hair may get dried out at first. But after a few weeks your scalp will start producing natural oils, leaving your hair softer and free of flakes.

Clean combs and brushes Freshen up your combs and hairbrushes by soaking them in a solution of 3 cups warm water and 2 teaspoons baking soda. Swirl them around in the water to loosen up all the debris caught between the teeth, then let them soak for about half an hour. Rinse well and dry before using.

Use as gargle or mouthwash Did the main course you ordered include a few too many onions or a bit too much garlic? Try gargling with 1 teaspoon baking soda in a half glass of water. The baking soda will neutralize the odors on contact. When used as a mouthwash, baking soda will also relieve canker-sore pain.

Scrub teeth and clean dentures If you run out of your regular toothpaste, or if you're looking for an all-natural alternative to commercial toothpaste, just dip your wet toothbrush in some baking soda and brush and rinse as usual. You can also use baking soda to clean retainers, mouthpieces, and dentures. Use a solution of 1 tablespoon baking soda dissolved in 1 cup warm water. Let the object soak for a half hour and rinse well before using.

Clean and sweeten toothbrushes Keep your family's toothbrushes squeaky clean by immersing them in a solution of 1/4 cup baking soda and 1/4 cup water. Let the brushes soak overnight about once every week or two. Be sure to give them a good rinsing before using.

Remove built-up gel, hair spray, or conditioner from hair When it comes to personal grooming, too much of a good thing can spell bad news for your hair. But a thorough cleansing with baking soda at least once a week will wash all of the gunk out of your hair. Simply add 1 tablespoon soda to your hair while shampooing. In addition to removing all the chemicals you put in your hair, it will wash away water impurities, and may actually lighten your hair.

Use as antiperspirant Looking for an effective, all-natural deodorant? Try applying a small amount—about a teaspoon's worth—of baking soda with a powder puff under each arm. You won't smell like a flower or some exotic spice. But then, you won't smell like anything from the opposite extreme, either.

Relieve itching inside a cast Wearing a plaster cast on your arm or leg is a misery any time of year, but wearing one in the summertime can be torture. The sweating and itchiness you feel underneath your "shell" can drive you nearly insane. Find temporary relief by using a hair dryer—on the coolest setting—to blow a bit of baking soda down the edges of the cast. *Note:* Have someone help you, to avoid getting the powder in your eyes.

Alleviate athlete's foot You can deploy wet or dry baking soda to combat a case of athlete's foot. First, try dusting your feet (along with your socks and shoes) with dry baking soda to dry out the infection. If that doesn't work, try making a paste of 1 teaspoon baking soda and 1/2 teaspoon water and rubbing it

SCIENCE FAIR

Use the gas produced by mixing **baking soda** and **vinegar** to blow up a balloon. First, pour 1/2 cup vinegar into the bottom of a narrow-neck **bottle** (such as an empty water bottle) or **jar.** Then insert a **funnel** into the mouth of an average-sized **balloon,** and fill it with 5 tablespoons baking soda. Carefully stretch the mouth of the balloon over the

opening of the bottle, then gently lift it up so that the baking soda empties into the vinegar at the bottom of the bottle. The fizzing and foaming you see is actually a chemical reaction between the two ingredients. This reaction results in the release of **carbon dioxide gas—** which will soon **inflate the balloon!**

between your toes. Let it dry, and wash off after 15 minutes. Dry your feet thoroughly before putting on your shoes.

Soothe tired, stinky feet When your dogs start barking, treat them to a soothing bath of 4 tablespoons baking soda in 1 quart (1 liter) warm water. Besides relaxing your aching tootsies, the baking soda will remove the sweat and lint that gathers between your toes. Regular footbaths can also be an effective treatment for persistent foot odor.

Deodorize shoes and sneakers A smelly shoe or sneaker is no match for the power of baking soda. Liberally sprinkle soda in the offending loafer or lace-up and let it sit overnight. Dump out the powder in the morning. (Be careful when using baking soda with leather shoes, however; repeated applications can dry them out.) You can also make your own reusable "odor eaters" by filling the toes of old socks with 2 tablespoons baking soda and tying them up in a knot. Stuff the 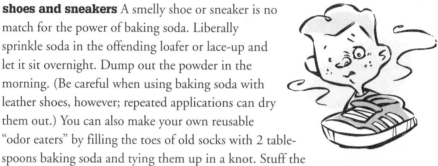 socks into each shoe at night before retiring. Remove the socks in the morning and breathe easier.

✳ BAKING SODA **IN THE LAUNDRY**

Boost strength of liquid detergent and bleach It may sound like a cliché, but adding 1/2 cup baking soda to your usual amount of liquid laundry detergent really will give you "whiter whites" and brighter colors. The baking soda also softens the water, so you can actually use less detergent. Adding 1/2 cup baking soda in top-loading machines (1/4 cup for front-loaders) also increases the potency of bleach, so you need only half the usual amount of bleach.

Remove mothball smell from clothes If your clothes come out of storage reeking of mothballs, take heed: Adding 1/2 cup baking soda during your washer's rinse cycle will get rid of the smell.

Wash new baby clothes Get all of the chemicals out of your newborn's clothing—without using any harsh detergents. Wash your baby's new clothes with some mild soap and 1/2 cup baking soda.

Rub out perspiration and other stains Pretreating clothes with a paste made from 4 tablespoons baking soda and 1/4 cup warm water can help vanquish a variety of stains. For example, rub it into shirts to remove perspiration stains; for really bad stains, let the paste dry for about two hours before washing. Rub out tar stains by applying the paste and washing in plain baking soda. For collar stains, rub in the paste and add a bit of vinegar as you're putting the shirt in the wash.

Wash mildewed shower curtains Just because your plastic shower curtain or liner gets dirty or mildewed doesn't mean you have to throw it away. Try cleaning it in your washing machine with two bath towels on the gentle setting. Add 1/2 cup baking soda to your detergent during the wash cycle and 1/2 cup vinegar during the rinse cycle. Let it drip-dry; don't put it in the dryer.

Clean battery terminals Eliminate the corrosive buildup on your car's battery terminals. Scrub them clean using an old toothbrush and a mixture of 3 tablespoons baking soda and 1 tablespoon warm water. Wipe them off with a wet towel and dry with another towel. Once the terminals have completely dried, apply a bit of petroleum jelly around each terminal to deter future corrosive buildup.

Use as deicer in winter Salt and commercial ice-melt formulations can stain—or actually eat away—the concrete around your house. For an equally effective, but completely innocuous, way to melt the ice on your steps and walkways during those cold winter months, try sprinkling them with generous amounts of baking soda. Add some sand for improved traction.

Tighten cane chair seats The bottoms of cane chairs can start to sag with age, but you can tighten them up again easily enough. Just soak two cloths in a solution of 1/2 cup baking soda in 1 quart (1 liter) hot water. Saturate the top surface of the caning with one cloth, while pushing the second up against the bottom of the caning to saturate the underside. Use a clean, dry cloth to soak up the excess moisture, then put the chair in the sun to dry.

Kids' Stuff Spies use it and so can you. Send a message or draw a picture with **invisible ink.** Here's how you do it: Mix 1 tablespoon each of **baking soda** and **water.** Dip a **toothpick** or **paintbrush** in the mixture and write your message or draw a picture or design on a piece of **plain white paper.** Let the paper and the "ink" dry completely. To reveal your message or see your picture, mix 6 drops **food coloring** with 1 tablespoon water. Dip a clean **paintbrush** in the solution, and lightly paint over the paper. Use different food-coloring combinations for a cool effect.

Remove tar from your car It may look pretty bad, but it's not that hard to get road tar off your car without damaging the paint. Make a soft paste of 3 parts baking soda to 1 part water and apply to the tar spots with a damp cloth. Let it dry for five minutes, then rinse clean.

Give your deck the weathered look You can instantly give your wooden deck a weathered look by washing it in a solution of 2 cups baking soda in 1 gallon (3.7 liters) water. Use a stiff straw brush to work the solution into the wood, then rinse with cool water.

Clean air-conditioner filters Clean washable air-conditioner filters each month they're in use. First vacuum off as much dust and dirt as possible, then wash in a solution of 1 tablespoon baking soda in 1 quart (1 liter) water. Let the filters dry thoroughly before replacing.

Keep your humidifier odor-free Eliminate musty smells from a humidifier by adding 2 tablespoons baking soda to the water each time you change it. *Note:* Check your owner's manual or consult the unit's manufacturer before trying this.

❋ BAKING SODA IN THE GREAT OUTDOORS

Keep weeds out of cement cracks Looking for a safe way to keep weeds and grasses from growing in the cracks of your paved patios, driveways, and walkways? Sprinkle handfuls of baking soda onto the concrete and simply sweep it into the cracks. The added sodium will make it much less hospitable to dandelions and their friends.

Clean resin lawn furniture Most commercial cleaners are too abrasive to be used on resin lawn furniture. But you won't have to worry about scratching or dulling the surface if you clean your resin furniture with a wet sponge dipped in baking soda. Wipe using circular motions, then rinse well.

Use as plant food Give your flowering, alkaline-loving plants, such as clematis, delphiniums, and dianthus, an occasional shower in a mild solution of 1 tablespoon baking soda in 2 quarts (2 liters) water. They'll show their appreciation with fuller, healthier blooms.

Maintain proper pool alkalinity Add 1 1/2 pounds (680 grams) baking soda for every 10,000 gallons (38,000 liters) of water in your swimming pool to raise the total alkalinity by 10 ppm (parts per million). Most pools require alkalinity in the 80-150 ppm range. Maintaining the proper pool alkalinity level is vital for minimizing changes in pH if acidic or basic pool chemicals or contaminants are introduced to the water.

Scour barbecue grills Keep your barbecue grill in top condition by making a soft paste of 1/4 cup baking soda and 1/4 cup water. Apply the paste with a wire brush and let dry for 15 minutes. Then wipe it down with a dry cloth and place the grill over the hot coals for at least 15 minutes to burn off any residue before placing any food on top.

Make deodorizing dog shampoo The next time Rover rolls around in your compost heap, pull out the baking soda to freshen him up. Just rub a few handfuls of the powder into his coat and give it a thorough brushing. In addition to removing the smell, it will leave his coat shiny and clean.

Wash insides of pets' ears If your pet is constantly scratching at his ears, it could indicate the presence of an irritation or ear mites. Ease the itch (and wipe out any mites) by using a cotton ball dipped in a solution of 1 teaspoon baking soda in 1 cup warm water to gently wash the inside of his ears.

Keep bugs away from pets' dishes Placing a border of baking soda around your pet's food bowls will keep away six-legged intruders. And it won't harm your pet if he happens to lap up a little (though most pets aren't likely to savor soda's bitter taste).

Deodorize the litter box Don't waste money on expensive deodorized cat litter. Just put a thin layer of baking soda under the bargain-brand litter to absorb the odor. Or mix baking soda with the litter as you're changing it.

✱ Balloons

Protect a bandaged finger Bandaging an injury on your finger is easy; keeping the bandage dry as you go about your day can be a different story. But here's the secret to skipping those wet-bandage changes: Just slip a small balloon over your finger when doing dishes, bathing, or even simply washing your hands.

Keep track of your child Those inexpensive floating helium-filled balloons sold in most shopping malls can be more than just a treat for a youngster; they could be invaluable in locating a child who wanders off into a crowd. Even if you keep close tabs on your kids, you can buy a little peace of mind by simply tying (though not too tightly) a balloon to your child's wrist on those weekend shopping trips.

Make a party invitation How's this for an imaginative invitation? Inflate a balloon (for sanitary purposes, use an electric pump, if possible). Pinch off the end, but don't tie a knot in it. Write your invitation details on the balloon with a bright permanent marker; make sure the ink is dry before you deflate it. Place the balloon in an envelope, and mail one out to each guest. When your guests receive it, they'll have to blow it up to see what it says.

Transport cut flowers Don't bother with awkward, water-filled plastic bags and such when traveling with freshly cut flowers. Simply fill up a balloon with about 1/2 cup water and slip it over the cut ends of your flowers. Wrap a rubber band several times around the mouth of the balloon to keep it from slipping off.

Use as a hat mold To keep the shape in your freshly washed knit cap or cloth hat, fit it over an inflated balloon while it dries. Use a piece of masking tape to keep the balloon from tilting over or falling onto the ground.

Mark your campsite Bring along several helium-filled balloons on your next camping trip to attach to your tent or a post. They'll make it easier for the members of your party to locate your campsite when hiking or foraging in the woods.

Make an ice pack Looking for a flexible ice pack you can use for everything from icing a sore back to keeping food cold in your cooler? Fill a large, durable balloon with as much water as you need and put it in your freezer. You can even mold it to a certain extent into specific shapes—for example, put it under something flat like a box of pizza if you want a flat ice pack for your back. Use smaller latex balloons for making smaller ice packs for lunch boxes, etc.

Freeze for cooler punch To keep your party punch bowl cold and well filled, pour juice in several balloons (use a funnel) and place them in your freezer. When it's party time, peel the latex off the ice, and periodically drop a couple into the punch bowl.

Repel unwanted garden visitors Put those old deflated shiny metallic balloons—the ones lying around your house from past birthday parties—to work in your garden. Cut them into vertical strips and hang them from poles around your vegetables and on fruit trees to scare off invading birds, rabbits, and squirrels.

Protect your rifle A dirty rifle can jam up and just be downright dangerous to use. But you can keep dust and debris from accumulating in your rifle barrel by putting a sturdy latex balloon over the barrel's front end.

SCIENCE FAIR

You experience a discharge of **static electricity** when you touch a doorknob after shuffling across a carpet. But you rarely see this phenomenon, with the exception of lightning, which is static electricity on a grand scale. Here's an experiment that offers a dazzling display of static electricity in action:

Empty the contents of a package of nonflavored **gelatin** powder onto a piece of **paper**. Blow up a **balloon**, rub it on a **woolen sweater**, and then hold it about an inch over the powder. The **gelatin particles will arch up** toward the balloon. The slightly negatively charged electrons—the built-up static electricity on the balloon—are attracting the positively charged protons in the gelatin powder.

✳ Bananas

Make a face mask Who needs Botox when you have bananas? That's right: You can use a banana as an all-natural face mask that moisturizes your skin and leaves it looking and feeling softer. Mash up a medium-sized ripe banana into a smooth paste, then gently apply it to your face and neck. Let it set for 10-20 minutes, then rinse it off with cold water. Another popular mask recipe calls for 1/4 cup plain yogurt, 2 tablespoons honey, and 1 medium banana.

Eat a frozen "banana-sicle" As a summer treat for friends and family, peel and cut four ripe bananas in half (across the middle). Stick a wooden ice-cream stick into the flat end of each piece. Place them all on a piece of wax paper, and then put it in the freezer. A few hours later, serve them up as simply yummy frozen banana-sicles. If you want to go all-out, quickly dip your frozen bananas in 6 ounces (170 grams) melted butterscotch or chocolate morsels (chopped nuts or shredded coconut are optional), then refreeze.

Tenderize a roast Banana leaves are commonly used in many Asian countries to wrap meat as it's cooking to make it more tender. Some folks in these areas say the banana itself also has this ability. So the next time you fear the roast you're cooking will turn tough on you, try softening it up by adding a ripe, peeled banana to the pan.

Polish silverware and leather shoes It may sound a bit like a lark, but using a banana peel is actually a great way to put the shine back into your silverware and leather shoes. First, remove any of the leftover stringy material from the inside of the peel, then just start rubbing the inside of the peel on your shoes or silver. When you're done, buff up the object with a paper towel or soft cloth. You might even want to use this technique to restore your leather furniture. Test it on a small section first before you take on the whole chair.

Brighten up houseplants Are the leaves on your houseplants looking dingy or dusty? Don't bother misting them with water—that just spreads the dirt around. Rather, wipe down each leaf with the inside of a banana peel. It'll remove all the gunk on the surface and replace it with a lustrous shine.

Deter aphids Are aphids attacking your rosebushes or other plants? Bury dried or cut-up banana peels an inch or two deep around the base of the aphid-prone plants, and soon the little suckers will pack up and leave. Don't use whole peels or the bananas themselves, though; they tend to be viewed as tasty treats by raccoons, squirrels, gophers, rabbits, and other animals, who will just dig them up.

Use as fertilizer or mulch Banana peels, like the fruit itself, are rich in potassium—an important nutrient for both you and your garden. Dry out banana peels on screens during the winter months. In early spring, grind them up in a food processor or blender and use it as a mulch to give new plants and seedlings a healthy start. Many cultivars of roses and other plants, like staghorn ferns, also benefit from the nutrients found in banana peels; simply cut up some peels and use them as plant food around your established plants.

Add to compost pile With their high content of potassium and phosphorus, whole bananas and peels are welcome additions to any compost pile—particularly in so-called compost tea recipes. The fruit breaks down especially fast in hot temperatures. But don't forget to remove any glued-on tags from the peels, and be sure to bury bananas deep within your pile—otherwise they may simply turn out to be a meal for a four-legged visitor.

Attract butterflies and birds Bring more butterflies and various bird species to your backyard by putting out overripe bananas (as well as other fruits such as mangos, oranges, and papayas) on a raised platform. Punch a few holes in the bananas to make the fruit more accessible to the butterflies. Some enthusiasts swear by adding a drop of Gatorade to further mush things up. The fruit is also likely to attract more bees and wasps as well, so make sure that the platform is well above head level and not centrally located. Moreover, you'll probably want to clear it off before sunset, to discourage visits from raccoons and other nocturnal creatures.

✳ Basters

Pour perfect batter To make picture-perfect pancakes, cookies, and muffins, simply fill your baster with batter so that you can pour just the right amount onto a griddle or cookie sheet or into a muffin pan.

Remove excess water from coffeemaker The perfect cup of coffee is determined by using the proper balance of water and ground coffee in your automatic coffeemaker. If you pour in too much water, however, you typically have to add more coffee or suffer through a weak pot. But there's another, often overlooked option: Simply use your kitchen baster to remove the excess water to bring it in at just the right level.

Water hard-to-reach plants Do you get drips all over yourself, the floor, or furniture when trying to water hanging plants or other difficult-to-reach houseplants? Instead, fill a baster with water and squeeze it directly into the pot. You can also use a baster to water a Christmas tree and to add small, precise amounts of water to cups containing seedlings or germinating seeds.

Refresh water in flower arrangements It's a fact: Cut flowers last longer with periodic water changes. But pouring out the old water and adding the new is not a particularly easy or pleasant task. Unless, that is, you use a baster to suck out the old water and then to squirt in fresh water.

> **TAKE CARE** Never use your kitchen baster for tasks such as cleaning out a fish tank or spreading or transferring chemicals.
>
> Basters are staples at discount stores, and it's worth a visit to pick up a few to keep around the house specifically for noncooking chores. Label them with a piece of masking tape to make sure you always use the same baster for the same task.

Place water in pet's bowl Are you getting tired of chasing the bunny, hamster, or other caged pet around the house whenever you change its water? Use a baster to fill the water dish. You can usually fit the baster between the slats without having to open the cage.

Clean your aquarium A baster makes it incredibly easy to change the water in your fish tank or to freshen it up a bit. Simply use the utensil to suck up the gunk that collects in the corners and in the gravel at the bottom of your tank.

Blow away roaches and ants If you've had it with sharing your living quarters with roaches or ants, give them the heave-ho by sprinkling boric acid along any cracks or crevices where you've spotted the intruders. Use a baster to blow small amounts of the powder into hard-to-reach corners and any deep voids you come across. *Note:* Keep in mind that boric acid can be toxic if ingested by young children or pets.

Transfer paints and solvents The toughest part of any touchup paint job is invariably pouring the paint from a large can into a small cup or container. To avoid the inevitable spills, and just to make life easier in general, use a baster to take the paint out of the can. In fact, it's a good idea to make a baster a permanent addition to your workshop for transferring any solvents, varnishes, and other liquid chemicals.

Cure a musty-smelling air conditioner If you detect a musty odor blowing out of the vents of your room air-conditioner, chances are it's caused by a clogged drain hole. First, unscrew the front of the unit and locate the drain hole. It's usually located under the barrier between the evaporator and compressor, or underneath the evaporator. Use a bent wire hanger to clear away  any obstacles in the hole or use a baster to flush it clean. You may also need to use the baster to remove any water that may be pooling up at the bottom of the unit to gain access to the drain.

Fix a leaky refrigerator Is water leaking inside your refrigerator? The most likely cause is a blocked drain tube. This plastic tube runs from a drain hole in the back of the freezer compartment along the back of your fridge and drains into an evaporation pan underneath. Try forcing hot water through the drain hole in the freezer with a baster. If you can't access the drain hole, try disconnecting the tube on the back to blow water through it. After clearing the tube, pour a teaspoon of ammonia or bleach into the drain hole to prevent a recurrence of algae spores, the probable culprit.

✳ Bath Oil

Remove glue from labels or bandages Get rid of those sticky leftover adhesive marks from bandages, price tags, and labels. Rub them away with a bit of bath oil applied to a cotton ball. It works great on glass, metal, and most plastics.

Use as a hot-oil treatment Heat 1/2 cup bath oil mixed with 1/2 cup water on High in your microwave for 30 seconds. Place the solution in a deep bowl and soak your fingers or toes in it for 10-15 minutes to soften cuticles or calluses. After drying, use a pumice stone to smooth over calluses or a file to push down cuticles. Follow up by rubbing in hand cream until fully absorbed.

Pry apart stuck drinking glasses When moisture seeps in between stacked glasses, separating them can get mighty tough—not to mention dangerous. But you can break the "ties that bond" by applying a few drops of bath oil along the sides of the glasses. Give the oil a few minutes to work its way down, then simply slide your glasses apart.

Loosen chewing gum from hair and carpeting If your child comes home with chewing gum in his or her hair—or tracks a wad onto your rug or carpet—

hold off on reaching for the scissors. Instead, rub a liberal amount of bath oil into the gum. It should loosen it up enough to comb out. On a carpet, test the oil on an inconspicuous area before applying to the spot.

Remove scuff marks You can get those annoying scuff marks off your patent-leather shoes or handbags. Apply a bit of bath oil to a clean, soft cloth or towel. Gently rub in the oil, then polish with another dry towel.

Soften a new baseball glove Apply several drops of bath oil in the midsection of the glove and a few more drops under each finger. Lightly spread the oil around with a soft cloth. Place a baseball in the pocket of the glove and fold the glove over the ball, keeping it in place with one or two belts or an Ace bandage. Let it sit for a couple of days, then release the constraints and remove any excess oil with a clean cloth. The glove should be noticeably more pliable.

Clean grease or oil from skin It doesn't take much tinkering around the inside of a car or mower engine to get your hands coated in grease or oil. But before you reach for any heavy-duty grease removers, try this: Rub a few squirts of bath oil onto your hands, then wash them in warm, soapy water. It works, and it's a lot easier on the dermis than harsh chemicals.

Revitalize vinyl upholstery Give your car's dreary-looking vinyl upholstery a makeover by using a small amount of bath oil on a soft cloth to wipe down the seats, dashboard, armrests, and other surfaces. Polish with a clean cloth to remove any excess oil. As an added bonus, a scented bath oil will make the interior smell better, too.

Slide together pipe joints Can't find the all-purpose lubricating oil or the WD-40 when you're trying to join pipes together? No problem. A few drops of bath oil should provide sufficient lubrication to fit pipe joints together with ease.

✳ Bathtub Appliqués

Place on the bottom of PC case Has your desktop computer case lost its "legs" (those four small rubber feet that invariably fall off over time from moving your PC around)? To steady your case, and to minimize vibrations, cut small squares from a bathtub appliqué, and apply them to the corners of your case where the feet used to be.

Apply to dance slippers, shoes, and pajamas Avoid nasty falls caused by slippery plastic dance slippers—and even new shoes. Cut small pieces of bathtub appliqués and apply them to the sole of each slipper or shoe. You can also sew cut pieces of an appliqué on the soles of your children's "feet" pajamas to prevent slips (and tears).

Stick to bottom of kids' wading pool A few bathtub appliqués applied to the floor of a kiddie pool will make it a lot less slippery for little feet and help prevent falls—especially when the water play turns rowdy. Also put a couple of appliqués along the edges of the pool to give kids easy places to grip onto.

Affix to sippy cups and high-chair seats Cut pieces of a bathtub appliqué and put them on toddlers' sippy cups to minimize spills. Also attach appliqués to high-chair seats to keep Junior from sliding down—or out.

✳ Beans (Dried)

Use for playing pieces We know you had your heart set on being the racing car in the next game of Monopoly, but if the car has taken a trip to parts unknown, would you settle for a bean? Beans work fine as replacement pieces for everything from checkers to Chutes and Ladders to bingo.

Treat sore muscles Is your bad back or tennis elbow acting up again? A hot beanbag may be just the cure you need. Place a couple of handfuls of dried beans in a cloth shoe bag, an old sock, or a folded towel (tie the ends tightly) and microwave it on High for 30 seconds to 1 minute. Let it cool for a minute or two, then apply it to your aching muscles.

Make a beanbag Pour 3/4 to 1 1/2 cups dried beans in an old sock, shaking them down to the toe section. Tie a loose knot and tighten it up as you work it down against the beans. Then cut off the remaining material about 1 inch (2.5 centimeters) above the knot. You now have a beanbag for tossing around or juggling. Or use it as a squeeze bag for exercising your hand muscles.

Practice your percussion Make a homemade percussion shaker or maraca for yourself or your youngster. Add 1/2 cup dried beans to a small plastic jar, or a soda or juice can—even an empty coconut shell. Cover any openings with adhesive or duct tape. You can use this noisemaker at sporting events or as a dog-training tool (give it a couple of shakes when the pooch misbehaves).

Decorate a jack-o'-lantern Embellish the fright potential of your Halloween jack-o'-lantern by gluing on various dried beans for the eyes and teeth.

Recycle a stuffed animal Make your own beanie creation by removing the stuffing from one of your child's old, unused stuffed animals. Replace the fluff with dried beans, and sew it closed. It's bound to rekindle your youngster's interest.

✳ Beer

Use as setting lotion Put some life back into flat hair with some flat beer. Before you get into the shower, mix 3 tablespoons beer in 1/2 cup warm water. After you shampoo your hair, rub in the solution, let it set for a couple of minutes, then rinse it off. You may be so pleased by what you see, you'll want to keep a six-pack in the bathroom.

Soften up tough meat Who needs powdered meat tenderizer when you have some in a can? You guessed it: Beer makes a great tenderizer for tough, inexpensive cuts of meat. Pour a can over the meat, and let it soak in for about an hour before cooking. Even better, marinate it overnight in the fridge or put the beer in your slow cooker with the meat.

Polish gold jewelry Get the shine back in your solid gold (i.e., minus any gemstones) rings and other jewelry by pouring a bit of beer (*not* dark ale!) onto a soft cloth and rubbing it gently over the piece. Use a clean second cloth or towel to dry.

Clean wood furniture Have you got some beer that's old or went flat? Use it to clean wooden furniture. Just wipe it on with a soft cloth, and then off with another dry cloth.

Make a trap for slugs and snails Like some people, some garden pests find beer irresistible—especially slugs and snails. If you're having problems with these slimy invaders, bury a container, such as a clean, empty juice container cut lengthwise in half, in the area where you've seen the pests, pour in about half a can of warm, leftover beer, and leave it overnight. You're likely to find a horde of them, drunk and drowned, the next morning.

Remove coffee or tea stains from rugs Getting that coffee or tea stain out your rug may seem impossible, but you can literally lift it out by pouring a bit of beer right on top. Rub the beer lightly into the material, and the stain should disappear. You may have to repeat the process a couple of times to remove all traces of the stain.

 DID **You** KNOW?

Some popular brands of beer proclaim their New England or Rocky Mountain pedigrees, or boast being "Milwaukee's finest." But, in fact, Pennsylvania has been home to more breweries throughout its history than any other state. One of its earliest breweries was opened in 1680 by none other than William Penn, the state's founder. And the Keystone State is still the home of the U.S.'s oldest active brewery, D. G. Yuengling & Son of Pottsville, Pennsylvania, founded in 1829.

✳ Berry Baskets

Keep peels out of drain Don't clog up your kitchen drain with peelings from potatoes or carrots. Use a berry basket as a sink strainer to catch those vegetable shavings as they fall.

Store soap pads and sponges Are you tired of throwing away prematurely rusted steel wool soap pads or smelly sponges? Place a berry basket near the corner of your kitchen sink and line the bottom with a layer of heavy-duty aluminum foil. Fashion a spout on a corner of the foil closest to the sink that can act as a drain to keep water from pooling up at the bottom of the basket. Now sit back and enjoy the added longevity of your soap pads and sponges.

Use as a colander Need a small colander to wash individual servings of fruits and vegetables or to drain off that child's portion of hot macaroni shells? Get your hands on an empty berry basket. It makes a dandy colander for these chores.

> *Kids' Stuff* **Berry baskets** can be particularly useful for all sorts of children's crafts. For example, you can cut apart the panels, and carve out geometric shapes for kids to use as **stencils.** You can also turn one into an **Easter basket** by adding some **cellophane grass** and a (preferably pink) **pipe cleaner** for a handle. Or use one as a multiple **bubble maker;** simply dip it in some **water** mixed with **dishwashing liquid** and wave it through the air to create swarms of bubbles. Lastly, let kids decorate the baskets with **ribbons** or **construction paper** and use them to store their own little trinkets and toys.

Hold recycled paper towels Don't toss out those lightly used paper towels in your kitchen. You can reuse them to wipe down countertops or to soak up serious spills. Keep a berry basket in a convenient location in your kitchen to have your recycled towels at the ready when needed.

Use as dishwasher basket If the smaller items you place in your dishwasher (such as baby bottle caps, jar lids, and food-processor accessories) won't stay put, try putting them in a berry basket. Place the items inside one basket, then cover over with a second basket. Fasten them together with a thick rubber band and place on your dishwasher's upper rack.

Organize your meds A clean berry basket could be just what the doctor ordered for organizing your vitamins and medicine bottles. If you're taking several medications, a berry basket offers a convenient way to place them all—or prepackaged individual doses—in one, easy-to-remember location. You can also use baskets to organize medications in your cupboard or medicine cabinet according to their expiration dates or uses.

Arrange flowers Droopy or lopsided flower arrangements just don't cut it. That's why the pros use something known as a frog to keep cut flowers in place. To make your own, insert an inverted berry basket into a vase (cut the basket to fit, if necessary). It will keep your stalks standing tall.

Protect seedlings Help young plants thrive in your garden by placing inverted berry baskets over them. The baskets will let water, sunlight, and air in, but keep raccoons and squirrels out. Make sure the basket is buried below ground level and tightly secured (placing a few good-sized stones around it may suffice).

Make a bulb cage Squirrels and other rodents view freshly planted flower bulbs as nothing more than tasty morsels and easy pickings. But you can put a damper on their meal by planting bulbs in berry baskets. Be sure to place the basket at the correct depth, then insert the bulb and cover with soil.

Build a hanging orchid planter Orchids are said to be addictive: Once you start collecting them, you can't stop. If you've got the bug, you can at least save yourself a bit of money by making your own hanging baskets for your orchids. Fill up a berry basket with sphagnum moss mixed with a bit of potting soil and suspend it with a length of monofilament fishing line.

Fashion a string dispenser or screwdriver holder If you don't want to bother untangling knots every time you need a piece of string, twine, or yarn, build your own string dispenser with two berry baskets. Place the ball inside one berry basket. Feed the cord through the top of a second, inverted basket, then tie the two baskets together with twist ties. You can also mount an 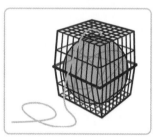 inverted berry basket on your workshop's pegboard and use it to hold and organize your screwdrivers; they'll fit neatly between the slats.

✳ Binder Clips

Strengthen your grip Does a weak grip or arthritis make it hard for you to open jars and do other tasks with your hands? Use a large binder clip to add some zip to your grip. Squeeze the folded-back wings of the clip, hold for a count of five, and relax. Do this a dozen or so times with each hand a few times a day. It will strengthen your grip and release tension too.

Mount a picture Here's a neat way to mount and hang a picture so that it has a clean frameless look. Sandwich the picture between a sheet of glass or clear plastic and piece of hardboard or stiff cardboard. Then use tiny binder clips along the edges to clamp the pieces together. Use two or three clips on each side. After the clips are in place, remove the clip handles at front. Tie picture wire to the rear handles for hanging the picture.

Keep your place A medium-sized binder clip makes an ideal bookmark. If you don't want to leave impression marks on the pages, tape a soft material like felt, or even just some adhesive tape, to the inside jaws of the clip before using.

Make a money clip To keep paper money in a neat bundle in your pocket or purse, stack the bills, fold them in half, and put a small binder clip over the fold.

Keep ID handy You're at the airport and you know you'll be asked to show your ID a few times. Instead of fishing in your wallet or trying to figure out which pocket you stuck your driver's license in, use a binder clip to firmly and conveniently attach your ID and other documents to your belt. You can also use a small binder clip to secure your office ID to your belt or a breast pocket.

✳ Bleach

Clean off mold and mildew Bleach and ammonia are both useful for removing mold and mildew both inside and outside your home. However, the two should *never* be used together. Bleach is especially suited for the following chores:

● Wash mildew out of washable fabrics. Wet the mildewed area and rub in some powdered detergent. Then wash the garment in the hottest water setting permitted by the clothing manufacturer using 1/2 cup chlorine bleach. If the garment can't be washed in hot water and bleach, soak it in a solution of 1/4 cup oxygen bleach (labeled "all fabric" or "perborate") in 1 gallon (3.7 liters) warm water for 30 minutes before washing.

● Remove mold and mildew from the grout between your bathroom tiles. Mix equal parts of chlorine bleach and water in a spray bottle, and spray it over grout. Let it sit for 15 minutes, then scrub with a stiff brush and rinse off. You can also do this just to make your grout look whiter.

● Get mold and mildew off your shower curtains. Wash them—along with a couple of bath towels (to prevent the plastic curtains from crinkling)—in warm water with 1/2 cup chlorine bleach and 1/4 cup laundry detergent. Let the washer run for a couple of minutes before loading. Put the shower curtain and towels in the dryer on the lowest temperature setting for 10 minutes, then immediately hang-dry.

● Rid your rubber shower mat of mildew. Soak in a solution of 1/8 cup chlorine bleach in 1 gallon (3.7 liters) water for 3-4 hours. Rinse well.

● Get mildew and other stains off unpainted cement, patio stones, or stucco. Mix a solution of 1 cup chlorine bleach in 2 gallons (7.5 liters) water. Scrub vigorously with a stiff or wire brush and rinse. If any stains remain, scrub again using 1/2 cup washing soda (this is sodium carbonate, not baking soda) dissolved in 2 gallons (7.5 liters) warm water.

● Remove mildew from painted surfaces and siding. Make a solution of 1/4 cup chlorine bleach in 2 cups water and apply with a brush to mildewed areas. Let the solution set for 15 minutes, then rinse. Repeat as necessary.

Sterilize secondhand items Remember Mom saying, "Put that down. You don't know where it's been"? She had a point—especially when it comes to toys or kitchen utensils picked up at thrift shops and yard sales. Just to be on the safe side, take your used, waterproof items and soak them for 5-10 minutes in a solution containing 3/4 cup bleach, a few drops of antibacterial dishwashing liquid, and 1 gallon warm water. Rinse well, then air-dry, preferably in sunlight.

Clean butcher block cutting boards and countertops Don't even think about using furniture polish or any other household cleaner to clean a butcher block cutting board or countertop. Rather, scrub the surface with a brush dipped in a solution of 1 teaspoon bleach diluted in 2 quarts (2 liters) water. Scrub in small circles, and be careful not to saturate the wood. Wipe with a slightly damp paper towel, then immediately buff dry with a clean cloth.

TAKE CARE Never mix bleach with ammonia, lye, rust removers, oven or toilet-bowl cleaners, or vinegar. Any combination can produce toxic chlorine gas fumes, which can be deadly. Some people are even sensitive to the fumes of undiluted bleach itself. Always make sure you have adequate ventilation in your work area before you start pouring.

Brighten up glass dishware Put the sparkle back in your glasses and dishes by adding a teaspoon of bleach to your soapy dishwater as you're washing your glassware. Be sure to rinse well, and dry with a soft towel.

Shine white porcelain Want to get your white porcelain sink, candleholder, or pottery looking as good as new? In a well-ventilated area on a work surface protected by heavy plastic, place several paper towels over the item (or across the bottom of the sink) and carefully saturate them with undiluted bleach. Let soak for 15 minutes to a half hour, then rinse and wipe dry with a clean towel. *Note:*

Do not try this with antiques; you can diminish their value or cause damage. And never use bleach on colored porcelain, because the color will fade.

Make a household disinfectant spray Looking for a good, all-purpose disinfectant to use around the house? Mix 1 tablespoon bleach in 1 gallon (3.7 liters) hot water. Then fill a clean, empty spray bottle and use it on a paper towel to clean countertops, tablecloths, lawn furniture—basically, wherever it's needed. Just be sure not to use it in the presence of ammonia or other household cleaners.

TAKE CARE Some folks skip the bleach when cleaning their toilets, fearing that lingering ammonia from urine—especially in households with young children—could result in toxic fumes. Unless you are sure there is no such problem, you may want to stick with ammonia for this job.

Disinfect trash cans Even the best housekeepers must confront a gunked-up kitchen garbage pail every now and then. On such occasions, take the pail outside, and flush out any loose debris with a garden hose. Then add 1/2 to 1 cup bleach and several drops of dishwashing liquid to 1 gallon (3.7 liters) warm water. Use a toilet brush or long-handled scrub brush to splash and scour the solution on the bottom and sides of the container. Empty, then rinse with the hose, empty it again, and let air-dry.

Increase cut flowers' longevity Freshly cut flowers will stay fresh longer if you add 1/4 teaspoon bleach per quart (1 liter) of vase water. Another popular recipe calls for 3 drops bleach and 1 teaspoon sugar in 1 quart (1 liter) water. This will also keep the water from getting cloudy and inhibit the growth of bacteria.

Clean plastic lawn furniture Is your plastic-mesh lawn furniture looking dingy? Before you place it curbside, try washing it with some mild detergent mixed with 1/2 cup bleach in 1 gallon (3.7 liters) water. Rinse it clean, then air-dry.

Kill weeds in walkways Do weeds seem to thrive in the cracks and crevices of your walkways? Try pouring a bit of undiluted bleach over them. After a day or two, you can simply pull them out, and the bleach will keep them from coming back. Just be careful not to get bleach on the grass or plantings bordering the walkway.

Get rid of moss and algae To remove slippery and unsightly moss and algae on your brick, concrete, or stone walkways, scrub them with a solution of 3/4 cup bleach in 1 gallon (3.7 liters) water. Be careful not to get bleach on your grass or ornamental plants.

Sanitize garden tools You cut that diseased stalk off your rosebush with your branch clipper. Unless you want to spread the disease the next time you use the tool, sterilize it by washing it with 1/2 cup bleach in 1 quart (1 liter) water. Let the tool air-dry in the sun, then rub on a few drops of oil to prevent rust.

✳ Blow-Dryer

Get wax off wood furniture It may have been a romantic evening, but that hardened candle wax on your wooden table or bureau is not the sort of lingering memory you had in mind. Melt it with a blow-dryer on its slowest, hottest setting. Remove the softened wax with a paper towel, then wipe the area with a cloth dipped in equal parts vinegar and water. Repeat if necessary. You can also remove wax from silver candlestick holders with a blow-dryer: Use the blow-dryer to soften the wax, then just peel it off.

Clean off radiators Are those dusty cast-iron radiators around your house becoming something of an eyesore? To clean them, hang a large, damp cloth behind each radiator. Then use your blow-dryer on its highest, coolest setting to blow dust and hidden dirt onto the cloth.

Remove bumper stickers Want to remove those cutesy stickers your kids used to decorate your car bumper to "surprise" you? Use a blow-dryer on its hottest setting to soften the adhesive. Move the dryer slowly back and forth for several minutes, then use your fingernail or credit card to lift up a corner and slowly peel off.

Dust off silk flowers and artificial houseplants They may require less care than their living counterparts, but silk flowers and artificial houseplants are apt to collect dust and dirt. Use your blow-dryer on its highest, coolest setting for a quick, efficient way to clean them off. Since this will blow the dust onto the furniture surfaces and floor around the plant, do this just before you vacuum those areas.

✳ Borax

Clear a clogged drain Before you reach for a caustic drain cleaner to unclog that kitchen or bathroom drain, try this much gentler approach: Use a funnel to insert 1/2 cup borax into the drain, then slowly pour in 2 cups boiling water. Let the mixture set for 15 minutes, then flush with hot water. Repeat for stubborn clogs.

Rub out heavy sink stains Get rid of those stubborn stains—even rust—in your stainless steel or porcelain sink. Make a paste of 1 cup borax and 1/4 cup lemon juice. Put some of the paste on a cloth or sponge and rub it into the stain, then rinse with running warm water. The stain should wash away with the paste.

Clean windows and mirrors Want to get windows and mirrors spotless *and* streakless? Wash them with a clean sponge dipped in 2 tablespoons borax dissolved in 3 cups water.

Remove mildew from fabric To remove mildew from upholstery and other fabrics, soak a sponge in a solution of 1/2 cup borax dissolved in 2 cups hot water, and rub it into the affected areas. Let it soak in for several hours until the stain disappears, then rinse well. To remove mildew from clothing, soak it in a solution of 2 cups borax in 2 quarts (2 liters) water.

Kids' Stuff Help your children brew up some **slime**—that gooey, stretchy stuff kids love to play with. First, mix 1 cup water, 1 cup **white glue,** and 10 drops **food coloring** in a medium bowl. Then, in a second, larger bowl, stir 4 teaspoons **borax** into 1 1/3 cups **water** until the powder is fully dissolved. Slowly pour the contents of the first bowl into the second. Use a wooden **mixing spoon** to roll (don't mix) the glue-based solution around in the borax solution four or five times. Lift out the globs of glue mixture, then knead it for 2-3 minutes. Store your homemade slime in an **airtight container** or a **self-sealing plastic storage bag.**

Get out rug stains Remove stubborn stains from rugs and carpets. Thoroughly dampen the area, then rub in some borax. Let the area dry, then vacuum or blot it with a solution of equal parts vinegar and soapy water and let dry. Repeat if necessary. Don't forget to first test the procedure on an inconspicuous corner of the rug or on a carpet scrap before applying it to the stain.

Sanitize your garbage disposal A garbage disposal is a great convenience but can also be a great breeding ground for mold and bacteria. To maintain a more sanitary disposal, every couple of weeks pour 3 tablespoons borax down the drain and let it sit for 1 hour. Then turn on the disposal and flush it with hot water from the tap.

Clean your toilet Want a way to disinfect your toilet bowl *and* leave it glistening without having to worry about dangerous or unpleasant fumes? Use a stiff brush to scrub it using a solution of 1/2 cup borax in 1 gallon (3.7 liters) water.

Eliminate urine odor on mattresses Toilet training can be a rough experience for all the parties involved. If your child has an "accident" in bed, here's how to get rid of any lingering smell: Dampen the area, then rub in some borax. Let it dry, then vacuum up the powder.

Make your own dried flowers Give your homemade dried flowers the look of a professional job. Mix 1 cup borax with 2 cups cornmeal. Place a 3/4-inch (2-centimeter) coating of the mixture in the bottom of an airtight container, like a large flat plastic food storage container. Cut the stems off the flowers you want to dry, then lay them on top of the powder, and lightly sprinkle more of the mixture on top of the flowers (be careful not to bend or crush the petals or other flower parts). Cover the container, and leave it alone for

7-10 days. Then remove the flowers and brush off any excess powder with a soft brush.

Keep away weeds and ants Get the jump on those weeds that grow in the cracks of the concrete outside your house by sprinkling borax into all the crevices where you've seen weeds grow in the past. It will kill them off before they have a chance to take root. When applied around the foundation of your home, it will also keep ants and other six-legged intruders from entering your house. But be very careful when applying borax—it is toxic to plants (see Take Care warning).

TAKE CARE Borax, like its close relative, boric acid, has relatively low toxicity levels, and is considered safe for general household use, but the powder can be harmful if ingested in sufficient quantities by young children or pets. Store it safely out of their reach.

Borax is toxic to plants, however. In the yard, be very careful when applying borax onto or near soil. It doesn't take much to leach into the ground to kill off nearby plants and prevent future growth.

Control creeping Charlie Is your garden being overrun by that invasive perennial weed known as creeping Charlie (*Glechoma hederacea*, also known as ground ivy, creeping Jenny and gill-over-the-ground)? You may be able to conquer Charlie with borax. First, dissolve 8-10 ounces (230-280 grams) borax in 4 ounces (120 milliliters) warm water. Then pour the solution into 2 1/2 gallons (9.5 liters) warm water—this is enough to cover 1,000 square feet (93 square meters). Apply this treatment only one time in each of two years. If you still have creeping Charlie problems, consider switching to a standard herbicide. (See Take Care warning about using borax in the garden.)

super item **26** *uses!* Bottles

Make a foot warmer Walking around on harsh winter days can leave you with cold and tired tootsies. But you don't need to shell out your hard-earned money on a heating pad or a hot-water bottle to ease your discomfort. Just fill up a 1- or 2-liter soda bottle with hot water, then sit down and roll it back and forth under your feet.

Use as a boot tree Want to keep your boot tops from getting wrinkled or folded over when you put them in storage? Insert a clean empty 1-liter soda bottle into each boot. For added tautness, put a couple of old socks on the bottles or wrap them in towels.

Recycle as a chew toy If Lassie has been chewing on your slippers instead of fetching them, maybe she's in need of some chew toys. A no-cost way to amuse your dog is to let her chew on an empty plastic 1-liter soda bottle. Maybe it's the crunchy sound they make, but dogs love them! Just be sure to remove the label and bottle cap (as well as the loose plastic ring under it). And replace it before it gets too chewed up—broken pieces of plastic are choke hazards.

Make a bag or string dispenser An empty 2-liter soda bottle makes the perfect container for storing and dispensing plastic grocery bags. Just cut off the bottom and top ends of the bottle, and mount it with screws upside down inside a kitchen cabinet or closet. Put washers under the screw heads to keep them from pulling through the plastic. Fill it with your recycled bags (squeeze the air out of them first) and pull them out as needed. You can make a twine dispenser the same way, using a 1-liter bottle and letting the cord come out the bottom.

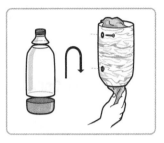

Place in toilet tank Unless your house was built relatively recently, chances are you have an older toilet that uses a lot of water each flush. To save a bit of money on your water bills, fill an empty 1-liter soda bottle with water (remove any labels first) and put it in the toilet tank to cut the amount of water in each flush.

Cut out a toy carryall If you're fed up with Lego or erector-set pieces underfoot, make a simple carryall to store them in by cutting a large hole in the side of a clean gallon jug with a handle. Cut the hole opposite the handle so you or your youngster can easily carry the container back to the playroom after putting the pieces away. For an easy way to store craft materials, crayons, or small toys, just cut the containers in half and use the bottom part to stash your stuff.

Store your sugar The next time you bring home a 5-pound (2.2-kilogram) bag of sugar from the supermarket, try pouring it into a clean, dry 1-gallon (3.7-liter) jug with a handle. The sugar is less likely to harden, and the handle makes it much easier to pour it out.

🖉 Tip Safe Rotary Cutter

> Cutting plastic containers can be a tricky, dangerous business—especially when you reach for your sharpest kitchen knife. But you can greatly minimize the risk by visiting your local fabric or crafts store and picking up a rolling cutter knife (this is not the same device used to slice pizza, by the way). The device shown in the picture in the hint "Make a scoop or boat bailer," facing page, usually sells for between $6 and $10. Be careful, though. These knives use blades that are razor sharp, but they make life much easier when it's time to cut into a hard plastic container.

Fashion a funnel To make a handy, durable funnel, cut a cleaned milk jug, bleach, or liquid detergent container with a handle in half across its midsection. Use the top portion (with the spout and handle) as a funnel for easy pouring of paints, rice, coins, and so on.

Make a scoop or boat bailer Cut a clean plastic half-gallon (2-liter) jug with a handle diagonally from the bottom so that you have the top three-quarters of the jug intact. You now have a handy scoop that can be used for everything from removing leaves and other debris from your gutters, to cleaning out the litter box and poop-scooping up after your dog. Use it to scoop dog food from the bag, spread sand or ice-melt on walkways in winter, or bail water out of your boat (you might want to keep the cap on for this last application).

Keep the cooler cold Don't let your cooler lose its cool while you're on the road. Fill a few clean plastic jugs with water or juice and keep them in the freezer for use when transporting food in your cooler. This is not only good for keeping food cold; you can actually drink the water or juice as it melts. It's also not a bad idea to keep a few frozen jugs in your freezer if you have extra space; a full freezer actually uses less energy and can save money on your electric bill. When filling a jug, leave a little room at the top for the water to expand as it freezes.

Use for emergency road kit in winter Don't get stuck in your car the next time a surprise winter storm hits. Keep a couple of clean gallon (3.7-liter) jugs with handles filled with sand or kitty litter in the trunk of your car. Then you'll be prepared to sprinkle the material on the road surface to add traction under your wheels when you need to get moving on a slippery road. The handle makes it easier to pour them.

Feed the birds Why spend money on a plastic bird feeder when you probably have one in your recycling bin? Take a clean 1/2-gallon (2-liter) juice or milk jug and carve a large hole on its side to remove the handle. (You might even drill a small hole under the large one to insert a sturdy twig or dowel for a perch.) Then poke a hole in the middle of the cap and suspend it from a tree with a piece of strong string or monofilament fishing line. Fill it up to the opening with birdseed, and enjoy the show.

Make a watering can No watering can? It's easy to make one from a clean 1-gallon (3.7-liter) juice, milk, or bleach jug with a handle. Drill about a dozen tiny (1/16-inch or 1.5-millimeter is good) holes just below the spout of the jug on the side opposite the handle. Or carefully punch the holes with an ice pick. Fill it with water, screw the cap on, and start sprinkling.

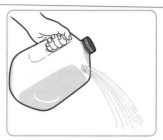

Create a drip irrigator for plants During dry spells, a good way to get water to the roots of your plants is to place several drip irrigators around your garden. You can make them from clean 1-gallon (3.7-liter) juice or detergent jugs. Cut a large hole in the bottom of a jug, then drill 2-5 tiny (about 1/16-inch or 1.5-millimeter) holes in or around the cap. Bury the capped jugs upside down about three-quarters submerged beneath the soil near the plants you need to water, and fill with water through the hole on top. Refill as often as needed.

Mark your plants Want an easy way to make ID badges for all the vegetables, herbs, and flowers in your garden? Cut vertical strips from a couple of clear 1-gallon (3.7-liter) water jugs. Make the strips the same width as your seed packets but double their length. Fold each strip over an empty packet to protect it from the elements, and staple it to a strong stick or chopstick.

Secure garden netting If you find yourself having to constantly re-stake the loose netting or plastic lining over your garden bed, place water-filled large plastic jugs around the corners to keep the material in place.

Use as an attachable trash can or harvest basket Here's a great tip for weekend gardeners and pros alike: Cut a large hole opposite the handle of a 1/2- or 1-gallon (2-or 3.7-liter) container, and loop the handle through a belt or rope on your waist. Use it to collect the debris—rocks, weeds, broken stems—you encounter as you mow the lawn or stroll through your garden. Use the same design to make an attachable basket for harvesting berries, cherries, and other small fruits or vegetables.

Space seeds in garden Want an easy way to perfectly space seeds in your garden? Use an empty soda bottle as your guide. Find the distance that the seed company recommends between seeds and then cut off the tapered top of the bottle so its diameter equals that distance. When you start planting, firmly press your bottle, cut edge down, into the soil and place a seed in the center of the circle it makes. Then line up the bottle so that its edge touches the curve of the first impression, and press down again. Plant a seed in the center, and repeat until you've filled your rows.

Build a bug trap Do yellow jackets, wasps, or moths swarm around you every time you set foot in the yard? Use an empty 2-liter soda bottle to make an environment-friendly trap for them. First, dissolve 1/2 cup sugar in 1/2 cup water in the bottle. Then add 1 cup apple cider vinegar and a banana peel (squish it up to fit it through). Screw on the cap and give the mixture a good shake before filling the bottle halfway with cold water. Cut or drill a 3/4-inch (2-centimeter) hole near the top of the bottle, and hang it from a tree branch where the bugs seem especially active. When the trap is full, toss it into the garbage and replace it with a new one.

Isolate weeds when spraying herbicides When using herbicides to kill weeds in your garden, you have to be careful not to also spray and kill surrounding plants. To isolate the weed you want to kill, cut a 2-liter soda bottle in half and place the top half over the weed you want to spray. Then direct your pump's spraying wand through the regular opening in the top of the bottle and blast away. After the spray settles down, pick up the bottle and move on to your next target. Always wear goggles and gloves when spraying chemicals in the garden.

Set up a backyard sprayer When temperatures soar out-doors, keep your kids cool with a homemade backyard sprayer. Just cut three 1-inch (2.5-centimeter) vertical slits in one side of a clean 2-liter soda bottle. Or make the slits at different angles so the water will squirt in different directions. Attach the nozzle of the hose to the bottle top with duct tape (make sure it's fastened on tight). Turn on the tap, and let the fun begin!

✳ BOTTLES **FOR THE DO-IT-YOURSELFER**

Build a paint bucket Tired of splattering paint all over as you work? Make a neater paint dispenser by cutting a large hole opposite the handle of a clean 1-gallon (3.7 liter) jug. Pour in the paint so that it's about an inch below the edge of the hole, and use the edge to remove any excess paint from your brush before you lift your brush. You can also cut jugs in half and use the bottom halves as disposable paint buckets when several people work on the same job.

Store your paints Why keep leftover house paints in rusted or dented cans when you can keep them clean and fresh in plastic jugs? Use a funnel to pour the paint into a clean, dry milk or water jug, and add a few marbles (they help mix the paint when you shake the container before your next paint job). Label each container with a piece of masking tape, noting the paint manufacturer, color name, and the date.

Use as workshop organizers Are you always searching for the right nail to use for a particular chore, or for a clothespin, picture hook, or small fastener? Bring some organization to your workshop with a few 1- or 1/2-gallon (3.7- or 2-liter) jugs. Cut out a section near the top of each jug on the side opposite the handle. Then use the containers to store and sort all the small items that seem to "slip through the cracks" of your workbench. The handle makes it easy to carry a jug to your worksite.

Use as a level substitute How can you make sure that shelf you're about to put up is straight if you don't have a level on hand? Easy. Just fill a 1-liter soda bottle about three-quarters full with water. Replace the cap, then lay the bottle on its side. When the water is level, so is the shelf.

Make a weight for anchoring or lifting Fill a clean, dry gallon (3.7-liter) jug with a handle with sand and cap it. You now have an anchor that is great for holding down a paint tarp, securing a shaky patio umbrella, or steadying a table for repair. The handle makes it easy to move or attach a rope. Or use a pair of sand-filled bottles as exercise weights, varying the amount of sand to meet your lifting capacity.

✳ Bottle Openers

Remove chestnut shells An easy way to remove the shells from chestnuts is to use the pointed end of a bottle opener to pierce the tops and bottoms of the shells and then boil the chestnuts for 10 minutes.

Cut packing tape on cartons Can't wait to open that long-awaited package on your doorstep? If you don't have a penknife handy, just run the sharp end of a bottle opener along the tape. It should do the job quite nicely.

Deploy as a shrimp de-veiner If you don't have a small paring knife on hand when you're getting ready to de-vein a batch of shrimp, don't worry. Just use the sharp end of a bottle opener. It just happens to be the perfect shape to make this messy chore a breeze.

DID **You** KNOW?

The old-fashioned bottle opener with one flat end and one pointed end is often referred to as a "church key." Although no one is exactly sure how or when this association came into being, it originated years ago in the brewery industry and was used to describe a flat opener with a hooked cutout used to lever off bottle caps—it is widely believed that the term derived from the early openers' resemblance to the heavy, ornate keys used to unlock big, old doors, such as those found on churches. Ironically, the term is now applied only to openers with both flat and pointed ends.

Scrape barbecue grill Looking for an easy way to clean off the burned remnants of last weekend's meal from your barbecue grill? If you have a bottle opener and a metal file, you're in luck. Simply file a notch about 1/8-inch (3 millimeters) wide into the flat end of the opener and you're ready to go.

Loosen plaster or remove grout It may not be the carpenter's best friend, but the sharp end of a bottle opener can be handy for removing loose plaster from a wall before patching it. It's great for running along cracks, and you can use to undercut a hole—that is, make it wider at the bottom than at the surface—so that the new plaster will "key" into the old. The sharp end of the opener is equally useful for removing old grout between your bathroom tiles before regrouting.

✳ Bread

Remove scorched taste from rice Did you leave the rice cooking too long and let it get burned? To get rid of the scorched taste, place a slice of white bread on top of the rice while it's still hot. Replace the pot lid and wait several minutes. When you remove the bread, the burned taste should be gone.

Soften up hard marshmallows You reach for your bag of marshmallows only to discover that they've gone stale. Put a couple of slices of fresh bread in the bag and seal it shut (you may want to transfer the marshmallows to a self-sealing plastic bag). Leave it alone for a couple of days. When you reopen the bag, your marshmallows should taste as good as new.

Absorb vegetable odors Love cabbage or broccoli, but hate the smell while it's cooking? Try putting a piece of white bread on top of the pot when cooking up a batch of "smelly" vegetables. It will absorb most of the odor.

Soak up grease and stop flare-ups To paraphrase a famous bear: Only you can prevent grease fires. One of the best ways to prevent a grease flare-up when broiling meat is to place a couple of slices of white bread in your drip pan to absorb the grease. It will also cut down on the amount of smoke produced.

Clean walls and wallpaper Most kids have a hard time understanding how easily the dirt on their hands can be transferred to walls. But you can remove most dirty or greasy fingerprints from painted walls by rubbing the area with a slice of white bread. Bread does a good job cleaning nonwashable wallpaper as well. Just cut off the crusts first to minimize the chance of scratching the paper.

Pick up glass fragments Picking up the large pieces of a broken glass or dish is usually easy enough, but getting up those tiny slivers can be a real pain (figuratively if not literally). The easiest way to make sure you don't miss any is to press a slice of bread over the area. Just be careful not to prick yourself when you toss the bread into the garbage.

Dust oil paintings You wouldn't want to try this with an original Renoir, or with any museum-quality painting for that matter, but you can clean off everyday dust and grime that collects on an oil painting by gently rubbing the surface with a piece of white bread.

✳ Bubble Pack

Prevent toilet-tank condensation If your toilet tank sweats in warm, humid weather, bubble pack could be just the right antiperspirant. Lining the inside of the tank with bubble pack will keep the outside of the tank from getting cold and causing condensation when it comes in contact with warm, moist air. To line the tank, shut off the supply valve under the tank and flush to drain the tank. Then wipe the inside walls clean and dry. Use silicone sealant to glue appropriate-sized pieces of bubble pack to the major flat surfaces.

Protect patio plants Keep your outdoor container plants warm and protected from winter frost damage. Wrap each container with bubble pack and use duct tape or string to hold the wrap in place. Make sure the wrap extends a couple of inches above the lip of the container. The added insulation will keep the soil warm all winter long.

Keep cola cold Wrap soft-drink cans with bubble pack to keep beverages refreshingly cold on hot summer days. Do the same for packages of frozen or chilled picnic foods. Wrap ice cream just before you leave for the picnic to help keep it firm en route.

Protect produce in the fridge Line your refrigerator's crisper drawer with bubble pack to prevent bruises to fruit and other produce. Cleanup will be easier, too—when the lining gets dirty, just throw it out and replace it with fresh bubble pack.

Add insulation Cut window-size pieces of wide bubble pack and duct-tape them to inside windows for added warmth and savings on fuel bills in winter. Lower the blinds to make it less noticeable.

Make a bedtime buffer Keep cold air from creeping into your bed on a chilly night by placing a large sheet of bubble pack between your bedspread or quilt and your top sheet. You'll be surprised at how effective it is in keeping warm air in and cold air out.

Cushion your work surface When repairing delicate glass or china, cover the work surface with bubble pack to help prevent breakage.

Protect tools Reduce wear and tear on your good-quality tools and extend their lives. Line your toolbox with bubble pack. Use duct tape to hold it in place.

Sleep on air while camping Get a better night's sleep on your next camping trip: Carry a 6-foot (2-meter) roll of wide bubble pack to use as a mat under your sleeping bag. No sleeping bag? Just fold a 12-foot-long (3.6-meter-long) piece of wide bubble pack in half, bubble side out, and duct-tape the edges. Then slip in and enjoy a restful night in your makeshift padded slumber bag.

Cushion bleachers and benches Take some bubble pack out to the ballgame with you to soften those hard stadium seats or benches. Or stretch a length along a picnic bench for more comfy dining.

❋ Buckets

Make a lobster pot If you don't have a large kettle, boil lobsters in an old metal bucket. Make sure to use pot holders and tongs when cooking and removing the lobster. Let the bucket cool before handling it again.

Kids' Stuff Add the beat of bucket **tom-toms** to create an exciting, fun atmosphere at your next family campfire. Cut **plastic buckets** to different lengths to create a distinct tone for each drum or use a mix of various-sized **plastic** and **galvanized buckets.** For more musical accompaniment, make a **broom-handle string bass** using a bucket as the sound box.

Create a food locker A tightly sealed 5-gallon (19-liter) bucket is an ideal waterproof (and animal-proof) food locker to bring with you on canoe trips.

Build a camp washing machine Here's a great way to wash clothes while camping. Make a hole in the lid of a 5-gallon (19-liter) plastic bucket and insert a new toilet plunger. Put in clothes and laundry detergent. Snap on the lid and move the plunger up and down as an agitator. You can safely clean even delicate garments.

Camp shower A bucket perforated with holes on the bottom makes an excellent campsite shower. Hang it securely from a sturdy branch, fill it using another bucket or jug, and then take a quick shower as the water comes out. Want to shower in warm water? Paint the outside of another bucket matte black. Fill it with water and leave it out in the sun all day.

Paint high Avoid messy paint spills when painting on a scaffold or ladder. Put your paint can and brush in a large bucket and use paint-can hooks to hang the bucket *and* the brush. If the bucket is large enough, you'll even have room for your paint scraper, putty knife, rags, or other painting tools you may need. A 5-gallon (19-liter) plastic bucket is ideal.

Paint low Use the lids from 5-gallon (19-liter) plastic buckets as trays for 1-gallon (3.78-liter) cans of paint. The lids act as platforms for the paint cans and are also large enough to hold a paintbrush.

Make stilts Make working on a ceiling less of a stretch. Use two sturdy buckets (minus handles) and a pair of old shoes to make your own mini-stilts. Drive screws through the shoe soles and into wood blocks inside the buckets. Or punch holes in the bucket bottoms and tie or strap down the shoes.

Keep extension cords tangle-free A 5-gallon (19-liter) bucket can help you keep a long extension cord free of tangles. Just cut or drill a hole near the bottom of the pail, making sure it is large enough for the cord's pronged end to pass through. Then coil the rest of the cord into the bucket. The cord will come right out when pulled and is easy to coil back in. Plug the ends of the cord together when it's not in use. You can use the center space to carry tools to a worksite.

Soak your saw The best way to clean saw blades is to soak them in acetone or turpentine in a shallow pan, with a lid on the pan to contain the fumes. You can make your own shallow pan by cutting the bottom two inches or so off a plastic 5-gallon (19-liter) bucket with a utility knife. The bucket's lid can serve as the cover. Remember to wear rubber gloves and use a stick to lever out the sharp blades.

Garden in a bucket Use a 5-gallon (19-liter) plastic bucket as a minigarden or planter. Use another as a composter for scraps and cuttings. Bucket gardens are just the right size for apartment balconies.

Tip **Where to Find Five-Gallon Buckets**

Five-gallon (19-liter) plastic buckets are versatile, virtually indestructible, and offer a myriad of handy uses. And you can usually get them for free. Ask nicely and your local fast-food restaurant or supermarket deli section may be happy to give you the buckets shortening or coleslaw came in. Or check with neighborhood plasterers, who use 5-gallon buckets of drywall compound. Also keep an eye open for neighbors doing home improvements. Don't forget to get the lids, too. Wash a bucket with water and household bleach, then let it dry in the sun for a day or two. Put some scented kitty litter, charcoal, or a couple of drops of vanilla inside to remove any lingering odors.

Make a Christmas tree stand Fill a bucket partway with sand or gravel and insert the base of the tree in it. Then fill it the rest of the way and pour water on the sand or gravel to help keep the tree from drying out.

✳ Butter

Keep mold off cheese Why waste good cheese by letting the cut edges get hard or moldy? Give semi-hard cheeses a light coat of butter to keep them fresh and free of mold. Each time you use the cheese, coat the cut edge with butter before you rewrap it and put it back in the fridge.

Make cat feel at home Is the family feline freaked out by your move to a new home? Moving is often traumatic for pets as well as family members. Here's a good way to help an adult cat adjust to the new house or apartment: Spread a little butter on the top of one of its front paws. Cats love the taste of butter so much they'll keep coming back for more.

Get rid of fishy smell Your fishing trip was a big success, but now your hands reek of fish. What to do? Just rub some butter on your hands, wash with warm water and soap, and your hands will smell clean and fresh again.

Swallow pills with ease If you have difficulty getting pills to go down, try rolling them in a small amount of butter or margarine first. The pills will slide down your throat more easily.

Soothe aching feet To soothe tired feet, massage them with butter, wrap in a damp, hot towel, and sit for 10 minutes. Your feet will feel revitalized … and they'll smell like popcorn too.

Remove sap from skin You've just gotten home from a pleasant walk in the woods, but your hand is still covered with sticky tree sap that feels like it will never come off. Don't worry. Just rub butter on your hand and the gunky black sap will wash right off with soap and water.

Keep leftover onion fresh The recipe calls for half an onion and you want to keep the remaining half fresh as long as possible. Rub butter on the cut surface and wrap the leftover onion in aluminum foil before putting it in the fridge. The butter will keep it fresh longer.

Zap ink stain on doll's face Uh-oh, one of the kids used a pen to draw a new smile on that favorite doll's face. Try eliminating the kiddy graffiti by rubbing butter on it and leaving the doll face-up in the sun for a few days. Wash it off with soap and water.

Cut sticky foods with ease Rub butter on your knife or scissor blades before cutting sticky foods like dates, figs, or marshmallows. The butter will act as a lubricant and keep the food from sticking to the blades.

Emergency shave cream If you run out of shaving cream, try slathering some butter onto your wet skin for a smooth, close shave.

Prevent pots from boiling over You take your eye off the pasta for two seconds, and the next thing you know, the pot is boiling over onto the stovetop. Keep the boiling water in the pot next time by adding a tablespoon or two of butter.

 DID *You* KNOW?

Butter is the semi-solid material that results from churning cream—a process that is depicted on a Sumerian tablet from 2500 B.C. A butter-filled churn was found in a 2,000-year-old Egyptian grave, and butter was plentiful in King Tut's day, when it was made from the milk of water buffaloes and camels. The Bible also contains many references to butter—as the product of cow's milk. Later, the Vikings are believed to have introduced butter to Normandy, a region world-renowned for its butter.

In the U.S.A., butter was the only food ever defined by an Act of Congress prior to the enactment of the Food, Drug, and Cosmetic Act of 1938. Butter made in North America must contain at least 80 percent milk fat. The remaining 20 percent is composed of water and milk solids. It may be salted or unsalted (sweet). The salt adds flavor and also acts as a preservative. It takes 21 pounds of fresh cow's milk to make a pound of butter (10 kilograms to make 500 grams).

Kids' Stuff Making **butter** is fun and easy, especially when there are several kids around to take turns churning. All you need is a **jar,** a **marble,** and 1 to 2 cups of heavy **whipping cream** or double cream (preferably without carrageenan or other stabilizers added). Use the freshest cream possible and leave it out of the refrigerator until it reaches a temperature of about 60°F (15°C). Pour the cream into the jar, add the marble, close the lid, and let the kids take turns shaking (churning), about one shake per second. It may take anywhere from 5 to 30 minutes, but the kids will see the cream go through various stages from sloshy to coarse whipped cream. When the whipped cream suddenly seizes and collapses, fine-grained bits of butter will be visible in the liquid buttermilk. Before long a glob of yellowish **butter** will appear. Drain off the **buttermilk** and enjoy the delightful taste of fresh-made butter.

Treat dry hair Is your hair dry and brittle? Try buttering it up for a luxuriant shine. Massage a small chunk of butter into your dry hair, cover it with a shower cap for 30 minutes, then shampoo and rinse thoroughly.

✳ Buttons

Decorate a dollhouse Use buttons as sconces, plates, and wall hangings in a child's dollhouse. The more variety, the better.

Beanbag filler Use small buttons the next time you make beanbags and save the dried beans for the soup.

Make a necklace String attractive buttons on two strands of heavy-duty thread or dental floss. Make an attractive design by alternating large and small buttons of various colors.

Decorate a Christmas tree Give your Christmas tree an old-fashioned look. Make a garland by knotting large buttons on a sturdy length of string or dental floss.

Use as game pieces or poker chips Don't let lost pieces stop you from playing games like backgammon, bingo, or Parcheesi. Substitute buttons for the lost pieces and keep playing to your heart's content. For an impromptu game of poker, use buttons as chips, with each color representing a different value.

Keep tape unstuck You're trying to wrap a present and you can't find the end of the tape roll. Instead of scratching in frustration trying to find that elusive end every time you use the tape, stick a button on the end of the tape. As you use the tape, keep moving the button.

C

✱ Cans

Keep tables together When you're having a large dinner party, lock card tables together by setting adjacent pairs of legs into empty cans. You won't have to clean up any spills caused by the tables moving this way and that.

Make light reflectors It's simple to make reflectors for your campsite or backyard lights. Just remove the bottom of a large empty can with a can opener and take off any label. Then use tin snips to cut the can in half lengthwise. You've just made two reflectors.

Quick floor patch Nail can lids to a wooden floor to plug knotholes and keep rodents out. If you can get access to the hole from the basement, nail the lid in place from underneath so the patch won't be obvious.

Tuna can egg poacher An empty 6-ounce (170-gram) tuna can is the perfect size to use as an egg poacher. Remove the bottom of the can as well as the top and remove any paper label. Then place the metal ring in a skillet of simmering water, and crack an egg into it.

Make a miniature golf course Arrange cans with both ends removed so the ball must go through them, go up a ramp into them, or ricochet off a board through them.

 DID **You** KNOW?

Tin cans are often described as "hermetically sealed," but do you know the origin of the term? The word *hermetic* comes from Hermes Trismegistus, a legendary alchemist who is reputed to have lived sometime in the first three centuries A.D. and to have invented a magic seal that keeps a vessel airtight.

The hermetically sealed can was invented in 1810 by British merchant Peter Durand. His cans were so thick they had to be hammered open! Two years later, Englishman Thomas Kensett set up America's first cannery on the New York waterfront to can oysters, meats, fruits, and vegetables.

Feed the birds A bird doesn't care if the feeder is plain or fancy as long as it is filled with suet. For a feeder that's about as basic as you can get, wedge a small can filled with suet between tree branches or posts.

Create decorative snowman Wrap an old soda can with white paper and tape with transparent tape. For a head use a styrene foam ball and tape it to the top of the can. Cover the body with cotton batting or cotton bandaging material and tape or glue it in place. Make a cone-shaped paper hat. Make eyes and a nose with buttons. To add arms, punch holes in the sides of the can and insert twigs. Use dots from a black marker pen to make buttons down the snowman's front. Make a scarf from a scrap of wooly fabric.

Make planters more portable Don't strain your back moving a planter loaded with heavy soil. Reduce the amount of soil and lighten the load by first filling one-third to one-half of the bottom of the planter with empty, upside-down aluminum cans. Finish filling with soil and add your plants. In addition to making the planter lighter, the rustproof aluminum cans also help it to drain well.

Protect young plants Remove both ends of an aluminum can and any paper label. Then push it into the earth to serve as a collar to protect young garden plants from cutworms. Use a soup can or a coffee can, depending on the size you need.

Make a tool tote Tired of fumbling around in your tool pouch to find the tool you need? Use empty frozen juice cans to transform the deep, wide pockets of a nail pouch into a convenient tote for wrenches, pliers, and screwdrivers. Make sure to remove the bottom of the can as well as the top. Glue or tape the cylinders together to keep them from shifting around, and slip them into the pouches to create dividers.

Make a pedestal Fill several wide identical-sized cans with rocks or sand and glue them together, one atop another. Screw a piece of wood into the bottom of the topmost can before attaching it, upside down, to the others. Paint your pedestal and place a potted plant, lamp, or statue on top. See the Tip on the following page for suggestions on the type of glue to use for this project.

Organize your desk If your office desk is a mess, a few empty cans can be the start of a nifty solution. Just attach several tin cans of assorted sizes together in a group to make an office-supplies holder for your desk. Start by cleaning and drying the cans and removing any labels. Then spray paint them (or wrap them in felt). When the paint is dry, glue them together using a hot glue gun. Your desk organizer is now ready to hold pens, pencils, paper clips, scissors, and such.

<mark>Tip</mark> **Glue for Cans**

> When gluing cans and other metal pieces together, use a glue that adheres well to metal, such as polyvinyl chloride (PVC), liquid solder, or epoxy. If the joint won't be subject to stress, you can use a hot glue gun. Make sure to wash and dry the cans and to remove any labels first. Also let any paint dry thoroughly before gluing.

Make pigeonholes Assemble half a dozen or more empty cans and paint them with bright enamel. After they dry, glue the cans together and place them on their sides on a shelf. Then store silverware, nails, office supplies, or other odds and ends in them.

* Candles

Unstick a drawer If you have a desk or chest drawer that sticks, remove it and rub a candle on the runners. The drawer will open more smoothly when you slip it back in place.

Make a pincushion A wide candle makes an ideal pincushion. The wax will help pins and needles glide more easily through fabric too.

Weatherproof your labels After you address a package with a felt-tip pen, weatherproof the label by rubbing a white candle over the writing. Neither rain, nor sleet, nor snow will smear the label now.

Quiet a squeaky door If a squeaky door is driving you batty, take it off its hinges and rub a candle over the hinge surfaces that touch each other. The offending door will squeak no more.

DID *You* KNOW?

Beeswax—the substance secreted by honeybees to make honeycombs—didn't make its debut in candles until the Middle Ages. Until then, candles were made of the rendered animal fat called tallow that produced a smoky flame and gave off acrid odors. Beeswax candles, by contrast, burned pure and clean. But they were not widely used at the time, being far too expensive for ordinary serfs and peasants.

The growth of whaling in the late 1700s brought a major change to candlemaking as spermaceti—a waxlike substance derived from sperm-whale oil—became available in bulk. The 19th century witnessed the advent of mass-produced candles and low-cost paraffin wax. Made from oil and coal shale, paraffin burned cleanly with no unpleasant odor.

Mend shoelace ends When the plastic or metal tips come off the ends of shoelaces, don't wait for the laces to fray. Do something to prevent the annoyance that comes from having to force a scraggly shoelace end through a teeny eyelet: Just dip the end into melted candle wax and the lace will hold until you can buy a new one.

Make a secret drawing Have a child make an "invisible" drawing with a white candle. Then let him or her cover it with a wash of watercolor paint to reveal the picture. The image will show up because the wax laid down by the candle will keep the paper in the areas it covers from absorbing the paint. If you have a few kids around, they can all make secret drawings and messages to swap and reveal.

Use puff-proof candle to ignite fires Don't let a draft blow out the flame when you're trying to light your fireplace or spark up the barbecue grill. Start your fire with one of those trick puff-proof birthday candles, designed to be a practical joke aid that prevents birthday celebrants from blowing out the candles on their cakes. Once your fire is up and roaring, smother the candle flame and save the trick candle for future use.

✳ Candy Tins

Emergency sewing kit A small candy tin is just the right size to hold a handy selection of needles, thread, and buttons in your purse or briefcase for on-the-spot repairs.

Store broken jewelry Don't lose all the little pieces of that broken jewelry you plan to have repaired someday. Keep the pieces together and safe in a small candy tin.

Prevent jewelry-chain tangles Keep necklaces and chain bracelets separate and tangle-free in their own individual tins.

Keep earrings together You are late for the party but you can only find one earring from the pair that matched your dress so nicely. To prevent pairs of small earrings from going their separate ways, store them together in a little candy tin and you'll be right on time for the next party.

Make a birthday keepsake Decorate the outside of a small candy tin, line it with felt or silk, and insert a penny or, if you can find one, a silver dollar from the birth year of your friend or loved one.

Organize your sewing gear Use a small candy tin to store snaps, sequins, buttons, and beads in your sewing box. Label the lids or glue on a sample for easy identification of the contents.

Store workshop accessories Candy tins are great for storing brads, glazing points, setscrews, lock washers, and other small items that might otherwise clutter up your workshop.

Store car fuses You'll always know where to find your spare car fuses if you store them in a little candy tin in the glove compartment of your car.

super item **24** *uses!* # Cardboard Boxes

* CARDBOARD BOXES **AROUND THE HOUSE**

Make a bed tray Have breakfast in bed on a tray made from a cardboard box. Just remove the top flaps and cut arches from the two long sides to fit over your lap. Decorate the bottom of the box—which is now the top of your tray—with adhesive shelf paper and you're ready for those bacon and eggs.

Shield doors and furniture Use cardboard shields to protect doors and furniture from stains when you polish doorknobs and furniture pulls. Cut out the appropriate-sized shield and slide it over the items you are going to polish. This works best when you make shields that slip over the neck of knobs or knoblike pulls. But you can also make shields for hinges and U-shaped pulls.

Create gift-wrap suspense Take a cue from the Russians and their nesting *matryoshka* dolls. Next time you are giving a small but sure-to-be appreciated gift to a friend, place the gift-wrapped little box inside a series of increasingly bigger gaily wrapped boxes.

DID *You* KNOW?

The Chinese invented cardboard in the early 1500s, thus anticipating the demand for containers for Chinese takeout food by several hundred years.

In 1871 New Yorker Albert Jones patented the idea of gluing a piece of corrugated paper between two pieces of flat cardboard to create a material rigid enough to use for shipping. But it wasn't until 1890 that another American, Robert Gair, invented the corrugated cardboard box. His boxes were pre-cut flat pieces manufactured in bulk that folded into boxes, just like the cardboard boxes that surround us today.

Make dustcovers Keep dust and dirt out of a small appliance, power tool, or keyboard. Cut the flaps off a cardboard box that fits over the item, decorate it or cover it with self-adhesive decorative paper, and use it as a dustcover.

Tip A Good Box Source

> Even if you don't drink alcohol, the proprietors of your local liquor store will often be happy to provide you with empty wine and liquor cartons. Don't forget to ask for the handy sections to be left intact.

Make an office in-box Making an in-box (or out-box) for your office desk is easy. Simply cut the top and one large panel off a cereal box; then slice the narrow sides at an angle. Wrap with self-adhesive decorative paper.

Make place mats Cut several 12 x 18-inch (30 x 45-centimeter) pieces of cardboard and cover them with colorful adhesive shelf paper or other decoration.

Play liquor box "ski ball" Transform your rec room or backyard into a carnival midway. Just leave the dividers in place in an empty wine or liquor carton. Place the carton at an angle and erect a small ramp in front (a rubber mat over a pile of books will do). Assign numbered values to each section of the carton, grab a few tennis or golf balls and you're ready to roll.

✳ CARDBOARD BOXES **FOR STORING THINGS**

Protect glassware or lightbulbs A good way to safely store fine crystal glassware is to put it in an empty wine or liquor carton with partitions. You can also use it for storing lightbulbs, but be sure to sort the bulbs by wattage so that it's easy to find the right one when you need a replacement.

Make a magazine holder Store your magazines in holders made from empty detergent boxes. Remove the top, then cut the box at an angle, from the top of one side to the bottom third of the other. Cover the holders with self-adhesive decorative paper.

Poster and artwork holder A clean liquor carton with its dividers intact is a great place to store rolled-up posters, drawings on paper, and canvases. Just insert the items upright between the partitions.

Store Christmas ornaments When you take down your Christmas tree, wrap each ornament in newspaper or tissue paper and store it in an empty liquor box with partitions. Each of the carton's segments can hold several of the wrapped holiday tree ornaments.

C

Create an impromptu sled Use a large cardboard box to pull a small child (or a load of firewood) over the snow.

Garage for toy vehicles Turn an empty large appliance box on its side and let the kids use it as a "garage" for their wheeled vehicles. They can also use a smaller box as a garage for miniature cars, trucks, and buses.

Make a puppet theater Stand a large cardboard box on end. Cut a big hole in the back for puppeteers to crouch in and a smaller one high up in the front for the stage. Decorate with markers or glue on pieces of fabric for curtains.

Organize kids' sporting goods Keep a decorated empty wine or liquor carton with partitions, and with the top cut off, in your child's room and use it for easy storage of tennis rackets, baseball bats, fishing poles, and such.

Make a play castle Turn a large appliance cardboard box into a medieval castle. Cut off the top flaps and make battlements by cutting notches along the top. To make a notch, use a utility knife to make a cut on either side of the section you want to remove, then fold the cut section forward and cut along the fold. To make a drawbridge, cut a large fold-down opening on one side that is attached at the bottom. Connect the top of the drawbridge to the sidewalls with ropes on either side, punching holes for the rope and knotting the rope on the other side. Use duct tape to reinforce the holes. Also cut

SCIENCE FAIR

Making a simple cardboard **sundial** is a great way for kids to observe how the sun's path changes every day. Just take a 10 x 10-inch (25 x 25-centimeter) piece of **cardboard** and poke a stick through the middle. If necessary, screw or nail a **small board** to the bottom of the stick to hold it upright. Place the sundial in a sunny spot. At **each**

hour, have the kids **mark** where the **stick's shadow** falls on the cardboard. Check again the next day, and sure enough, the sundial seems pretty accurate. Check a week later, though, and the shadows won't align to the marks at the right times. When the curious kids start searching the Internet for a reason, give them a hint: The earth is tilted on its axis.

out narrow window slits in the walls. Let the kids draw stones and bricks on the walls.

Repair a roof For temporary repair on your roof, put a piece of cardboard into a plastic bag and slide it under the shingles.

Organize your workshop A sectioned wine or liquor carton is a great place to store dowels, moldings, furring strips, weather stripping, and metal rods.

Store tall garden tools Turn three empty liquor cartons into a sectioned storage bin for your long-handled garden tools. Put a topless box on the floor with the dividers left in. Then cut the tops and bottoms off two similar boxes and stack them so the dividers match up. Use duct tape to attach the boxes to each other. Use the bin to store hoes, rakes, and other long-handled garden tools.

Protect work surfaces Keep work surfaces from being damaged. Flatten a large box or cut a large flat piece from a box and use it to protect your countertop, workbench, table, or desk from ink, paint, glue, or nicks from knives and scissors. Just replace it when it becomes messed up.

Protect your fingers Ouch! You just hammered your finger instead of the tiny nail you were trying to drive. To keep this from happening again, stick the little nail through a small piece of thin cardboard before you do your hammering. Hold the cardboard by an edge, position the nail, and pound it home. When you're done, use your bruise-free fingers to tear away the cardboard.

Keep upholstery tacks straight Reupholstering a chair or sofa? Here's a neat way to get a row of upholstery tacks perfectly straight and evenly spaced. Mark the spacing along the edge of a lightweight cardboard strip and press the tacks into it. After driving all of the tacks most of the way in, tug on the strip to pull the edge free before driving in the rest of the way.

Make a drip pan Prevent an oil leak from soiling your garage floor or driveway. Make a drip pan by placing a few sheets of corrugated cardboard in a cookie sheet and placing the pan under your car's drip. For better absorption, sprinkle some cat litter, sawdust, or oatmeal into the pan on top of the cardboard. Replace with fresh cardboard as needed.

Help your mechanic *Something* is dripping from your car's engine, but you don't know what. Instead of blubbering helplessly to your mechanic about it, place a large piece of cardboard under the engine overnight and bring it with you when you take the car in for service. The color and location of the leaked fluid will help the mechanic identify the problem.

✳ Cardboard Tubes

Extend vacuum cleaner reach Can't reach that cobweb on the ceiling with your regular vacuum cleaner attachment? Try using a long, empty wrapping paper tube to extend the reach. You can even crush the end of the paper tube to create a crevice tool. Use duct tape to make the connection airtight.

Make a sheath Flatten a paper towel tube, duct tape one end shut, and you have a perfect sheath for a picnic/camp knife. Use toilet paper rolls for smaller cutlery.

Keep electrical cords tangle-free Keep computer and appliance cords tangle-free. Fanfold the cord and pass it through a toilet paper tube before plugging in. You can also use the tubes to store extension cords when they're not in use. Paper towel tubes will also work. Just cut them in half before using them to hold the cords.

Make a fly and pest strip Get rid of pesky flies and mosquitoes with a homemade pest strip. Just cover an empty paper towel or toilet paper roll with transparent tape, sticky side out, and hang where needed.

Use as kindling and logs Turn toilet paper and paper towel tubes into kindling and logs for your fireplace. For fire starter, use scissors to cut the cardboard into 1/8-inch (3-millimeter) strips. Keep the strips in a bin near the fireplace so they'll be handy to use next time you make a fire. To make logs, tape over one end of the tube and pack shredded newspaper inside. Then tape the other end. The tighter you pack the newspaper, the longer your log will burn.

Make boot trees To keep the tops of long, flexible boots from flopping over and developing ugly creases in the closet, insert cardboard mailing tubes into them to help them hold their shape.

 DID **You** KNOW?

It took nearly 500 years for toilet paper to make the transition from sheets to rolls. Toilet paper was first produced in China in 1391 for the exclusive use of the emperor—in sheets that measured a whopping 2 x 3 feet (60 x 90 centimeters) each. Toilet paper in rolls was first made in the U.S.A. in 1890 by Scott Paper Company. Scott began making paper towels in 1907, thanks to a failed attempt to develop a new crepe toilet tissue. This paper was so thick it couldn't be cut and rolled into toilet paper, so Scott made larger rolls, perforated into 13 x 18-inch (33 x 45-centimeter), 13 x 18-inch (33 x 45-centimeter) sheets and sold them as Sani-Towels.

Make a plant guard It's easy to accidentally scar the trunk of a young tree when you are whacking weeds around it. To avoid doing this, cut a cardboard mailing tube in half lengthwise and tie the two halves around the trunk while you work around the tree. Then slip it off and use it on another tree.

Protect important documents Before storing diplomas, marriage certificates, and other important documents in your cedar chest, roll them tightly and insert them in paper towel tubes. This prevents creases and keeps the documents clean and dry.

Start seedlings Don't go to the garden supply store to buy biodegradable starting pots for seedlings. Just use the cardboard tubes from paper towels and toilet paper. Use scissors to cut each toilet paper tube into two pots, or each paper towel tube into four. Fill a tray with the cut cylinders packed  against each other so they won't tip when you water the seedlings. This will also prevent them from drying out too quickly. Now fill each pot with seed-starting mix, gently pack it down, and sow your seeds. When you plant the seedlings, make sure to break down the side of the roll and make sure all the cardboard is completely buried.

Store knitting needles To keep your knitting needles from bending and breaking, try this: Use a long cardboard tube from kitchen foil or plastic wrap. Cover one end with cellophane tape. Pinch the other end closed and secure it tightly with tape. Slide the needles in through the tape on the taped end. The tape will hold them in place for secure, organized storage.

Store fabric scraps Roll up leftover fabric scraps tightly and insert them inside a cardboard tube from your bathroom or kitchen. For easy identification, tape or staple a sample of the fabric to the outside of the tube.

Store string Nothing is more useless and frustrating than tangled string. To keep your string ready to use, cut a notch into each end of a toilet paper tube. Secure one end of the string in one notch, wrap the string tightly around the tube, and then secure the other end in the other notch.

Keep linens crease-free Wrap tablecloths and napkins around cardboard tubes after laundering to avoid the creases they would get if they were folded. Use long tubes for tablecloths and paper towel or toilet paper tubes for napkins. To guard against stains, cover the tubes with plastic wrap first.

Keep pants crease-free You go to your closet for that good pair of pants you haven't worn in a while, only to find an ugly crease at the fold site from the hanger rack. It won't happen again if you cut a paper towel tube lengthwise, fold it in half horizontally, and place it over the rack before you hang up your pants. Before hanging pants, tape the sides of the cardboard together at the bottom to keep it from slipping.

Keep Christmas lights tidy Spending more time untangling your Christmas lights than it takes to put them up? Make yuletide prep easier by wrapping your lights around a cardboard tube. Secure them with masking tape. Put small strands of lights or garlands *inside* cardboard tubes, and seal the ends of the tubes with masking tape.

Tip Carpet Tubes

Carpet stores discard long, thick cardboard tubes that store workers will probably be happy to provide to you free for the asking. Because the tubes can be up to 12 feet (3.6 meters) long, you might want to ask for them to cut one to the size you want before you cart it away.

Protect fluorescent lights Keep fluorescent light tubes from breaking before you use them. They will fit neatly into long cardboard tubes sealed with tape at one end.

Make a kazoo Got a bunch of bored kids driving you crazy on a rainy day? Cut three small holes in the middle of a paper towel tube. Then cover one end of the tube with wax paper secured with a strong rubber band. Now hum into the other end, while using your fingers to plug one, two, or all three holes to vary the pitch. Make one for each kid. They may still drive you crazy, but they'll have a ball doing it!

Instant megaphone Don't shout yourself hoarse when you're calling outside for a child or pet to come home *right now*. Give your vocal cords a rest by using a wide cardboard tube as a megaphone to amplify your voice.

Make a hamster toy Place a couple of paper towel or toilet paper tubes in the hamster (or gerbil) cage. The little critters will love running and walking through them, and they like chewing on the cardboard too. When the tubes start looking ragged, just replace them with fresh ones.

Preserve kids' artwork You want to save some of your kids' precious artwork for posterity (or you don't want it to clutter up the house). Simply roll up the artwork and place it inside a paper towel tube. Label the outside with the child's name and date. The tubes are easy to store, and you can safely preserve the work of your budding young artists. Use this method to hold and store your documents, such as certificates and licenses, too.

Build a toy log cabin Notch the ends of several long tubes with a craft knife and then help the kids build log cabins, fences, or huts with them. Use different-sized tubes for added versatility. For added realism, have the kids paint or color the tubes before construction begins.

Make English crackers Keep the spirit of holiday firecrackers but cut out the dangers associated with burning explosives. Use toilet paper tubes to make English crackers, which "explode" into tiny gifts. For each cracker, tie a string about 8 inches (20 centimeters) long around a small gift such as candy, a balloon, or a figurine. After tying, the string should have about 6 inches (15 centimeters) to spare. Place the gift into the tube so the string dangles out one end. Cover the tube with bright-colored crepe paper or tissue and twist the ends. When you pull the string, out pops the gift.

✳ Car Wax

Fix skips on CDs Don't throw out that scratched compact disc. Try fixing it first with a small dab of car wax. Spread a cloth on a flat surface and place the CD on it damaged side up. Then, holding the disc with one hand, use the other to wipe the polish into the affected area with a soft cloth. Wait for it to dry and buff using short, brisk strokes along the scratch, not across it. A cloth sold to wipe eyeglasses or camera lenses will work well. When you can no longer see the scratch, wash the disc with water and let it dry before playing.

Keep bathroom mirrors fog-free Prevent your bathroom mirror from steaming up after your next hot shower. Apply a small amount of car paste wax to the mirror, let it dry, and buff with a soft cloth. Next time you step out of the shower, you'll be able to see your face in the mirror immediately. Rub the wax on bathroom fixtures to prevent water spots too.

Eliminate bathroom mildew To chase grime and mildew from your shower, follow these two simple steps: First clean the soap and water residue off the tiles or shower wall. Then rub on a layer of car paste wax and buff with a clean, dry cloth. You'll only need to reapply the wax about once a year. Don't wax the bathtub—it will become dangerously slippery.

Eradicate furniture stains Someone forgot to use a coaster and now there's an ugly white ring on the dining room table. When your regular furniture polish doesn't work, try using a dab of car wax. Trace the ring with your finger to apply the wax. Let it dry and buff with a soft cloth.

Keep snow from sticking When it's time to clear the driveway after a big snowstorm, you don't want snow sticking to your shovel. Apply two thick coats of car paste wax to the work surface of the shovel before you begin shoveling. The snow won't stick and there will be less wear and tear on your cardiovascular system. If you use a snow thrower, wax the inside of the chute.

✳ Carpet Scraps

Muffle clunky appliance noise Does your washer or dryer shake, rattle, and roll when you're doing a load? Put a piece of scrap carpet underneath it, and that may be all you need to calm things down.

Catch a falling sock You may never be able to stop socks and other articles of clothing from falling to the floor en route from washer to dryer. But you can make retrieval a lot easier by placing a narrow piece of carpet on the floor between the two appliances. When something falls, just pull out the strip and the article comes with it.

Keep Fido's home dry Don't let the raindrops keep falling on your dog's head. Weatherproof the doghouse: Make a rain flap by nailing a carpet remnant over the entrance to your doggy's domicile. In colder areas, you can also use small pieces of carpet to line interior walls and the floor to add insulation.

Make a scratching post If your cat is clawing up the living room sofa, this might do the trick. Make a scratching post by stapling carpet scraps to a post or board and place it near kitty's favorite target. If you want it to be freestanding, nail a board to the bottom of the post to serve as a base.

Keep garden paths weed-free Place a series of carpet scraps upside down and cover them with bark mulch or straw for a weed-free garden path. Use smaller scraps as mulch around your vegetable garden.

Exercise in comfort Make an instant exercise mat. Cut a length of old carpet around 3 feet (1 meter) wide and as long as your height. When you're not using it for yoga or sit-ups, roll it up and store it under your bed.

Make your own car mats Why buy expensive floor mats for your car when you can make your own? Cut carpet remnants to fit the floorboards of your car and drive off in comfort.

Protect your knees To protect your knees when you're washing the floor, weeding, or doing other work on all fours, make your own kneepads. Cut two pieces of carpeting 10 inches (25 centimeters) square and then cut two parallel slits or holes in each. Run old neckties or scarves through the slits and use them to tie the pads to your knees.

Keep floors dry Don't let the floor get soaked when you water your indoor plants. Place 12-inch (30-centimeter) round carpet scraps under houseplants to absorb any overwatering excess.

Prevent scratched floors Stop screeching chairs from scratching or making black marks on wood or vinyl floors. Glue small circles of carpet remnants to the bottom of chair and table legs.

Make a buffer Use epoxy resin to glue an old piece of carpet to a block of wood to make a buffer. Make several and use one to buff shoes, another to wipe blackboards, and one to clean window screens.

Cushion kitchen shelves Reduce the noisy clattering when putting away pots and pans: Cushion kitchen shelves and cabinets with pieces of carpet.

Add traction Keep good-sized carpet scraps in the trunk of your car to add traction when you're stuck in snow or ice. Keep one piece with your spare tire: When you have a flat, you won't have to kneel or lie on the dirty ground when you have to look under the carriage.

Protect workshop tools Does your workshop have a floor made of concrete or another hard material? If so, put down a few carpet remnants in the area closest to your workbench. Now when tools or containers accidentally fall to the floor, they will be far less likely to break.

✳ Castor Oil

Soften cuticles If you were ever forced to swallow castor oil as a child, this may be a pleasant surprise: The high vitamin-E content of that awful-tasting thick oil can work wonders on brittle nails and ragged cuticles. And you don't have to swallow the stuff. Just massage a small amount on your cuticles and nails each day and within three months you will have supple cuticles and healthy nails

Soothe tired eyes Before going to bed, rub odorless castor oil all around your eyes. Rub some on your eyelashes, too, to keep them shiny. Be careful not to get the oil in your eyes.

Lubricate kitchen scissors Use castor oil instead of toxic petroleum oil to lubricate kitchen scissors and other utensils that touch food.

Repel moles If moles are destroying your garden and yard, try using castor oil to get rid of them. Mix 1/2 cup castor oil and 2 gallons (7.5 liters) water and drench the molehill with it. It won't kill them, but it will get them out looking for another neighborhood to dig up.

Enjoy a massage Castor oil is just the right consistency to use as a soothing massage oil. For a real treat, warm the oil on the stovetop or on half-power in the microwave. Ahhh!

DID *You* KNOW?

Castor oil is more than an old-fashioned medicine cabinet staple. It has hundreds of industrial uses. Large amounts are used in paints, varnishes, lipstick, hair tonic, and shampoo. Castor oil is also converted into plastics, soap, waxes, hydraulic fluids, and ink. And it is made into lubricants for jet engines and racing cars because it does not become stiff with cold or unduly thin with heat. North American manufacturers now use about 40 percent of the entire world's crop of castor oil.

117

Perk up ailing ferns Give your sickly ferns a tonic made by mixing 1 tablespoon castor oil and 1 tablespoon baby shampoo with 4 cups lukewarm water. Give the fern about 3 tablespoons of the tonic, then follow with plain water. Your plants should be perky by the time you use up your supply of tonic.

Condition your hair For healthy, shiny hair, mix 2 teaspoons castor oil with 1 teaspoon glycerin and one egg white. Massage it into your wet hair, wait several minutes, and wash out.

✳ Cat Litter

Make a mud mask Make a deep-cleansing mud mask. Mix two handfuls of fresh cat litter with enough warm water to make a thick paste. Smear the paste over your face, let it set for 20 minutes, and rinse clean with water. The clay from cat litter detoxifies your skin by absorbing dirt and oil from the pores. When your friends compliment you on your complexion and ask how you did it, just tell them it's your little secret.

Sneaker deodorizer If your athletic shoes reek, fill a couple of old socks with scented cat litter, tie them shut, and place them in the sneakers overnight. Repeat if necessary until the sneakers are stink-free.

Add traction on ice Keep a bag of cat litter in the trunk of your car. Use it to add traction when you're stuck in ice or snow.

Prevent grease fires Don't let a grease fire spoil your next barbecue. Pour a layer of cat litter into the bottom of your grill for worry-free outdoor cooking.

Stop musty odors Get rid of that musty smell when you open the closet door. Just place a shallow box filled with cat litter in each musty closet or room. Cat litter works great as a deodorant.

DID *You* KNOW?

Ed Lowe might not have gotten the idea for cat litter if a neighbor hadn't asked him for some sand for her cat box one day in 1947. Ed, who worked for his father's company selling industrial absorbents, suggested clay instead because it was more absorbent and would not leave tracks around the house. When she returned for more, he knew he had a winner. Soon he was criss-crossing the country, selling bags of his new Kitty Litter from the back of his Chevy Coupe. By 1990 Edward Lowe Industries, Inc., was the nation's largest producer of cat box filler with retail sales of more than $210 million annually.

Preserve flowers The fragrance and beauty of freshly cut flowers is such a fleeting thing. You can't save the smell, but you can preserve their beauty by drying your flowers on a bed of cat litter in an airtight container for 7-10 days.

Remove foul stench Just because your garbage cans hold garbage doesn't mean they have to smell disgusting. Sprinkle some cat litter into the bottom of garbage cans to keep them smelling fresh. Change the litter after a week or so or when it becomes damp. If you have a baby in the house, use cat litter the same way to freshen diaper pails.

Keep tents must-free Keep tents and sleeping bags fresh smelling and free of must when not in use. Pour cat litter into an old sock, tie the end, and store inside the bag or tent.

Repel moles Moles may hate the smell of soiled cat litter even more than you do. Pour some down their tunnels to send them scurrying to find new homes.

Make grease spots disappear Get rid of ugly grease and oil spots in your driveway or on your garage floor. Simply cover them with cat litter. If the spots are fresh, the litter will soak up most of the oil right away. To remove old stains, pour some paint thinner on the stain before tossing on the cat litter. Wait 12 hours and then sweep clean.

Freshen old books You can rejuvenate old books that smell musty by sealing them overnight in a can with clean cat litter.

❋ Chalk

Repel ants Keep ants at bay by drawing a line around home entry points. The ants will be repelled by the calcium carbonate in the chalk, which is actually made up of ground-up and compressed shells of marine animals. Scatter powdered chalk around garden plants to repel ants and slugs.

Polish metal and marble To make metal shine like new, put some chalk dust on a damp cloth and wipe. (You can make chalk dust by using a mortar to pulverize pieces of chalk.) Buff with a soft cloth for an even shinier finish. Wipe clean marble with a damp soft cloth dipped in powdered chalk. Rinse with clear water and dry thoroughly.

Keep silver from tarnishing You love serving company with your fine silver, but polishing it before each use is another story. Put one or two pieces of chalk in the drawer with your good silver. It will absorb moisture and slow tarnishing. Put some in your jewelry box to delay tarnishing there too.

Remove grease spots Rub chalk on a grease spot on clothing or table linens and let it absorb the oil before you brush it off. If the stain lingers, rub chalk into it again before laundering. Get rid of ring-around-the-collar stains too. Mark the stains heavily with chalk before laundering. The chalk will absorb the oils that hold dirt in.

Stop screwdriver slips Does your screwdriver slip when you try to tighten a screw? It won't slip nearly as much if you rub some chalk on the tip of the blade.

Reduce closet dampness Tie a dozen pieces of chalk together and hang them up in your damp closet. The chalk will absorb moisture and help prevent mildew. Replace with a fresh bunch every few months.

Hide ceiling marks Temporarily cover up water or scuff marks on the ceiling until you have time to paint or make a permanent repair. Rub a stick of white chalk over the mark until it lightens or disappears.

Keep tools rust-free You can eliminate moisture and prevent rust from invading your toolbox by simply putting a few pieces of chalk in the box. Your tools will be rust-free and so will the toolbox.

DID **You** KNOW?

The first "street painting" took place in 16th-century Italy, when artists began using chalk to make drawings on pavement. The artists often made paintings of the Virgin Mary (Madonna in Italian) and thus they became known as *madonnari*. The *madonnari* of old were itinerant artists known for a life of freedom and travel. But they always managed to attend the many regional holidays and festivals that took place in each Italian province. Today *madonnari* and their quaint street paintings continue to be a colorful part of the celebrations that take place every day in modern Italy.

✳ Charcoal Briquettes

Make a dehumidifier A humid closet, attic, or basement can wreak havoc on your health as well as your clothes. Get rid of all that humidity with several homemade dehumidifiers. To make one, just put some charcoal briquettes in a coffee can, punch a few holes in the lid, and place in the humid areas. Replace the charcoal every few months.

Keep root water fresh Put a piece of charcoal in the water when you're rooting plant cuttings. The charcoal will keep the water fresh.

Banish bathroom moisture and odors Hide a few pieces of charcoal in the nooks and crannies of your bathroom to soak up moisture and cut down on unpleasant odors. Replace them every couple of months.

Keep books mold-free Professional librarians use charcoal to get rid of musty odors on old books. You can do the same. If your bookcase has glass doors, it may provide a damp environment that can cause must and mold. A piece of charcoal or two placed inside will help keep the books dry and mold-free.

✳ Cheesecloth

Remove turkey stuffing with ease To keep turkey dressing from sticking to the bird's insides, pack the dressing in cheesecloth before you stuff it into the turkey's cavity. When the turkey is ready to serve, pull out the cheesecloth and the stuffing will slide out with it.

Make a homemade butterfly net Just sew cheesecloth into a bag and glue or staple it to a hoop formed from a wire coat hanger—and send the kids a-hunting. Or make a smaller cheesecloth net for when you take the kids fishing and let them use it as a bait-net to catch minnows. For an inexpensive Halloween costume, wrap a child in cheesecloth from head to toe and send your mini-mummy out to collect candy.

Convert a colander into a strainer If you can't find a strainer when you need one, a colander lined with cheesecloth will serve in a pinch.

Cut vacuuming time Here is a neat, time-saving way to vacuum the contents of a drawer filled with small objects without having to remove the contents. Simply cover the nozzle of your vacuum cleaner with cheesecloth, secured with a strong rubber band, and the vacuum will pick up only the dust.

Reduce waste drying herbs When drying fresh herbs, wrap them in cheesecloth to prevent seeds and smaller crumbled pieces from falling through.

Picnic food tent Keep bugs and dirt away from your picnic food serving plates. Wrap a piece of cheesecloth around an old wire umbrella form and place it over the plates. Use a hacksaw to remove the umbrella handle and tack the cheesecloth to the umbrella ribs with a needle and thread.

Make instant festive curtains Brighten any room with inexpensive, colorful, and festive cheesecloth curtains. Dye inexpensive cheesecloth (available in bulk from fabric vendors) in bright colors and cut it to the lengths and widths you need. Attach clip-on café-curtain hooks and your new curtains are ready to hang.

✳ Chest Rub

Repel ticks and other bugs Going for a walk in the woods? Smear some chest rub on your legs and pants before you leave the house. It will keep ticks from biting and may spare you from getting Lyme disease. Pesky biting insects like gnats and mosquitoes will look elsewhere for victims if you apply chest rub to your skin before venturing outdoors. They hate the smell.

Lunsford Richardson, the pharmacist who created Vick's VapoRub in 1905, also originated America's first "junk mail." Richardson was working in his brother-in-law's drugstore when he blended menthol and other ingredients into an ointment to clear sinuses and ease congestion. He called it Richardson's Croup and Pneumonia Cure Salve, but soon realized he needed something catchier to sell successfully. He changed the name to Vick's after his brother-in-law, Joshua Vick, and convinced the U.S. Post Office to institute a new policy allowing him to send advertisements addressed only to "Boxholder." Sales of Vick's first surpassed a million dollars during the Spanish flu epidemic of 1918.

Make calluses disappear Coat calluses with chest rub and then cover them with an adhesive bandage overnight. Repeat the procedure as needed. Most calluses will disappear after several days.

Soothe aching feet Are your feet aching after that long walk in the woods? Try applying a thick coat of chest rub and cover with a pair of socks before going to bed at night. When you wake up, your feet will be moisturized and rejuvenated.

Stop insect-bite itch fast Apply a generous coat of chest rub for immediate relief from itchy insect bites. The eucalyptus and menthol in the ointment are what do the trick.

Treat toenail fungus If you have a toenail fungus (onychomycosis), try applying a thick coat of chest rub to the affected nail several times a day. Many users and even some medical pros swear that it works (just check the Internet). But if you don't see results after a few weeks, consult a dermatologist or podiatrist.

✳ Chewing Gum

Retrieve valuables Oops, you just lost an earring or other small valuable down the drain. Try retrieving it with a just-chewed piece of gum stuck to the bottom of a fishing weight. Dangle it from a string tied to the weight, let it take hold, and reel it in.

Lure a crab You'll be eating plenty of crab cakes if you try this trick: Briefly chew a stick of gum so that it is soft but still hasn't lost its flavor, then attach it to a crab line. Lower the line and wait for the crabs to go for the gum.

Fill cracks Fill a crack in a clay flowerpot or a dog bowl with piece of well-chewed gum.

Use as makeshift window putty Worried that a loose pane of glass may tumble and break before you get around to fixing it? Hold it in place temporarily with a wad or two of fresh-chewed gum.

Repair glasses When your glasses suddenly have a lens loose, put a small piece of chewed gum in the corner of the lens to hold it in place until you can get the glasses properly repaired.

Treat flatulence and heartburn Settle stomach gases and relieve heartburn by chewing a stick of spearmint gum. The oils in the spearmint act as an antiflatulent. Chewing stimulates the production of saliva, which neutralizes stomach acid and corrects the flow of digestive juices. Spearmint also acts as a digestive aid.

✳ Chicken Wire

Repel deer Are the deer tearing up your garden again? Here's a simple method to keep them away: Stake chicken wire *flat* around the perimeter of your garden. Deer don't like to walk on it, and it is not an eyesore like a chicken-wire fence.

Crown catnip plants If you are growing catnip for your cat, put a crown of chicken wire over the plant, close to the ground. As the catnip grows through the wire and gets eaten, the roots will remain intact, growing new catnip. Make sure the edges of the wire are tucked in securely. Catnip is a hardy plant, even in frigid temperatures, so if the roots remain, you will see it year after year.

Protect bulbs from rodents Keep pesky burrowing rodents from damaging your flower bulbs. Line the bottom of a prepared bed with chicken wire, plant the bulbs, and cover with soil.

Flower holder Keep cut flowers aligned in a vase. Squish some chicken wire together and place it in the bottom of the vase before inserting the flowers.

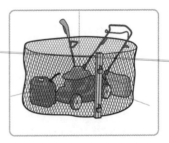

Make a childproof corral Your garage or shed is full of dangerous tools and toxic substances. Keep kids away from these hazardous items by enclosing them in a childproof corral. Make it by first attaching standard-width chicken wire to the walls in a corner. Then staple 1 x 2s to the cut ends of the wire and install screw eyes in the wood to accommodate two padlocks.

Firmer fence posts Before setting a fence post in concrete, wrap the base with chicken wire. This will make the anchoring firmer and the post more secure.

Secure insulation After you place fiberglass batting between roof rafters or floor joists, staple chicken wire across the joists to secure it and, in the case of the rafters, to keep it from sagging.

✳ Clipboards

Makeshift pants hanger Can't find a hanger for a pair of pants? Use a clipboard instead. Just suspend the clipboard from a hook inside the closet or on the bedroom door. Hang the trousers overnight by clipping the cuffs to the board.

Keep recipes at eye level When you are following a recipe clipped from a magazine or newspaper, it's hard to read and keep clean when the clipping is lying on the counter. Solve the problem by attaching a clipboard to a wall cabinet at eye level. Just snap the recipe of the day onto the clipboard and you are ready to create your kitchen magic.

Hold place mats Hang a clipboard inside a kitchen cabinet or pantry door and use the clamp as a convenient, space-saving way to store your place mats.

Keep sheet music in place Flimsy pages of sheet music are susceptible to drafts and sometimes seem to spend more time on the floor than on the music stand. To eliminate this problem, attach the music sheets to a clipboard before placing it in the stand. The pages will remain upright and in place.

Aid road-trip navigation Before starting out on a long motor trip, fold the map to the area you will be traveling in. Attach it to a clipboard and keep it nearby to check your progress at rest stops.

Organize your sandpaper Most of the time, sandpaper is still good after the first or second time you use it. The trick is to find that used sandpaper again. Hang a clipboard on a hook on your workshop pegboard. Just clip still-usable sandpaper to the board when you are done and the sandpaper will be handy next time you need it.

✳ Clothespins

Fasten Christmas lights Keep your outdoor Christmas lights in place and ready to withstand the elements. As you affix your lights to gutters, trees, bushes (or even your spouse!) fasten them securely with clip-on clothespins.

Make a clothespin clipboard Organize your workshop, kitchen, or bathroom with a homemade rack made with straight clothespins. Space several clothespins evenly apart on a piece of wood, and screw them on with screws coming through from the back of the board (pre-drill the holes so you don't split the clothespin). Now your rack is ready to hang.

Keep snacks fresh Tired of biting into stale potato chips from a previously opened bag? Use clip-on clothespins to reseal bags of chips and other snacks, cereal, crackers, and seeds. The foods will stay fresh longer and you won't have as many spills in the pantry, either. Use a clothespin for added freshness insurance when you store food in a freezer bag too.

Organize your closet Okay, you found one shoe. Now, where the heck is the other one? From now on use clip-on clothespins to hold together pairs of shoes, boots, or sneakers, and put an end to those unscheduled hunting expeditions in your closets. It's a good idea for gloves, too.

Keep gloves in shape After washing wool gloves, insert a straight wooden clothespin into each finger. The clothespins will keep the gloves in their proper shape.

Prevent vacuum cord "snapback" Whoops! You're vacuuming the living room floor when suddenly the machine stops. You've accidentally pulled out the plug and the cord is automatically retracting and snapping back into the machine. To avoid similar annoyance in the future, simply clip a clothespin to the cord at the length you want.

Make an instant bib Make bibs for your child by using a clip-on clothespin to hold a dish towel around the child's neck. Use bigger towels to make lobster bibs for adults. It's much faster than tying on a bib.

Make clothespin puppets Traditional straight clothespins without the metal springs are ideal for making little puppets. Using the knob as a head, have kids paste on bits of yarn for hair, and scraps of cloth or colored paper for clothes to give each one its own personality.

Hold leaf bag open Ever try filling a large leaf bag all by your lonesome, only to see half the leaves fall to the ground because the bag won't stay open? Next time enlist a couple of clip-on clothespins as helpers. After you shake open the bag and

spread it wide, use the clothespins to clip one side of the bag to a chain-link fence or other convenient site. The bag will stay open for easy filling.

Mark a bulb spot What to do when a flower that blooms in the spring … doesn't? Just push a straight clothespin into the soil at the spot where it didn't grow. In the fall you will know exactly where to plant new bulbs to avoid gaps.

Grip a nail Hammer the nail and not your fingers. Just remember to use a clip-on clothespin to hold nails when hammering in hard-to-reach places.

Clamp thin objects Use clip-on clothespins as clamps when you're gluing two thin objects together. Let the clothespin hold them in place until the glue sets.

Keep paintbrush afloat Keep your paintbrush from sinking into the solvent residue when you soak it. Clamp the brush to the container with a clothespin.

✳ Club Soda

Make pancakes and waffles fluffier If you like your pancakes and waffles on the fluffy side, substitute club soda for the liquid called for in the recipes. You'll be amazed at how light and fluffy your breakfast treats turn out.

? DID You KNOW?

Bubbling water has been associated with good health since the time of the ancient Romans, who enjoyed drinking mineral water almost as much as they liked bathing in it. The first club soda was sold in North America at the end of the 1700s. That's when pharmacists figured out how to infuse plain water with carbon dioxide, which they believed was responsible for giving natural bubbling water health-inducing qualities. Club soda and seltzer are essentially the same. However, seltzer is a natural effervescent water (named for a region in Germany where it is plentiful) whereas club soda is manufactured.

Give your plants a mineral bath Don't throw out that leftover club soda. Use it to water your indoor and outdoor plants. The minerals in the soda water help green plants grow. For maximum benefit, try to water your plants with club soda about once a week.

Remove fabric stains Clean grease stains from double-knit fabrics. Pour club soda on the stain and scrub gently. Scrub more vigorously to remove stains on carpets or less delicate articles of clothing.

Help shuck oysters If you love oysters but find shucking them to be a near-impossible chore, try soaking them in club soda before you shuck. The oysters won't exactly jump out of their shells, but they will be much easier to open.

Clean precious gems Soak your diamonds, rubies, sapphires, and emeralds in club soda to give them a bright sheen. Simply place them in a glass full of club soda and let them soak overnight.

Clean your car windshield Keep a spray bottle filled with club soda in the trunk of your car. Use it to help remove bird droppings and greasy stains from the windshield. The fizzy water speeds the cleaning process.

Restore hair color If your blond hair turns green when you swim in a pool with too much chlorine, don't panic. Rinse your hair with club soda and it will change back to its original color.

Tame your tummy Cold club soda with a dash of bitters will work wonders on an upset stomach caused by indigestion or a hangover.

Clean countertops and fixtures Pour club soda directly on stainless steel countertops, ranges, and sinks. Wipe with a soft cloth, rinse with warm water, and wipe dry. To clean porcelain fixtures, simply pour club soda over them and wipe with a soft cloth. There's no need for soap or rinsing, and the soda will not mar the finish. Give the inside of your refrigerator a good cleaning with a weak solution of club soda and a little bit of salt.

Remove rust To loosen rusty nuts and bolts, pour some club soda over them. The carbonation helps to bubble the rust away.

Eliminate urine stains Did someone have an accident? After blotting up as much urine as possible, pour club soda over the stained area and immediately blot again. The club soda will get rid of the stain and help reduce the foul smell.

Ease cast-iron cleanup Food tastes delicious when it's cooked in cast iron, but cleaning those heavy pots and pans with the sticky mess inside is no fun at all. You can make the cleanup a lot easier by pouring some club soda in the pan while it's still warm. The bubbly soda will keep the mess from sticking.

✳ Coat Hangers

Stop caulk-tube ooze To prevent caulk from oozing from the tube once the job is done, cut a 3-inch (7.5-centimeter) piece of coat hanger wire; shape one end into a hook and insert the other, straight end into the tube. Now you can easily pull out the stopper as needed.

Secure a soldering iron Keeping a hot soldering iron from rolling away and burning something on your workbench is a real problem. To solve this, just twist a wire coat hanger into a holder for the iron to rest in. To make the holder, simply bend an ordinary coat hanger in half to form a large **V**. Then bend each half in half so that the entire piece is shaped like a **W**.

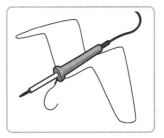

Extend your reach Can't reach that utensil that has fallen behind the refrigerator or stove? Try straightening a wire coat hanger (except for the hook at the end), and use it to fish for the object.

Make a giant bubble wand Kids will love to make giant bubbles with a homemade bubble wand fashioned from a wire coat hanger. Shape the hanger into a hoop with a handle and dip it into a bucket filled with 1 part liquid dishwashing detergent in 2 parts water. Add a few drops of food coloring to make the bubbles more visible.

Create arts and crafts Make mobiles for the kids' room using wire coat hangers; paint them in bright colors. Or use hangers to make wings and other accessories for costumes.

Unclog toilets and vacuum cleaners If your toilet is clogged by a foreign object, fish out the culprit with a straightened wire coat hanger. Use a straightened hanger to unclog a jammed vacuum cleaner hose.

Make a mini-greenhouse To convert a window box into a mini-greenhouse, bend three or four lengths of coat hanger wire into **U**'s and place the ends into the soil. Punch small holes in a dry-cleaning bag and wrap it around the box before putting it back in the window.

SCIENCE FAIR

Here's a fun way to demonstrate **Newton's first law of motion.** Bend a wire **coat hanger** into a large loopy **M**, as shown. Holding the wire in the middle, attach a same-sized **modeling-clay ball** to each of the hooks. Then place the low center point of the **M** on top of your head. If you **turn your head** to the left or right, the **inertia** of the balls will be enough to **keep them in place,** demonstrating Newton's law that "objects at rest tend to stay at rest." With practice, you can actually turn all the way around and the balls will remain still.

Hang a plant Wrap a straightened wire coat hanger around a 6- to 8-inch (15- to 20-centimeter) flowerpot, just below the lip; twist it back on itself to secure it, then hang.

Make plant markers Need some waterproof markers for your outdoor plants? Cut up little signs from a milk jug or similar rigid but easy-to-cut plastic. Write the name of the plant with an indelible marker. Cut short stakes from wire hangers. Make two small slits in each marker and pass the wire stakes through the slits. Neither rain nor sprinkler will obscure your signs.

Make a paint can holder When you are up on a ladder painting your house, one hand is holding on while the other is painting. How do you hold the paint can? Grab a pair of wire snips and cut the hook plus 1 inch (2.5 centimeters) of wire from a wire hanger. Use a pair of pliers to twist the 1-inch section firmly around the handle of your paint can. Now you have a handy hanger.

Light a hard-to-reach pilot light The pilot light has gone out way inside your stove or furnace. You'd rather not risk a burn by lighting a match and sticking your hand all the way in there. Instead, open up a wire hanger and tape the match to one end. Strike the match and use the hanger to reach the pilot.

DID *You* KNOW?

All Albert J. Parkhouse wanted to do when he arrived at work was to hang up his coat and get busy doing his job. It was 1903, and Albert worked at Timberlake Wire and Novelty Company in Jackson, Michigan. But when he went to hang his clothes on the hooks the company provided for workers, all were in use. Frustrated, Albert picked up a piece of wire, bent it into two large oblong hoops opposite each other, and twisted both ends at the center into a hook. He hung his coat on it and went to work. The company thought so much of the idea they patented it and made a fortune. Alas, Albert never got a penny for inventing the wire coat hanger.

✱ Coffee Beans

Freshen your breath What to do when you're all out of breath mints? Just suck on a coffee bean for a while and your mouth will smell clean and fresh again.

Remove foul odor from hands If your hands smell of garlic, fish or other strong foods you've been handling, a few coffee beans may be all you need to get rid of the odor. Put the beans in your hands and rub them together. The oil released from the coffee beans will absorb the foul smell. When the odor is gone, wash your hands in warm, soapy water.

Fill a beanbag They don't call them beanbags for nothing. Coffee beans are ideal as beanbag filler, but with the price of coffee nowadays it's a good idea to wait for a sale and then buy the cheapest beans available.

✳ Coffee Cans

Bake perfectly round bread Use small coffee cans to bake perfectly cylindrical loaves of bread. Use your favorite recipe but put the dough in a well-greased coffee can instead of a loaf pan. For yeast breads use two cans and fill each only half full. Grease the inside of the lids and place them on the cans. For yeast breads, you will know when it is time to bake when the rising dough pushes the lids off. Place the cans—without the lids—upright in the oven to bake.

Separate hamburgers Before you put those hamburger patties in the freezer, stack them with a coffee-can lid between each and put them in a plastic bag. Now, when the patties are frozen you'll be able to easily peel off as many as you need.

Hold kitchen scraps Line a coffee can with a small plastic bag and keep it near the sink to hold kitchen scraps and peelings. Instead of walking back and forth to the garbage can, you'll make one trip to dump all the scraps at the same time.

Make a bank To make a bank for the kids or a collection can for a favorite charity, use a utility knife to cut a 1/8-inch (3-millimeter) slit in the center of the plastic lid of a coffee can. Tape decorative paper or adhesive plastic to the sides of the kids' bank; for a collection can, use the sides of the can to highlight the charity you are helping.

Create a toy holder Make a decorative container for kids' miniature books and small toys. Wash and dry a coffee can and file off any sharp edges. Sponge on two coats of white acrylic paint, letting it dry between coats. Cut out a design from an old sheet or pillowcase to wrap around the can. Mix 4 tablespoons white glue with enough water to the consistency of paint. Paint on the glue mixture and gently press the fabric onto the can. Trim the bottom and tuck top edges

DID **You** KNOW?

Ground coffee loses its flavor immediately unless it is specially packaged or brewed. Freshly roasted and ground coffee is often sealed in combination plastic-and-paper bags, but the coffee can is by far the most common container in North America. Vacuum-sealed cans keep coffee fresh for up to three years. The U.S. is the world's largest consumer of coffee, importing up to 2.5 million pounds (1.1 million kilograms) each year. More than half the U.S. population consumes coffee. The typical coffee drinker has 3.4 cups of coffee per day. That translates into 350 million cups of coffee guzzled daily.

inside the can. Apply two coats of glue mixture over the fabric overlay, letting it dry between coats.

Store belts If you have more belts than places to hang them up, just roll them up and store them in a cleaned-out coffee can with a clear lid. Coffee cans are just the right size to keep belts from creasing, and clear lids will let you find each belt easily.

Keep the laundry room neat Have an empty coffee can nearby as you're going through the kids' pockets before putting up a load of wash. Use it to deposit gum and candy wrappers, paper scraps, and other assorted items that kids like to stuff into their pockets. Keep another can handy for coins and bills.

Make a dehumidifier If your basement is too damp, try this easy-to-make dehumidifier. Fill an empty coffee can with salt and leave it in a corner where it will be undisturbed. Replace the salt at monthly intervals or as needed.

Keep carpets dry Place plastic coffee-can lids under houseplants as saucers. They will protect carpets or wood floors and catch any excess water.

Keep toilet paper dry when camping Bring a few empty coffee cans with you on your next camping trip. Use them to keep toilet paper dry in rainy weather or when you're carrying supplies in a canoe or boat.

Gauge rainfall or sprinkler coverage Find out if your garden is getting enough water from the rain. Next time it starts to rain, place empty coffee cans in several places around the garden. When the rain stops, measure the depth of the water in the cans. If they measure at least an inch, there's no need for additional watering. This is also a good way to test if your sprinkler is getting sufficient water to the areas it is supposed to cover.

Make a coffee-can bird feeder To fashion a coffee can into a sturdy bird feeder, begin with a full can and open the top only halfway. (Pour the coffee into an airtight container.) Then open the bottom of the can halfway the same way. Carefully bend the cut ends down inside the can so the edges are not exposed to cut you. Punch a hole in the side of the can at both ends, where it will be the "top" of the feeder, and put some wire through each end to make a hanger.

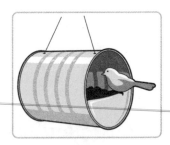

Make a spot lawn seeder When it's time to reseed bare spots on your lawn, don't use a regular spreader. It wastes seed by throwing it everywhere. For precision seeding, fashion a spot seeder from an empty coffee can and a pair of plastic lids. Drill small holes in the bottom of the can, just big enough to let grass seeds pass through. Put one lid over the bottom of the can, fill the can with seeds, and cap it with the other lid. When you're ready to spread the seeds, take off the bottom lid. When you're finished, replace it to seal in any unused seed for safe storage.

Eliminate workshop clutter You want small items like screws, nuts, and nails to be handy, but you don't want them to take up workbench space. Here's a way to get the small stuff up out of the way. Drill a hole near the top of empty coffee cans so you can hang them on nails in your workshop wall. Label the cans with masking tape so you will know what's inside.

Soak a paintbrush An empty coffee can is perfect for briefly soaking a paintbrush in thinner before continuing a job the next day. Cut an **X** into the lid and insert the brush handles so the bristles clear the bottom of the can by about 1/2 inch (12 millimeters). If the can has no lid, attach a stick to the brush handle with a rubber band to keep the bristles off the bottom of the can.

Catch paint drips Turn the plastic lids from old coffee cans into drip catchers under paint cans and under furniture legs when you're painting. Protect cupboard shelves by putting them under jars of cooking oil and syrup too.

✳ Coffee Filters

Cover food in the microwave Coffee filters are microwave-safe. Use them to cover bowls or dishes to prevent splatter when cooking or baking in your microwave oven.

Filter cork crumbs from wine Don't let cork droppings ruin your enjoyment of a good glass of wine. If your attempt at opening the bottle results in floating cork crumbs, just decant the wine through a coffee filter.

DID *You* KNOW?

The coffee filter was invented in 1908 by a housewife from Dresden, Germany. Melitta Bentz was looking for a way to brew a perfect cup of coffee without the bitterness often caused by overbrewing. She decided to try making a fil- tered coffee, pouring boiling water over ground coffee, and filtering out the grinds. Melitta experimented with different materials, until she found that the blotter paper that her son used for school worked best. She cut a round piece of blotting paper, put it in a metal cup, and the first Melitta coffee filter was born. Shortly thereafter, Melitta and her husband, Hugo, launched the company that still bears her name.

Line a sieve If you save your cooking oil for reuse after deep-fat frying, line your sieve with a basket-style coffee filter to remove smaller food remnants and impurities.

Hold a taco Serve tacos, hot dogs, popcorn, and other messy foods in cone or basket-style coffee filters. The filter is a perfect sleeve and will help keep fingers clean and cleanup a snap.

Catch ice-cream drips Next time the kids scream for ice-cream bars or ice pops, serve it to them with a drip catcher made from basket-style coffee filters. Just poke the stick through the center of two filters and the drips will fall into the paper, not on the child or your carpet.

Make an instant funnel Cut the end off a cone-style coffee filter to make an instant funnel. Keep a few in your car and use them to avoid spillage when you add a quart of oil or two.

Clean your specs Next time you clean your glasses, try using a coffee filter instead of a tissue. Good-quality coffee filters are made from 100 percent virgin paper, so you can use them to clean your glasses without leaving lint. You can also use them safely to polish mirrors and TV and computer-monitor screens.

Keep skillets rust-free Prolong the life of your good cast-iron cookware. Put a coffee filter in the skillet when it's not in use. The filter will absorb moisture and prevent rusting.

Prevent soil leakage When you're repotting a plant, line the pot with a coffee filter to keep the soil from leaking out through the drain hole.

Make an air freshener Fill a coffee filter with baking soda, twist-tie it shut, and you have just made an air freshener. Make several and tuck them into shoes, closets, the fridge, or wherever else they may be needed.

✱ Coffee Grounds

Don't raise any dust Before you clean the ashes out of your fireplace, sprinkle them with wet coffee grounds. They'll be easier to remove, and the ash and dust won't pollute the atmosphere of the room.

Deodorize a freezer Get rid of the smell of spoiled food after a freezer failure. Fill a couple of bowls with used or fresh coffee grounds and place them in the freezer overnight. For a flavored-coffee scent, add a couple of drops of vanilla to the grounds.

Fertilize plants Don't throw out those old coffee grounds. They're chock-full o' nutrients that your acidic-loving plants crave. Save them to fertilize rosebushes, azaleas, rhododendrons, evergreens, and camellias. It's better to use grounds from a drip coffeemaker than the boiled grounds from a percolator. The drip grounds are richer in nitrogen.

Keep worms alive A cup of used coffee grounds will keep your bait worms alive and wiggling all day long. Just mix the grounds into the soil in your bait box before you dump in the worms. They like coffee almost as much as we do, and the nutrients in the grounds will help them live longer.

Keep cats out of the garden Kitty won't think of your garden as a latrine anymore if you spread a pungent mixture of orange peels and used coffee grounds around your plants. The mix acts as great fertilizer too.

Boost carrot harvest To increase your carrot harvest, mix the seeds with fresh-ground coffee before sowing. Not only does the extra bulk make the tiny seeds easier to sow, but the coffee aroma may repel root maggots and other pests. As an added bonus, the grounds will help add nutrients to the soil as they decompose around the plants. You might also like to add a few radish seeds to the mix before sowing. The radishes will be up in a few days to mark the rows, and when you cultivate the radishes, you will be thinning the carrot seedlings and cultivating the soil at the same time.

DID *You* KNOW?

Coffee grows on trees that reach a height of up to 20 feet (6 meters), but growers keep them pruned to about 6 feet (2 meters) to simplify picking and encourage heavy berry production. The first visible sign of a coffee tree's maturity is the appearance of small white blossoms, which fill the air with a heady aroma reminiscent of jasmine and orange. The mature tree bears cherry-size oval berries, each containing two coffee beans with their flat sides together. A mature coffee tree will produce one pound (450 grams) of coffee per growing season. It takes 2,000 hand-picked Arabica coffee berries (4,000 beans) to make a pound of roasted coffee.

✳ Coins

Test tire tread Let old Abe Lincoln's head tell you if it's time to replace the tires on your car. Insert an American penny into the tread. If you can't cover the top of Honest Abe's head inside the tread, it's time to head for the tire store. Check tires regularly and you will avoid the danger and inconvenience of a flat tire on a busy road.

Give carpet a lift When you move a chair, sofa, table, or bed, you will notice the deep indentations in your carpet made by the legs. To fluff it up again, simply hold a coin on its edge and scrape it against the flattened pile. If it still doesn't pop back up, hold a steam iron a couple of inches (5 centimeters) above the affected spot. When the area is damp, try fluffing again with the coin.

Keep cut flowers fresh Your posies and other cut flowers will stay fresh longer if you add a copper penny and a cube of sugar to the vase water.

Instant measure If you need to measure something but you don't have a ruler, just reach into your pocket and pull out a quarter. It measures exactly 1 inch (2.54 centimeters) in diameter. Just line up quarters to measure the length of a small object.

Make a noisemaker Drop a few coins into an empty aluminum soda can, seal the top with duct tape, and head for the stadium to root for your favorite team. Take your noisemaker with you when you walk the dog and use it as a training aid. When the pooch is naughty, just shake the noisemaker.

Decorate a barrette Use shiny pennies to decorate a barrette for a little girl. Gather enough pennies to complete the project (5 pennies for each large barrette; fewer for smaller barrettes). Arrange pennies as you like on the barrette and use hot-melt glue to attach them. Allow 24 hours to dry.

Hang doors perfectly Next time you hang an entry door, nickel-and-dime it to ensure proper clearance between the outside of the door and the inside of the frame. When the door is closed, the gap at the top should be the thickness of a nickel, and the gap at the sides should be that of a dime. If you do it right, you will keep the door from binding and it won't let in drafts.

SCIENCE FAIR

Scientists use **optical illusions** to show how the brain can be tricked. This simple experiment uses **two coins,** but you'll think you are seeing three. Hold two coins on top of each other between your **thumb and index finger.** Quickly slide the coins back and forth and you will **see a third coin!**

How it works: Scientists say that everything we see is actually light reflected from objects. Our eyes use the light to create images on our retinas, the light-sensitive linings in our eyeballs. Because images don't disappear instantly, when something moves quickly you may see both an object and an after-image of it at the same time.

Make a paperweight If you have ever traveled abroad, you have probably come home with a few odd-looking coins from foreign lands. Instead of leaving them lying around in a desk drawer, use them to make an interesting paperweight. Just put the coins into a small glass jar with a closable lid and cover the lid with decorative cloth or paper.

?? DID *You* KNOW?

Coins were first produced around 700 B.C. by Lydians, a people who lived in what is now Turkey. From there, they spread to ancient Greece and Rome. However, worldwide use of coins (and paper money) took centuries to occur. Even in early America, bartering remained the popular way to exchange goods and services. On April 2, 1792, after the ratification of the U.S. Constitution, Congress passed the Mint Act. This established the coinage system in the United States and the dollar as the official U.S. currency. The first U.S. coins were produced by the Philadelphia Mint in 1793.

✳ Colanders

Prevent grease splatters Sick of cleaning grease splatters on the stovetop after cooking your famous burgers? Prevent them by inverting a large metal colander over the frying pan. The holes will let heat escape but the colander will trap the splatters. Be careful! The metal colander will be hot—use an oven mitt to remove it.

Heat a pasta bowl Does your pasta get too cold too fast? To keep it warm longer, heat the bowl first. Place a colander in the bowl, pour the pasta and water into the colander, and let the hot water stand in the bowl for a few seconds to heat it. Pour out the water, add the pasta and sauce, and you're ready to serve.

Keep berries and grapes fresh Do your berries and grapes get moldy before you've had a chance to enjoy their sweet taste? To keep them fresher longer, store them in a colander, not a closed plastic container, in the refrigerator. The cold air will circulate through the holes in the colander, keeping them fresh for days.

Corral bathtub toys Don't let the bathtub look like another messy toy box. After each bath, corral your child's small playthings in a large colander and store it in the tub. The water will drain from the toys, keeping them ready for next time, and the bathtub will stay tidy.

Use as sand toy Forget spending money on expensive sand toys for your budding archeologist. A simple inexpensive plastic colander is perfect for digging at the beach or in the sandbox.

*Cold Cream

Erase temporary tattoos Kids love temporary tattoos, but getting them off can be a painful, scrubbing chore. To make removal easier, loosen the tattoo by rubbing cold cream on it and then gently rub it off with a facecloth. Voilà!

Remove bumper stickers Does your bumper sticker still say "Honk for Gore"? Erase the past by rubbing cold cream on the sticker and letting it soak in. Once it does, you should be able to peel it right off.

Make face paint Need a safe, easy recipe for Halloween face paint? Mix 1 teaspoon cornstarch, 1/2 teaspoon water, 1/2 teaspoon cold cream, and 2 drops food coloring (depending on the costume) together. Use a small paintbrush to paint designs on your face or your child's. Remove it with soap and water.

DID *You* KNOW?

Yes, cold cream really is cold. That's because it's made with a lot of water that evaporates and cools your warm face. Cold cream is the granddaddy of all facial ointments. It was invented by the Greek physician Galen in A.D. 157. It's not known exactly why Galen created his mixture, but according to Michael Boylan, a professor at Marymount College in Arlington, Virginia, and an expert on Galen, ancient medicine was based on treating with opposites. And Galen might have been seeking a cure for a hot and dry skin condition like eczema or psoriasis. But the women of ancient Greece soon discovered the soothing white cream was great for taking off makeup, which remains the primary use for cold cream to this day.

*Compact Discs

Use as holiday ornaments Decorate your Christmas tree in style! Hang CDs shiny side out to create a flickering array of lights—or paint and decorate the label side to create inexpensive personalized ornaments. For variety, cut the CDs into stars and other shapes with sharp scissors. Drill a 1/4-inch (6-millimeter) hole through the CD and thread ribbon through to hang.

Make wall art in teen's room Old CDs make inexpensive and quirky wall art for your teenager's room. Attach the CDs with thumbtacks and use them to create a border at the ceiling or halfway up the wall. Or let your teen use them to frame his or her favorite posters.

Catch candle drips You should always use a candleholder specifically designed to catch melting wax. However, if one is not available, a CD is great in a pinch. Make sure it's a short candle that can stand on its own with a flat bottom. It should also be slightly larger than the CD hole. Place the candleholder on a stable, heat-resistant surface and keep a watchful eye on it.

Make artistic bowls Looking for a funky, decorative bowl? Place a CD in the oven on low heat over a metal bowl until the CD is soft. Wearing protective gloves, gently bend the CD into the shape desired. Seal the hole by gluing the bottom edge to another surface such as a flat dish using expoxy or PVC glue. Don't use the bowl for food.

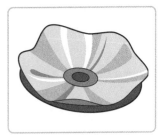

Use as sidewalk/driveway reflectors Forget those ugly orange reflectors. Instead, drill small holes in a CD and screw it onto your mailbox post or onto a wood stake and push it into the ground. Install several of them to light a nighttime path to your front door.

Kids' Stuff Use an **old CD** to make a **picture frame** for someone you love. You need a CD, a **picture** of you that is larger than the CD hole, a **large bead, ribbon,** and **glue.** Glue the picture in the middle of the CD on the shiny side. If you wish, decorate the CD with **markers** or **stickers.** Use **hot-melt glue** to attach the bead at the top of the CD, let dry, and thread ribbon through the bead.

Use as template for perfect circle Need to draw a perfect circle? Forget tracing around cups or using cumbersome compasses. Every CD provides two circle sizes— trace around the inner hole or the outer circumference.

Tip **CD Repair**

> Before throwing away or recycling a scratched-up CD, try to repair it. First, clean it thoroughly with a lint-free cloth or mild soap and a little bit of water. Hold the CD by the edge to keep from getting fingerprints on it. Polish it from the middle to the edge, not in a circular motion. If your CD still skips, try fixing it with a little non-gel toothpaste. Dab some toothpaste on the end of your finger and rub it lightly onto the entire CD. Use a damp paper towel to remove the toothpaste and dry it with a fresh paper towel. The fine abrasive in the toothpaste might smooth out the scratch. You might also want to use car wax on a scratch (see page 115).

Make a decorative sun catcher Sun catchers are attractive to watch, and all you need to make one is a couple of CDs. Glue two CDs together, shiny side out, wrap yarn or colored string through the hole, and hang them in a window. The prism will make a beautiful light show.

Create a spinning top Turn an old CD into a fun toy for the kids (and adults too!). With a knife, make two slits across from each other in the CD hole. Force a penny halfway through the hole, and then spin the CD on its edge.

Make a CD clock Old CDs can be functional! Turn a disc into a funky clock face for clockwork sold by arts-and-crafts stores. Paint and design one side of the CD and let it dry. Write or use stickers to create the numbers around its edge. Assemble the clockwork onto the CD.

Cover with felt and use as coasters CDs can help to prevent those unsightly stains from cups left on the table. Simply cut a round piece of felt to fit over the CD and glue it onto the label side of the CD so that the shiny side will face up when you use the coaster.

✳ Cooking Spray

Prevent rice and pasta from sticking Most cooks know that a little cooking oil in the boiling water will keep rice or pasta from sticking together when you drain it. If you run out of cooking oil, however, a spritz of cooking oil spray will do the job just as well.

Grating cheese Put less elbow grease into grating cheese by using a nonstick cooking spray on your cheese grater for smoother grating. The spray also makes for easier and faster cleanup.

Prevent tomato sauce stains Sick of those hard-to-clean tomato sauce stains on your plastic containers? To prevent them, apply a light coating of nonstick cooking spray on the inside of the container before you pour in the tomato sauce.

Keep car wheels clean. You know that fine black stuff that collects on the wheels of your car and is so hard to clean off? That's brake dust—it's produced every time you apply your brakes and the pads wear against the brake disks or cylinders. The

DID You KNOW?

Ever wondered where PAM, the name of the popular cooking spray, comes from? It stands for "Product of Arthur Meyerhoff." The first patent for a nonstick cooking spray was issued in 1957 to Arthur and his partner, Leon Rubin, who began marketing PAM All Natural Cooking Spray in 1959. After appearing on local Chicago TV cooking shows in the early '60s, the product developed a loyal following, and it quickly became a household world. By the way, PAM is pretty durable stuff—it has a shelf life of two years.

next time you invest the elbow grease to get your wheels shiny, give them a light coating of cooking spray. The brake dust will wipe right off.

De-bug your car When those bugs smash into your car at 55 miles (88 kilometers), per hour, they really stick. Give your grille a spritz of nonstick cooking spray so you can just wipe away the insect debris.

Lubricate your bicycle chain Is your bike chain a bit creaky and you don't have any lubricating oil handy? Give it a shot of nonstick cooking spray instead. Don't use too much—the chain shouldn't look wet. Wipe off the excess with a clean rag.

Cure door squeak Heard that door squeak just one time too many? Hit the hinge with some nonstick cooking spray. Have paper towels handy to wipe up the drips.

Remove paint and grease Forget smelly solvents to remove paint and grease from your hands. Instead, use cooking spray to do the job. Work it in well and rinse. Wash again with soap and water.

Dry nail polish Need your nail polish to dry in a hurry? Spray it with a coat of cooking spray and let dry. The spray is also a great moisturizer for your hands.

Quick casting Pack a can of cooking spray when you go fishing. Spray it on your fishing line and the line will cast easier and farther.

Prevent grass from sticking Mowing the lawn should be easy, but cleaning stuck grass from the mower is tedious. Prevent grass from sticking on mower blades and the underside of the housing by spraying them with cooking oil before you begin mowing.

Prevent snow sticks Shoveling snow is hard enough, but it can be more aggravating when the snow sticks to the shovel. Spray the shovel with nonstick cooking spray before shoveling—the snow slides right off! If you use a snow thrower, spray inside the discharge chute to prevent it from clogging.

✳ Corks

Create a fishing bobber It's an idea that's as old as Tom Sawyer, but worth remembering: A cork makes a great substitute fishing bobber. Drive a staple into the top of the cork, then pull the staple out just a bit so you can slide your fishing line through it.

Make an impromptu pincushion Need a painless place to store pins while you sew? Save corks from wine bottles—they make great pincushions!

Prevent pottery scratches Your beautiful pottery can make ugly scratches on furniture. To save your tabletops, cut thin slices of cork and glue them to the bottom of your ceramic objects.

Replace soda bottle caps Lost the cap to your soda bottle and need a replacement? Cork it! Most wine corks fit most soda bottles perfectly.

Make a pour spout Don't have one of those fancy metal pour spouts to control the flow from your oil or vinegar bottle? You don't need one. Make your own spout by cutting out a wedge of the cork along its length. Use a utility or craft knife. Stick the cork in the bottle and pour away. When you're through, cover the hole with a tab of masking tape.

Use as Halloween face paint Kids love to dress up as a hobo for Halloween. To create that scruffy look, char the end of a piece of cork by holding it over a candle. Let it cool a little, then rub it on the kid's face.

Block sun glare In the olden days of football and baseball, players would burn cork and rub it under their eyes to reduce glare from the sun and stadium lights. These days, ballplayers use commercial products to do the same, but you can still use cork to get the job done.

Prevent chair scratches The sound of a chair scraping across your beautiful floor can make your skin crawl. Solve the problem by cutting cork into thin slices and attaching them to the bottom of the chair legs with a spot of wood glue.

Create craft stamps You can use cork to create a personalized stamp. Carve the end of a cork into any shape or design you want. Use it with ink from a stamp pad to decorate note cards. Or let the kids dip carved corks in paint to create artwork.

DID *You* KNOW?

Cork, the bark of the cork oak, has been used to seal wine bottles and other vessels for more than 400 years. The bark has a unique honeycomb cell structure—each cell is sealed, filled with air, and not connected to any other cell. This makes it waterproof and a poor conductor of heat and vibration. Plus cork contains suberin, a natural waxy substance that makes it impermeable to liquids and gases and prevents the cork from rotting. No wonder it's still the material of choice for sealing up your favorite cabernet or bubbly.

Create a cool bead curtain. Want a creative, stylish beaded curtain for a child's or teen's room? Drill a hole through corks and string them onto a cord along with beads and other decorations. Make as many strings as you need and tie them onto a curtain rod.

Fasten earrings Earring backs always get lost, and you can't always find a perfect-sized stand-in when you need it. Instead, use a snippet of cork as a temporary substitute. Slice a small piece about the size of the backing and push it on. An eraser cut off the end of a pencil will also work.

> **TAKE CARE** Should you use a corkscrew to open a bottle of wine? Yes, but don't use it on a bottle of champagne! Pushing a corkscrew down into a bottle of champagne against the pressure of the carbonation can actually make the bottle explode! If possible, wait a day before opening and let the carbonation settle a bit. Wrap the cork in a towel and twist the bottle, not the cork, slowly.
>
> To open wine, use a traditional corkscrew that twists into the stopper. Peel the top of the plastic to expose the cork. Insert the corkscrew in the center. Twist it straight down and pull the cork straight out with even pressure.

Picture-perfect frames If you're always straightening picture frames on the wall, cut some small flat pieces of cork—all the same thickness—and glue them to the back of the frame. The cork will grip the wall and stop the sliding. It will also prevent the frame from marring the wall.

Mass-produce sowing holes Here's a neat trick for quickly getting your seeds sown in straight rows of evenly spaced holes. Mark out the spacing you need on a board. Drill drywall screws through the holes, using screws that will protrude about 3/4 inch (2 centimeters) through the board. Now twist wine corks onto the screws. Just press the board, corks down, into your garden bed, and voilà—instant seed holes.

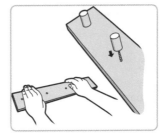

✳ Cornstarch

Dry shampoo Fido needs a bath, but you just don't have time. Rub cornstarch into his coat and brush it out. The dry bath will fluff up his coat until it's tub time.

Untangle knots Knots in string or shoelaces can be stubborn to undo, but the solution is easy. Sprinkle the knot with a little cornstarch. It will then be easy to work the segments apart.

Soak up furniture polish residue You've finished polishing your furniture, but there's still a bit left on the surface. Sprinkle cornstarch lightly on furniture after polishing. Wipe up the oil and cornstarch, then buff the surface.

Remove ink stains from carpet Oh no, ink on the carpet! In this case a little spilt milk might save you from crying. Mix the milk with cornstarch to make a paste. Apply the paste to the ink stain. Allow the concoction to dry on the carpet for a few hours, then brush off the dried residue and vacuum it up.

Give carpets a fresh scent Before vacuuming a room, sprinkle a little cornstarch on your carpeting. Wait about half an hour and then vacuum normally.

Make your own paste The next time the kids want to go wild with construction paper and paste, save money by making the paste yourself. Mix 3 teaspoons cornstarch for every 4 teaspoons cold water. Stir until you reach a paste consistency. This is especially great for applying with fingers or a wooden tongue depressor or Popsicle stick. If you add food coloring, the paste can be used for painting objects.

Make finger paints This simple recipe will keep the kids happy for hours. Mix together 1/4 cup cornstarch and 2 cups cold water. Bring to a boil and continue boiling until the mixture becomes thick. Pour your product into several small containers and add food coloring to each container. You've created a collection of homemade finger paints.

Clean stuffed animals To clean a stuffed animal toy, rub a little cornstarch onto the toy, wait about 5 minutes, and then brush it clean. Or place the stuffed animal (or a few small ones) into a bag. Sprinkle cornstarch into the bag, close it tightly, and shake. Now brush the pretend pets clean.

Separate marshmallows Ever buy a bag of marshmallows only to find them stuck together? Here's how to get them apart: Add at least 1 teaspoon cornstarch to

DID *You* KNOW?

Cornstarch has been made into biodegradable packing "peanuts" sold in bulk. If you receive an item shipped in this material, you can toss the peanuts on the lawn. They'll dissolve with water, leaving no toxic waste. To test if the peanuts are made from cornstarch, wet one in the sink to see if it dissolves.

the bag and shake. The cornstarch will absorb the extra moisture and force most of the marshmallows apart. Repackage the remaining marshmallows in a container and freeze them to avoid sticking in future.

Lift a scorch mark from clothing You moved the iron a little too slowly and now you have a scorch mark on your favorite shirt. Wet the scorched area and cover it with cornstarch. Let the cornstarch dry, then brush it away along with the scorch mark.

Remove grease spatters from walls Even the most careful cook cannot avoid an occasional spatter. A busy kitchen takes some wear and tear but here's a handy remedy for that unsightly grease spot. Sprinkle cornstarch onto a soft cloth. Rub the grease spot gently until it disappears.

Get rid of bloodstains The quicker you act, the better. Whether it's on clothing or table linens, you can remove or reduce a bloodstain with this method. Make a paste of cornstarch mixed with cold water. Cover the spot with the cornstarch paste and rub it gently into the fabric. Now put the cloth in a sunny location to dry. Once dry, brush off the remaining residue. If the stain is not completely gone, repeat the process.

Polish silver Is the sparkle gone from your good silverware? Make a simple paste by mixing cornstarch with water. Use a damp cloth to apply this to your silverware. Let it dry, then rub it off with cheesecloth or another soft cloth to reveal that old shine.

Make windows sparkle Create your own streak-free window cleaning solution by mixing 2 tablespoons cornstarch with 1/2 cup ammonia and 1/2 cup white vinegar in a bucket containing 3-4 quarts (3-4 liters) warm water. Don't be put off by the milky concoction you create. Mix well and put the solution in a trigger spray bottle. Spray on the windows, then wipe with a warm-water rinse. Now rub with a dry paper towel or lint-free cloth. Voilà!

Say good riddance to roaches There's no delicate way to manage this problem. Make a mixture that is 50 percent plaster of Paris and 50 percent cornstarch. Spread this in the crevices where roaches appear. It's a killer recipe.

✳ Correction Fluid

Cover scratches on appliances Daub small nicks on household appliances with correction fluid. Once it dries, cover your repair with clear nail polish for staying power. This works well on white china, too, but only for display. Now that correction fluid comes in a rainbow of colors, its uses go beyond white. You may easily find a match for your beige or yellow household stove or refrigerator.

Touch up a ceiling Hide marks on white or beige ceilings with judiciously applied brush strokes of correction fluid. You can tone down the brightness, if you need to, by buffing the repaired area with a paper towel once it has dried.

C

Erase scuffs Need a quick fix for scuffed white shoes? Correction fluid will camouflage the offensive marks. On leather, buff gently once the fluid dries. No need to buff on patent leather.

Paint the town Decorate your windows for any occasion. Paint snowflakes, flowers, or Welcome Home signs using correction fluid. Later you can remove your art with nail polish remover, an ammonia solution, vinegar and water, or a commercial window cleaner. Or you can scrape it off with a single-edged razor blade in a holder made for removing paint from glass.

DID *You* KNOW?

Correction fluid was invented in 1951 by Bette Nesmith Graham, mother of Michael Nesmith of the Monkees musical group. Graham was working as an executive secretary in Texas. She used water-based paint and began supplying little bottles of it to other secretaries, calling it Mistake Out. Five years later, she improved the formula and changed the name to Liquid Paper. Despite its proven use, Graham was turned down when she tried to sell it to IBM, so she marketed it on her own. In the 1960s her invention began to generate a tidy profit; by 1979, when she sold the product to the Gillette Corp, she received $47.5 million plus a royalty on every bottle sold until 2000. Today, with the ease of correcting documents on a computer, correction fluid is no longer the office essential it once was.

✳ Cotton Balls

Scent the room Saturate a cotton ball with your favorite cologne and drop it into your vacuum cleaner bag. Now, as you vacuum, the scent will be expressed and gently permeate the room.

Deodorize the refrigerator Sometimes the refrigerator just doesn't smell fresh. Dampen a cotton ball with vanilla extract and place it on a shelf. You'll find it acts as a deodorizer, offering its own pleasant scent.

Fight mildew There are always hard-to-reach spots in the bathroom, usually around the fixtures, where mildew may breed in the grout between tiles. Forget about becoming a contortionist to return the sparkle to those areas. Soak a few cotton balls in bleach and place them in those difficult spots. Leave them to work their magic for a few hours. When you remove them, you'll find your job has been done. Finish by rinsing with a warm-water wash.

Protect little fingers Pad the ends of drawer runners with a cotton ball. This will prevent the drawer from closing completely and keep children from catching their fingers as the drawer slides shut.

Rescue your rubber gloves If your long, manicured nails sometimes puncture the fingertips of your rubber dishwashing gloves, here's a solution you'll appreciate. Push a cotton ball into the fingers of your gloves. The soft barrier should prolong the gloves' life.

✳ Crayons

Use as a floor filler Crayons make great fill material for small gouges or holes in resilient flooring. Get out your crayon box and select a color that most closely matches the floor. Melt the crayon in the microwave over wax paper on medium power, a minute at a time until you have a pliant glob of color. Now, with a plastic knife or putty knife, fill the hole. Smooth it over with a rolling pin, a book, or some other flat object. You'll find the crayon cools down quickly. Now wax the floor, to provide a clear protective coating over your new fill.

Fill furniture scratches Do your pets sometimes treat your furniture like … well, a scratching post? Don't despair. Use a crayon to cover scratches on wooden furniture. Choose the color most like the wood finish. Soften the crayon with a hair dryer or in the microwave on the defrost setting. Color over the scratches, then buff your repair job with a clean rag to restore the luster.

Carpet cover-up Even the most careful among us manage to stain the carpet. If you've tried to remove a stain and nothing works, here's a remedy you might be able

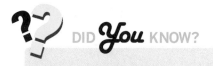

DID **You** KNOW?

Jazberry Jam and Mango Tango. Those aren't ice-cream flavors, they are recently introduced Crayola crayon colors. When Edwin Binney and C. Harold Smith introduced the first crayons safe for children to use in 1903, a box of eight sold for a nickel and included colors with more pedestrian names: black, brown, blue, red, violet, orange, yellow, and green. Since then, the manufacturer, Binney and Smith, has introduced more than 400 colors, retiring many along the way. Currently there are 120 colors available. Inch Worm and Wild Blue Yonder are other recent introductions.

to live with. Find a crayon that matches or will blend with your carpet. Soften the crayon a bit with a hair dryer or in the microwave on the defrost setting. Now color over the spot. Cover your repair with wax paper and gently iron the color in. Keep the iron on a low setting. Repeat as often as necessary.

Colorful decoration Here's a fun project to do with the kids. Make a multicolored sun catcher by shaving crayons onto a 4- or 5-inch (10- or 12-centimeter) sheet of wax paper. Use a potato peeler or grater for this task. Place another sheet of wax paper over the top and press with a hot iron until the shavings melt together. Poke a hole near the top through the layers of wax and crayon while still warm. Once your ornament cools, peel away the papers and thread a ribbon through it to hang in a window.

✳ Cream of Tartar

Tub scrubber Let this simple solution of cream of tartar and hydrogen peroxide do the hard work of removing a bathtub stain for you. Fill a small, shallow cup or dish with cream of tartar and add hydrogen peroxide drop by drop until you have a thick paste. Apply to the stain and let it dry. When you remove the dried paste, you'll find that the stain is gone too.

Brighten cookware Discolored aluminum pots will sparkle again if you clean them with a mixture of 2 tablespoons cream of tartar dissolved into 1 quart (1 liter) water. Bring the mixture to a boil inside the pot and boil for 10 minutes.

Make play clay for kids Here's a recipe for fun dough that's like the famous commercial stuff: Add together 2 tablespoons cream of tartar, 1 cup salt, 4 cups plain flour (without rising agents), and 1-2 tablespoons cooking oil. Stir well with a wooden spoon to mix together, then slowly stir while adding 4 cups water. Cook the mixture in a saucepan over a medium flame, stirring occasionally until it thickens. It's ready when it forms a ball that is not sticky. Work in food coloring, if you want. Let it cool, then let the kids get creative. It dries out quicker than the commercial variety, so store it in an airtight container in the fridge.

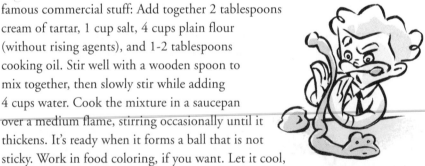

✳ Curtain Rings

Get hooked On a camping trip or a hike, when you don't want to carry a backpack, it's easy to lash a few items to your belt loop with the help of a curtain ring. Mountain climbers rely on expensive carabiners, which they use to hold items and to control ropes. But you don't need to carry along anything so heavy. Attach your sneakers to your sleeping bag with a metal curtain ring; your gloves and canteen can dangle from a metal shower curtain ring or a brass key ring.

Keep curiosity at bay It's a natural stage of development, but not always one you want to encourage. Curious toddlers can't help poking around in your kitchen cupboards. If you've got a toddler visiting, lock up your accessible cupboards by clicking shower curtain rings over the latches. Then when baby leaves, it's easy to remove the rings.

Hold your hammer Sometimes you need three hands when you're doing household repair jobs. Attach a sturdy metal shower curtain ring to your belt and slip your hammer through it. Now you can climb a ladder or otherwise work with both hands and just grab the hammer when needed.

Store nuts and washers Keep nuts and washers on metal shower curtain rings hung from a hook in your workshop. The ring's pear shape and latching action ensure secure storage. Put nuts and washers of similar size on their own rings so that you can find the right size quickly.

Keep track of kids' mittens "Where are my mittens, Ma?" "Where did you leave them?" "I dunno." Something as simple as a curtain ring can help you do away with this dialogue: Drive a nail in the mudroom wall. Hand Junior a curtain ring and tell him to use it to clip his mittens together and hang them on the nail.

✳ Dental Floss

Remove a stuck ring Here's a simple way to slip off a ring that's stuck on your finger. Wrap the length of your finger from the ring to the nail tightly with dental floss. Now you can slide the ring off over the floss "carpet."

Lift cookies off baking tray Ever fought with a freshly baked cookie that wouldn't come off the pan? Crumbled cookies may taste just as good as those in one piece, but they sure don't look as nice on the serving plate. Use dental floss to easily remove cookies from the baking tray. Hold a length of dental floss taut and slide it neatly between the cookie bottom and the pan.

Slice cake and cheese Use dental floss to cut cakes, especially delicate and sticky ones that tend to adhere to a knife. Just hold a length of the floss taut over the cake and then slice away, moving it slightly side to side as you cut through the cake. You can also use dental floss to cut small blocks of cheese cleanly.

Repair outdoor gear Because dental floss is strong and resilient but slender, it's the ideal replacement for thread when you are repairing an umbrella, tent, or backpack. These items take a beating and sometimes get pinhole nicks. Sew up the small holes with floss. To fix larger gouges, sew back and forth over the holes until you have covered the space with a floss patch.

Extra-strong string for hanging things Considering how thin it is, dental floss is strong stuff. Use it instead of string or wire to securely hang pictures, sun catchers, or wind chimes. Use it with a needle to thread together papers you want to attach or those you want to display, in clothesline fashion.

Secure a button permanently Did that button fall off again? This time, sew it back on with dental floss—it's much stronger than thread, which makes it perfect for reinstalling buttons on coats, jackets, and heavy shirts.

Separate photos Sometimes photos get stuck to each other and it seems the only way to separate them is to ruin them. Try working a length of dental floss between the pictures to gently pry them apart.

* Denture Tablets

Re-ignite your diamond's sparkle Has your diamond ring lost its sparkle? Drop a denture tablet into a glass containing a cup of water. Follow that with your ring or diamond earrings. Let it sit for a few minutes. Remove your jewelry and rinse to reveal the old sparkle and shine.

Vanish mineral deposits on glass Fresh flowers often leave a ring on your glass vases that seems impossible to remove no matter how hard you scrub. Here's the answer. Fill the vase with water and drop in a denture tablet. When the fizzing has stopped, all of the mineral deposits will be gone. Use the same method to clean thermos bottles, cruets, glasses, and coffee decanters.

Clean a coffeemaker Hard water leaves mineral deposits in the tank of your electric drip coffeemaker that not only slows the perking but also affects the taste of your brew. Denture tablets will fizz away these deposits and give the tank a bacterial clean-out too. The tablets were designed to clean and disinfect dentures, and they'll do the same job on your coffeemaker. Drop two denture tablets in the tank and fill it with water. Run the coffeemaker. Discard that potful of water and follow up with one or two rinse cycles with clean water.

Clean your toilet Looking for a way to make the toilet sparkle again? Porcelain fixtures respond to the cleaning agent in denture tablets. Here's a solution that does the job in the twinkling of an eye. Drop a denture tablet in the bowl. Wait about 20 minutes and flush. That's it!

Clean enamel cookware Stains on enamel cookware are a natural for the denture tablet cleaning solution. Fill the pot or pan with warm water and drop in a tablet or two, depending on its size. Wait a bit—once the fizzing has stopped, your cookware will be clean.

DID You KNOW?

Bleaching agents are a common component of denture cleaner tablets, providing the chemical action that helps the tablets to remove plaque and to whiten and bleach away stains. This is what makes them surprisingly useful for cleaning toilets, coffeemakers, jewelry, and enamel cookware, among other things.

Unclog a drain Slow drain got you down? Reach for the denture tablets. Drop a couple of tablets into the drain and run water until the problem clears. For a more stubborn clog, drop 3 tablets down the sink, follow that with 1 cup white vinegar, and wait a few minutes. Now run hot water in the drain until the clog is gone.

* Disposable Diapers

Make a heating pad Soothe your aching neck. Or, for that matter, your aching back or shoulder. Use a disposable diaper's high level of absorbency to your advantage by creating a soft, pliant heating pad. Moisten a disposable diaper and place it in the microwave on medium-high setting for about 2 minutes. Check that it's not too hot for comfort and then apply to your achy part.

Keep a plant watered longer Before potting a plant, place a clean disposable diaper in the bottom of the flowerpot—absorbent side up. It will absorb water that would otherwise drain out the bottom and will keep the plant from drying out too fast. You'll also cut back on how often you have to water the plant.

Pad a package You want to mail your friend that lovely piece of china you know she'll love. But you don't have any protective wrapping on hand. If you have disposable diapers, wrap the item in the diapers or insert them as padding before sealing the box. Diapers cost more than regular protective packaging wrap, but at least you will have gotten the package out today, and you can be assured your gift will arrive in one piece.

DID *You* KNOW?

It took a mother to invent disposable diapers. Looking for an alternative to messy cloth diapers, Marion Donovan first created a plastic covering for diapers. She made her prototype from a shower curtain and later parachute fabric. Manufacturers weren't interested, but when she created her own company and debuted the product in 1949 at Saks Fifth Avenue in New York City, it was an instant success. Donovan soon added disposable absorbent material to create the first disposable diaper and, in 1951, sold her company for $1 million.

✱ DUCT TAPE **AROUND THE HOUSE**

Temporarily hem your pants You've found a terrific pair of jeans, but the length isn't right. You expect a little shrinkage anyway, so why spend time hemming? Besides, thick denim jeans are difficult to sew through. Fake the hem with duct tape. The new hem will last through a few washes too.

Remove lint on clothing You're all set to go out for the night and suddenly you notice pet hairs on your outfit. Quick, grab the duct tape and in no time, you'll be ready to go. Wrap your hand with a length of duct tape, sticky side out. Then roll the sticky tape against your clothing in a rocking motion until every last hair has been picked up. Don't wipe, since that may affect the nap.

Make a bandage in a pinch You've gotten a bad scrape. Here's how to protect it until you get a proper bandage. Fold tissue paper or paper towel to cover the wound and cover this with duct tape. It may not be attractive, but it works in a jam.

Reseal bags of chips Tired of stale potato chips? To keep a half-finished bag fresh, fold up the top and seal it tight with a piece of duct tape.

Pocket folder protector Old pocket folders may lose their resiliency but are otherwise useful. Cover your old folder with duct tape; reinforce between sections and it's as good as new.

Bumper sticker Got something you want to say? Make your own bumper sticker. Cut a length of duct tape, affix it to your bumper and with a sharp marker, pen your message.

Keep a secret car key You'll never get locked out of your car again if you affix an extra key to the undercarriage with duct tape.

Catch pesky flies You've just checked into a rustic cabin on the lake and you're ready to start your vacation. Everything would be perfect if only the flying insects were not part of the deal. Grab your roll of duct tape and roll off a few foot-long strips. Hang them from the rafters as flypaper. Soon you'll be rid of the bugs and you can roll up the tape to toss it in the trash.

Replace a shower curtain grommet How many times have you yanked the shower curtain aside only to rip through one of the delicate eyelets? Grab the duct tape to make a simple repair. Once the curtain is dry, cut a rectangular piece and fold it from front to back over the torn hole. Slit the tape with a mat knife, razor blade, or scissors, and push the shower curtain ring back in place.

Repair a vacuum hose Has your vacuum hose cracked and developed a leak? It doesn't spell the end of your vacuum. Repair the broken hose with duct tape. Your vacuum will last until the motor gives out.

DUCT TAPE✱

Reinforce book binding Duct tape is perfect for repairing a broken book binding. Using a nice-colored tape, run the tape down the length of the spine and cut shorter pieces to run perpendicular to that if you need extra reinforcement.

Cover a book Use duct tape in an interesting color to create a durable book cover for a school textbook or a paperback that you carry to the beach. Make a pattern for the cover on a sheet of newspaper; fit the pattern to your book, then cover the pattern, one row at a time, with duct tape, overlapping the rows. The resulting removable cover will be waterproof and sturdy.

Repair a photo frame Many people enjoy displaying family photos in easel-type frames on mantels and side tables throughout the house. But sometimes the foldout leg that holds a frame upright pulls away from the back of the frame and your photo won't stand up properly. Don't despair! Just use duct tape to reattach the broken leg to the frame back.

Hang Christmas lights Festive holiday lights are fun in season, but a real chore when it's time for them to come down. Use duct tape to hang your lights and the removal job will be much easier. Tear duct tape into thin strips. At intervals, wrap strips around the wire and then tape the strand to the gutter or wherever you hang your lights.

Wrap holiday presents Here's a novel way to wrap a special gift. Don't bother with the paper. Go straight for the tape. Press duct tape directly on the gift box. Make designs or cover in stripes and then add decorative touches by cutting shapes, letters, and motifs from tape to attach to the "wrapped" surface.

 DID *You* KNOW?

DUCT TAPE*

Make Halloween costumes Want to be the Tin Man for Halloween? How about a robot? These are just two ideas that work naturally with the classic silver duct tape. Make a basic costume from brown paper grocery bags, with openings in the back so the child can easily put on and take off the costume. Cover this pattern with rows of duct tape. For the legs, cover over an old pair of pants, again giving your little robot or Tin Man an easy way to remove the outfit for bathroom breaks. Duct tape comes in an array of colors, so let your imagination lead your creativity.

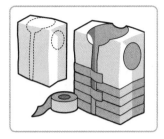

Make a toy sword Got a couple of would-be swashbucklers around the house? Make toy swords for the junior Errol Flynns by sketching a kid-size sword on a piece of cardboard. Use two pieces if you haven't got one thick enough. Be sure to make a handle the child's hand can fit around comfortably once it's been increased in thickness by several layers of duct tape. Wrap the entire blade shape in silver duct tape. Wrap the handle in black tape.

Make play rings and bracelets Make rings by tearing duct tape into strips about 1/2-inch (1.2-centimeter) wide, then folding the strips in half lengthwise— sticky sides together. Continue to put more strips over the first one until the ring is thick enough to stand on its own. You can adjust the size with a scissors and tape the ends closed. To make a stone for the ring, cover a small item such as a pebble and attach it to the ring. Make a bracelet by winding duct tape around a stiff paper pattern.

Make hand puppets Duct tape is great for puppet making. Use a small paper lunch bag as the base for the body of your puppet. Cover the bag with overlapping rows of duct tape. Make armholes through which your fingers will poke out. Create a head from a tape-covered ball of wadded paper and affix buttons or beads for eyes and mouth.

Make bicycle streamers Add snazzy streamers to your kids' handlebars. Make them using duct tape in various colors. Cut the tape into strips about 1/2-inch (1.2-centimeter) wide by 10 inches (25 centimeters) long. Fold each strip in half, sticky sides together. Once you have about half a dozen for each side, stick them into the end of the handlebar and secure them with wraps of duct tape. Be sure your child will still have a good grip on the handlebar.

❋ DUCT TAPE **FOR THE DO-IT-YOURSELFER**

Repair a taillight Someone just backed into your car and smashed the taillight! Here's a quick repair that will last until you have time to get to the repair shop.

Depending on where the cracks lie, use yellow or red duct tape to hold the remaining parts together. In some states this repair will even pass inspection.

Short-term auto hose fix Until you can get to your mechanic, duct tape makes a strong and dependable temporary fix for broken water hoses on your automobile. But don't wait too long. Duct tape can only withstand temperatures up to 200°F (93°C). Also, don't use it to repair a leak in your car's gas line—the gasoline dissolves the adhesive.

Make a temporary roof shingle If you've lost a wooden roof shingle, make a temporary replacement by wrapping duct tape in strips across a piece of 1/4-inch (6-millimeter) plywood you've cut to size. Wedge the makeshift shingle in place to fill the space. It will close the gap and repel water until you can repair the roof.

Fix a hole in your siding Stormy weather damaged your vinyl siding? A broken tree limb tossed by the storm, hailstones, or even an errant baseball can rip your siding. Patch tears in vinyl siding with duct tape. Choose tape in a color that matches your siding and apply it when the surface is dry. Smooth your repair by hand or with a rolling pin. The patch should last at least a season or two.

Replace lawn chair webbing Summertime is here, and you go to the shed to fetch your lawn furniture, only to discover the webbing on your favorite backyard chair has worn through. Don't throw it out. Colorful duct tape makes a great, sturdy replacement webbing. Cut strips twice as long as you need. Double the tape, putting sticky sides together, so that you have backing facing out on both sides. Then screw it in place with the screws on the chair.

Tape a broken window Before removing broken window glass, crisscross the broken pane with duct tape to hold it all together. This will ensure a shard doesn't fall out and cut you.

DID *You* KNOW?

As most Canadians know, the star of *The Red Green Show* on the Canadian Broadcasting Corporation—and the Public Broadcasting System in the United States—has been known to use duct tape for everything from fixing a spare tire to re-webbing a lawn chair. Red's real-life persona, Steve Smith, admits he doesn't use "the handyman's secret weapon" as much as his screen character. "I live in a pretty nice neighborhood, where duct tape is discouraged as a renovation tool," he says. Nevertheless, when he had to prevent his front door from locking, he put a small strip of duct tape across the bolt. He points out that this was the first time he'd used duct tape "to *stop* something from working."

Repair outdoor cushions Don't let a little rip in the cushions for your outdoor furniture bother you. Repair the tear with a closely matched duct tape and it will hold up for several seasons.

Repair a trash can Plastic trash cans often split or crack along the sides. But don't toss out the can with the trash. Repair the tear with duct tape. It's strong enough to withstand the abuses a trash can takes, and easy to manipulate on the curved or ridged surface of your can. Put tape over the crack both outside and inside the can.

Quick fix for a toilet seat You're giving a party and someone taps you on the shoulder to tell you the toilet seat has broken. You don't have to make a mad dash to the home center. Grab the duct tape and carefully wrap the break for a neat repair. Your guests will thank you.

Mend a screen Have the bugs found the tear in your window or door screen? Thwart their entrance until you make a permanent fix by covering the hole with duct tape.

✳ DUCT TAPE **FOR SPORTS AND OUTDOOR GEAR**

Tighten shin guards Hockey players need a little extra protection. Use duct tape to attach shin guards firmly in place. Put on all your equipment, including socks. Now split the duct tape to the width appropriate for your size—children might need narrower strips than adults—and start wrapping around your shin guard to keep it tight to your leg.

Add life to a hockey stick Street hockey sticks take a beating. If yours is showing its age, breathe a little more life into it by wrapping the bottom of the stick with duct tape. Replace the tape as often as needed.

Extend the life of skateboard shoes Kids who perform fantastic feats on their skateboards find their shoes wear out very quickly because a lot of the jumps involve sliding the toe or side of the foot along the board. They wear holes in new shoes fast. Protect their feet and prolong the life of their shoes by putting a layer or two of duct tape on the area that scrapes along the board.

Repair your ski gloves Ski glove seams tearing open? Duct tape is the perfect solution to ripped ski gloves because it's waterproof, incredibly adhesive, strong, and can easily be torn into strips of any width. Make your repair lengthwise or around the fingers and set out on the slopes again.

Repair a tent You open your tent at the campsite and oops—a little tear. No problem as long as you've brought your duct tape along. Cover the hole with a patch; for double protection mirror the patch inside the tent. You'll keep insects and weather where they belong.

Extra insulation Make your winter boots a little bit warmer by taping the insoles with duct tape, silver side up. The shiny tape will reflect the warmth of your feet back into your boots.

Stay afloat You're out for a paddle, when you discover a small hole in your canoe. Thank goodness you thought to pack duct tape in your supply kit. Pull the canoe out of the water, dry the area around the hole, and apply a duct tape patch to the outside of the canoe. You're ready to finish your trip.

Waterproof footwear Need a waterproof pair of shoes for fishing, gardening, or pushing off the canoe into the lake? Cover an old pair of sneakers with duct tape, overlapping the edges of each row. As you round corners, cut little **V**'s in the edges of the tape so that you can lap the tape smoothly around the corner.

Pool patch Duct tape will repair a hole in your swimming pool liner well enough to stand up to water for at least a season. Be sure to cover the area thoroughly.

Protect yourself from ticks When you're out on a hike, on your way to your favorite fishing hole, or just weeding in the yard, protect your ankles from those pesky ticks. Wrap duct tape around your pant cuffs to seal out the bugs. This is a handy way to keep your pant leg out of your bicycle chain too!

Create a clothesline Whether you're out in the wilderness on a camping trip or in your own backyard, when you need a clothesline and you're without rope, think: duct tape. Twist a long piece of duct tape into a rope and bind it between trees for a clothesline. It makes a dandy jump rope as well or a basic rope sturdy enough to lash two items together. You can even use your creation to drag a child's wagon.

DID *You* KNOW?

The folks at 3M's product information lines handle a lot of calls about duct tape. Three of the most commonly asked questions are:
1. Can duct tape be used for removing warts?
2. Can it be used to secure the duct from the household dryer to the outdoors?
3. Is it waterproof?

The official answers:
1. Duct tape is not recommended for removing warts, because it hasn't been scientifically tested.
2. The company does not recommend using duct tape for the dryer duct, because the temperatures may exceed 200°F (93°C), the maximum temperature duct tape can withstand.

3. The backing of the duct tape is waterproof, but the adhesive is not. Duct tape will hold up to water for a while, but eventually the adhesive will give out.

Protect your gas grill hose For some reason, mice and squirrels love to chew on rubber, and one of their favorite snacks is often the rubber hose that connects the propane tank to your gas grill. Protect the hose by wrapping it in duct tape.

Make an emergency sneaker lace You're enjoying a game of driveway hoops when you bust a sneaker lace. Ask for a brief time-out while you grab the duct tape from the garage. Cut off a piece of tape that's as long as you need and rip off twice the width you need. Fold the tape in half along its length, sticky side in. Thread your new lace onto your sneaker, tie it up, and you are ready for your next jump shot.

Repair your ski pants Oh no, you ripped your ski pants and the wind is whipping into the nylon outer layer. No need to pay inflated lodge shop prices for a new pair if you have a roll of duct tape in the car. Just slip a piece of tape inside the rip, sticky side out, and carefully press both sides of the rip together. The repair will be barely detectable.

✳ Dustpans

Decorate your door for fall Gather dried fall foliage, such as Indian corn, bittersweet branches with orange berries, and other decorative greens. Tie them together as a bouquet with a rubber band or tape. Spread them out in a fan shape and cover the binding with a ribbon. Now set this against a copper dustpan. Use super glue or a glue gun to attach your bouquet to the pan. Hang this homage to fall on your front door.

Enlist the littlest shoveler Youngsters enjoy mimicking their elders. While you shovel snow, let the little one help by your side using a dustpan as a shovel.

Use as a sand toy Pack a clean dustpan with your beach toys. It's a great sand scoop and will really help the castle builders in their task.

Speed toy cleanup Picking up all those little toys gets tiresome. Scoop them up with a dustpan and deposit them in the toy bin. It's a real time-saver, not to mention a back-saver.

✱ Earrings

Use as a bulletin board tack Lend a little personal style to your bulletin board. Use mateless pierced earrings to tack up pictures, notes, souvenirs, and clippings.

Create a brooch Got a batch of mateless pierced earrings collecting dust in a box? Use wire cutters to snip off the stems and get creative: Arrange the earrings on a swatch of cardboard or foam core, and secure them with hot-melt glue. Add a pin backing and, voilà! a new brooch. Or use the same method to jazz up a plain picture frame.

Make a magnet Give your fridge some glitz. Use wire cutters to cut the stem off an orphan earring and glue it to a magnet. What a great way to emphasize how pleased you are with that perfect report card when you stick it on the refrigerator.

Clip your scarf Did you lose one of your very favorite earrings? Oh well, at least you can still work the survivor into an ensemble by using it to secure a scarf. Just tie the scarf as desired, then clip or pierce it with the earring.

Make an instant button. Oh, darn! You're dressed to go out and you discover a button missing. No need to re-invent your whole outfit. Just dip into your collection of clip-on earrings. Clip the earring on the button side of the clothing to create

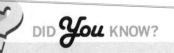

DID You KNOW?

People have been wearing—and probably losing—earrings for nearly 5,000 years. According to historians who have studied jewelry, the tiny baubles were likely introduced in western Asia in about 3000 B.C. The oldest earrings that have been discovered date to 2500 B.C. and were found in Iraq. The popularity of earrings over time has grown or receded, depending on hairstyles and clothing trends. The clip-on earring was introduced in the 1930s, and by the 1950s, fashionable women simply did not pierce their ears. But twenty years later, pierced ears were back.

a new "button," then button as usual with the buttonhole. If you have time, move the top button on that favorite blouse to replace the lost one and then use the earring at the top of the blouse.

Decorate your Christmas tree Scatter clip-on earrings around the boughs of your Christmas tree as an eye-catching accent to your larger tree decorations. Or use them as the main adornment on a small tree or wreath.

✳ Eggs

Make a facial Who has time or money to spend at the local day spa, paying someone to tell you how awful your skin looks? For a little pampering, head to the refrigerator and grab an egg. If you have dry skin that needs moisturizing, separate the egg and beat the yolk. Oily skin takes the egg white, to which a bit of lemon or honey can be added. For normal skin, use the entire egg. Apply the beaten egg, relax and wait 30 minutes, then rinse. You'll love your new fresh face.

Use as glue Out of regular white glue? Egg whites can act as a glue substitute when gluing paper or light cardboard together.

Add to compost Eggshells are a great addition to your compost because they are rich in calcium—a nutrient that helps plants. Crushing them before you put them in your compost heap will help them break down faster.

Water your plants After boiling eggs, don't pour the water down the drain. Instead, let it cool; then water plants with the nutrient-filled water.

Start seeds Plant seeds in eggshells. Place the eggshell halves in the carton, fill each with soil, and press seeds inside. The seeds will draw extra nutrients from the eggshells. Once the seedlings are about 3 inches (7.5 centimeters) tall, they are ready to be transplanted into your garden. Remove them from the shell before you put them in the ground. Then crush the eggshells and put them in your compost or plant them in your garden.

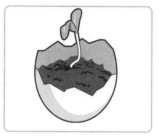

✳ Egg Cartons

Use for storing and organizing With a dozen handy compartments, egg cartons are a natural for storing and organizing small items. Here are some ideas to get you going. You're sure to come up with more of your own.

- Instead of emptying the coins in your pocket into a jar for later sorting, cut off a four-section piece of an egg carton and leave it on your dresser. Sort your quarters, dimes, nickels, and pennies as you pull them out of your pockets. (Dump pennies in a larger container, such as a jar, or put them in a piggy bank.)

- Organize buttons, safety pins, threads, bobbins, and fasteners on your sewing table.

- Organize washers, tacks, small nuts and bolts, and screws on your workbench. Or use to keep disassembled parts in sequence.

- Keep small Christmas ornaments from being crushed in handy, stackable egg cartons.

Start a fire Fill a cardboard egg carton with briquettes (and a bit of leftover candle wax if it's handy), place in your barbecue grill, and light. Egg cartons can also be filled with tinder, such as small bits of wood and paper, and used as a fire starter in a fireplace or a woodstove.

Start seedlings An egg carton can become the perfect nursery for your seeds. Use a cardboard egg carton, not a polystyrene one. Fill each cell in the carton with soil and plant a few seeds in each one. Once the seeds have sprouted, divide the carton into individual cells and plant, cardboard cells and all.

Make ice Making a bunch of ice for a picnic or party? Use the bottom halves of clean polystyrene egg cartons as auxiliary ice trays.

Reinforce a trash bag Yuck! You pull the plastic trash bag out of the kitchen trash container and gunk drips out. Next time, put an opened empty egg carton at the bottom of the trash bag to prevent tears and punctures.

Create shippable homemade goodies Here's a great way to brighten the day of a soldier, student, or any faraway friend or loved one. Cover an egg carton with bright wrapping paper. Line the individual cells with candy wrappers or shredded coconut. Nestle homemade treats inside each. Include the carton in your next care package or birthday gift, and rest assured the treats will arrive intact.

Golf ball caddy An egg carton in your golf bag is a great way to keep golf balls clean and ready for teeing off.

✳ Emery Boards

Sand deep crevices If you are refinishing an elaborate piece of wood such as turned table legs or chair spindles, you can use emery boards to gently smooth those hard-to-reach crevices before applying stain or finish. These filelike nail sanders are easy to handle and provide a choice of two sanding grits.

Ever wonder about emery boards, those little sticks that we tuck into our drawers and can never seem to find when we need to file down a torn nail? Emery is a natural mixture of corundum and magnetite. Diamond is the only mineral harder than corundum. Sapphires and rubies are also varieties of corundum. Makes it easy to understand why a manicurist's magazine would urge women to "treat their nails like jewels, not tools." Emery boards have changed a lot since 1910, when they were introduced. They now come with bright designs, give off scents, or are shaped as hearts and stars.

Remove dirt from an eraser Do you have a fussy student who doesn't like dirt on the end of the pencil? Take an emery board and rub lightly over the eraser until the dirt is filed off.

Prep seeds for planting Use an emery board to remove the hard coating on seeds before you plant them. This will speed sprouting and help them absorb moisture.

Save your suede Did somebody step on your blue suede shoes? Or worse, spill some wine on them? Don't check into Heartbreak Hotel. Rub the stain lightly with an emery board, and then hold the shoe over steam from a teakettle or pan to remove the stain. This works for suede clothing too.

✳ Envelopes

Shred old receipts faster The best way to get rid of receipts that may have your credit card number or other personal information is to shred them. But feeding tiny receipts into a shredder is tedious. Instead, place all the old receipts into a few old envelopes and shred the envelopes.

Make a small funnel You save money by buying your spices in bulk and you want to transfer them to smaller, handier bottles for use in the kitchen, but you don't have a small funnel to do the job. Make a couple of disposable funnels from an envelope. Seal the envelope, cut it in half diagonally, and snip off one corner on each half. Now you have two funnels for pouring spices into your smaller jars.

Sort and store sandpaper You know how sheets of sandpaper love to curl themselves up into useless tubes? Prevent that problem and keep your sandpaper sheets organized by storing them in standard letter-size cardboard mailing envelopes. Use one envelope for each grit and write the grit on the envelopes.

Make bookmarks Recycle envelopes by making them into handy bookmarks of different sizes. Cut off the gummed flap and one end of the envelope. Then slip the remainder over the corner of the page where you stopped reading for a quick placeholder that doesn't damage your book. Give a batch to the kids to decorate for their own set or to give as a homemade gift.

Make file folders Don't let papers get disorganized just because you ran out of file folders. Cut the short ends off a light cardboard mailing envelope. Turn it inside out so you have a blank cardboard on the outside. Cut a 3/4-inch (2-centimeter) wide strip lengthwise off the top of one side. The other edge becomes the place where you label your file.

✳ Epsom Salt

Get rid of raccoons Are the masked night marauders poking around your trash can, creating a mess and raising a din? A few tablespoons of Epsom salt spread around your garbage cans will deter the raccoons, who don't like the taste of the stuff. Don't forget to reapply after it rains.

Deter slugs Are you tired of visiting your yard at night only to find the place crawling with slimy slugs? Sprinkle Epsom salt where they glide and say good-bye to the slugs.

Fertilize tomatoes and other plants Want those Big Boys to be big? Add Epsom salt as a foolproof fertilizer. Every week, for every foot of height of your tomato plant, add one tablespoon. Your tomatoes will be the envy of the neighborhood. Epsom salt is also a good fertilizer for houseplants, roses and other flowers, and trees.

Make your grass greener How green is your valley? Not green enough, you say? Epsom salt, which adds needed magnesium and iron to your soil, may be the answer. Add 2 tablespoons to 1 gallon (3.7 liters) of water. Spread on your lawn and then water it with plain water to make sure it soaks into the grass.

Clean bathroom tiles Is the tile in your bathroom getting that grungy look? Time to bring in the Epsom salt. Mix it in equal parts with liquid dish detergent, then dab it onto the offending area and start scrubbing. The Epsom salt works with the detergent to scrub and dissolve the grime.

Regenerate a car battery Is your car battery starting to sound as if it won't turn over? Worried that you'll be stuck the next time you try to start your car? Give your battery a little more life with this potion. Dissolve about an ounce of Epsom salt in warm water and add it to each battery cell.

Get rid of blackheads Here's a surefire way to dislodge blackheads: Mix 1 teaspoon Epsom salt and 3 drops iodine in 1/2 cup boiling water. When the mixture cools enough to stick your finger in it, apply it to the blackhead with a cotton ball. Repeat this three or four times, reheating the solution if necessary. Gently remove the blackhead and then dab the area with an alcohol-based astringent.

Frost your windows for Christmas If you are dreaming of a white Christmas, but the weather won't cooperate, at least you can make your windows look frosty. Mix Epsom salt with stale beer until the salt stops dissolving. Apply the mixture to your windows with a sponge—for a realistic look, sweep the sponge in an arc at the bottom corners. When the mixture dries, the windows will look frosted.

Kids' Stuff Here are two fun winter-inspired projects using Epsom salt for the holiday season:

Make snowflakes by folding a piece of **blue paper** several times and snipping shapes into the resulting square of paper. Unfold your snowflake. Brush one side with a thick mixture of **water** and **Epsom salt**. After it dries, turn it over and brush the other side. When it's finished, you'll have a **frosty-looking snowflake** you can hang in your window.

To make a **snowy scene**, use crayons to draw a picture on **construction paper**. Mix equal parts of **Epsom salt** and **boiling water**. Let it cool; then use a wide artist's paintbrush to paint the picture. When it dries, "snow" crystals will appear.

✳ Fabric Softener

End clinging dust on your TV Are you frustrated to see dust fly back onto your television screen, or other plastic surfaces, right after cleaning them? To eliminate the static cling that attracts dust, simply dampen your dust cloth with fabric softener straight from the bottle and dust as usual.

Remove old wallpaper Removing old wallpaper is a snap with fabric softener. Just stir 1 capful liquid softener into 1 quart (1 liter) water and sponge the solution onto the wallpaper. Let it soak in for 20 minutes, then scrape the paper from the wall. If the wallpaper has a water-resistant coating, score it with a wire-bristle brush before treating with the fabric softener solution.

Abolish carpet shock To eliminate static shock when you walk across your carpet, spray the carpet with a fabric softener solution. Dilute 1 cup softener with 2 1/2 quarts (2.5 liters) water; fill a spray bottle and lightly spritz the carpet. Take care not to saturate it and damage the carpet backing. Spray in the evening and let the carpet dry overnight before walking on it. The effect should last for several weeks.

Remove hair-spray residue Dried-on overspray from hair spray can be tough to remove from walls and vanities, but even a buildup of residue is no match for a solu-

DID **You** KNOW?

How does fabric softener reduce cling as well as soften clothes? The secret is in the electrical charges. Positively charged chemical lubricants in the fabric softener are attracted to your load of negatively charged clothes, softening the fabric. The softened fabrics create less friction, and less static, as they rub against each other in the dryer, and because fabric softener attracts moisture, the slightly damp surface of the fabrics makes them electrical conductors. As a result, the electrical charges travel through them instead of staying on the surface to cause static cling and sparks as you pull the clothing from the dryer.

tion of 1 part liquid fabric softener to 2 parts water. Stir to blend, pour into a spray bottle, spritz the surface, and polish it with a dry cloth.

Clean now, not later Clean glass tables, shower doors, and other hard surfaces, and repel dust with liquid fabric softener. Mix 1 part softener into 4 parts water and store in a squirt bottle, such as an empty dishwashing liquid bottle. Apply a little solution to a clean cloth, wipe the surface, and then polish with a dry cloth.

Float away baked-on grime Forget scrubbing. Instead, soak burned-on foods from casseroles with liquid fabric softener. Fill the casserole with water, add a squirt of liquid fabric softener, and soak for an hour, or until residue wipes easily away.

Keep paintbrushes pliable After using a paintbrush, clean the bristles thoroughly and rinse them in a coffee can full of water with a drop of liquid fabric softener mixed in. After rinsing, wipe the bristles dry and store the brush as usual.

Untangle and condition hair Liquid fabric softener diluted in water and applied after shampooing can untangle and condition fine, flyaway hair, as well as curly, coarse hair. Experiment with the amount of conditioner to match it to the texture of your hair, using a weaker solution for fine hair and a stronger solution for coarse, curly hair. Comb through your hair and rinse.

Remove hard-water stains Hard-water stains on windows can be difficult to remove. To speed up the process, dab full-strength liquid fabric softener onto the stains and let it soak for 10 minutes. Then wipe the softener and stain off the glass with a damp cloth and rinse.

Make your own fabric softener sheets Fabric softener sheets are convenient to use, but they're no bargain when compared to the price of liquid softeners. You can make your own dryer sheets and save money. Just moisten an old washcloth with 1 teaspoon liquid softener and toss it into the dryer with your next load.

✳ Fabric Softener Sheets

Pick up pet hair Pet hair can get a pretty tenacious grip on furniture and clothing. But a used fabric softener sheet will suck that fur right off the fabric with a couple of swipes. Just toss the fuzzy wipe into the trash.

End car odors Has that new-car smell gradually turned into that old-car stench? Tuck a new dryer fabric softener sheet under each car seat to counteract musty odors and cigarette smells.

Lift burned-on casserole residue Those sheets will soften more than fabric. The next time food gets burned onto your casserole dish, save the elbow grease. Instead fill the dish with hot water and toss in three or four used softener sheets. Soak overnight, remove the sheets, and you'll have no trouble washing away the residue. Be sure to rinse well.

Freshen drawers There's no need to buy scented drawer-liner paper; give your dresser drawers a fresh-air fragrance by tucking a new dryer fabric softener sheet under existing drawer liners, or tape one to the back of each drawer.

Wipe soap scum from shower door Tired of scrubbing scummy shower doors? It's easy to wipe the soap scum away with a used dryer fabric softener sheet.

> **TAKE CARE** People with allergies or chemical sensitivities may develop rashes or skin irritations when they come into contact with laundry treated with some commercial fabric softeners or fabric softener sheets. If you are sensitive to softeners, you can still soften your laundry by substituting 1/4 cup white vinegar or the same amount of your favorite hair conditioner to your washer's last rinse cycle for softer, fresher-smelling washables.

Repel dust from electrical appliances Because television and PC screens are electrically charged, they actually attract dust, making dusting them a never-ending chore, but not if you dust them with used dryer softener sheets. These sheets are designed to reduce static cling, so they remove the dust, and keep it from resettling for several days or more.

Do away with doggy odor If your best friend comes in from the rain and smells like a … well … wet dog, wipe him down with a used dryer softener sheet, and he'll smell as fresh as a daisy.

Freshen laundry hampers and wastebaskets There's still plenty of life left in used dryer fabric softener sheets. Toss one into the bottom of a laundry hamper or wastebasket to counteract odors.

Tame locker-room and sneaker smells Deodorizing sneakers and gym bags calls for strong stuff. Tuck a new dryer fabric softener sheet into each sneaker and leave overnight to neutralize odors (just remember to pull them out before wearing the sneaks). Drop a dryer sheet into the bottom of a gym bag and leave it there until your nose lets you know it's time to renew it.

Prevent musty odors in suitcases Place a single, unused dryer fabric softener sheet into an empty suitcase or other piece of luggage before storing. The bag will smell great the next time you use it.

Buff chrome to a brilliant shine After chrome is cleaned, it can still look streaky and dull, but whether it's your toaster or your hubcaps, you can easily buff up the shine with a used dryer softener sheet.

Use as a safe mosquito repellent For a safe mosquito repellent, look no farther than your laundry room. Save used dryer fabric softener sheets and pin or tie one to your clothing when you go outdoors to help repel mosquitoes.

Use an inconspicuous air freshener Don't spend hard-earned money on those plug-in air fresheners. Just tuck a few sheets of dryer fabric softener into closets, behind curtains, and under chairs.

Do away with static cling You'll never be embarrassed by static cling again if you keep a used fabric softener sheet in your purse or dresser drawer. When faced with static, dampen the sheet and rub it over your pantyhose to put an end to clinging skirts.

Keep dust off blinds Cleaning venetian blinds is a tedious chore, so make the results last by wiping them down with a used dryer fabric softener sheet to repel dust. Wipe them with another sheet whenever the effect wears off.

Renew grubby stuffed toys Wash fake-fur stuffed animals in the washing machine set on gentle cycle, then put the stuffed animals into the clothes dryer along with a pair of old tennis shoes and a fabric softener sheet, and they will come out fluffy and with silky-soft fur.

Substitute a dryer sheet for a tack cloth Sticky tack cloths are designed to pick up all traces of sawdust on a woodworking project before you paint or varnish it, but they are expensive and not always easy to find at the hardware store. If you find yourself in the middle of a project without a tack cloth, substitute an unused dryer fabric softener sheet; it will attract sawdust and hold it like a magnet.

Consolidate sheets and make them smell pretty To improve sheet storage, store the sheet set in one of the matching pillowcases, and tuck a new dryer fabric softener sheet into the packet for a fresh fragrance.

Abolish tangled sewing thread To put an end to tangled thread, keep an unused dryer fabric softener sheet in your sewing kit. After threading the needle, insert it into the sheet and pull all of the thread through to give it a nonstick coating.

✳ Film Canisters

Rattle toy for the cat Cats are amused by small objects that rattle and shake, and they really don't care what they look like. To provide endless entertainment for your cat, drop a few dried beans, a spoonful of dry rice, or other small objects that can't harm a cat, into an empty film canister, snap on the lid, and watch the fun begin.

Handy stamp dispenser To keep a roll of stamps from being damaged, make a stamp dispenser from an empty film canister. Hold the canister steady by taping it to a counter with duct tape, and use a utility knife to carefully cut a slit into the side of the canister. Drop the roll of stamps in, feed it out through the slit, snap the cap on, and it's ready to use.

Use as hair rollers You can collect all the hair rollers you'll ever need if you save your empty plastic film canisters. To use, pop the top off, roll damp hair around the canister, and hold it in place by fastening a hair clip over the open end of the canister and your hair.

Emergency sewing kit You'll never be at a loss if you pop a button or your hem unravels if you fill an empty film canister with buttons, pins, and a pre-threaded needle. Make several; tuck one into each travel bag, purse, or gym bag, and hit the road.

On-the-road pill dispensers Use empty film canisters as travel-size pill bottles for your purse or overnight bag. If you take more than one medication, use a separate canister for each. Write the medication and dosage on a peel-and-stick label and attach to each canister. For at-a-glance identification, color the labels with different-colored highlighter pens.

Tip **The Vanishing Film Canister**

> Plastic film canisters have myriad uses, from emergency ashtrays to spice bottles. But with the rise of digital cameras, these small wonders are rapidly going the way of the rotary dial phone or the phonograph needle. A good source for free film canisters has always been the neighborhood one-hour photo shop. But these days you may find that even they have a canister shortage. If so, check the yellow pages for a professional film developer, because most high-quality, professional photographers still use film—and film canisters.

Store fishing flies You can save a lot of money and grief by storing fishing flies and hooks in film canisters. They don't take up much room in a fishing vest, and if you do drop one in a stream, the airtight lid will keep it floating long enough for you to … well … fish it out.

Carry spices for camp cooking Just because you are roughing it, doesn't mean that you have to eat bland food. You can store a multitude of seasonings in individual film canisters to take along when you go camping, and you'll still have plenty of room for the food itself in your backpack or car trunk. It's a good idea for your RV or vacation cabin too.

Carry small change for laundry and tolls Film canisters are just the right size to hold quarters and smaller change. Tuck a canister of change into your laundry bag or your car's glove compartment, and you'll never have to hunt for change when you're at a self-service laundry or a tollbooth.

Bring your own diet aids If you are on a special diet, you can easily and discreetly transport your favorite salad dressings, artificial sweetener, or other condiments to restaurants in plastic film canisters. Clean, empty canisters hold single-sized servings, have snap-on, leakproof lids, and are small enough to tuck into a purse.

Keep jewelry close at hand An empty film canister doesn't take up much room in your gym bag, and it'll come in handy for keeping your rings and earrings from being misplaced while you work out.

Emergency nail polish remover Create a small, spillproof carry case for nail polish remover by tucking a small piece of sponge into a plastic film canister. Saturate the sponge with polish remover and snap on the lid. For an emergency repair, simply insert a finger and rub the nail against the fluid-soaked sponge to remove the polish.

✳ Flour

Repel ants with flour Sprinkle a line of flour along the backs of pantry shelves and wherever you see ants entering the house. Repelled by the flour, ants won't cross over the line.

Freshen playing cards After a few games, cards can accumulate a patina of snack residue and hand oil, but you can restore them with some all-purpose flour in a paper bag. Drop the cards into the bag with enough flour to cover, shake vigorously, and remove the cards. The flour will absorb the oils, and it can be easily knocked off the cards by giving them a vigorous shuffle.

DID *You* KNOW?

Ever wondered why the word *flour* is pronounced exactly like the word *flower*? Well, you may be surprised to learn that *flour* is actually derived from the French word for flower, which is *fleur*. The French use the word to describe the most desirable, or floury (flowery) and protein-rich, part of a grain after processing removes the hull. And, because much of our food terminology comes from the French, we still bake and make sauces with the flower of grains, such as wheat, which we call flour.

Safe paste for children's crafts Look no farther than your
kitchen canister for an inexpensive, nontoxic paste
that is ideal for children's paper craft projects,
such as papier-mâché and scrap-booking. To
make the paste, add 3 cups cold water to a
saucepan and blend in 1 cup all-purpose flour.
Stirring constantly, bring the mixture to a boil.
Reduce heat and simmer, stirring until smooth and
thick. Cool and pour into a plastic squeeze bottle to use.
This simple paste will keep for weeks in the refrigerator, and cleans up easily
with soap and water.

Make modeling clay Keep the kids busy on a rainy day with modeling clay—they can
even help you make the stuff. Knead together 3 cups all-purpose flour,
1/4 cup salt, 1 cup water, 1 tablespoon vegetable oil, and 1 or 2 drops food
coloring. If the mixture is sticky, add more flour; if it's too stiff, add more
water. When the "clay" is a workable consistency, store it until needed in a
self-sealing plastic bag.

Polish brass and copper No need to go out and buy cleaner for your brass and silver.
You can whip up your own at much less cost. Just combine equal parts of flour,
salt, and vinegar, and mix into a paste. Spread the paste onto the metal, let it
dry, and buff it off with a clean, dry cloth.

Bring back luster to a dull sink To buff your stainless steel sink back to a warm glow,
sprinkle flour over it and rub lightly with a soft, dry cloth. Then rinse the sink
to restore its shine.

✳ Flowerpots

Container for baking bread Want to give the staff of life an interesting shape? Take a
new, clean medium-sized clay flowerpot, soak it in water for about 20 minutes, and then lightly grease the inside with butter. Place your bread dough,

DID *You* KNOW?

For thousands of years people
have been plopping plants
into pots to transport a native
plant to a new land or to bring
an exotic plant home. In 1495
B.C., Egyptian queen
Hatshepsut sent workers to
Somalia to bring back incense
trees in pots. And in 1787
Captain Bligh reportedly had
more than 1,000 breadfruit
plants in clay pots aboard the
H.M.S. *Bounty*. The
plants were destined
for the West Indies,
where they were to be
grown as food for the
slaves.

prepared as usual, in the pot and bake. The clay pot will give your bread a crusty outside and keep the inside moist.

Create a firewood container Who needs an expensive metal or brass rack to hold firewood by the fireplace? Spare yourself the expense and put an extra-large empty ceramic or clay flowerpot beside the hearth. It's a perfect—and cheap—place to keep kindling and small logs ready for when the weather outside gets frightful.

Unfurl yarn knot-free That sweater you're knitting will take forever if you're constantly stopping to pull out tangles in the yarn. To prevent this, place your ball of yarn under an upturned flowerpot and thread the end through the drain hole. Set it next to where you are sitting for more pleasurable purling.

Create an aquarium fish cave Some fish love to lurk in shadowy corners of their home aquariums, keeping themselves safe from imagined predators. Place a mini flowerpot on its side on the aquarium floor to create a cave for spelunking fish.

Kill fire ants If fire ants plague your yard or patio and you're tired of getting stung by the tiny attackers, a flowerpot can help you quench the problem. Place the flowerpot upside down over the anthill. Pour boiling water through the drain hole and you'll be burning down their house.

Help container plant roots The plants that you want to put in that beautiful new deep container you ordered for your patio have a shallow root system, and you don't want to go to the bother—and expense—of filling that huge container completely with potting soil. What do you do? When planting shallow-rooted plants in a deep container, one easy solution is to find  another smaller flowerpot that will fit upside down in the base of the deeper pot and occupy a lot of that space. After you insert it, fill around it with soil before putting in your plants.

Keep soil in your flowerpot Soil from your houseplant won't slip-slide away if you place broken clay flowerpot shards in the bottom of the pot before re-planting. When watering your plants, you'll find that the water drains out, but not the soil.

✳ Foam Food Trays

Make knee pads for gardening If you find gardening is a pain in the knees when you tend your little patch of green, tape foam food trays to your knees. Or attach them to your legs using the top halves of old tube socks. The trays give you extra padding while you pull out weeds and fertilize your plants.

Release your innersoles If your tired old dogs need a little padding, grab a couple of clean meat trays and cut them to fit inside the sole of your shoes or boots. You'll have happy feet and some extra cushioning for free.

Produce a disposable serving dish If you need a quick disposable serving platter while you're on a cookout or camping trip, you can make one from a foam food tray. Wash it with soap and water, cover it entirely with foil, and load it up with food. Use these serving dishes to bring goodies to the church potluck, local bake sale, or sick neighbor. No worries about losing your own platters.

Provide an art palette Create a paint palette for your budding Picasso. A thoroughly cleaned and dried food tray is the perfect place for kids to squirt their tempera or oil paints. Are they experimenting with watercolors? Use two trays: Put watercolor paint in one and water in the other. At the end of the art session, you can just throw them away.

Protect pictures in the mail Why buy expensive padded envelopes to send photographs to loved ones? Cut foam trays slightly smaller than your mailing envelope. Insert your photographs between the trays, place in the envelope, and mail. The photos will arrive without creases or bends.

✳ Freezer

Eliminate unpopped popcorn Don't you just hate the kernels of popcorn that are left at the bottom of the bowl? Eliminate the popcorn duds by keeping your unpopped supply in the freezer.

Remove wax from candlesticks Grandma's heirloom silver candlesticks will get a new life if you place them in the freezer and then pick off the accumulated wax drippings. But don't do this if your candlesticks are made from more than one type of metal. The metals can expand and contract at different rates and damage the candlesticks.

Extend candle life Place candles in the freezer for at least two hours before burning. They will last longer.

Unstick photos Picture this: Water spills on a batch of photographs, causing them to stick together. If you pull them apart, your pictures will be ruined. Don't be so hasty. Stick them in the freezer for about 20 minutes. Then use a butter knife to gingerly separate the photos. If they don't come free, place them back in the freezer. This works for envelopes and stamps too.

Clean a pot Your favorite pot has been left on the stove too long, and now you've got a burned-on mess to clean up. Place the pot in the freezer for a couple of hours. When the burned food becomes frozen, it will be easier to remove.

Tip **Freezer Tactics**

> Here are some ways to get the most out of your freezer or your refrigerator's freezer compartment:
>
> ● To prevent spoilage, keep your freezer at 0°F (-18°C). To check the temperature, stick a freezer thermometer (sold at hardware stores) between two frozen food containers.
>
> ● A full freezer runs the compressor less often and stays colder longer. Good to remember the next time there's a blackout.
>
> ● The shelves on a freezer door are a little warmer than the freezer interior, making them ideal for storing items such as bread and coffee.
>
> ● When defrosting your freezer, place a large towel or sheet on the bottom. Water drips onto it, making cleanup much easier.
>
> ● The next time you defrost your freezer, apply a thin coat of petroleum jelly to the walls to keep frost from sticking.

Remove odors Got a musty-smelling book or a plastic container with a fish odor? Place them in the freezer overnight. By morning they'll be fresh again. This works with almost any other small item that has a bad smell you want to get rid of.

✳ Funnels

Make a string dispenser Don't get yourself tied up in knots over tangled string. Nail a large funnel to the wall, with the stem pointing down. Place a ball of string in the funnel and thread the end through the funnel's stem. You have an instant knot-free string dispenser.

Separate eggs Want an egg-ceptional egg separator? Try a funnel. Simply crack the egg into the funnel. The white will slide out the spout into another container, while the yolk stays put. Of course, you have to be careful not to break the yolk when you're cracking the egg.

Make a kids' telephone Just because you choke every time you open your phone bill doesn't mean the kids have to, too. Use two small plastic funnels to make them a durable string telephone. For each funnel, tie a button to one end of a length of kite string and thread it through the large end of the funnel. Tie another button at the bottom of the spout to keep the string in place and let the kids start yakking.

✳ Garden Hose

Snake decoy to scare birds If flocks of annoying, messy birds are invading your yard, try replicating their natural predator to keep them away. Cut a short length of hose, lay it in your grass—poised like a snake—and the birds will steer clear.

Stabilize a tree A short length of old garden hose is a good way to tie a young tree to its stake. You'll find that the hose is flexible enough to bend when the tree does, but at the same time, it's strong enough to keep the tree tied to its stake until it can stand on its own. Also, the hose will not damage the bark of the young tree as it grows.

Capture earwigs Pesky garden earwigs will find their final resting place in that leaky old hose. Cut the hose into 12-inch (30-centimeter) lengths, making sure the inside is completely dry. Place the hose segments where you have seen earwigs crawling around and leave them overnight. By the morning the hoses should be filled with the earwigs and ready for disposal. One method is to dunk the hoses in a bucket of kerosene.

Tip **Buying a Hose**

It's just a garden-variety hose, right? Actually, there are a few important points to keep in mind when you buy this important outdoor tool:

● To determine how long a hose you need, measure the distance from the faucet to the farthest point in your yard. Add several feet to allow for watering around corners; this will help you avoid annoying kinks that cut water pressure.

● Vinyl and rubber hoses are generally more sturdy and weather resistant than ones made of cheaper forms of plastic. If a hose flattens when you step on it, it is not up to gardening duties.

● Buy a hose with a lifetime warranty; only good-quality hoses have one.

Unclog a downspout When leaves and debris clog up your rainspout and gutters, turn to your garden hose to get things flowing again. Push the hose up the spout and poke through the blockage. You don't even have to turn the hose on, because the water in the gutters will flush out the dam.

Cover swing set chains No parent wants to see his or her child hurt on the backyard swing set. Put a length of old hose over each chain to protect little hands from getting pinched or twisted. If you have access to one end of the chains, just slip the chain through the hose. Otherwise, slit the hose down the middle, and slip it over the swing set chains. Close the slit hose with a few wraps of duct tape.

Make a play phone Transform your old garden hose into a fun new telephone for the kids. Cut any length of hose you desire. Stick a funnel at each end and attach it with glue or tape. Now the kids can talk for as long as they want, with no roaming charges.

Protect your handsaw and ice skate blades Keep your handsaw blade sharp and safe by protecting it with a length of garden hose. Just cut a piece of hose to the length you need, slit it along its length, and slip it over the teeth. This is a good way to protect the blades of your ice skates on the way to the rink and your cooking knives when you pack them for a camping trip.

Make a paint can grip You don't want that heavy paint can to slip and spill. Plus those thin wire handles can really cut into your hand. Get a better grip by cutting a short length of hose. Slit it down the middle and encase the paint can handle.

Make a sander for curves If you've got a tight concave surface to sand—a piece of cove molding, for example—grab a 10-inch (25-centimeter) length of garden hose. Split open the hose lengthwise and insert one edge of the sandpaper. Wrap it around the hose, cut it to fit, and insert the other end in the slit. Firmly close the slit with a bit of duct tape. Get stroking!

✻ Gloves

Grip a stubborn jar lid It's a jarring experience when you can't open a jar of peanut butter or olives. If the lid just won't come loose, don some rubber gloves. You'll get a better grip to unscrew the top.

Make an ice pack If you need an ice pack in a hurry, fill a kitchen rubber glove with ice. Close the wrist with a rubber band to contain water from the melting ice. When you're done, turn the glove inside out to dry.

Paper-sorting finger Don't fancy licking your finger when you riffle through a stack of papers or dollar bills? Cut off the index finger piece from an old rubber glove and you have an ideal sheath for your finger the next time you have to quickly sort through some papers.

Make strong rubber bands If you need some extra-strong rubber bands, cut up old rubber gloves. Make horizontal cuts in the finger sections for small rubber bands and in the body of the glove for large ones.

Latex surgical gloves for extra insulation You've got a good pair of gloves or mittens, but your hands still get cold while shoveling the snow or doing other outdoor activities. Try slipping on a pair of latex surgical gloves underneath your usual mittens or gloves. The rubber is a super insulator, so your hands will stay toasty, and dry too.

Clean your knickknacks Need to dust that collection of glass animals or other delicate items? Put on some fabric gloves—the softer the better—to clean your bric-a-brac thoroughly.

Dust a chandelier If your chandelier has become a haven for spiderwebs and dust, try this surefire dusting tip. Soak some old fabric gloves in window cleaner. Slip them on and wipe off the lighting fixture. You'll beam at the gleaming results.

Remove cat hair Here's a quick and easy way to remove cat hair from upholstery: Put on a rubber glove and wet it. When you rub it against fabric, the cat hair will stick to the glove. If you are worried about getting the upholstery slightly damp, test it in an inconspicuous area first.

✳ Glycerin

Make your own soap Homemade soap is a great gift and snap to make if you have glycerin and a microwave. Here's how: Cut the glycerin material, usually sold in blocks, into 2-inch (5-centimeter) cubes. Using a microwave set at half-power, zap several cubes in a glass container for 30 seconds at a time—checking and stirring as needed—until the glycerin melts. Add drops of color dye or scents at this point,

if you wish. Pour the melted glycerin into soap or candy molds. If you don't have any molds, fill the bottom 3/4 inch (2 centimeters) of a polystyrene cup. Let harden for 30 minutes.

Clean a freezer spill Spilled sticky foods that are frozen to the bottom of your freezer don't have a chance against glycerin. Unstick the spill and wipe it clean with a rag dabbed with glycerin, a natural solvent.

Remove tar stains Do you think it's impossible to remove a tar or mustard stain? It's not, if you use glycerin. Rub glycerin into the spot and leave it for about an hour. Then, with paper towels, gently remove the spot using a blot-and-lift motion. You may need to do this several times.

Make new liquid soap Wondering what to do with those little leftover slivers of soap? Add a bit of glycerin and crush them together with some warm water. Pour the mixture into a pump bottle. You'll have liquid soap on the cheap.

✳ Golf Gear

Make a golf-tee tie rack If your ties are scattered about the closet or your room, try using golf tees to get them organized. Sand and paint a length of pine board. Drill 1/8-inch (3-millimeter) holes every 2 inches (5 centimeters). Dip the tip of each tee in yellow carpenter's glue and tap it into a hole. Hang the tie rack on the closet wall or inside the door. A perfect gift for the golfer in your life.

Aerate your lawn Kill two birds with one stone by wearing your golf shoes to aerate your lawn the next time you mow. The grip that a golf shoe gives you is also a good idea if you have to push the mower up a hill.

Fill stripped screw holes You're replacing a rusty door hinge when you discover that a screw won't grip because its hole has gotten too big. The fix is easy. Dip the tip of a golf tee in yellow carpenter's glue and tap the tee into the hole. Cut the tee flush with the door frame surface with a utility knife. When the glue dries, you can drill a new pilot hole for the screw in the same spot.

H

❋ Hair Conditioner

Take off makeup Put your face first. Why buy expensive makeup removers when a perfectly good substitute sits in your shower stall? Hair conditioner quickly and easily removes makeup for much less money than name-brand makeup removers.

Unstick a ring Grandma's antique ring just got stuck on your middle finger. Now what? Grab a bottle of hair conditioner and slick down the finger. The ring should slide right off.

Protect your shoes in foul weather Here's a way to keep salt and chemicals off your shoes during the winter: Lather your shoes or boots with hair conditioner to protect them from winter's harsh elements. It's a good leather conditioner too.

Lubricate a zipper You're racing out the door, throwing on your jacket, and dang! Your zipper's stuck, so you yank and pull until it finally zips up. A dab of hair conditioner rubbed along the zipper teeth can help you avoid this bother next time.

Smooth shave-irritated legs After you shave your legs, they may feel rough and irritated. Rub on hair conditioner; it acts like a lotion and can soothe the hurt away.

 DID **You** KNOW?

Hair conditioner has been around for about 50 years. While researching ways to help World War II burn victims, Swiss chemists developed a compound that improved the health of hair. In the 1950s other scientists developing fabric softeners found that the same material could soften hair.

Despite our efforts to keep hair healthy with hair conditioner, we still lose on average between 50 and 100 strands a day. For most of us, thankfully, there are still many more strands left: People with blond hair have an average of 140,000 strands of hair, brown-haired people, 100,000, and redheads, 90,000.

Smooth-sliding shower curtain Tired of yanking on the shower curtain? Instead of closing smoothly, does it stutter along the curtain rod, letting the shower spray water onto the floor? Rub the rod with hair conditioner, and the curtain will glide across it.

Prevent rust on tools Every good do-it-yourselfer knows how important it is to take care of the tools in your toolbox. One way to condition them and keep rust from invading is to rub them down with hair conditioner.

Clean and shine your houseplants Do your houseplants need a good dusting? Feel like your peace lily could use a makeover? Put a bit of hair conditioner on a soft cloth and rub the plant leaves to remove dust and shine the leaves.

Oil skate wheels Do your child's skateboard wheels whine? Or are the kids complaining about their in-line and roller skates sticking? Try this trick: Rub hair conditioner on the axles of the wheels, and they'll be down the block with their rehabilitated equipment in no time.

Shine stainless steel Forget expensive stainless steel polishers. Apply hair conditioner to your faucets, golf clubs, chrome fixtures, or anything else that needs a shine. Rub it off with a soft cloth, and you'll be impressed with the gleam.

Clean silk garments Do you dare to ignore that "dry clean only" label in your silk shirt? Here's a low-cost alternative to sending it out. Fill the sink with water (warm water for whites and cold water for colors). Add a tablespoon of hair conditioner. Immerse the shirt in the water and let it sit for a few minutes. Then pull it out, rinse, and hang it up to dry. The conditioner keeps the shirt feeling silky smooth.

✳ Hair Spray

Exterminate houseflies An annoying, buzzing housefly has been bobbing and weaving around your house for two days. Make it bite the dust with a squirt of hair spray. Take aim and fire. Watch the fly drop. But make sure the hair spray is water-soluble so that, if any spray hits the walls, you'll be able to wipe it clean. Works on wasps and bees too.

Reduce runs in pantyhose Often those bothersome runs in your pantyhose or stockings start at the toes. Head off a running disaster by spraying hair spray on the toes of a new pair of pantyhose. The spray strengthens the threads and makes them last longer.

Remove lipstick from fabric Has someone been kissing your shirts? Apply hair spray to the lipstick stain and let it sit for a few minutes. Wipe off the hair spray and the stain should come off with it. Then wash your shirts as usual.

Preserve a Christmas wreath When you buy a wreath at your local Christmas tree lot, it's fresh, green, and lush. By the time a week has gone by, it's starting to shed needles and look a little dry. To make the wreath last longer, grab your can of hair spray and spritz it all over as soon as you get the fresh wreath home. The hair spray traps the moisture in the needles.

Protect children's artwork Picture this: Your preschooler has just returned home with a priceless work of art demanding that it find a place on the refrigerator door. Before you stick it up, preserve the creation with hair spray, to help it last longer. This works especially well on chalk pictures, keeping them from being smudged so easily.

Preserve your shoes' shine After you've lovingly polished your shoes to give them the just-from-the-store look, lightly spray them with hair spray. The shoe polish won't rub off so easily with this coat of protection.

Keep recipe cards splatter-free Don't let the spaghetti sauce on the stove splatter on your favorite recipe card. A good coating of hair spray will prevent the card from being ruined by kitchen eruptions. With the protection, they wipe off easily.

DID *You* KNOW?

Here are some great moments in hair-spray history:
- A Norwegian inventor developed the technology that became the aerosol can in the early 1900s. What would hair spray be without aerosol cans?
- L'Oréal introduced its hair spray, called Elnett, in 1960.

The next year Alberto VO5 introduced its version.
- In 1964 hair spray surpassed lipstick as women's most popular cosmetic aid. Must have been all those beehive hairdos.
- Hair spray makes possible the bumper sticker that reads

"The Higher the Hair, the Closer to God."
- In 1984 the hair spray on Michael Jackson's hair ignited while he was rehearsing a commercial for Pepsi.

Keep drapes dirt-free Did you just buy new drapes or have your old ones cleaned? Want to keep that like-new look for a while? The trick is to apply several coats of hair spray, letting each coat dry thoroughly before the next one.

Remove ink marks on garments Your toddler just went wild with a ballpoint pen on your white upholstery and your new shirt. Squirt the stain with hair spray and the pen marks should come right off.

Extend the life of cut flowers A bouquet of cut flowers is such a beautiful thing, you want to do whatever you can to postpone wilting. Just as it preserves your hairstyle, a spritz of hair spray can preserve your cut flowers. Stand a foot away from the bouquet and give them a quick spray, just on the undersides of the leaves and petals.

✳ Hydrogen Peroxide

Remove stains of unknown origin Can't tell what that stain is? Still want to remove it? Try this sure-fire remover: Mix a teaspoon of 3% hydrogen peroxide with a little cream of tartar or a dab of non-gel toothpaste. Rub the paste on the stain with a soft cloth. Rinse. The stain, whatever it was, should be gone.

> **TAKE CARE** Hydrogen peroxide is considered corrosive—even in the relatively weak 3% solution sold as a household antiseptic. Don't put it in your eyes or around your nose. Don't swallow it or try to set it on fire either.

Remove wine stains Hydrogen peroxide works well to remove wine stains so don't worry if you spill while you quaff.

Remove grass stains If grass stains are ruining your kids' clothes, hydrogen peroxide may bring relief. Mix a few drops of ammonia with just 1 teaspoon 3% hydrogen peroxide. Rub on the stain. As soon as it disappears, rinse and launder.

Remove mildew The sight and smell of mildew is a bathroom's enemy. Bring out the tough ammunition: a bottle of 3% hydrogen peroxide. Don't water it down, just attack directly by pouring the peroxide on the offending area. Wipe it clean. Mildew surrender.

Remove bloodstains This works only on fresh bloodstains: Apply 3% hydrogen peroxide directly to the stain, rinse with fresh water, and launder as usual.

Sanitize your cutting board Hydrogen peroxide is a surefire bacteria-killer—just the ally you need to fight the proliferation of bacteria on your cutting board, especially after you cut chicken or other meat. To kill the germs on your cutting board, use a paper towel to wipe the board down with vinegar, then use another paper towel to wipe it with hydrogen peroxide. Ordinary 3% peroxide is fine.

?? DID *You* KNOW?

Hydrogen peroxide, (H_2O_2) was discovered in 1818. The most common household use for it is as an antiseptic and bleaching agent. (It's the key ingredient in most teeth-whitening kits and all-fabric oxygen bleaches, for example). Textile manufacturers use higher concentrations of hydrogen peroxide to bleach fabric.

During World War II, hydrogen peroxide solutions fueled torpedoes and rockets.

✱ Ice-Cream Scoops

Scoop meatballs and cookie dough If you want uniform-size meatballs every time, use an ice-cream scoop to measure out the perfect orbs. This method works well for cookies too. Dip the scoop in the dough, and plop the ball on the cookie sheet. You'll end up with cookies all the same size—no tiffs over which one is the largest.

Make butter balls At your next large family gathering, scoop out large globes of butter or margarine to serve to your guests. A smaller scoop, or melon baller, can create individual-size balls of butter.

Create sand castles On your next trip to the beach, throw an ice-cream scoop into your bag. Your kids will have a fun tool for making their sand castles down by the shore. The scoop allows them to make interesting rounded shapes with the sand.

DID *You* KNOW?

Spade, dipper, spatula, or spoon—the styles of ice-cream scoop you can buy are almost as varied as the flavors of ice cream you'll put in them. One Web site lists 168 choices of the device! Here's some more dish on ice-cream scoops that you might not know:

▪ A scoop introduced during the Depression, called the slicer, helped the ice-cream parlor owner scoop out the same amount every time and not give away any extra.

▪ Many ways have been developed to help the ice cream plop out of a scoop. Some scoops split apart; others have a wire scraper to nudge the stuff out. Still others have antifreeze in the handle or a button on the back to make it pop out.

▪ Some ice-cream scoops, also called molds, can imprint symbols on the ice cream, for fraternal organizations and others.

▪ Most scoops come in two standard sizes—#10 and #20, indicating the number of level scoops you'll get from a quart of ice cream. But since most people make rounded scoops, it's more practical to think of a #10 as giving you about seven rounded scoops and a #20, about 12.

Plant seeds If you're out in the garden faced with a plot of earth that needs seeding, turn to your kitchen drawer for help. An ice-cream scoop will make equal-sized planting holes for the seeds for your future harvest.

Repot a houseplant Does dirt scatter everywhere when you are repotting your houseplants? An ice-cream scoop is the perfect way to add soil to the new pot without making a mess.

Pre-scoop ice cream If you're tiring of constantly being bugged by your kids for a scoop of ice cream, try this tip. Scoop several scoops of ice cream onto a wax-paper-lined cookie sheet, spaced apart. Place the sheet with the scoops back in your freezer to re-harden. Remove the scoops from the wax paper and pile them up in a self-sealing plastic bag. The next time the kids want a scoop of strawberry ice cream, they can help themselves.

✳ Ice Cubes

Water hanging plants and Christmas trees If you're constantly reaching for the step stool to water hard-to-reach hanging plants, ice cubes can help. Just toss several cubes into the pots. The ice melts and waters the plants and does it without causing a sudden downpour from the drain hole. This is also a good way to water your Christmas tree, whose base may be hard to reach with a watering can.

Remove dents in carpeting If you've recently rearranged the furniture in your living room, you know that heavy pieces can leave ugly indents in your carpet. Use ice cubes to remove them. Put an ice cube, for example, on the spot where the chair leg stood. Let it melt, then brush up the dent. Rug rehab completed.

Smooth caulk seams You're caulking around the bathtub, but the sticky caulk compound keeps adhering to your finger as you try to smooth it. If you don't do something about it, the finished job will look pretty awful. Solve the problem by running an ice cube along the caulk line. This forms the caulk into a nice even bead and the caulk will never stick to the ice cube.

Help iron out wrinkles So your ready-to-wear shirt is full of wrinkles and there's no time to wash it again. Turn on the iron and wrap an ice cube in a soft cloth. Rub over the wrinkle just before you iron and the shirt will smooth out.

Mask the taste of medicine No matter what flavor your local pharmacist offers in children's medicine, kids can still turn up their noses at the taste. Have them suck on an ice cube before taking the medicine. This numbs the taste buds and allows the medicine to go down, without the spoonful of sugar.

Pluck a splinter Parental challenge #573: removing a splinter from the hand of a screaming, squirming toddler. Before you start jabbing with that needle, grab an ice cube and numb the area. This should make splinter removal more painless and quicker.

Prevent a blister from a burn Have you burned yourself? An ice cube applied to the burn will stop it from blistering.

Cool water for your pets Imagine what it's like to wear a fur coat in the middle of summer. Your rabbits, hamsters, and gerbils will love your thoughtfulness if you place a few cubes in their water dish to cool down. This is also a good tip for your cat, who's spent the hot morning lounging on your bed, or your dog, who's just had a long romp in the park.

Unstick a sluggish disposal If your garbage disposal is not working at its optimum because of grease buildup (not something stuck inside), ice cubes may help. Throw some down the disposal and grind them up. The grease will cling to the ice, making the disposal residue-free.

Make creamy salad dressing Do you want to make your homemade salad dressing as smooth and even as the bottled variety? Try this: Put all the dressing ingredients in a jar with a lid, then add a single ice cube. Close the lid and shake vigorously. Spoon out the ice cube and serve. Your guests will be impressed by how creamy your salad dressing is.

Stop sauces from curdling Imagine this: Your snooty neighbors are over for a Sunday brunch featuring eggs Benedict. But when you mixed butter and egg yolks with lemon juice to make hollandaise sauce for the dish, it curdled. What do you do? Place an ice cube in the saucepan, stir, and watch the sauce turn back into a silky masterpiece.

DID *You* KNOW?

Here are some cold, hard facts about ice cubes:
- To make clear ice cubes, use distilled water and boil it first. It's the air in the water that causes ice cubes to turn cloudy.

- A British Columbian company sells fake ice cubes that glow and blink in your drink.
- Those aren't ice cubes in that inviting drink in the print advertisement, because they'd never last under hot studio lights. They're plastic or glass.

- The word ice cube has been commercially co-opted over the years. To name two examples: a vintage candy (the chocolate pat wrapped in silver paper) and a well-known rapper/actor.

De-fat soup and stews Want to get as much fat as possible out of your homemade soup or stew as quickly as possible? Fill a metal ladle with ice cubes and skim the bottom of the ladle over the top of the liquid in the soup pot. Fat will collect on the ladle.

Reheat rice Does your leftover rice dry out when you reheat it in the microwave? Try this: Put an ice cube on top of the rice when you put it in the microwave. The ice cube will melt as the rice reheats, giving the rice much-needed moisture.

Remove gum from clothing You're just about to walk out the door when Junior points to the gum stuck to his pants. Keep your cool and grab an ice cube. Rub the ice on the gum to harden it, then scrape it off with a spoon.

✳ Ice Cube Trays

Divide a drawer If your junk drawer is an unsightly mess, insert a plastic ice cube tray for easy, low-cost organization. One "cube" can hold paper clips, the next, rubber bands, another, stamps. It's another small way to bring order to your life.

Organize your workbench If you're looking through your toolbox for that perfect-sized fastener that you know you have somewhere, here's the answer to your problem. An ice cube tray can help you organize and store small parts you may need at one time or another, such as screws, nails, bolts, and other diminutive hardware.

Keep parts in sequence You're disassembling your latest swap-meet acquisition that has lots of small parts and worry that you'll never be able to get them back together again in the correct sequence. Use an old plastic ice cube tray to help keep the small parts in the right order until you get around to reassembling it. If you really want to be organized, mark the sequence by putting a number on a piece of masking tape in each compartment. The bottom half of an egg carton will also work.

A painter's palette Your child, a budding Mary Cassatt or Picasso, requires a palette to mix colors. A plastic ice cube tray provides the perfect sturdy container for holding and mixing small amounts of paints and watercolors.

Freeze extra eggs Are you overstocked on bargain-priced eggs? Freeze them for future baking projects. Medium eggs are just the right size to freeze in plastic ice cube trays with one egg in each cell, with no spillover. After they freeze, pop them out into a self-sealing plastic bag. Defrost as many as you need when the time comes.

Freeze foods in handy cubes An ice cube tray is a great way to freeze small amounts of many different kinds of food for later use. The idea is to freeze the food in the tray's cells, pop out the frozen cubes, and put them in a labeled self-sealing plastic bag for future use. Some ideas:

- Your garden is brimming with basil, but your family can't eat pesto as quickly as you're making it. Make a big batch of pesto (without the cheese) and freeze it in ice cube trays. Later, when you're ready to enjoy summer's bounty in the middle of winter, defrost as many cubes as you need, add cheese, and mix with pasta.

- There's only so much sweet potato your growing baby will eat at one sitting. Freeze the rest of it in trays for a future high-chair meal.

- The recipe calls for 1/2 cup chopped celery, but you have an entire head of celery and no plans to use it soon. Chop it all, place in an ice cube tray, add a little water, and freeze. The next time you need chopped celery, it's at your fingertips. This works well for onions, carrots, or any other vegetable you'd use for stew and such.

- Are you always throwing out leftover parsley? Just chop it up, put it in an ice cube tray with a little water, and freeze for future use. Works with other fresh herbs.

- There's a bit of chicken soup left in the bottom of the pot. It's too little for another meal, but you hate to throw it out. Freeze the leftovers, and the next time you make soup or another dish that needs some seasoning, grab a cube or two.

- If you are cooking a homemade broth, make an extra-large batch and freeze the excess in ice cube trays. You'll have broth cubes to add instant flavor to future no-time-to-cook dishes. You can do the same with a leftover half-can of broth.

- Here's what to do with that half-drunk bottle of red or white wine: Freeze the wine into cubes that can be used later in pasta sauce, casseroles, or stews.

Kids' Stuff This is a great summertime project. Collect a bunch of small objects around your house: **buttons, beads, tiny toys**. Then get an **ice cube tray** and place one or more of the items in each tray cube. Fill the tray with water. Then cut a length of **yarn** (long enough to make a comfortable **necklace, bracelet, or anklet**). Lay the yarn in the ice cube tray, making sure it hits every cube and is submerged. **Freeze**. When frozen, pop out and tie on the jewelry. The kids will cool off while they see how long their creation takes to melt.

✳ Ice Scrapers

Remove splattered paint If you just painted your bathroom and have gotten paint splatters all over
your acrylic bathtub, use an ice scraper to
remove them without scratching the tub surface.
Use ice scrapers to remove paint specks from any
other nonmetallic surfaces.

Smooth wood filler Do you have small gouges in your wood floors? Want to use wood
filler to make them smooth again? An ice scraper can help you do the job right.
Once you've packed wood filler into a hole, the ice scraper is the perfect tool to
smooth and level it.

Remove wax from skis Every experienced skier knows that old wax buildup on skis can
slow you down. An ice scraper can swiftly and neatly take off that old wax and
prepare your plows for the next coat.

Scrape out your freezer Your windshield isn't the only place ice and frost build up. If the
frost is building up in your freezer and you want to delay the defrosting chore
for a while, head out to the car and borrow the scraper.

Clean up bread dough No matter how much flour you put on your work surface, some
of that sticky bread dough always seems to stick to it. A clean ice scraper is just
the tool for skimming the sticky stuff off the work surface. In a pinch, a plastic
scraper can also substitute for a spatula for nonstick pans.

✻ Jars

Waterproof camping storage When you're boating or camping, keeping things like matches and paper money dry can be a challenge. Store items that you don't want to get wet in clear jars with screw tops that can't pop off. Even if you're backpacking, plastic peanut butter jars are light enough not to weigh you down, plus they provide more protection for crushable items than a resealable plastic bag.

Create workshop storage Don't let workshop hardware get mixed up. Keep all your nails, screws, nuts, and bolts organized by screwing jar lids to the underside of a wooden or melamine shelf. (Make sure the screw won't poke through the top of the shelf.) Then put each type of hardware in its own jar, and screw each jar onto its lid. You'll keep everything off the counters, and  by using clear jars, you can find what you need at a glance. Works great for storing seeds in the potting shed too!

Stamp out cookies Just about any clean, empty wide-mouthed jar is just the right size for cutting cookies out of any rolled dough.

Use to dry gloves or mittens You took a break from shoveling snow to come in for soup and a sandwich, and want to get back to work. To help your gloves or mittens dry out during lunch, pull each one over the bottom of an empty jar, then stand the jar upside down on a radiator or hot-air vent. Warm air will fill the jar and radiate out to dry damp clothing in a jiffy.

Make a piggy bank You can encourage thriftiness in your child by making a piggy bank out of any jar with a metal lid. Take the lid off the jar, place it on a flat work surface like a cutting board, and tap a screwdriver with a hammer to carefully punch a slot hole in the center. Then use the hammer or a rasp to smooth the rough edges on the underside of the slot to protect fingers from scratches. Personalizing the mini-bank with paints or collage makes a fun rainy-day project.

Collect insects Help the kids observe nature by gently collecting fireflies and other interesting bugs in clear jars. Punch a few small airholes in the lids for ventilation. Don't make the holes too large, or your bugs will escape! Don't forget to let the critters go after you've admired them.

Make baby-food portions Take advantage of the fact that baby-food jars are already the perfect size for baby's portions. Clean them thoroughly before reuse, and fill them with anything from pureed carrots to vanilla pudding. Attach a spoon with a rubber band, and you've got a perfect take-along meal when you travel with your little one.

Bring along baby's treats Dry cereal can be a nutritious snack for your baby. No need to bring the whole box when you leave the house; pack individual servings in clean, dry baby-food jars. If they get spilled, the mess is minimal.

SCIENCE FAIR

Turn a large **wide-mouthed jar** into a **miniature biosphere**. Clean the jar and lid, then place a handful of **pebbles** and **charcoal chips** in the bottom. Add several trowelfuls of slightly damp, sterilized **potting soil**. Select a few **plants** that like similar conditions (such as ferns and mosses, which both like moderate light and moisture). Add a few colorful **stones, seashells,** or a piece of **driftwood**. Add **water** to make the terrarium humid. Tighten the lid and place the jar in dim light for two days. Then display in bright light but not direct sunlight. You shouldn't need to add water—it cycles from the plants to the soil and back again.

It's important to use sterilized soil to avoid introducing unwanted organisms. The charcoal chips filter the water as it recycles.

✱ Jar Lids

Make safety reflectors Is your driveway difficult to maneuver after dark? With some scrap wood and jar lids you can make inexpensive reflectors to guide drivers. Spray the lids with reflective paint, screw them to the sides of stakes cut from the scrap wood, and drive the stakes into the ground. Voilà! No more dinged fenders or flattened flowers!

Save half-eaten fruit Got half a peach, apple, or orange you'd like to save for later? Wrap a jar lid in plastic wrap or wax paper and then set the fruit cut side down on it in the refrigerator. A bit of lemon juice on the cut surface of the fruit will help prevent discoloration. And why throw out the contents of a partially consumed glass of milk or juice? Just cover it with a lid and refrigerate to keep it fresh.

Cut biscuits Yum, homemade biscuits! Lids with deep rims or canning jar bands (the part with the cut-out center) make impromptu biscuit cutters. Use different-sized lids for Papa, Mama, and Baby biscuits. Dip the bottom edge of the lid in flour to keep it from sticking when you press it into the dough. Avoid lids whose rims are rolled inward; the dough can get stuck inside and be hard to extract.

Create a spoon rest Place a jar lid on the stove or the countertop next to the stove while cooking. After stirring a pot, rest the spoon on the lid, and there'll be less to clean up later.

Drip catcher under honey jar Honey is delicious, but it can be a sticky mess. At the table, place the honey jar on a plastic lid to stop drips from getting on the tabletop. Store it that way, too, and your cabinet shelf will stay cleaner.

Make coasters to protect furniture Wet drinking glasses and hot coffee mugs can really do a number on furniture finishes. The simple solution is to keep plenty of coasters on hand. Glue rounds of felt or cork to both sides of a jar lid (especially flat canning jar lids, which shouldn't be reused for canning, anyhow), and keep a stack wherever cups and glasses accumulate in your house. Your furniture will thank you!

Kids' Stuff What's on your fridge door? Probably a bunch of magnets and children's artwork. Combine the two and you've got something both useful and beautiful. For a stimulating **craft project**, set out a bunch of **fun materials**—paints, glue, fabrics, family photos, googly eyes, glitter, pompoms, or even just paper and markers—and let your child decorate several **jar lids**. Glue some strong **magnets** from the hardware store on the backs (**hot-melt glue** works well), and when they're done, have an unveiling—with refreshments, of course!

Saucers for potted plants Lids with a rim are perfect for catching excess water under small potted plants, and unlike your ceramic saucers, if they get encrusted with minerals, you won't mind throwing them out.

Organize your desk Corral those paper clips and other small office items that clutter up your desk, by putting them in jar lids with deep rims. Works great to hold loose change or earrings on your dresser or bureau too. A quick coat of matte spray paint and an acrylic sealant will make them more attractive and water-resistant.

✳ Ketchup

Get rid of chlorine green If chlorine from swimming pools is turning your blond tresses green or just giving your hair an unwanted scent, eliminate the problem with a ketchup shampoo. To avoid a mess, do it in the shower. Massage ketchup generously into your hair and leave it for fifteen minutes, then wash it out, using baby shampoo. The odor and color should be gone.

Make copper pots gleam When copper pots and pans—or decorative molds—get dull and tarnished, brighten them with ketchup. It's cheaper than commercial tarnish removers and safe to apply without gloves. Coat the copper surface with a thin layer of the condiment. Let it sit for five to thirty minutes. Acids in the ketchup will react with the tarnish and remove it. Rinse the pan and dry immediately.

Keep silver jewelry sparkling Let ketchup do the work of shining tarnished silver. If your ring, bracelet, or earring has a smooth surface, dunk it in a small bowl of ketchup for a few minutes. If it has a tooled or detailed surface, use an old toothbrush to work ketchup into the crevices. To avoid damaging the silver, don't leave the ketchup on any longer than necessary. Rinse your jewelry clean, dry it, and it's ready to wear.

❓ DID *You* KNOW?

Ketchup originated in the Far East as a salty fish sauce. The word *ketchup* (also spelled *catsup*) probably comes from Chinese or Malay. Brought to the West, it was transformed by the 1700s into a huge variety of sauces with vegetable and animal main ingredients. To this day, you can still find banana ketchup, mushroom ketchup, and other variants. Tomato ketchup is a relative newcomer, first sold in 1837, but it is now found in more than 90 percent of North American homes.

✳ Keys

Weigh down drapery Need to keep your draperies hanging properly? Just slip a few old keys in the hems. If you are worried about them falling out, tack them in place with a few stitches going through the holes in the keys. You can also keep blind cords from tangling by using keys as weights on their bottoms.

Make fishing sinkers Old unused keys make great weights for your fishing line. Since they already have a hole in them, attaching them to the line is a cinch. Whenever you come across an unidentified key, toss it into your tackle box.

Create an instant plumb bob You are getting ready to hang wallpaper and you need to draw a perfectly vertical line on the wall to get you started. Take a length of cord or string and tie a key or two to one end. You've got a plumb bob that will give you a true vertical. You can do the same with a pair of scissors too.

✳ Kool-Aid

Clean your dishwasher Is the inside of your dishwasher rusty brown? The cause is a high iron content in your water. Dump a packet of unsweetened lemonade Kool-Aid into the soap drawer and run the washer through a hot-water cycle. When you open the door, the inside will be as white as the day you bought the machine.

Clean rust from concrete Nasty rust stains on your concrete? Mix unsweetened lemonade Kool-Aid with hot water. Scrub and the rust stain should come right out.

Color wall paints Mix any flavor of unsweetened Kool-Aid into water-based latex paint to alter its color. Or mix unsweetened Kool-Aid with water to create your own watercolors, but don't give them to the kids—Kool-Aid stains can be tough to remove.

Make play makeup lip gloss Make some tasty lip gloss for little girls playing dress-up. Let the girls pick their favorite presweetened Kool-Aid flavor. Blend a package of the drink mix with 3 tablespoons vegetable shortening, then microwave for one minute. Transfer to a 35mm film canister and refrigerate overnight.

* Ladders

Make display shelving Convert a short wooden
stepladder to shelving for displaying plants and
collectibles. It's as easy as one, two, three:

1. Remove the folding metal spreader that holds
the front and rear legs of the ladder together.
Then position the ladder's rear legs upright
against the wall and attach two 1 x 2 cleats to
fix the distance between the front and rear legs.
Position the cleats so that their tops are level with the top of a rung.

2. Each shelf will be supported at front by an existing rung. To support the
back of each shelf, attach a cleat between the rear legs, positioning it at the
same level as a rung.

3. Cut plywood or boards to fit as shelves and screw them to the rungs and
cleats. Now screw the centermost rear cleat to the wall and you're done.

Construct a rustic indoor trellis Give your vines and trailing plants something to climb
on. Using wall anchors, attach vinyl-covered hooks to your wall and hang an
attractive straight ladder (or a segment of one) from the hooks, positioning the
ladder's legs on the floor a couple of inches from the wall. It's easy to train
potted plants to grow up and around this rustic support. It looks nice on a
porch too.

Display quilts and more Don't let your fancy stitching languish in the closet! For that
homespun feel, a ladder is a great way to display lacework, crochet, quilts,
and throws. To prevent rough surfaces from damaging delicate fabrics,
smooth wooden ladder rungs with sandpaper or metal rungs with steel wool
if necessary.

Create a garden focal point Got some old wooden straight ladders around that you no
longer trust? Show your whimsical side by using them to create a decorative
garden archway. Cut two sections of old ladder to the desired height and position them opposite one another along a path. Screw the legs of each one to two

strong posts sunk deeply into the soil. Cut a
third ladder section to fit across the top of the
two others and tie it to them using supple
grapevine, young willow twigs, or heavy jute
twine. Festoon your archway with fun and fan-
ciful stuff, such as old tools, or let climbing
plants clamber up and over it. It also works well
as the entryway to an enclosed area.

Plop it down and plant it When a ladder is truly on its last legs, it can still be of service
lying down. On the ground, a straight ladder or the front part of a stepladder
makes a shallow planter with ready-made sections that look sweet filled with
annuals, herbs, or salad greens. After a couple of years of contact with soil, a
wooden ladder will decompose, so don't expect to use it again.

Make a temporary table The big family picnic is a summertime staple, but where to put
all the food? You can cook up a makeshift table in no time by placing a straight
ladder across two sawhorses. Top it with plywood and cover it with a tablecloth. The ladder will provide strength to support your buffet, as well as any
guests who might lean on it.

Make a pot rack Accessorize your country kitchen with a
pot rack made from a sawed-off section of a
wooden straight ladder with thin, round rungs.
Sand the cut ends smooth; then tie two pieces
of sturdy rope to the rungs at either end. To suspend your pot rack, screw four large metal eye
hooks into the ceiling, going into the joists;
then tie the other ends of the ropes to them.

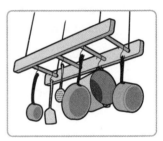

Hang some S-hooks from the rungs to hold your kitchenware. Leave the rack
unfinished if you want a rustic look. Or paint or stain it if you want a more
finished look.

super item
34 *uses!* Lemons

Eliminate fireplace odor There's nothing cozier on a cold winter night than a warm fire
burning in the fireplace—unless the fire happens to smell horrible. Next time
you have a fire that sends a stench into the room, try throwing a few lemon
peels into the flames. Or simply burn some lemon peels along with your firewood as a preventive measure.

Get rid of tough stains on marble You probably think of marble as stone, but it is
really petrified calcium (also known as old seashells). That explains why it is so

porous and easily stained and damaged. Those stains can be hard to remove. If washing won't remove a stubborn stain, try this: Cut a lemon in half, dip the exposed flesh into some table salt, and rub it vigorously on the stain. But do this only as a last resort; acid can damage marble. Rinse well.

Make a room scent/humidifier Freshen and moisturize the air in your home on dry winter days. Make your own room scent that also doubles as a humidifier. If you have a wood-burning stove, place an enameled cast-iron pot or bowl on top, fill with water, and add lemon (and/or orange) peels, cinnamon sticks, cloves, and apple skins. No wood-burning stove? Use your stovetop instead and just simmer the water periodically.

Neutralize cat-box odor You don't have to use an aerosol spray to neutralize foul-smelling cat-box odors or freshen the air in your bathroom. Just cut a couple of lemons in half. Then place them, cut side up, in a dish in the room, and the air will soon smell lemon-fresh.

DID *You* KNOW?

With all due respect to Trini Lopez and his rendition of "Lemon Tree," a lemon tree actually isn't very pretty—and its flower isn't sweet either. The tree's straggly branches bear little resemblance to an orange tree's dense foliage, and its purplish flowers lack the pleasant fragrance of orange blossoms. Yes, the fruit of the "poor lemon" is sour—thanks to its high citric acid content—but it is hardly "impossible to eat." Sailors have been sucking on vitamin-C-rich lemons for hundreds of years to prevent scurvy. To this day, the British navy requires ships to carry enough lemons so that every sailor can have one ounce of juice daily.

Deodorize a humidifier When your humidifier starts to smell funky, deodorize it with ease: Just pour 3 or 4 teaspoons lemon juice into the water. It will not only remove the off odor but will replace it with a lemon-fresh fragrance. Repeat every couple of weeks to keep the odor from returning.

Clean tarnished brass Say good-bye to tarnish on brass, copper, or stainless steel. Make a paste of lemon juice and salt (or substitute baking soda or cream of tartar for the salt) and coat the affected area. Let it stay on for 5 minutes. Then wash in warm water, rinse, and polish dry. Use the same mixture to clean metal kitchen sinks too. Apply the paste, scrub gently, and rinse.

Polish chrome Get rid of mineral deposits and polish chrome faucets and other tarnished chrome. Simply rub lemon rind over the chrome and watch it shine! Rinse well and dry with a soft cloth.

Prevent potatoes from turning brown Potatoes and cauliflower tend to turn brown when boiling, especially when you're having company for dinner. You can make sure the white vegetables stay white by squeezing a teaspoon of fresh lemon juice into the cooking water.

Freshen the fridge Remove refrigerator odors with ease. Dab lemon juice on a cotton ball or sponge and leave it in the fridge for several hours. Make sure to toss out any malodorous items that might be causing the bad smell.

Brighten dull aluminum Make those dull pots and pans sparkle, inside and out. Just rub the cut side of half a lemon all over them and buff with a soft cloth.

> *Kids' Stuff* Kids love to send and receive secret messages, and what better way to do it than by writing them in **invisible ink**? All they need is **lemon juice** (fresh-squeezed or bottled) to use as ink, a **cotton swab** to write with, and a sheet of **white paper** to write on. When the ink is dry and they are ready to read the invisible message, have them hold the paper up to bright sunlight or a lightbulb. The heat will cause the writing to darken to a pale brown and the message can be read! Make sure they don't overdo the heating and ignite the paper.

Keep rice from sticking To keep your rice from sticking together in a gloppy mass, add a spoonful of lemon juice to the boiling water when cooking. When the rice is done, let it cool for a few minutes, then fluff with a fork before serving.

Refresh cutting boards No wonder your kitchen cutting board smells! After all, you use it to chop onions, crush garlic, cut raw and cooked meat and chicken, and prepare fish. To get rid of the smell and help sanitize the cutting board, rub it all over with the cut side of half a lemon or wash it in undiluted juice straight from the bottle.

Keep guacamole green You've been making guacamole all day long for the big party, and you don't want it to turn brown on top before the guests arrive. The solution: Sprinkle a liberal amount of fresh lemon juice over it and it will stay fresh and green. The flavor of the lemon juice is a natural complement to the avocados in the guacamole. Make the fruit salad hours in advance too. Just squeeze some lemon juice onto the apple slices, and they'll stay snowy white.

Make soggy lettuce crisp Don't toss that soggy lettuce into the garbage. With the help of a little lemon juice you can toss it in a salad instead. Add the juice of half a lemon to a bowl of cold water. Then put the soggy lettuce in it and refrigerate for 1 hour. Make sure to dry the leaves completely before putting them into salads or sandwiches.

Keep insects out of the kitchen You don't need insecticides or ant traps to ant-proof your kitchen. Just give it the lemon treatment. First squirt some lemon juice on door thresholds and windowsills. Then squeeze lemon juice into any holes or cracks where the ants are getting in. Finally, scatter small slices of lemon peel around the outdoor entrance. The ants will get the message that they aren't welcome. Lemons are also effective against roaches and fleas: Simply mix the juice of 4 lemons (along with the rinds) with 1/2 gallon (2 liters) water and wash your floors with it; then watch the fleas and roaches flee. They hate the smell.

Clean your microwave Is the inside of your microwave caked with bits of hardened food? You can give it a good cleaning without scratching the surface with harsh cleansers or using a lot of elbow grease. Just mix 3 tablespoons lemon juice into 1 1/2 cups water in a microwave-safe bowl. Microwave on High for 5-10 minutes, allowing the steam to condense on the inside walls and ceiling of the oven. Then just wipe away the softened food with a dishrag.

Deodorize your garbage disposal If your garbage disposal is beginning to make your sink smell yucky, here's an easy way to deodorize it: Save leftover lemon and orange peels and toss them down the drain. To keep it smelling fresh, repeat once every month.

✳LEMONS **IN THE LAUNDRY**

Bleach delicate fabrics Ordinary household chlorine bleach can cause the iron in water to precipitate out into fabrics, leaving additional stains. For a mild, stain-free bleach, soak your delicates in a mixture of lemon juice and baking soda for at least half an hour before washing.

Remove unsightly underarm stains Avoid expensive dry-cleaning bills. You can remove unsightly underarm stains from shirts and blouses simply by scrubbing them with a mixture of equal parts lemon juice (or white vinegar) and water.

Tip **Before You Squeeze**

> To get the most juice out of fresh lemons, bring them to room temperature and roll them under your palm against the kitchen counter before squeezing. This will break down the connective tissue and juice-cell walls, allowing the lemon to release more liquid when you squeeze it.

Boost laundry detergent To remove rust and mineral discolorations from cotton T-shirts and briefs, pour 1 cup lemon juice into the washer during the wash cycle. The natural bleaching action of the juice will zap the stains and leave the clothes smelling fresh.

Rid clothes of mildew You unpack the clothes you've stored for the season and discover that some of the garments are stained with mildew. To get rid of mildew on clothes, make a paste of lemon juice and salt and rub it on the affected area, then dry the clothes in sunlight. Repeat the process until the stain is gone. This works well for rust stains on clothes too.

Whiten clothes Diluted or straight, lemon juice is a safe and effective fabric whitener when added to your wash water. Your clothes will also come out smelling lemon-fresh.

✴LEMONS **FOR HEALTH AND BEAUTY**

Lighten age spots Before buying expensive medicated creams to lighten unsightly liver spots and freckles, try this: Apply lemon juice directly to the area, let sit for 15 minutes, and then rinse your skin clean. Lemon juice is a safe and effective skin-lightening agent.

Create blond highlights For blond highlights worthy of the finest beauty salon, add 1/4 cup lemon juice to 3/4 cup water and rinse your hair with the mixture. Then sit in the sun until your hair dries. Lemon juice is a natural bleach. Don't forget to put on plenty of sunscreen before you sit out in the sun. To maximize the effect, repeat once daily for up to a week.

Clean and whiten nails Pamper your fingernails without the help of a manicurist. Add the juice of 1/2 lemon to 1 cup warm water and soak your fingertips in the mixture for 5 minutes. After pushing back the cuticles, rub some lemon peel back and forth against the nail.

SCIENCE FAIR

Turn a **lemon into a battery**! It won't start your car, but you will be able to feel the current with your tongue. Roll the lemon on a flat surface to "activate" the juices. Then cut two small slices in the lemon about 1/2 inch (1.25 centimeters) apart. Place a **penny** into one slot and a **dime** into the other. Now touch your **tongue** to the penny

and the dime at the same time. You'll feel a slight **electric tingle**. Here's how it works: The acid in the lemon reacts differently with each of the two metals. One coin contains positive electric charges, while the other contains negative charges. The charges create current. Your tongue conducts the charges, causing a small amount of electricity to flow.

Cleanse your face Clean and exfoliate your face by washing it with lemon juice. You can also dab lemon juice on blackheads to draw them out during the day. Your skin should improve after several days of treatment.

Freshen your breath Make an impromptu mouthwash using lemon juice straight from the bottle. Rinse with the juice and then swallow it for longer-lasting fresh breath. The citric acid in the juice alters the pH level in your mouth, killing the bacteria that cause bad breath. Rinse after a few minutes, because long-term exposure to the acid in the lemon can harm tooth enamel.

Treat flaky dandruff If itchy, scaly dandruff has you scratching your head, relief may be no farther away than your refrigerator. Just massage 2 tablespoons lemon juice into your scalp and rinse with water. Then stir 1 teaspoon lemon juice into 1 cup water and rinse your hair with it. Repeat this daily until your dandruff disappears. No more itchy scalp, and your hair will smell lemon-fresh.

Soften dry, scaly elbows It's bad enough that your elbows are dry and itchy, but they look terrible too. Your elbows will look and feel better after a few treatments with this regimen: Mix baking soda and lemon juice to make an abrasive paste. Then rub the paste into your elbows for a soothing, smoothing, and exfoliating treatment.

Remove berry stains Sure it was fun to pick your own berries, but now your fingers are stained with berry juice that won't come off with soap and water. Try washing your hands with undiluted lemon juice. Wait a few minutes and wash with warm, soapy water. Repeat if necessary until the stain is completely gone.

Disinfect cuts and scrapes Stop bleeding and disinfect minor cuts and scrapes. Pour a few drops of lemon juice directly on the cut or apply the juice with a cotton ball and hold firmly in place for one minute.

Soothe poison ivy rash You won't need an ocean of calamine lotion the next time poison ivy comes a-creeping around. Just apply lemon juice full-strength directly to the affected area to soothe itching and alleviate the rash.

Relieve rough hands and sore feet You don't have to take extreme measures to soothe your extremities. If you have rough hands or sore feet, rinse them in a mixture of equal parts lemon juice and water, then massage with olive oil and dab dry with a soft cloth.

Remove warts You've tried countless remedies to get rid of your warts, and nothing seems to work. Next time, try this: Apply a dab of lemon juice directly to the wart, using a cotton swab. Repeat for several days until the acids in the lemon juice dissolve the wart completely.

✳ Lighter Fluid

Wipe away rust Rust marks on stainless steel will come off in a jiffy. Just pour a little lighter fluid onto a clean rag and rub the rust spot away. Use another rag to wipe away any remaining fluid.

Get gum out of hair It happens to the best of us, not to mention the kids. Gum in the hair is a pain in the neck to remove. Here is an easy solution that really works: Apply a few drops of lighter fluid directly to the sticky area, wait a few seconds, and comb or wipe away the gum. The solvents in the fluid break down the gum, making it easy to remove from many surfaces besides hair.

Remove labels with ease Lighter fluid will remove labels and adhesives from almost any surface. Use it to quickly and easily remove the strapping tape from new appliances or to take stickers off book covers.

Take out crayon marks Did the kids leave their mark with crayons on your walls during that last visit? No problem. Dab some lighter fluid on a clean rag and wipe till the marks vanish.

> **TAKE CARE** Lighter fluid is inexpensive, easy to find (look for a small plastic bottle next to the larger bottles of barbecue starter) and has many surprising uses. But it is highly flammable and can be hazardous to your health if inhaled or ingested. Always use it in a well-ventilated area. Do not smoke around it or use it near an open flame.

Remove heel marks from floors You don't have to scrub to remove those black heel marks on the kitchen floor. Just pour a little lighter fluid on a paper towel and the marks will wipe right off.

Rid cooking-oil stain from clothes When cooking-oil stains won't wash out of clothes, try pouring a little lighter fluid directly onto the stain before washing it the next time. The stain will come out in the wash.

✳ Lip Balm

Prevent windburn You love to ski, but you hate wearing a ski mask. Next time you go snow skiing, try rubbing lip balm, such as ChapStick, on your face before you hit the slopes. The lip balm will protect your skin from windburn.

Remove a stuck ring No need to pull and tug on your poor beleaguered finger to try to remove that stuck ring. Simply coat the finger with lip balm and gently wriggle the ring loose.

Groom wild eyebrows Use lip balm as a styling wax to groom unruly mustaches, eyebrows, or other wild hairs.

 Lip Balm and Lipstick

> During the dry winter months you may be tempted to apply a layer of lip balm before you put on your lipstick. Beauty experts say this is not a good idea because the lip balm could interfere with the adherence of the lipstick. Instead of using lip balm during the day, the experts recommend that you switch to a moisturizing lipstick. Save the lip balm for moisturizing your lips before you go to bed.

Zap bleeding from shaving cuts Ouch! You just cut yourself shaving and you've no time to spare. Just dab a bit of lip balm directly onto the nick and the bleeding from most shaving cuts will quickly stop.

Lubricate a zipper Rub a small amount of lip balm up and down the teeth of a sticky or stuck zipper. Then zip and unzip it a few times. The lip balm will act as a lubricant to make the zipper work smoothly.

Simplify carpentry Rub some lip balm over nails and screws being drilled or pounded into wood. The lip balm will help them slide in a little easier.

Keep a lightbulb from sticking Outdoor lightbulbs, which are exposed to the elements, often get stuck in place and become hard to remove. Before screwing a lightbulb into an outdoor socket, coat the threads on the bulb with lip balm. This will prevent sticking and make removal easier.

Lubricate tracks for sliding things Apply lip balm to the tracks of drawers and windows, or to the ridges on a medicine cabinet, for easier opening and shutting.

Magazines

No-cost gift wrap Cut out pages with colorful magazine advertisements and use them to make lovely gift wrap for small gifts.

Keep wet boots in shape Roll up a couple of old magazines and use them as boot trees inside a pair of damp boots. The magazines will help the boots maintain their shape as they dry.

Use in kids' craft projects Save up your old magazines for use in rainy-day craft projects with the kids. Let them go through the magazines to find pictures and words to use in collages. Suggest themes for the collages if you like.

Line drawers Pages from large magazines with heavy coated paper make wonderful liners for small dresser and desk drawers. Look for advertisements with especially colorful designs or pictures. Clip the page, place inside the drawer, and press around the edges to define where to trim with scissors.

Magnets

Clean up a nail spill Keep a strong magnet on your workbench. Next time you spill a jar of small items like nails, screws, tacks, or washers, save time and energy and let the magnet help pick them up for you.

DID *You* KNOW?

Ancient Chinese and Greeks discovered that certain rare stones, called lodestones, seem to magically attract bits of iron and always pointed in the same direction when allowed to swing freely.

Manmade magnets come in many shapes and sizes, but every magnet has a north pole and a south pole. If you break a magnet into pieces, each piece, no matter how small, will have a north and south pole. The magnetic field, which every magnet creates, has long been used to harness energy, although scientists still don't know for sure what it is!

Prevent a frozen car lock Here's a great way to use refrigerator magnets during the bitter cold of winter. Place them over the outside door locks of your car overnight and they will keep the locks from freezing.

Keep desk drawer neat Are your paper clips all over the place? Place a magnet in your office desk drawer to keep the paper clips together.

Store a broom in a handy place Why run to the hall closet every time you need to sweep the kitchen? Instead, just use a screw to attach a magnet about halfway down the broom handle. Then store the broom attached to the side of your refrigerator between the fridge and the wall, where it will remain hidden until you are ready to use it.

* Margarine Tubs

Corral those odds and ends Loose thumbtacks in every room? Odd bolts and nails in a broken cup? Stray superball under the couch? These are just some of the items waiting to be organized into your extra plastic margarine tubs. Get your board game going faster and easier by storing the loose pieces in a tub until the next time. You've sorted out all the sky pieces for a puzzle, so keep them separate and safe in their own tub. With or without their lids, a few clean margarine tubs can do wonders for a junk drawer in need of organization.

Make a baby footprint paperweight Make an enduring impression of your baby's foot, using quick-drying modeling clay—which comes in lots of great colors. Put enough clay in a margarine tub to hold a good impression. Put a thin layer of petroleum jelly on baby's foot and press it firmly into the clay. Let the clay dry as directed, then flex the tub away from the edges until the clay comes free. Years from now you'll be able to show Johnny that his size 13s were once smaller than the palm of your hand! You can also preserve your pet's paw print the same way.

Use as a paint container Want to touch up the little spots here and there in the living room, but don't want to lug around a gallon of paint? Pour a little paint into a margarine tub to carry as you make your inspection. Hold it in a nest of paper towels to catch any possible drips. The tubs with lids are also perfect for storing that little bit of leftover paint for future touch-ups.

Make individual ice-cream portions Small margarine tubs are just the right size for a quick ice-cream snack. And when it comes home from the store, a gallon of ice cream is the perfect consistency to portion out into the tubs. No more time-consuming getting out the bowls, finding the scoop, and waiting for the ice cream to soften up enough to dish out. When Johnny and Janey want their ice cream *now*, they can get it themselves and everyone has an equal portion—they just go to the freezer and pull out a tub.

Mold gelatin desserts Don't buy a fancy mold for your next birthday party or barbecue. Use a large margarine tub as the mold for a gelatin or mousse centerpiece. For individual fun gelatin dessert molds, use the smaller tubs and put a surprise gummy or mini-marshmallow face on the top, which will show through from the bottom when the mold is inverted. The flexible tubs are easy to squeeze to release the dessert.

Make frugal freezer storage Reuse your clean, sturdy margarine and other plastic containers for freezing measured portions of soups and stocks, and to break up leftovers into single servings. A 2-pound (1 kilogram) container, for example, stores the perfect amount of sauce for 1 pound (.5 kilogram) of pasta. *Hint:* Before freezing, let the food cool just enough to reduce condensation.

Give kids some lunch box variety As a break from the usual sandwich, put some fruit salad, rice mix, or other interesting fare in one or two recycled margarine tubs for your child's lunch. The tubs are easy to open and will keep the food from getting crushed.

Bring fast food for baby Need to bring your home cooking for Junior on the road? Use a disposable margarine tub for a container that won't break in your baby bag. It's also a handy food bowl, and you won't have to wrap it up and bring it home for cleaning.

Make a piggy bank Use a tall tub as a homemade bank for your little one. Cut out a piece of paper that will fit wrapped around the side, tape it in place and encourage him or her to decorate it with flair. Cut a slit in the top, and start saving!

Travel light with your pet Lightweight, disposable margarine tubs make the perfect pet food containers and double as food and water bowls. And those valuable dog cookies won't get crushed if you put them in a plastic tub. If your pet is vacationing at a friend's house, make things a little easier for the caregiver by putting one serving in each container, to be used and discarded as needed.

Create thrifty seed starters Starting your seeds indoors is supposed to save you money, so don't spend your savings on lots of big seed trays. Take a margarine tub, poke a few holes in the bottom, add moistened seed-starting mix, and sow your seeds following packet instructions. Use permanent marker on the side of the tub to help you remember what you've sown, and use the tub's lid as a drip saucer. Small tubs are space savers as well, especially if you want to start only one or two of each type of plant.

✳ Marshmallows

Separate toes when applying polish Get the comfort of a salon treatment when giving yourself a home pedicure. Just place marshmallows between your toes to separate them before you apply the nail polish.

Keep brown sugar soft Ever notice how brown sugar seems to harden overnight once you've opened the bag? Next time you open a bag of brown sugar, add a few marshmallows to the bag before closing it. The marshmallows will add enough moisture to keep the sugar soft for weeks.

Stop ice-cream drips Here's an easy way to keep a leaky ice-cream cone from staining your clothes. Just place a large marshmallow in the bottom of the cone before you add the ice cream.

Keep wax off birthday cakes If one of your birthday wishes is to keep candle wax off the frosting on the cake, try this trick: Push each candle into a marshmallow and set the marshmallow atop the frosting. The wax will melt onto the marshmallow, which you can discard. Meanwhile, the marshmallows will add a festive look to the cake.

DID *You* KNOW?

Ancient Egyptians made the first marshmallow candy—a honey-based concoction flavored and thickened with the sap of the root of the marshmallow plant (*Althaea* *officinalis*). Marshmallow grows in salt marshes and on banks near large bodies of water. Its sap was used to make marshmallow candy and medicine until the mid-1800s. Today's commercial marshmallows are a mixture of corn syrup or sugar, gelatin, gum arabic, and flavoring.

Impromptu cupcake frosting You're already mixing the batter for the cupcakes when you realize you're out of frosting. No problem—if you happen to have some marshmallows on hand. Just pop a marshmallow on top of each cupcake about a minute or so before they come out of the oven. It will make a delicious, instant, gooey frosting.

✳ Masking Tape

Label foods and school supplies You don't need to buy labels or a fancy machine that makes them. Use inexpensive masking tape instead to mark food containers and freezer bags before putting them in the refrigerator or freezer, and don't forget to write the date! You can also use masking tape to conveniently mark kids' schoolbooks and supplies.

Fix a broken umbrella rib If a strong wind breaks a rib on your umbrella, it's easy to fix it. Use a piece of masking tape and a length of wire cut from a coat hanger to make a splint.

Reuse a vacuum cleaner bag Save money by using a vacuum cleaner bag twice. Here's how: After the bag is full the first time, do not empty it the usual way through the hole in front. Take out the bag and cut a slit down the middle of the back. After you empty the bag, hold the cut edges together, fold them closed, and seal them with masking tape. Your bag is ready to be used again. Take care not to overfill during the second use.

Hang party streamers Use masking tape instead of transparent tape to put up streamers and balloons for your next party. The masking tape won't leave a residue on the wall like transparent tape does. Always remember to remove the masking tape within a day or two. If you wait too long, it could take paint off the wall when it comes off.

Keep paint can neat To prevent paint from filling the groove at the top of a paint can, simply cover the rim of the can with masking tape.

Make a road for toy cars Make a highway for those tiny toy cars your little ones love to play with. Just tape two strips of masking tape to a floor or tabletop. Add a little handmade cardboard stop sign or two and they're off to the races. Carefully guiding a toy car along the taped roadway is more than just fun for small children, it also helps them gain motor control of their fingers for skills they will need later, such as writing.

* Mayonnaise

Condition your hair Hold the mayo ... and massage it into your hair and scalp just as you would any fine conditioner! Cover your head with a shower cap, wait several minutes, and shampoo. The mayonnaise will moisturize your hair and give it a lustrous sheen.

Give yourself a facial Why waste money on expensive creams when you can treat yourself to a soothing facial with whole-egg mayonnaise from your own refrigerator? Gently spread the mayonnaise over your face and leave it on for about 20 minutes. Then wipe it off and rinse with cool water. Your face will feel clean and smooth.

Strengthen your fingernails To add some oomph to your fingernails, just plunge them into a bowl of mayonnaise every so often. Keep them bathed in the mayo for about 5 minutes and then wash with warm water.

Relieve sunburn pain Did someone forget to put on sunscreen? To treat dry, sunburned skin, slather mayonnaise liberally over the affected area. The mayonnaise will relieve the pain and moisturize the skin.

Remove dead skin Soften and remove dead skin from elbows and feet. Rub mayonnaise over the dry, rough tissue, leave it on for 10 minutes, and wipe it away with a damp cloth.

Safe way to kill head lice Many dermatologists now recommend using mayonnaise to kill and remove head lice from kids instead of toxic prescription drugs and over-the-counter preparations. What's more, lice are becoming more resistant to such chemical treatments. To treat head lice with mayonnaise, massage a liberal amount of mayonnaise into the hair and scalp before bedtime. Cover  with a shower cap to maximize the effect. Shampoo in the morning and then use a fine-tooth comb to remove any remaining lice and nits. To completely eradicate the infestation, repeat the treatment in 7-10 days.

Make plant leaves shiny Professional florists use this trick to keep houseplant leaves shiny and clean. You can do the same thing at home. Just rub a little mayonnaise on the leaves with a paper towel, and they will stay bright and shiny for weeks and even months at a time.

Remove crayon marks Did the kids leave crayon marks on your wood furniture? Here's a simple way to remove them that requires hardly any elbow grease: Simply rub some mayonnaise on the crayon marks and let it soak in for several minutes. Then wipe the surface clean with a damp cloth.

Clean piano keys If the keys to your piano are starting to yellow, just tickle the ivories with a little mayonnaise applied with a soft cloth. Wait a few minutes, wipe with a damp cloth, and buff. The piano keys will look like new.

Remove bumper stickers Time to get rid of that Nixon for President bumper sticker on your car? Instead of attacking it with a razor and risk scratching the bumper, rub some mayonnaise over the entire sticker. Let it sit for several minutes and wipe it off. The mayonnaise will dissolve the glue.

Get tar off your car To get road tar or pine sap off your car with ease, slather some mayonnaise over the affected area, let it sit for several minutes, and wipe it away with a clean, soft rag.

✳ Meat Tenderizer

Ease backache To relieve your aching back, mix sufficient water with meat tenderizer to make a paste and rub it on your back where it hurts. The enzymes in the tenderizer will help soothe those aching back muscles.

Relieve wasp-sting pain Make a paste of meat tenderizer and water and apply it directly to the sting from a bee or wasp. Be careful not to push any remaining part of the stinger deeper into your skin. The enzymes in the meat tenderizer will break down the proteins in the insect venom.

Remove protein-based stains Try a little tenderness to remove protein-based stains like milk, chocolate, and blood from clothes. For fresh wet stains, sprinkle on enough meat tenderizer to cover the area and let it sit for an hour. Then brush off the dried tenderizer and launder as usual. For stains that are already set, mix water and meat tenderizer to make a paste and rub it into the stain. Wait an hour before laundering as usual.

 DID *You* KNOW?

When Lloyd Rigler and Lawrence Deutsch dined at Adolph Rempp's Los Angeles restaurant one night in 1949, they had no clue that their fortunes were about to change forever. But the two partners were so impressed by the tender, flavorful meat that they soon bought the rights to the product now known as Adolph's Meat Tenderizer. Rigler toured the country—visiting 63 cities in 60 days—demonstrating the product, winning over skeptical food critics by sending them home with tenderized meat to cook themselves. Rave reviews led to windfall sales and profits, allowing the partners to sell the business in 1974 and turn their attention to philanthropy and the arts for the rest of their lives.

"Tenderize" tough perspiration stains Tenderize away hard-to-remove perspiration stains. Before you wash that sweat-stained sweatshirt (or any other perspiration-stained garment) dampen the stain and then sprinkle some meat tenderizer on it. Then just wash as usual.

✳ Milk

Make frozen fish taste fresh If you want fish from your freezer to taste like it was fresh caught, try this trick: Place the frozen fish in a bath of milk until it thaws. The milk will make it taste fresher.

Boost corn on the cob flavor Here's a simple way to make corn on the cob taste sweeter and fresher. Just add 1/4 cup powdered milk to the pot of boiling water before you toss in the corn.

Repair cracked china Before you throw out that cracked plate from your grandmother's old china set, try mending it with milk. Place the plate in a pan, cover it with milk (fresh or reconstituted powdered milk), and bring to a boil. As soon as it starts to boil, lower the heat and simmer for about 45 minutes. The protein in the milk will miraculously meld most fine cracks.

Polish silverware Tarnished silverware will look like new with a little help from some sour milk. If you don't have any sour milk on hand, you can make some by adding vinegar to fresh milk. Then simply soak the silver in the milk for half an hour to loosen the tarnish, wash in warm, soapy water, and buff with a soft cloth.

Soothe sunburn and bug bites If your skin feels like it's burning up from too much sun exposure or if itchy bug bites are driving you crazy, try using a little milk paste for soothing relief. Mix one part powdered milk with two parts water and add a pinch or two of salt. Dab it on the burn or bite. The enzymes in the milk powder will help neutralize the insect-bite venom and help relieve sunburn pain.

Impromptu makeup remover When you run out of makeup remover and you can't get to the store, use powdered milk instead. Just mix 3 tablespoons powdered milk with 1/3 cup warm water in a jar and shake well. Add more water or powder as necessary to achieve the consistency of heavy cream. Now you are ready to apply your makeshift makeup remover with a facecloth. When you're done, wipe it off and rinse with water.

Give yourself a facial Here's another way to give yourself a fancy spa facial at home. Make a mask by mixing 1/4 cup powdered milk with enough water to form a thick paste. Thoroughly coat your face with the mixture, let dry completely, then rinse with warm water. Your face will feel fresh and rejuvenated.

Soften skin Treat yourself to a luxurious foamy milk bath. Toss 1/2 cup or so of powdered milk into the tub as it fills. Milk acts as a natural skin softener.

Clean and soften dirty hands You come back from the garden with stained and gritty hands. Regular soap just won't do, but this will: Make a paste of oatmeal and milk and rub it vigorously on your hands. The stains will be gone and the oatmeal-and-milk mixture will soften and soothe your skin.

Clean patent leather Make your patent-leather purses or shoes look like new again. Just dab on a little milk, let it dry, and buff with a soft cloth.

Remove ink stains from clothes To remove ink stains from colored clothes, an overnight milk bath will often do the trick. Just soak the affected garment in milk overnight and launder as usual the next day.

✱ Milk Cartons

Make ice blocks for parties Keep drinks cold at your next barbecue or party with ice blocks made from empty milk cartons. Just rinse out the old cartons, fill them with water, and put them in the freezer. Peel away the container when you're ready to put the blocks in the cooler or punch bowl.

Make a lacy candle Here's an easy way to make a delicate, lacy candle. Coat the inside of a milk carton with cooking spray, put a taper candle in the middle, anchoring it with a base of melted wax, then fill it with ice cubes. Pour in hot wax; when the wax cools, peel off the carton. The melting ice will form beautiful, lacy voids in the wax.

Instant kids' bowling alley Make an indoor bowling alley for the kids with pins made from empty milk and juice cartons. Just rinse the cartons (use whatever sizes you like) and let them dry. Then take two same-sized cartons and slide one upside down into the other, squeezing it a little to make it fit. Once you've made ten, set your pins up at the end of the hall and let the kids use a tennis ball to roll for strikes and spares.

Feed birds in winter To make an attractive wintertime treat for feathered visitors, combine melted suet and birdseed into an empty milk carton. Suet is beef fat; you can get it from a butcher. To render it, chop or grind the fat and heat it over a

DID *You* KNOW?

John Van Wormer, an Ohio toy factory owner, didn't cry over spilt milk when he dropped a bottle of the stuff on the floor one morning in 1915. Instead, he was inspired to patent a paper-based milk carton he named Pure-Pak. It took him 10 years to perfect a machine that coated the paper with wax and sealed the carton with animal glues. Those early waxy containers were slow to catch on with skeptical consumers and bore little resemblance to today's milk cartons, but now some 30,000 million Pure-Pak cartons are sold annually.

low flame until it melts. Then strain it through cheesecloth into the carton. Insert a loop of string into the mixture while it is still melted. After it hardens, tear away the carton and tie your new mass of bird food to a branch. Do this only in cold weather. Once the temperature gets above about 70°F (20°C), the suet will turn rancid and melt.

Make seed starters Milk cartons are the perfect size to use for seed starters. Simply cut off the top half of a carton, punch holes in the bottom, fill with potting mix, and sow the seeds according to instructions on the packet.

Make vegetable garden collars Use empty milk cartons to discourage grubs and cut-worms from attacking your young tomato and pepper plants. Just cut off the tops and bottoms of the containers, and when the ground is soft, push them into the ground around the plants when you set them out.

Collect food scraps for compost Keep an empty milk carton handy near the kitchen sink and use it to collect food scraps for your compost heap.

Disposable paint holder If you have a small paint project and you don't want to save the leftover paint (or lug a heavy can), an empty milk carton can help. Just cut off the top of the carton and pour in the amount of paint you need. When the job is finished, throw the carton into the trash, leftover paint and all.

✳ Mothballs

Rinse woolens for storage Of course it is a good idea to store woolens with mothballs to ward off moths. To give your favorite sweaters even more protection, dissolve a few mothballs in the final rinse when you wash them before storage.

213

Kill bugs on potted plants To exterminate bugs on a potted plant, put the plant in a clear plastic bag, such as a cleaning bag, add a few mothballs, and seal for a week. When you take the plant out of the bag, your plant will be bug-free. It will also keep moths away for a while.

Repel mice from garage or shed Don't let mice spend their winter vacation in your garage. Place a few mothballs around the garage, and the mice will seek other quarters. To keep mice out of your potting shed, put the mothballs around the base of wrapped or covered plants.

Keep dogs and cats away from garden Don't throw out old mothballs. Scatter them around your gardens and flowerbeds to keep cats, dogs, and rodents away. Animals hate the smell!

Keep bats at bay Bats won't invade your belfry (or attic) if you scatter a few mothballs around. Add some mothballs to the boxes you store in the attic and silverfish will stay away too.

✳ Mouse Pads

Pad under table legs When you get a new mouse pad for your computer, don't throw out the old one. Use it to make pads for table legs and chairs to prevent them from scratching wood and other hard-surface floors. Just cut the foam and cloth pad into small pieces and superglue each piece to the bottom of a leg.

Make knee pads for the garden Old computer mouse pads are just the right size to cushion your knees when you're working in the garden. Kneel on them loose as is or attach them directly to your pant legs with duct tape.

Pad under houseplants Keep potted plant containers from scratching or damaging your hard floors. Just set the pot atop an old mouse pad and your floor will remain scratch-free. Use four pads for large pots.

Hot pad for the table Protect your table from hot casseroles, coffeepots, and serving dishes. Use old PC mouse pads as hot pads. The cloth-topped foam mouse pad is the perfect size to hold most hot containers you bring to the table.

✳ Mouthwash

Clean computer monitor screen Out of glass cleaner? A strong, alcohol-based mouthwash will work as well as, or better than, glass cleaner on your computer monitor or TV screen. Apply with a damp, soft cloth and buff dry. Remember to use only on glass screens, not liquid crystal displays! The alcohol can damage the material used in LCDs.

Cleanse your face An antiseptic mouthwash makes a wonderful astringent for cleansing your face. Check the ingredients to make sure it does not contain sugar, then use as follows. Wash your face with warm, soapy water and rinse. Dab a cotton ball with mouthwash and gently wipe your face as you would with any astringent. You should feel a pleasant, tingling sensation. Rinse with warm water followed by a splash of cold water. Your face will look and feel clean and refreshed.

Treat athlete's foot A sugarless antiseptic mouthwash may be all you need to treat mild cases of athlete's foot or toenail fungus. Use a cotton ball soaked in mouthwash to apply to the affected area several times a day. Be prepared: It will sting a bit! Athlete's foot should respond after a few days. Toenail fungus may take up to several months. If you do not see a response by then, make an appointment with a dermatologist or podiatrist.

Add to wash water Smelly gym socks are often full of bacteria and fungi that may not all come out in the wash—unless you add a cup of alcohol-based, sugarless mouthwash during the regular wash cycle.

Tip **Homemade Mouthwash**

> Freshen your breath with your own alcohol-free mouthwash. Place 1 ounce (30 grams) whole cloves and/or 3 ounces (85 grams) fresh rosemary in a pint-size (half-liter) jar and pour in 2 cups boiling water. Cover the jar tightly and let it steep overnight before straining. Need a mouthwash immediately? Dissolve 1/2 teaspoon baking soda in 1/2 cup warm water.

Cure underarm odor Regular deodorants mask unpleasant underarm odors with a heavy perfume smell but do little to attack the cause of the problem. To get rid of the bacteria that cause perspiration odor, dampen a cotton ball with a sugarless, alcohol-based mouthwash and swab your armpits. If you've just shaved your armpits, it's best to wait for another day to try this.

Disinfect a cut When you need to clean out a small cut or wound, use an alcohol-based mouthwash to disinfect your skin. Remember that before it became a mouthwash, it was successfully used as an antiseptic to prevent surgical infections.

Get rid of dandruff To treat a bad case of dandruff, wash your hair with your regular shampoo; then rinse with an alcohol-based mouthwash. You can follow with your regular conditioner.

Clean your toilet All out of your regular toilet bowl cleaner? Try pouring 1/4 cup alcohol-based mouthwash into the bowl. Let it stand in the water for 1/2 hour, then swish with a toilet brush before flushing. The mouthwash will disinfect germs as it leaves your toilet bowl sparkling and clean.

✳ Mustard

M

Soothe an aching back Take a bath in yellow mustard to relieve an aching back or arthritis pain. Simply pour a regular 6- to 8-ounce (175- to 240-milliliter) bottle of mustard into the hot water as the tub fills. Mix well and soak yourself for 15 minutes. If you don't have time for a bath, you can rub some mustard directly on the affected areas. Use only mild yellow mustard and make sure to apply it to a small test area first. Undiluted mustard may irritate your skin.

Relax stiff muscles Next time you take a bath in Epsom salt, throw in a few tablespoons yellow mustard too. The mustard will enhance the soothing effects of the Epsom salt and also help to relax stiff, sore muscles.

Relieve congestion Relieve congestion with a mustard plaster just like Grandma used to make. Rub your chest with prepared mustard, soak a washcloth in hot water, wring it out, and place it over the mustard.

Make a facial mask Pat your face with mild yellow mustard for a bracing facial that will soothe and stimulate your skin. Try it on a small test area first to make sure it will not be irritating.

Remove skunk smell from car You didn't see the skunk in the road until it was too late, and now your car exudes that foul aroma. Use mustard powder to get rid of those awful skunk odors. Pour 1 cup dry mustard into a bucket of warm water, mix well, and splash it on the tires, wheels, and underbody of the car. Your passengers will thank you.

Remove odor from bottles You've got some nice bottles you'd like to keep, but after washing them, they still smell like whatever came in them. Mustard is a sure way to kill the smell. After washing, just squirt a little mustard into the bottle, fill with warm water, and shake it up. Rinse well, and the smell will be gone.

❓ DID *You* KNOW?

Ancient Romans brought mustard back from Egypt and used the seeds to flavor unfermented grape juice, called *must*. This is believed to be how the mustard plant got its name. The Romans also made a paste from the ground seeds for medicinal purposes and may have used it as a condiment. But the mustard we use today was first prepared in Dijon, France, in the 13th century. Dijon-style mustard is made from darker seeds than yellow mustard.

super item
38 uses!

Nail Polish

Make buttons glow in the dark It happens all the time. The lights are dimmed, you grab the remote control to increase the TV volume, and darn, you hit the wrong button and change the channel instead. To put an end to video flubs, dab glow-in-the-dark nail polish onto frequently used remote buttons. You can also use phosphorescent polish to mark keys and keyholes and other hard-to-spot items.

Mark your thermostat setting When you wake up with a chill and don't have your glasses, it's easy to return to your comfort zone if you've marked your dial-type thermostat. Simply set it to your preferred temperature and then make a thin mark with colored nail polish from the dial into the outside ring.

Tip Using Nail Polish

- To keep nail polishes fresh and easy to use, store them in the refrigerator. Keep them together in a little square plastic container.
- Shaking a polish bottle to mix the color can cause bubbles. Roll the bottle between your palms instead.
- Wipe the inside threads of your nail polish bottle and cap with a cotton swab dipped in polish remover before closing them. It'll open more easily.

Mark temperature settings on shower knobs Don't waste precious shower time fiddling with the water temperature. With the shower on, select your ideal settings, then turn off the flow to the shower and make a small mark with bright nail polish onto the stationary lip of both the hot and cold knob indicating the handle position that's best. Once it's set, no sweat!

Make cup measurements legible Find your measuring cup markings faster, especially if you like to measure "on the fly" while cooking. Use a very visible color of nail polish to trace over the basic measurement levels. This also works great for those dimly lit, late-night bottle feedings, when you need to see how well

Junior has tanked up. And you won't have to squint to find the correct dosage on little plastic medicine cups if you first mark them with a thin line of dark polish.

Mark levels inside a bucket When you're mixing in a big bucket, you don't typically have the opportunity to lift the bucket to check the quantity. Besides, the bucket you use for mixing might not have the measurements clearly marked at all. Make sure you know you're using the right amounts by marking pint, quart, and gallon (or half, full, and other liter) levels with lines of nail polish. Use a color that stands out against the bucket's color.

Label your sports gear You share a lot of interests with your golf partner, including the same brand of golf balls. Make it clear who got on the green first, by putting a dot of bright nail polish on your ball supply. This also works well with batting gloves and other items that don't have enough room to fit your name.

Label poison containers If everyone in your home has easy access to your cupboard, prevent someone from grabbing dangerous items in haste. Use dark red or other easily visible nail polish to label the poisons. Draw an unmistakable X on the label as well as the lid or spout.

Seal an envelope Do you have a mild distrust of those self-sealing envelopes? Brush a little nail polish along the underside of the flap, seal it, and it won't even open over a teakettle! Add some flair to a special card by brushing your initial (or any design) in nail polish over the sealed flap tip, as a modern type of sealing wax that doesn't need to be melted first.

Smudgeproof important drug labels Preserve the important information on your prescription medicine and other important medicine labels with a coat of clear polish, and they won't be smudged as you grab them after getting your glass of water.

Waterproof address labels When you're sending a parcel on a rainy day, a little clear polish brushed over the address information will make sure your package goes to the right place.

Prevent rust rings from metal containers If your guests are going to peek into your medicine cabinet, you don't want them to see rust rings on your shelves. Brush nail lacquer around the bottom of shaving cream cans and other metal containers to avoid those unsightly stains.

Make a gleaming paperweight To create paperweights that look like gemstones, or interesting rocks for the base of your potted cactus, try this: Find some palm-size, smooth clean rocks. Put about 1/2 inch (1.25 centimeters) water into a pie pan, and put 1 drop clear nail polish onto the water. The polish will spread out over the water surface. Holding a rock with your fingertips, slowly roll it in the water to coat it with the polish. Set the rock on newspaper to dry.

Prevent rusty toilet seat screws If you're installing a new toilet seat, keep those screws from quickly rusting. Paint them with a coat or two of clear nail lacquer; it will also help prevent seat wobble by keeping the screws in place.

Paint shaker holes to restrict salt If your favorite saltshaker dispenses a little too generously, paint a few of the holes shut with nail polish. It is a good idea for those watching their salt.

Tarnish-proof costume jewelry Inexpensive costume jewelry can add sparkle and color to an everyday outfit, but not if it tarnishes and the tarnish rubs off the jewelry and onto your skin. To keep your fake jewelry and your skin sparkling clean, brush clear nail polish onto the back of each piece and allow it to dry before wearing.

Protect your belt buckle's shine Cover new or just-shined belt buckles with a coat of clear polish. You'll prevent oxidation and guarantee a gleaming first impression.

Seal out scuffs on shoes On leather shoes, it's the back and toes that really take the brunt of the wear and tear that leaves scratches on the surface. Next time you buy a new pair of shoes—especially ones for a kid or an active adult—give these areas the extra measure of protection they need. Paint a little clear nail polish on the outside of the back seam and over the toes. Rub the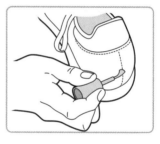
polish in a little to feather out the shine of the polish. After it dries, you'll be a step ahead of those perennial shoe problems "driver's heel" and "jump rope toe."

Keep laces from unraveling Neaten the appearance of frayed shoelaces, and extend their life. Dip the ends in clear nail polish and twist the raveled ends together. Repair laces in the evening so that the polish will dry overnight.

DID *You* KNOW?

Nail polish is certainly not a recent concept. As early as 3000 B.C., ancient Chinese nobility are believed to have colored their long nails with polishes, made from gum arabic, beeswax, gelatin, and pigments. The nobility wore shades of gold, silver, red, or black, while lesser classes were restricted to pastel shades. Colored nails were also popular with ancient Egyptians, who often dyed their nails with henna or stained them with berries. Polish wasn't just for women. In Egypt and Rome, military commanders painted their nails red before going into battle.

Get rid of a wart Warts are unsightly, embarrassing, and infectious. In order to get rid of warts and prevent spreading the virus to others, cover them with nail polish. The wart should be gone or greatly diminished in one week.

Protect pearl buttons Delicate pearl buttons will keep their brand-new sparkle with a protective coat of clear nail polish. It will keep costume pearl buttons from peeling as well.

Prevent loss of buttons Keep that brand-new shirt in good shape by putting a drop of clear nail polish on the thread in the buttons. It prevents the thread from fraying, so taking this precaution in advance could save you some embarrassment later. Put a dab on just-repaired buttons as well.

DID You KNOW?

Unless you work in a lab, you probably don't know that clear nail polish is the respected workhorse used in mounting microscopic slides. Officially referred to as NPM (nail polish mountant) it is the preferred and inexpensive substance used around a cover glass to seal it onto a slide, protecting the specimen from air and moisture.

Make needle threading easier Do you fumble with your needle and thread, licking and re-licking the frayed thread end until it's too floppy to go through the eye? Try dragging the cut thread end through the application brush of nail polish once or twice, and then roll the thread end between your thumb and forefinger. It will dry in a second, and your thread end stays stiff enough to thread in a flash. Your sewing box is a great retirement home for a nail color you no longer use.

Prevent frayed fabric from unraveling Do you have wisps peeking out from the bottom of your skirt? Is the nylon lining of your jacket fraying at the cuffs? You can tame those fraying strays by brushing them into place with some clear nail polish.

Keep ribbons from fraying The gift is perfect, so make sure the wrapping is just as nice. Brush the cut ends of ribbon with a little clear nail polish to stop them from unraveling. This is also the perfect solution for your little girl's hair ribbons on special occasions; at least one part of her will stay together all day!

Stop a run in your hose It's a helpless feeling, realizing that a small run in your stocking is about to turn into a big embarrassment. Happily you can stop runs permanently and prolong the life of fragile stockings with a dab of clear nail polish. Simply apply polish to each end of a run (no need to remove hose), and let it dry. This invisible fix stops runs, and lasts through many hand launderings.

Mend a fingernail You just split a nail, but don't have a nail repair kit handy? Grab an unused tea bag instead. Cut the bag open, dump the tea, cut a piece of the bag into the shape of your nail, and cover it with clear nail polish. Press it onto your nail, then apply colored nail polish. You'll be good to go until the break grows out.

Temporarily repair eyeglasses So you sat on your glasses and one lens has a small crack, but you can't get to the optometrist right away? Seal the crack on both sides with a thin coat of clear nail polish. That will hold it together until you can see your way to the doctor's office.

Stop a windshield crack from spreading If you've developed a small crack in your windshield, stop it cold with some clear polish. Working in the shade, brush the crack on both sides of the glass with polish to fill it well. Move the car into the sun so the windshield can dry. You will eventually need to repair your windshield, but this will give you time to shop around for the best estimate.

Fill small nicks on floors and glass Have the children been playing hockey on your hardwood floors? Fill those little nicks by dabbing them with some clear nail polish. It will dry shiny, so sand the spot gently with some 600-grit sandpaper. A thick coat of clear nail polish also helps to soften the sharp edge of a nicked mirror or glass pane.

Reset loose jewelry stones If your jewelry has popped a stone or two, you don't have to put it in the "play dress-up" box yet. The stone can be reset using a little drop of clear nail polish as the "glue." It dries quickly, and the repair will be invisible.

Repair lacquered items Did you chip a favorite lacquered vase or other lacquered item? Try mixing colors of nail polish to match the piece. Paint over the chipped area to make it less noticeable. *Caution:* You may lower the value of an antique by doing this, so you probably only want to try this with inexpensive items.

Plug a hole in your cooler A small hole inside your cooler doesn't make it trash-worthy yet. Seal the hole with two coats of nail polish to hold in ice and other melted substances.

Fill washtub nicks It's a mystery how they got there, but your washing machine tub has one or two nicks near the holes, and now you're concerned about snags in your clothes or even rust spots. Seal those nicks with some nail polish, feathering the edges so there is no lip.

Keep chipped car paint from rusting If your car suffers small dings and chips, you can keep them from rusting or enlarging by dabbing clear nail polish onto the damaged areas.

Smooth wooden hangers If you've noticed a few splinters or nicks in your wooden hangers, no need to toss them out. Brush some nail polish over the rough edges to smooth the surface again and keep your coat linings safe.

Tighten loose screws You're not rough with your drawers and cabinets, but you find yourself tightening certain pull screws once too often. Keep them in place by brushing a little clear polish on the screw threads, insert the screws, and let dry before using again. This is also a great solution if you've been keeping a Phillips screwdriver in the kitchen for loose pot handles. You can also use clear nail polish to keep nuts on machine screws or bolts from coming loose, and if you need to take the nuts off, a twist with a wrench will break the seal.

Mend holes in window screens You notice a small hole has been poked in your window or door screen. If the hole is no more than about 1/4 inch (6 millimeters) in diameter, you can block the bugs and keep the hole from getting bigger by dabbing on a bit of clear nail polish.

Fix torn window shades Got a little tear in your window shade? Don't worry. You can usually seal it with a dab of clear nail polish.

✳ Nail Polish Remover

Remove stains from china Your bone china has assorted stains from years of use. Spruce up your set by rubbing soiled areas with nail polish remover. Clean spots with a cotton swab and then wash dishes as usual.

TAKE CARE Frequent use of nail polish remover containing acetone—check the label—can cause dry skin and brittle nails. All nail polish removers are flammable and potentially hazardous if inhaled for a long time; use them in a well-ventilated area away from flames. And work carefully; they can damage synthetic fabrics, wood finishes, and plastics.

Eliminate ink stains If the ink stains on your skin won't come off with soap and water, they are probably not water-soluble. Try using nail polish remover instead. Take a cotton ball and wipe the affected areas with the solution. Once the ink stains are gone, wash skin with soap and water. Nail polish remover can also eliminate ink stains on the drum of your clothes dryer.

Rub paint off windows Spare your nails the next time you want to remove paint on a window. Working in a well-ventilated area, dab on nail polish remover in small sections. Let the solution remain on the painted areas for a few minutes before rubbing it off with a cloth. Once finished, take a damp cloth and go over the areas again.

Remove stickers from glass Scraping price stickers from glass objects can be messy, and it often leaves behind a gummy adhesive that attracts dirt and is sticky to the touch. Remove the stickers and clean up the residual glue by wiping the area with acetone-based nail polish remover. The same method can be used for removing stickers and sticky residue from metal surfaces.

Dissolve melted plastic Ever get too close to a hot metal toaster with a plastic bag of bread or bagels? The resulting mess can be a real cleaning challenge. But don't let a little melted plastic ruin a perfectly good appliance. Eliminate the sticky mess with nail polisher remover. First unplug the toaster and wait for it to cool. Then pour a little nail polish remover on a soft cloth and gently rub over the damaged areas. Once the melted plastic is removed, wipe with a damp cloth and dry with a paper towel. Your toaster is now ready for the next round of bagels. The same solution works for melted plastic on curling irons.

Unhinge superglue Superglue will stick tenaciously to just about anything, including your skin. And trying to peel it off your fingers can actually cause skin damage. Instead, soak a cotton ball with acetone-based nail polish remover and hold it on the skin until the glue dissolves.

Clean vinyl shoes Patent-leather shoes may not reflect up, but they *do* show off scuff marks, as will white or other light-colored vinyl shoes. To remove the marks,

SCIENCE FAIR

Some kids love to study insects, and just like the pros, your budding entomologist can kill and **preserve bugs**, using nail polish remover. Use a **nail polish remover** that contains the solvent acetone. (Check the label or sniff it for a banana-like odor.) To preserve the insects, soak some **cotton balls** with the polish remover and place them in a **glass or plastic jar** along with several **tissues** and the selected insects. A wide-mouthed peanut butter jar works well. The tissues prevent the insects from damaging their wings. Seal the jar tightly with a lid, and the specimens will quickly dehydrate. Use a **straight pin** stuck through the insect's body to mount it on a corkboard or corrugated **cardboard**.

rub them lightly but briskly with a soft cloth or paper towel dipped in nail polish remover. Afterward, remove any residue with a damp cloth.

Keep watches clean Tired of looking at your watch and seeing unsightly scratches when you check the time? Get rid of them with nail polish remover. If the face of your watch is made from unbreakable plastic, rub the remover over the scratches until they diminish or disappear.

Clean computer keyboards You can keep computer keyboards clean with nail polish remover and an old toothbrush. Simply moisten the brush with remover and lightly rub the keys.

Dilute correction fluid To take the goop out of correction fluid or old nail polish, dilute it with nail polish remover. Pour just a few drops into the bottle and then shake. Add a little more polish remover to the solution, if needed, to attain the desired consistency.

Prep brass for re-lacquering Old or damaged lacquer coatings on brass can be safely removed with nail polish remover. Take a soft cloth and pour a small amount of remover on it. Rub the brass object until the old lacquer has been lifted. Your brass item is now ready to be polished or professionally re-lacquered.

✳ Newspaper

Encase your glassware for moving Are you relocating or packing up items for long-term storage? Use several sheets of soaking-wet newspapers to wrap up your glass dishes, bowls, drinking glasses, and other fragile items, and then let them thoroughly dry before packing. The newspaper will harden and form a protective cast around the glass that will dramatically improve its chances of surviving the move without breaking.

Store sweaters and blankets Don't treat moths to a fine meal of your homemade or store-bought woolen sweaters and blankets. When putting them into storage,

DID *You* KNOW?

America's first newspaper was called *Publick Occurrences, Both Foreign and Domestick*. It was a folded three-panel sheet of paper printed in Boston on September 25, 1690, by Richard Pierce and Benjamin Harris. Unfortunately, British colonial authorities closed it after its first and only issue and quickly issued a decree banning "unlicensed" publications. Ironically, the only known copy isn't found in the United States. It's in the Public Records Office in London.

wrap your woolens in a few sheets of newspaper (be sure to tape up the corners). It will keep away the moths, and keep out dust and dirt.

Clean and polish your windows If you're like most folks, you probably use a lot of absorbent paper towels for drying off your just-washed windows. Did you know that crumpled-up newspaper dries and polishes windows even better than paper towels? And it's a lot cheaper too.

Deodorize luggage and containers Do you have a plastic container or wooden box with a persistent, unpleasant odor? Stuff in a few sheets of crumpled newspaper and seal it closed for three or four days. You can also use this technique to deodorize trunks and suitcases (using more newspaper, of course).

Dry wet shoes If your shoes get soaked after walking through the rain or slogging through the snow, stuff them with dry, balled-up newspaper to prevent any long-term damage. Place the shoes on their sides at room temperature so the moisture can be thoroughly absorbed. For severe sogginess, you may need to replace the stuffing a few times.

Make an impromptu ironing board If you always take along a travel iron—just in case you end up in a motel that doesn't provide irons and ironing boards—it's a cinch to make your own on-the-road ironing board. Simply fill a pillowcase with a short stack of newspapers, keeping it as level as possible. Then place it on a countertop or the floor and get pressing.

Create an emergency splint If someone you're with takes a nasty fall—and you suspect there may be a bone injury to an arm or leg—it's important to immobilize the limb to prevent pain and additional damage. Fashion a makeshift splint by folding up several sheets of newspaper until stiff and attach it beneath the limb using a few pieces of adhesive tape. You may need to overlap a couple of folded sheets to make a splint long enough for a leg injury.

Remove oven residue They may call it a self-cleaning oven, but when it's done cleaning, you always have to contend with mopping off that ashlike residue. Don't waste a roll of paper towels on the flaky stuff; clean it up with a few sheets of moistened, crumpled newspaper.

Pick up broken glass shards Okay, so everyone breaks a big glass bowl at least once in a lifetime. It's no big thing. A safe way to get up the small shards of glass that remain after you remove the large pieces is to blot the area with wet newspapers. The tiny fragments will stick to the paper, which makes for easy disposal. Just carefully drop the newspaper in your garbage can.

Unscrew a broken lightbulb To remove a broken lightbulb, wad up several sheets of newspaper, press the paper over the bulb, and turn it counterclockwise. (Make sure you're wearing protective gloves and that the power is off.) The bulb should loosen up enough to remove from the socket. Wrap it in the paper and toss it into the garbage.

Slow-ripen tomatoes in late fall Is there an early frost predicted and you still have a bunch of tomatoes on the vine? Relax. Pick your tomatoes and wrap each one in a couple of sheets of newspaper. Store them in airtight containers inside a dark cabinet or closet at room temperature. Check each one every three to four days; they will all eventually ripen to perfection.

Line your trash compactor Putting a few layers of newspapers at the bottom of your trash compactor will not only soak up the nasty odors caused by rotting foods, it will also protect the unit against damage caused by any sharp objects that manage to squeeze through.

Use as mulch Newspaper makes terrific mulch for veggies and flowers. It's excellent at retaining moisture and does an equally fine job at fighting off and suffocating weeds. Just lay down several sheets of newspaper. Then cover the paper with about 3 inches (7.5 centimeters) of wood mulch so it doesn't blow away. *Warning:* Avoid using glossy stock and colored newsprint for mulching (or composting); color inks may contain lead or harmful dyes that can leach into the ground. To check your newsprint, contact your local paper and ask about the inks they use; many papers now use only safe vegetable-based inks.

Add to compost Adding moderate amounts of wet, shredded newsprint—printed in black ink only—to your compost heap is a good and relatively safe way to reduce odor and to give earthworms a tasty treat.

Adios, earwigs If your garden is under siege by earwigs—those creepy-looking insects with the sharp pincers on their hindquarters—get rid of them by making your own environmentally friendly traps. Tightly roll up a wet newspaper, and put a rubber band around it to keep it from unraveling. Place it in the area you've seen the insects, and leave it overnight. By morning, it will be

DID *You* KNOW?

What we call newsprint—the type of paper used by newspapers around the world—was invented around 1838 by a Nova Scotia teenager, Charles Fenerty. After hearing frequent complaints from local paper mills about maintaining adequate supplies of rags to make rag paper, Fenerty hit upon the idea of making paper from spruce pulp. Unfortunately, Fenerty didn't go public with his discovery until 1844. By then, a consortium of European investors had already patented a process for creating paper solely from wood fiber.

standing room only for the bugs. Place the newspaper in a plastic grocery bag, tie a knot at the top of the bag, and toss it into the trash. Repeat until your traps are free of earwigs.

Winterize outdoor faucets If you live in an older home without frost-free outdoor spigots, it's a good idea to insulate the outdoor faucets. To prevent damage from ice and cold temperatures, make sure you shut off the valve to each faucet, and drain off any excess water from the spigots. Then insulate each faucet by wrapping it with a few sheets of newspaper covered with a plastic bag (keep the bag in place by wrapping it with duct tape or a few rubber bands).

Protect windows when painting Don't bother buying thick masking or carpenter tape when painting around the windows of your home. Simply wet several long strips of newspaper and place them on the glass alongside the wood you're painting. The newspaper will easily adhere to the surface and keep the paint off the glass or frames, and it is much easier to remove than tape.

Roll your own fireplace logs Bad winter on the way? Bolster your supply of fireplace logs by making a few of your own out of old newspapers. Just lay out a bunch of sheets end to end, roll them up as tightly as you can, tie up the ends with twine or wire, and wet them in a solution of slightly soapy water. Although it will take a while, let them dry thoroughly, standing on end, before using. *Note:* Do not use newspaper logs in a woodstove unless the manufacturer specifies that it is okay.

Put traction under your wheels Unless your vehicle has four-wheel drive, it's always a good idea to keep a small stack of newspapers in the trunk of your car during the winter months to prevent getting stranded on a patch of ice or slush. Placing a dozen or two sheets of newspaper under each rear wheel will often provide just the traction you need to get your car back on the road.

* Oatmeal

Treat itchy poison ivy or chicken pox Take the itch out of a case of chicken pox or a poison ivy rash with a relaxing, warm oatmeal bath. Simply grind 1 cup oatmeal in your blender until it is a fine powder, then pour it into a piece of cheesecloth, the foot section of a clean nylon stocking, or the leg of an old pantyhose. Knot the material, and tie it around the faucet of your bathtub so the bag is suspended under the running water. Fill the tub with lukewarm water and soak in it for 30 minutes. You may find additional relief by applying the oatmeal pouch directly to the rash or pox.

Add luxury to a regular bath You don't have to have itchy skin to make a luxurious bath mix with oatmeal. And it beats buying expensive bath oils. All you need is 1 cup oatmeal and your favorite scented oil, such as rose or lavender. Grind the oatmeal in a blender, put it in a cheesecloth bag, add a few drops of the scented oil, and suspend the bag under the running water as you fill your bathtub. You'll not only find it sweetly soothing, you can also use the oatmeal bag as a washcloth to exfoliate your skin.

Make a facial mask If you're looking for a quick pick-me-up that will leave you feeling *and* looking better, give yourself an oatmeal facial. Combine 1/2 cup hot—

 DID *You* KNOW?

Thirty minutes. Five minutes. One minute! Oatmeal cooking times depend on how the oats were made into oatmeal. After the inedible hull is removed, the oat is called a groat. If the groats are just cut into about four pieces, the oatmeal takes up to 30 minutes to cook. If the groats are steamed and rolled but not cut, it takes about five minutes. If they are steamed, rolled, *and* cut, the cooking time drops to a minute or so. Steaming, rolling, and cooking breaks down the fiber, so if you want a lot of fiber, use 30-minute oatmeal and cook it until it is chewy, not mushy.

not boiling—water and 1/3 cup oatmeal. After the water and oatmeal have settled for two or three minutes, mix in 2 tablespoons plain yogurt, 2 tablespoons honey, and 1 small egg white. Apply a thin layer of the mixture to your face, and let it sit for 10-15 minutes. Then rinse with warm water. (Be sure to place a metal or plastic strainer in your sink to avoid clogging the drain with the granules.)

Make a dry shampoo Do you sometimes need to skip washing your hair in order to get to work on time? Keep a batch of dry shampoo on hand in an airtight container specifically for those occasions when your alarm clock "malfunctions." Put 1 cup oatmeal in the blender and grind it into a fine powder. Add 1 cup baking soda, and mix well. Rub a bit of the mixture into your hair. Give it a minute or two to soak up the oils, then brush or shake it out of your hair (preferably over a towel or bag to avoid getting it all over). This dry shampoo mixture is also ideal for cleaning the hair of bedridden people who are unable to get into a shower or bathtub. Plus, it's equally effective for deodorizing that big ol' bath-hating mutt of yours.

✳ Olive Oil

Remove paint from hair Did you get almost as much paint in your hair as you did on the walls in your last paint job? You can easily remove that undesirable tint by moistening a cotton ball with some olive oil and gently rubbing it into your hair. The same approach is also effective for removing mascara—just be sure to wipe your eyes with a tissue when done.

Make your own furniture polish Restore the lost luster of your wooden furniture by whipping up some serious homemade furniture polish that's just as good as any of the commercial stuff. Combine 2 parts olive oil and 1 part lemon juice or white vinegar in a clean recycled spray bottle, shake it up, and spritz on. Leave on the mixture for a minute or two, then wipe off with a clean terry-cloth or paper towel. In a hurry? Get fast results by applying olive oil straight from the bottle onto a paper towel. Wipe off the excess with another paper towel or an absorbent cloth.

Use as hair conditioner Is your hair as dry and brittle as sagebrush in the desert? Put the moisture back into it by heating 1/2 cup olive oil (don't boil it), and then liberally applying it to your hair. Cover your hair with a plastic grocery bag, then wrap it in a towel. Let it set for 45 minutes, then shampoo and thoroughly rinse.

Clear up acne Okay, the notion of applying oil to your face to treat acne does sound a bit wacky. Still, many folks swear this works: Make a paste by mixing 4 tablespoons salt with 3 tablespoons olive oil. Pour the mixture onto your hands and fingers and work it around your face. Leave it on for a minute or two, then rinse it off with warm, soapy water. Apply daily for one week, then cut back to two or three times weekly. You should see a noticeable improvement in your condition. (The principle is that the salt cleanses the pores by exfoliation, while the olive oil restores the skin's natural moisture.)

Substitute for shaving cream If you run out of shaving cream, don't waste your time trying to make do with soap—it could be rough on your skin. Olive oil, on the other hand, is a dandy substitute for shaving cream. It not only makes it easier for the blade to glide over your face or legs, but it will moisturize your skin as well. In fact, after trying this, you may swear off shaving cream altogether.

Tip Buying Olive Oil

Expensive extra virgin olive oil is made from olives crushed soon after harvest and processed without excessive heat. It's great for culinary uses where the taste of the oil is important. But for everyday cooking and non-food applications, lower grades of olive oil—light, extra light, or just plain olive oil—work fine and save you money.

Clean your greasy hands To remove car grease or paint from your hands, pour 1 teaspoon olive oil and 1 teaspoon salt or sugar into your palms. Vigorously rub the mixture into your hands and between your fingers for several minutes; then wash it off with soap and water. Not only will your hands be cleaner, they'll be softer as well.

Recondition an old baseball mitt If your beloved, aging baseball glove is showing signs of wear and tear—cracking and hardening of the leather—you can give it a second lease on life with an occasional olive oil rubdown. Just work the oil into the dry areas of your mitt with a soft cloth, let it set for 30 minutes, then wipe off any excess. Your game may not improve, but at least it won't be your glove's fault. Some folks prefer to use bath oil to recondition their mitts (see page 81).

✳ Onions

Remove rust from knives Forget about using steel wool or harsh chemicals—how's this for an easy way to get the rust off your kitchen or utility knives? Plunge your rusty knife into a large onion three or four times (if it's very rusty, it may require a few extra stabs). The only tears you shed will be ones of joy over your rust-free blade.

Eliminate new paint smell Your bedroom's new shade of paint looks great, but the smell is keeping you up all night. What to do? Place several freshly cut slices of onion in a dish with a bit of water. It will absorb the smell within a few hours.

Correct pet "mistakes" If Rover or Kitty is still not respecting your property—whether it be by chewing, tearing, or soiling—you may be able to get the message across by leaving several onion slices where the damage has been done. Neither cats nor dogs are particularly fond of *"eau de onion,"* and they'll avoid returning to the scene of their crimes.

Soothe a bee sting If you have a nasty encounter with a bee at a barbecue, grab one of the onion slices intended for your burger and place it over the area where you got stung. It will ease the soreness. (If you are severely allergic to bee or other insect stings, seek medical attention at once.)

Use as smelling salts If you happen to be with someone at a party or in a restaurant who feels faint—and you don't normally carry smelling salts in your pocket—reach for a freshly cut onion. The strong odor is likely to bring him around.

Use as a natural pesticide Whip up an effective insect and animal repellent for the flowers and vegetables in your garden. In a blender, puree 4 onions, 2 cloves garlic, 2 tablespoons cayenne pepper, and 1 quart water (1 liter). Set the mixture aside. Now dilute 2 tablespoons soap flakes in 2 gallons (7.5 liters) water. Pour in the contents of your blender, shake or stir well, and you have a potent, environment-friendly solution to spray on your plants.

? DID *You* KNOW?

How can you keep your eyes from tearing when cutting onions? Suggestions range from wearing protective goggles while chopping, to placing a fan behind you to blow away the onion's tear-producing vapors, to rubbing your hands with vinegar before you start slicing. The National Onion Association, however, advises chilling onions in the freezer for 30 minutes prior to slicing them. The association also suggests cutting off the top portion and peeling off the outer layers. The idea is to leave the root end intact, because it has the highest concentrations of the sulfur compounds that cause your eyes to tear.

Make mosquito repellent Some people find that increasing their intake of onions or garlic in the summer—or rubbing a slice of onion over their exposed skin—is a good way to keep away mosquitoes and other biting insects (not to mention friends and family).

✳ Oranges

Use for kindling Dried orange and lemon peels are a far superior choice for use as kindling than newspaper. Not only do they smell better and produce less creosote than newspaper, but the flammable oils found inside the peels enable them to burn much longer than paper.

Make a pomander Pomanders have been used for centuries to fill small spaces with a delightful fragrance as well as to combat moths. They are also incredibly easy to make: Take a bunch of cloves and stick them into an orange, covering the whole surface. That's it. Pretty simple, huh? Now suspend your pomander using a piece of string, twine, or monofilament fishing line inside a closet or cupboard, and it will keep the space smelling fresh for years.

Simmer for stovetop potpourri Fill your abode with a refreshing citrus scent by simmering several orange and/or lemon peels in 1-2 cups of water in an aluminum pot for a few hours. Add water as needed during the simmering. This process freshens up the pot as well as the air in your home.

Keep kitties off your lawn Are the neighbor's cats still mistaking your lawn for their litter box? Gently point them elsewhere by making a mixture of orange peels and coffee grounds and distributing it around the cats' "old haunts." If they don't take the hint, lay down a second batch and try moistening it with a bit of water.

Apply as mosquito repellent If you're not crazy about the idea of rubbing onions all over yourself to keep away mosquitoes (see previous page), you may be happy to know that you can often get similar results by rubbing fresh orange or lemon peels over your exposed skin. It's said that mosquitoes and gnats are totally repulsed by either scent.

Show ants the door Get rid of the ants in your garden, on your patio, and along the foundation of your home. In a blender, make a smooth puree of a few orange peels in 1 cup warm water. Slowly pour the solution over and into anthills to send the little pests packing.

✳ Oven Cleaner

Put the style back in your curling iron Is your curling iron buried under a layer of caked-on styling gel or conditioner? Before the next time you use it, spray on a light coating of oven cleaner. Let it sit for one hour, then wipe it off with a damp rag, and dry with a clean cloth. *Warning:* Do not use iron until it is thoroughly dry.

Wipe away bathtub ring Got a stubborn stain or ring around your white porcelain tub that refuses to come clean? Call out the big guns by spraying it with oven cleaner. Let it sit for a few hours, then give it a thorough rinsing. *Warning:* Do not apply oven cleaner to colored porcelain tubs; it could cause fading. And be careful not to get the oven cleaner on your shower curtain; it can ruin both plastic and fabric.

Clean grimy tile grout lines Ready for an all-out attack on grout grunge? First, make sure you have plenty of ventilation—it's a good idea to use your exhaust fan to suck air out of a small bathroom. Put on your rubber gloves and spray oven cleaner into the grout lines. Wipe the cleaner off with a sponge within five seconds. Rinse thoroughly with water to reveal sparkling grout lines.

> **TAKE CARE** Most oven cleaners contain highly caustic lye, which can burn the skin and damage the eyes. Always wear long rubber gloves and protective eyewear when using oven cleaner. The mist from oven cleaner spray can irritate nasal membranes. Ingestion can cause corrosive burns to the mouth, throat, and stomach that require immediate medical attention. Store oven cleaner well out of children's reach.

Clean ovenproof glass cookware You've tried everything to scrub those baked-on stains off your Pyrex or CorningWare cookware. Now try this: Put on rubber gloves and cover the cookware with oven cleaner. Then place the cookware in a heavy-duty garbage bag, close it tightly with twist ties, and leave overnight. Open the bag outdoors, keeping your face away from the dangerous fumes. Use rubber gloves to remove and wash the cookware.

Clean a cast-iron pot If you need to clean and re-season that encrusted secondhand cast-iron skillet you found at a yard sale, start by giving it a good spraying with oven cleaner and placing it in a sealed plastic bag overnight. (This keeps the cleaner working by preventing it from drying.) The next day, remove the pot and scrub it with a stiff wire brush. Then, wash it thoroughly with soap and water, rinse well, and immediately dry it with a couple of clean, dry cloths. *Note:* This technique eliminates built-up gunk and grease, but not rust. For that, you'll need to use vinegar. Don't leave it on too long, though. Prolonged exposure to vinegar can damage your cast-iron utensil.

Remove stains from concrete Get those unsightly grease, oil, and transmission fluid stains off your concrete driveway or garage floor. Spray them with oven cleaner. Let it settle for 5-10 minutes, then scrub with a stiff brush and rinse it off with your garden hose at its highest pressure. Severe stains may require a second application.

Strip paint or varnish For an easy way to remove paint or varnish from wooden or metal furniture, try using a can of oven cleaner; it costs less than commercial paint strippers and is easier to apply (that is, if you spray rather than brush it on). After applying, scrub off the old paint with a wire brush. Neutralize the stripped surface by coating it with vinegar, and then wash it off with clean water. Allow the wood or metal to thoroughly dry before repainting. Don't use oven cleaner to strip antiques or expensive furnishings; it can darken the wood or discolor the metal.

✳ Oven Mitts

Use as beverage cozy or egg warmer Keep that mug of java or tea from getting cold when you're called away by placing an oven mitt over it. The glove's insulation will keep it warm until you get back. You can also use an oven mitt to keep boiled eggs warm for up to half an hour. Conversely, an oven mitt will help keep a cold drink colder longer.

Use for dusting and polishing Although oven mitts are typically confined to kitchen duty, they're actually great for dusting and polishing around your house. Use one side of the mitt to apply wax or polish to your furniture, and the other side to buff it up. It's a great way to use old mitts or all those extra ones you've collected.

When pruning thorny plants Although oven mitts may be a bit too awkward to use for weeding or planting seedlings in your garden, they can come in awfully handy when it comes time to prune trees, hedges, and bushes—particularly those thorny devils such as holly, firethorn, and rosebushes.

Remove hot engine parts Keeping an oven mitt in your car's glove compartment or trunk can make life a lot easier when you need to handle hot radiator caps and the like during an on-the-road emergency.

Change a hot lightbulb Did the lightbulb on your reading lamp just blow out? Don't scorch your fingers when replacing it. Once you've removed the lampshade, put on an oven mitt, remove the dead bulb from the socket, and toss it into the garbage. That way, you won't still be blowing on your fingertips when screwing in the new bulb.

* Paintbrushes

Use for delicate dusting A feather duster or dust rag is fine for cleaning shelves and such, but neither one is much good when you need to get into the tiny cracks and crevices of chandeliers, wicker furniture or baskets, and all sorts of knick-knacks. That's when a small natural-bristle paintbrush can be indispensable. The soft bristles are perfect for cleaning out areas that are otherwise impossible to reach. It's also excellent for dusting delicate items such as porcelain or carved-wood figurines.

Brush off beach chairs Keep a clean, dry paintbrush in your car specifically for those return trips from the beach. Use it to remove sand from beach chairs, towels, toys, the kids, and even yourself before you open the car door or trunk. You'll wind up with a lot less to vacuum the next time you clean your vehicle.

Brush on the sauce A small synthetic-bristle paintbrush can be invaluable in the kitchen. You can use it to brush on pie glaze, marinades, and sauces while baking or roasting. You can also use it to paint on the barbecue sauce when grilling burgers and steaks in the great outdoors. To top it all off, a paintbrush is easier to clean than most conventional pastry brushes.

Apply stain remover to clothes Let's face it: Pouring detergent or stain remover onto a soiled garment is often a hit-or-miss proposition—and when you miss, it usually involves grabbing the paper towels to soak up a spill. Make life easier for yourself. Use a small paintbrush to apply liquid stain remover to dirty shirt collars and such. It's neater and a lot more accurate.

Clean your window screens Are your window screens screaming out for a good cleaning? Use a large, clean paintbrush to give them a good dusting. Then shake off the brush, dip it into a small dish of kerosene, and "paint" both sides of your screens. Dry off the mesh with a clean cloth.

Cover up seeds when sowing Sow your seeds with a little TLC. When planting seeds in rows, use a large paintbrush to gently brush them over with soil. This lets you distribute the exact amount of soil needed and prevents overpacking.

P

Natural-bristle brushes work best with alkyd/oil-based paint. But use a synthetic-bristle brush with latex paint because the water in the paint can ruin natural bristles. Before cleaning any brush, wipe excess paint onto newspaper. Clean a brush used with alkyd paint in mineral spirits until you get out all the paint, then shake out. To clean out latex paint, wash the brush thoroughly with soapy water, rinse clean, and shake out. Many latex paints contain acrylics that won't wash out completely with soap and water. In this case, finish up with mineral spirits.

super item
33 uses! **Pantyhose**

❋ PANTYHOSE **AROUND THE HOUSE**

Find lost small objects Have you ever spent hours on your hands and knees searching through a carpet for a lost gemstone, contact lens, or some other tiny, precious item? If not, count yourself among the lucky few. Should you ever be faced with this situation, try this: Cut a leg off an old pair of pantyhose, make sure the toe section is intact, and pull it up over the nozzle of your vacuum cleaner hose. (If you want additional security, you can even cut off the other leg and slip that over as well.) Secure the stocking in place with a tightly wound rubber band. Turn on the vacuum, *carefully* move the nozzle over the carpet, and you'll soon find your lost valuable attached to the pantyhose filter.

Vacuum your fish tank If you have a wet-dry shop vacuum, you can change the water in your fish tank without disturbing the gravel and tank accessories. (You'll still have to relocate the fish, of course.) Just pull the foot of an old nylon stocking over the end of the vacuum's nozzle, secure it with a rubber band, and you are ready to suck out the water.

Buff your shoes Bring out the shine in your freshly polished shoes by buffing them with a medium-length strip of pantyhose. It works so well, you may retire that chamois cloth for good.

Keep your hairbrush clean If you dread the prospect of cleaning out your hairbrush, here's a way to make the job much easier. Cut a 2-inch (5-centimeter) strip from the leg section of a pair of pantyhose, and stretch it over and around the bristles of your new (or newly cleaned) hairbrush. If necessary, use a bobby pin or a comb to push the hose down over the bristles. The next time your brush needs cleaning, simply lift up and remove the pantyhose layer—along with all the dead hair, lint, etc. on top—and replace it with a fresh strip.

Wrap up wrapping paper Keep your used rolls of wrapping paper from tearing and unraveling by storing them in tubes made by cutting the leg sections off old pairs of pantyhose. (Don't forget to leave the foot section intact.) Or, if you have a bunch of used rolls, you can simply put one in each leg of a pair of pantyhose and hang them over a hanger in your closet.

Remove nail polish Can't find the cotton balls? Moisten strips of recycled pantyhose with nail polish remover to take off your old nail polish. Cut the material into 3-inch (7.5-centimeter) squares, and store a stack of them in an old bandage container or makeup case.

Keep spray bottles clog-free If you recycle your spray bottles to use with homemade cleaners or furniture polishes, you can prevent any potential clogs by covering the open end of the tube—the part that goes inside the bottle—with a small, square-cut piece of pantyhose held in place with a small rubber band. This works especially well for filtering garden sprays that are mixed from concentrates.

Substitute for stuffing Is your kid's teddy bear or doll losing its stuffing? Get out a needle and thread and prepare the patient for an emergency "stuffing transplant." Replace the lost filler with narrow strips of clean, worn-out pantyhose (ball them up, if possible). Stitch the hole up well, and a complete recovery is guaranteed. This works well with throw pillows and seat cushions too.

Organize your suitcase As any seasoned traveler knows, you can squeeze more of your belongings into any piece of luggage by rolling up your clothes. To keep your bulkier rolls from unwrapping, cover them in flexible nylon tubes. Simply cut the legs off a pair of old pantyhose, snip off the foot sections, and stretch the stockings over your rolled-up garments. Happy travels!

Take a citrus bath Make your own scented bath oil by drying and grinding up orange and/or lemon peels and then pouring them into the foot section of a recycled pantyhose. Put a knot about 1 inch (2.5 centimeters) above the peels, and leave another 6 inches (15 centimeters) or so of hose above that before cutting off

? DID You KNOW?

Nylon, the world's first synthetic fiber, was invented at E. I. DuPont de Nemours, Inc., and unveiled on October 28, 1938. Instead of calling a press conference, company vice president Charles Stine chose to make the landmark announcement to 3,000 women's club members at the New York World's Fair, introducing it with live models wearing nylon stockings. Stine's instincts were right on the money: By the end of 1940, DuPont had sold 64 million pairs of stockings. Nylon actually made its big-screen debut a year earlier, when it was used to create the tornado that lifted Dorothy out of Kansas in *The Wizard of Oz.*

PANTYHOSE*

the remainder. Tie the stocking to the bathtub faucet with the peels suspended below the running water. In addition to giving your bath a fresh citrus fragrance, you can use the stocking to exfoliate your skin.

Hold mothballs or potpourri Looking for an easy way to store mothballs in your closet or to make sachets of potpourri to keep in your dresser drawers? Pour either ingredient into the toe section of your recycled nylons. Knot off the contents, then cut off the remaining hose. If you plan to hang up the mothballs, leave several inches of material before cutting.

Make a ponytail scrunchy Why buy a scrunchy for your ponytail when you can easily make one for nothing? Just cut a horizontal strip about 3-inches (7.5 centimeters) wide across a pantyhose leg, wrap it a few times around your ponytail, and you're done.

Use to hang-dry sweaters Avoid getting clothespin marks on your newly washed sweaters by putting an old pair of pantyhose through the neck of the sweater and running the legs out through the arms. Then hang the sweater to dry on your clothesline by clipping the clothespins onto the pantyhose instead of the wool.

Bundle blankets for storage For an effortless and foolproof way to keep blankets and quilts securely bundled before they go into temporary storage, wrap them up in large "rubber bands" made from the waistbands from your used pantyhose. You can reuse the bands year after year if needed.

Tie up boxes, newspapers, magazines If you run out of twine (or need something stronger—say, for a large stack of glossy magazines), tie up your bundles of boxes, newspapers, and other types of recyclable paper goods using an old pair of pantyhose. Cut off the legs and waistband, and you'll be able to get everything curbside without any snags.

✳ PANTYHOSE **IN THE KITCHEN**

Store onions in cutoff bundles Get the maximum shelf life out of your onions by hanging them in nylon holders that provide the good air circulation needed to keep them fresh. Place the onions one at a time into the leg of a clean pair of pantyhose. Work the first one down to the foot section. Tie a knot above it and add the next one—repeat until done. Cut off the remaining hose, and then hang the stocking in a cool, dry area of your kitchen. You can easily remove your onions when needed by snipping off each knot, starting from the bottom.

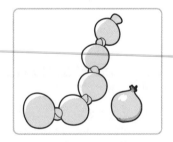

Make a pot or dish scrubber Clean those stains off your nonstick cookware by making a do-it-yourself scrub pad. Crumple up a pair of clean old pantyhose, moisten it with a bit of warm water, add a couple of drops of liquid dishwashing detergent, and you're good to go. You can also make terrific scrubbers for dishes—as well as walls and other nonporous surfaces—by cutting off the foot or toe section, fitting it over a sponge, and knotting off the end.

Make a flour duster Looking for a simple way to dust baking pans and surfaces with exactly the right amount of flour? Just cut the foot section off a clean old pantyhose leg, fill it with flour, tie a knot in it, and keep it in your flour jar. Give your new flour dispenser a few gentle shakes whenever you need to dust flour onto a baking pan or prepare a surface for rolling out dough for breads or pastries.

Keep a rolling pin from sticking Getting pie dough to the perfect consistency is an art form in itself. Although you can always add water to dough that's too dry, it often results in a gluey consistency that winds up sticking to your rolling pin. Avoid the hassle of scraping clean your rolling pin by covering it with a piece of pantyhose. It will hold enough flour to keep even the wettest pie dough from sticking to the pin.

Secure trash bags How many times have you opened your kitchen trash can only to discover that the liner has slipped down (and that someone in your house has covered it over with fresh garbage anyway)? You can prevent such "accidents" by firmly securing the garbage bag or liner to your trash can with the elastic waistband from a recycled pair of pantyhose; tie a knot in the band to keep it tight. You can also use this method to keep garbage bags from slipping off the edge of your outdoor garbage bins.

Dust under the fridge Having trouble catching those dust bunnies residing underneath and alongside your refrigerator? Round them up by balling up a pair of old pantyhose and attaching it with a rubber band to a coat hanger or yardstick. The dust and dirt will cling to the nylon, which can easily be washed off before being called back for dusting duty.

DID You KNOW?

You have probably heard that you can temporarily replace a broken fan belt with pantyhose in an emergency. Well, don't believe it—it won't work! Jim Kerr, automotive technician instructor at the Saskatchewan Institute of Applied Arts and Sciences and "Tech Talk" columnist for CanadianDriver.com, says, "Pulleys in most vehicles require flat belts, not the rounded shape pantyhose would present. Even on a V-belt pulley, they fly off as soon as the engine starts. We know; we've tried it." A much better idea is to replace the belts before they get in bad condition.

Stake delicate plants Give your young plants and trees the support they need. Use strips of pantyhose to attach them to your garden stakes. The nylon's flexibility will stretch as your seedlings or saplings fill out and mature—unlike string or twine, which can actually damage plant stalks if you tie it too tightly.

Store flower bulbs in winter Pantyhose legs make terrific sacks for storing your flower bulbs over winter, since they let air freely circulate around the bulbs to prevent mold and rot. Simply cut a leg off a pair of pantyhose and place your bulbs inside, knot off the end, and place ID tags on each sack using a strip of masking tape. Hang them up in a cool, dry space, and they'll be ready for planting in the spring.

Prevent soil erosion in houseplants When moving a houseplant to a larger or better accommodation, put a piece of pantyhose at the bottom of the new pot. It will act as a liner that lets the excess water flow out without draining the soil along with it.

Support melons Keep small melons such as cantaloupe and muskmelons off the ground—and free of pests and disease—by making protective sleeves for them from your old pantyhose. Cut the legs off the pantyhose. As your young melons start to develop, slide each one into the foot section, and tie the leg to a stake to suspend the melon above the ground. The nylon holders will stretch as the melons mature, while keeping them from touching the damp soil, where they would be susceptible to rot or invasion by hungry insects and other garden pests.

Keep deer out of your garden If you've been catching Bambi and her friends nibbling on your crops, put up a "No Trespassing" sign they will easily understand. Simply fill the foot sections of some old pantyhose with human hair clippings collected from hairbrushes or your local barbershop—or, even better, use Rover's fur after a good brushing. Tie up the ends, and hang up the nylon satchels where the deer tend to snack. They won't be back for seconds. The hair or fur will lose its scent after a while, so replace every four or five days as needed.

Clean up after gardening Here are two recycling tips in one: Save up your leftover slivers of soap, and place them in the foot section of an old nylon stocking. Knot it off, and hang it next to your outdoor faucet. Use the soap-filled stocking to quickly wash off your hands after gardening and other outdoor work without worrying about getting dirt on door handles or bathroom fixtures inside your house.

P

Cover a kids' bug jar What child doesn't like to catch fireflies—and hopefully release them—on a warm summer night? When making a bug jar for your youngster, don't bother using a hammer and nail to punch holes in the jar's metal lid (in fact, save the lids for other projects). It's much easier to just cut a 5- or 6-inch (15-centimeter) square from an old pair of pantyhose and affix it to the jar with a rubber band. The nylon cover lets plenty of air enter the jar, and makes it easier to get the bugs in and out.

✱ PANTYHOSE **FOR THE DO-IT-YOURSELFER**

Apply stain to wood crevices Getting wood stain or varnish into the tight corners and crevices of that unfinished bookcase or table that you just bought can be a maddening task. Your brush just won't fit into them and give them an even coating. But there's really nothing to it once you know the secret. Just cut a strip from an old pair of pantyhose, fold it over a few times, and use a  rubber band to affix it to the tip of a wooden Popsicle stick. Dip your homemade applicator into the stain or varnish, and you'll have no trouble getting it into those hard-to-reach spots.

Test a sanded surface for snags Think you did a pretty good job sanding down that woodworking project? Put it to the pantyhose test. Wrap a long piece of pantyhose around the palm of your hand and rub it over the wood. If the pantyhose snags onto any spots, sand them until you're able to freely move the nylon over the surface without any catches.

Patch a hole in a screen Don't invite the bugs in for a bite; use a small square of pantyhose to temporarily patch that hole in your window screen. You can secure the

 DID *You* KNOW?

According to the Toy Industry Association, legendary doll maker Madame Alexander came up with the concept for pantyhose in the early 1950s, when she started sewing tiny pairs of silk stockings onto her dolls' underpants to keep them from slipping down. But Allen Gant, Sr., of Burlington, North Carolina, invented pantyhose as we know them, and they were first produced in 1959 by Glen Raven Mills, his family's textile business. Another pantyhose pioneer is Hollywood actress Julie Newmar, best known as the original Catwoman on the old *Batman* TV series in the late 1960s, who holds a patent for "ultra-sheer, ultra-snug" pantyhose.

patch by simply applying some rubber cement around the hole before pressing the patch in place. When you're ready to fix the hole with a piece of screening, peel off the nylon and the glue. If you want the patch to last a bit longer, sew it onto the screen with thread.

Clean your pool Want a more effective way to skim the debris off the surface of your pool water? Cut a leg off a pair of pantyhose and fit it over your pool's skimmer basket. It will catch a lot of tiny dirt particles and hairs that would otherwise make their way into—and possibly clog—your pool's filter unit.

Make a paint strainer Strain your paint like the pros: Use a pantyhose filter to remove the lumps of paint from an old can of paint. First, cut a leg off a pair of old pantyhose, clip the foot off the leg, and make a cut along the leg's length so that you have a flat piece of nylon. Then cut the leg into 12- to 14-inch (30- to 32-centimeter) sections to make the filters. Stretch the nylon over  a clean bucket or other receptacle and hold it in place with a rubber band or perhaps even the waistband from that pair of pantyhose. Now slowly pour the paint into the bucket.

super item 25 uses! Paper Bags

✳ PAPER BAGS **AROUND THE HOUSE**

Dust off your mops Dust mops make it a breeze to get up the dust balls and pet hair around your home, but how do you get the stuff off your mop? Place a large paper bag over the mop head; use a piece of string or a rubber band to keep it from slipping off. Now give it several good shakes (a few gentle bumps wouldn't hurt either). Lay the mop on its side for a few minutes to let the dust in the bag settle. Then carefully remove the bag for easy disposal of your dusty dirt.

Clean artificial flowers Authentic silk flowers are actually pretty rare these days; most are now made of nylon or some other man-made material. But regardless of whether they're silk or something else, you can easily freshen them up by placing them in a paper bag with 1/4 cup salt. Give the bag a few gentle shakes, and your flowers will emerge as clean as the day you purchased them.

Carry your laundry If your laundry basket is already overflowing, or (gasp!) the plastic handle suddenly gives out, you can always use a sturdy shopping bag to pick up the slack. A bag with handles will probably make the job easier, but any large bag will do in a pinch. Just be sure your laundry is completely dry before using the bag on the return trip. Otherwise, your freshly cleaned clothes could wind up under your feet.

Cover your kids' textbooks Helping your children make book covers for their textbooks isn't only fun, it's also a subtle way to teach kids to respect public property. And few materials rival a paper bag when it comes to making a rugged book cover. First, cut the bag along its seams to make it a flat, wide rectangle, then place the book in the center. Fold in the top and bottom edges so the bag is only slightly wider than the book's height. Next, fold over the sides to form sleeves over the book covers. Cut off the excess, leaving a couple of inches on either side to slide over the front and back covers. Put a piece of masking tape on the top and bottom of each sleeve (over the paper, not the book) to keep it on tight, and you're done. Lastly, let your child put his or her personal design on each cover.

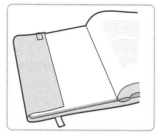

Create a table decoration Use a small designer shopping bag with handles to make an attractive centerpiece for your dining room table or living room mantel. Fill a small cup with some water and place it in the middle of the bag. Place a few fresh-cut flowers in the glass, and presto! All done.

Make your own wrapping paper Need to wrap a present in a hurry? You don't have to rush out to buy wrapping paper. Just cut a large paper bag along the seams until it's a flat rectangle. Position it so that any printing is facing up at you, put your gift on top and fold, cut, and tape the paper around your gift. If you wish, personalize your homemade wrapping paper by decorating it with markers, paint, or stickers.

DID *You* KNOW?

Are paper shopping bags better for the environment than their plastic counterparts? Not really, according to the U.S. Environmental Protection Agency. Paper bags generate 70 percent more air pollutants and 50 times more water pollutants than plastic bags. What's more, it takes four times as much energy to make a paper bag as it does to manufacture a plastic bag, and 91 percent more energy to recycle paper than plastic. On the other hand, paper bags come from a renewable resource (trees), while most plastic bags are made from nonrenewable resources (polyethylene, a combination of crude oil and natural gas). So what's the answer? Bring your own cloth shopping bags with you to the market!

PAPER BAGS*

Reuse as gift bags ~~What to do with those small gift bags~~ with handles favored by most boutiques? Why not use them to package your own gifts? They're ideal for holding items such as bath supplies, jewelry, perfume, and even most books. Simply add some shredded crepe paper, a personalized card, and you're all set.

Recycle as towel or tissue dispensers Add a simple but elegant touch to your guest bathrooms by using small "boutique bags" as paper towel or tissue dispensers. You can even embellish them with your own personal touches, such as ribbons or stickers that match your decor.

Reshape knits after washing Put the shape back into your wool sweater or mittens by tracing the contours of the item on a paper bag before you wash it. Then use your outline to stretch the item back to its original shape after washing it.

Store linen sets Have you ever emptied the contents of your linen closet looking for the flat sheet to match the fitted one you just pulled out? You can easily spare yourself some grief by using medium-sized paper bags to store your complete linen sets. Not only will your shelves be better organized, but you can also keep your linens smelling fresh by placing a used fabric softener sheet in each bag.

Use as a pressing cloth If your ironing board's cover appears to have seen its last steam iron, don't sweat it. You can easily make a temporary pressing cloth by splitting open one or two paper bags. Dampen the bags and lay them over your ironing board to get those last few shirts or skirts pressed for the workweek.

Pack your bags Getting ready to leave on a family vacation? Don't forget to pack a few large shopping bags—the kind with handles—in your luggage. They're guaranteed to come in handy to bring home the souvenirs you pick up, or perhaps your soiled laundry or beach towels.

Bag your recycled newspapers Double up on your recycling efforts by using large paper bags to hold your newspapers for collection. It not only spares you the time and effort needed to tie up your bundles with string, but it also makes it easier to sort out your magazines, newsprint, and glossy pages.

✳ PAPER BAGS **IN THE KITCHEN**

Make cleanups easier Cut open one or two paper bags and spread them out over your countertop when peeling vegetables, husking corn, shelling peas, or any other messy task. When you're done, simply fold up the paper, and toss it into the trash for a fast and easy cleanup.

Keep bread fresh If you live in a high-humidity area, your bread will stay fresher when stored inside a paper bag rather than a plastic one. The paper's ability to "breathe" will keep the bread's crust crisp while allowing the center of the loaf to stay soft and moist.

Use to ripen fruit Many fruits—including avocados, bananas, pears, peaches, and tomatoes—will ripen better when placed in a paper bag. To hasten the ripening process of any fruit, place an already ripe apple or banana peel in the same bag and store it at room temperature. To ripen green bananas, wrap them in a damp dishtowel before placing them in the bag. Once your fruits have adequately ripened, you can halt the process by putting them in the refrigerator.

Store mushrooms Remove your store-bought mushrooms from their mesh packaging and place them in a paper bag inside your refrigerator to keep them fresh for up to five days.

✸ PAPER BAGS **IN THE GARDEN**

Store geraniums in winter Although they're considered to be annuals, geraniums are easy to overwinter. First, remove the plants from their pots or carefully dig them up from your garden bed, shake off as much soil as possible, and place each plant in its own paper bag. Cover each bag with a second paper bag turned upside down and store them in a cool, dry place. When spring arrives, cut off all but 1 inch (2.5 centimeters) of stem and repot. Place them in a sunny spot, water regularly, and watch your plants "spring" back to life.

Feed your plants Bonemeal is an excellent source of nutrients for all the plants in your garden. You can easily make your own by first drying your leftover chicken bones in a microwave oven (depending on the quantity, cook them for 1-4 minutes on High). Then place the dried bones in a sturdy paper bag and grind them up using a mallet, hammer, or rolling pin. When done, distribute the powder around your plants and watch them thrive.

Add to compost Brown paper bags are a great addition to any garden compost heap. Not only do they contain less ink and pigment than newsprint, but they will also attract more earthworms to your pile (in fact, the only thing the worms like better than paper bags is cardboard). It's best to shred and wet the bags before adding to your pile. Also, be sure to mix them in well to prevent them from blowing away after they dry.

Dry your herbs To dry fresh herbs, first wash each plant under cold water and dry thoroughly with paper towels. Make sure the plants are completely dry before you proceed to reduce the risk of mold. Take five or six plants, remove the lower leaves, and place them upside down inside a large paper bag. Gather the end of the bag around the stems and tie it up. Punch a few holes in the bag for ventilation, then store it in a warm, dry area for at least two weeks. Once the plants have dried, inspect them carefully for any signs of mold. If you find any, toss out the whole bunch. You can grind them up, once you've removed the stems, with a rolling pin or a full soda bottle, or keep them whole to retain the flavor longer. Store your dried herbs in airtight containers and away from sunlight.

> *Kids' Stuff* Make a **life-size body poster** of your child. Start by cutting up 4-6 **paper bags** so they lie completely flat (any print should be facing down). Arrange them into one big square on the floor and **tape** the undersides together. Then have your child lie down in the middle, and use a **crayon** to trace the outline of his or her entire body. Give him or her **crayons or watercolor paints** to fill in the face, clothing, and other details. When your kid is finished, hang it up in his or her room as a terrific **wall decoration**.

✳ PAPER BAGS **FOR THE DO-IT-YOURSELFER**

Move snow off your windshield If you're tired of having to constantly scrape ice and snow off your car's windshield during the winter months, keep some paper bags on hand. When there's snow in the forecast, go out to your car and turn on the wipers. Then, shut off the engine with the wipers positioned near the middle of your windshield. Now, split open a couple of paper bags and use your car's wipers to hold them in place. After the last snowflake falls, pull off the paper to instantly clear your windshield. *Note:* To prevent damaging your car's wipers, *do not* turn on the ignition until you've removed the snow and paper from the windshield.

Make a fire starter Looking for an easy way to get a fire going in your fireplace? Simply fill a paper bag with some balled-up newspaper and perhaps some bits of candle wax. Stick the bag under your logs, light it, then sit back and enjoy your roaring fire.

Spray-paint small items You don't have to make a mess every time you need to spray-paint a small item. Just place the object to be painted inside a large shopping bag and spray away; the bag will contain the excess spray. Once the item has dried, simply remove it and toss away the bag.

Build a bag kite Make a simple bag kite for your children to play with by folding over the top of a paper bag to keep it open. Glue on pieces of party streamers under the fold. Reinforce the kite by gluing in some strips of balsa wood or a few thin twigs along the length of the bag. Poke a couple of holes above the opened end, and attach two

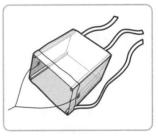

pieces of string or yarn (put a piece of masking or transparent tape over the holes to prevent them from tearing) and tie the ends onto a roll of kite string. It should take off when the kids start running.

✳ Paper Clips

Open shrink-wrapped CDs Opening shrink-wrap, especially on CDs, can be a test of skill and patience! Save your fingernails and teeth from destruction. Twist out the end of a paper clip and slice the wrap. To prevent scratches, slip the clip under the folded section of wrap and lift up.

Use as hooks for hanging Paper clips make great impromptu hooks. Making a hanging ceramic plaque? Insert a large, sturdy paper clip on the back before the clay hardens.

Use as zipper pull Don't throw away your jacket or pocketbook just because the zipper pull broke. Untwist a small paper clip enough to slip it through the hole. Twist it closed and zip! For a more decorative look, thread beads over the paper clip or glue on sequins before closing.

Hold the end of transparent tape Got a roll of transparent tape without a dispenser? Don't drive yourself nuts trying to locate and lift the end of the tape. Stick a paper clip under the end the next time you use the roll.

Make a bookmark Paper clips make great bookmarks because they don't fall out. A piece of ribbon or colorful string attached to the clip will make it even easier to use and find.

Pit cherries Need a seedless cherry for a recipe? Don't like to pit the cherry while you're eating it? Clip it to pit it! Over a bowl or sink, unfold a clean paper clip at the

SCIENCE FAIR

Want to amaze your friends? Challenge them to make a **paper clip float on water**. Give them a cup of water and a paper clip. When they fail, you show them how to do it. Tear off a piece of **paper towel**—larger than the clip—and place it on top of the water. Put the **paper clip** on top of the paper towel and wait a few seconds. The towel will sink, leaving the clip floating. It's magic! Actually, it's the surface tension of the water that allows the clip to float. As the paper towel sinks, it lowers the paper clip onto the water without breaking the surface tension.

center and, depending on cherry size, insert either the clip's large or small end through the top. Loosen pit and pull. To de-pit cherries but leave stems intact, insert the clip in the bottom. Cherry juice stains, so watch your clothing.

Extend a ceiling fan chain Put away the step stool and put an end to your ballet routine while trying to reach a broken or too-short ceiling fan chain. To extend the chain, just fasten a chain of paper clips to its end.

✳ Paper Plates

Make index cards It's inevitable—at the eleventh hour your child will say, "I need index cards for school tomorrow." If you don't have any, use paper plates and a ruler. Measure out a 3 x 5 or 4 x 6 (A7 or A6) card on the plate and cut. Use the first card as a template for the rest.

Protect stored dishes Prevent stored dishes from clattering and breaking, especially when you are moving, by inserting a paper plate between each dish when packing.

Paint can drip catcher Painters scrape the paintbrush on the side of the can to remove excess paint. To prevent drips from falling on the floor, place a paper plate under the can.

Make Frisbee flash cards Drilling your kids with flash cards can be a drag, but here's a way to make it fun. Write the numbers, letters, words or shapes you are teaching on paper plates and let the kids toss them like Frisbees across the room when they get a correct answer.

Make a snowman decoration When the cold wind blows and cabin fever peaks, paper plates can provide an inexpensive, creative outlet for kids. They can use them to make masks, mobiles, and seasonal decorations. To create a cute winter snowman, use two paper plates. Cut the rim off one plate to make it smaller. Staple the smaller plate to the larger plate, creating a head and body. Make boots and hat out of  black construction paper and mittens out of red paper and glue on. Decorate the face with googly eyes, buttons, pipe cleaners, or draw on features with crayon or marker.

✳ Paper Towels

Mess-free bacon zapping Here's a sure-fire way to cook bacon in your microwave oven. Layer two paper towels on the bottom of your microwave. Lay slices of bacon side by side, on the paper towels. Cover with two more paper towels. Run your microwave on High at 1-minute intervals, checking for crispness. It should take 3-4 minutes to cook. There's no pan to clean, and the towels absorb the grease. Toss them for easy cleanup.

Clean silk from fresh corn If you hate picking the silk off a freshly husked ear of corn, a paper towel can help. Dampen one and run it across the ear. The towel picks up the silk, and the corn is ready for the boiling pot or the grill.

Strain grease from broth That pot of chicken broth has been bubbling for hours, and you don't want to skim off the fat. Instead, use a paper towel to absorb the fat. Place another pot in the sink. Put a colander (or a sieve) in the new pot and put a paper towel in the colander. Now pour the broth through the towel into the waiting pot. You'll find that the fat stays in the towel, while the cleaner broth streams through. Of course, be sure to wear cooking mitts or use potholders to avoid burning your hands with the boiling-hot liquid.

Keep produce fresh longer Don't you hate it when you open the vegetable bin in the refrigerator and find last week's moldy carrots mixed with the now-yellow lettuce? Make your produce last long enough so you can eat it. Line your vegetable bins with paper towels. They absorb the moisture that causes your fruits and vegetables to rot. Makes cleaning up the bin easier too.

Keep frozen bread from getting soggy If you like to buy bread in bulk from the discount store, this tip will help you freeze and thaw your bread better. Place a paper towel in each bag of bread to be frozen. When you're ready to eat that frozen loaf, the paper towel absorbs the moisture as the bread thaws.

Clean a can opener Have you ever noticed that strange gunk that collects on the cutting wheel of your can opener? You don't want that in your food. Clean your can opener by "opening" a paper towel. Close the wheel on the edge of a paper towel, close the handles, and turn the crank. The paper towel will clean off the gunk as the wheel cuts through it.

SCIENCE FAIR

Learn how all other colors are actually mixes of the **primary colors** of red, blue, and yellow. Cut a **paper towel** into strips. With a **marker**, draw a rectangle or large circle on one end of each strip. Try interesting shades of **orange, green, purple, or brown**. Black is good too. Place the other end of the strip into a **glass jar**

filled with **water**, leaving the colored end dry and draped over the side of the jar. As the water from the jar slowly (about 20 minutes) moves down the towel and into the color blot, you'll see the **colors separate**. This also demonstrates **capillary attraction**— the force that allows the porous paper to soak up the water and carry it over the side of the jar.

Keep cast-iron pots rust-free Stop rust from invading your prized collection of cast-iron pots. After they're clean, place a paper towel in each to absorb any moisture. Store lids separately from the pots, separated by a lining of paper towels. No more ugly surprises when you reach for the pot again.

Make a place mat for kids Your darling grandchildren are coming for an extended visit, and though they are adorable, they're a disaster at mealtime. Paper towels can help you weather the storm. Use a paper towel as a place mat. It will catch spills and crumbs during the meal and makes cleaning up easy.

Test viability of old seeds You've just found a packet of watermelon seeds dated from two springs back. Should you bother to plant them or has their shelf life expired and they're best planted in the garbage can? To find out for sure, dampen two paper towels and lay down a few seeds. Cover with two more dampened paper towels. Over the next two weeks, keep the towels damp and keep checking on the seeds. If most of the seeds sprout, then plant the rest of the batch in the garden.

Clean a sewing machine Your sewing machine is good as new after its recent tune-up, but you're worried about getting grease from the machine onto the fabric for that new vest you're sewing. Thread the sewing machine and stitch several lines up a paper towel first. That should take care of any residual grease so you'll be ready to resume your sewing projects.

Make a beautiful kids' butterfly Use colored markers to draw a bold design on a paper towel. Then lightly spray water on the towel. It should be damp so that the colors start to run, but do not soak. When the towel is dry, fold it in half, open it up, and then gather it together using the fold line as your guide. Loop a pipe cleaner around the center to make the body of the but-

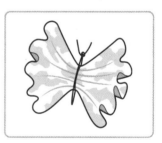

terfly and twist it closed. To make antennae, fold another pipe cleaner into a **V** shape and slip it under the first pipe cleaner at the top of the butterfly.

✳ Peanut Butter

Get chewing gum out of hair There it is. The piece of chewing gum you gave to your child not ten minutes ago is now a wadded mess in his hair. Apply some peanut butter and rub the gum until it comes out. Your child's hair may smell like peanut butter until you shampoo it, but it's better than cutting the gum out.

Remove price-tag adhesive You've removed the price tag from that new vase you've just purchased but you're left with that pesky gummy glue on the glass. Remove it easily by rubbing peanut butter on it.

Bait a mouse trap You know the mice are out there, scurrying around your kitchen at night. It's time to get tough. Lay traps, but bait them with peanut butter. They can't resist, and it's nearly impossible for them to swipe without tripping the trap. You'll be rid of the critters in no time.

Eliminate stinky fish smell If you're trying to eat more fish for health reasons, but hate the smell that hangs in your house after you've cooked it, try this trick. Put a dollop of peanut butter in the pan with the frying fish. The peanut butter absorbs the odor instead of your furnishings.

Plug an ice-cream cone Ice-cream cones are fun to eat but a bit messy too. Here's a delectable solution: Plug up the bottom of an ice-cream cone with a bit of peanut butter. Now, when munching through that scoop of double chocolate fudge, you'll be protected from leaks. And there's a pea-nutty surprise at the end of the treat.

✳ Pencils

Ease a new key into a lock You just had a new house key made, but you can't seem to fit it into your front door lock. Rub a pencil over the teeth of the key. The graphite powder should help the key open the door.

Use as hair accessory Take a pencil to school to help with your … hair. A pencil can help give lift to curly hair if you don't have a pick. Two pencils crossed in an **X** also can stabilize and decorate a hair bun, plus provide you a new writing tool if you lose yours during the day.

Decorate a picture frame Dress up the frame for this year's class picture with pencils. Glue two sharpened pencils lengthwise to the frame. Sharpen down two other pencils to fit the width of the frame.

SCIENCE FAIR

Are your eyes deceiving you? Cut a small **piece of paper**, about 2 inches (5 centimeters) square. Turn the square so it's a diamond. On one side, draw an animal or a person. On the other side, draw a setting for the animal, or a hat and hair for the person. Examples are a cheetah and

grasslands or a boy with a hat. Next **tape** the bottom point of the diamond onto the point of a **pencil**. Then, holding the pencil so the picture is upright, **twirl** the pencil rapidly between your hands. You should see **both images** from the two sides of the paper **at the same time**.

Repel moths with pencil shavings ~~If you're tired of finding~~ your winter sweaters filled with moth holes after you've stored them for the season, this may help. Empty your electric pencil sharpener into little cloth sacks and use as sachets and in your closet. The cedar shavings will signal the moths to skedaddle.

Stake a small plant Got a small plant that needs some support? Don't know if it needs watering? A pencil can help with both problems. It's the perfect-sized stake for a small plant, tied with piece of old pantyhose or a cloth strip. Or stick a pencil in the pot of that house-plant to see if the soil needs watering yet.

Lubricate a sticky zipper Your zipper is refusing to budge, no matter how hard you tug and pull. Pick up a pencil and end your frustration. Run the pencil lead along the teeth of the zipper to unstick it. In no time you'll be zipping out the door with your jacket safely zipped up.

✳ Pencil Erasers

Shine your coins If you've just inherited a rather grimy coin collection from your uncle, but you'd like to see it with more luster, try an eraser to shine up the coins. But don't do this to rare and valuable coins—you can erase their value along with their surface patina.

Store pins or drill bits A box is not the most handy place to keep sewing pins. What if the box spills? What if you have a hard time grabbing just one when you're laying out pattern pieces? Here's the solution: Stick pins in an eraser. They won't fall out, and it's easy to grab the ones you need. This is also a good tip if you're storing several small drill bits.

Clean off crayon marks Your toddler has gone wild with the crayons, but he drew on the walls and not on paper. You've tried everything to get it off, but not this: an eraser. Try "erasing" the crayon marks to get the wall back to a clean slate.

Remove scuff marks on vinyl floors Those new shoes of your husband's have left black streak marks all over the kitchen floor. An eraser will take them off in no time. Give him the eraser and have him do it.

Clean your piano keys Whether it's a baby grand piano that fills the corner of the living room, a more conventional upright, or just a fold-away elec-tronic keyboard, cleaning the keys can be a nightmare project of dust and finger marks. And when you clean it, it's hard to reach some spots to remove dirt. The sides of the black keys are especially difficult to clean. Find an

eraser that fits between the ivories and the black keys and you'll have 86'ed the dirt on the 88s. This works well whether you have a piano with real ivory keys or the more common plastic ones.

Cushion picture frames Don't you hate it when that heavy mirror or picture frame gets slightly crooked? Tired of worrying about the black marks and scrapes the frame is making on the wall? Glue erasers to the bottom corners of the frame. The pictures will now hang straighter and not leave their mark.

Remove residue from stick-on labels That gray gummy substance on the new picture frame you just purchased is a sight to behold and not coming off with plain soap and water. Rub the residue with an eraser and watch the stuff just peel away.

* Pepper

Stop a car radiator leak A heat wave has hit your town, and your aging, leaking car radiator isn't too happy about it. If it's overheating because of a small leak, pepper can help. Before you bring your car to a mechanic for a more thorough repair, pour a handful of pepper into your radiator. It will temporarily plug the leaks until you can get some help.

Use as a decongestant Is your nose stopped up? Are your ears plugged? Do you have a cold? Forget the over-the-counter medications. Nothing gets things flowing again faster than some cayenne pepper. Sprinkle it on your food and grab some tissues.

Keep colors bright That new cherry-red shirt you just purchased is fantastic, but just think how faded the color will look after the shirt has been washed a few times. Add a teaspoon of pepper to the wash load. Pepper keeps bright colors bright and prevents them from running too.

Get bugs off plants There's nothing more frustrating than a swarm of bugs nibbling at your fledgling garden. Just when things are starting to pop up, the bugs are there, chowing down. Mix black pepper with flour. Sprinkle around your plants. Bugs take a hike.

DID You KNOW?

The black pepper on your table actually starts out as a red berry on a bush. When the pea-size berry is placed in boiling water for ten minutes, it shrinks and turns black, becoming the familiar peppercorn that we fill our pepper grinders with. Of course, some of us skip that step and buy pepper already ground. Either way, black pepper is an ancient spice and the most common one in the world.

Deter deer from your garden Your freshly budding garden seems as if it's ringing the dinner bell for the neighborhood deer. They'll find another place to dine if you spray your bushes with a cayenne and water mixture.

Keep ants out of the kitchen Two or three of your annual summer visitors have invaded your kitchen. Those ants are looking for sugar. Give them some pepper instead. Cayenne pepper sprinkled in spots where the ants are looking, such as along the backs of your countertops or on your baseboards, will tell them that no sugar is ahead.

Kill an ant colony If you find the ants' home colony a little too close to yours and it is causing them to relocate to your kitchen, cayenne pepper can help get rid of it. Pour the pepper down the ant hole and say so long to ants.

super item
31 *uses!* **Petroleum Jelly**

❋PETROLEUM JELLY **FOR PERSONAL GROOMING**

Moisturize your lips and more If you don't want to pay a lot for expensive lip balm, makeup remover, or even facial moisturizer, then your answer is a tube of petroleum jelly. It can soothe lips, take off foundation, eye shadow, mascara, and more. It will even act as a moisturizer on your face.

Make emergency makeup Oh no! You've run out of your favorite shade of eye shadow. What do you do now? It's easy—make your own. Add a bit of food coloring to petroleum jelly and apply as usual. This is a quick way to make stopgap blush, lipstick, or eye shadow.

Lengthen the life of perfume You've picked out a great scent to wear on your night out, but it's got to last. Worry not. Dab a bit of petroleum jelly on your pulse points. Then spray on the perfume. Now you can dance the night away and not worry about your perfume turning in early.

Remove a stuck ring Is your wedding ring stuck? Trying to get it off can take a lot of tug and pull. Apply some petroleum jelly and it will glide right off.

Soften chapped hands If you're constantly applying hand lotion to your tired, chapped hands, but then taking it off again so you can get more work done, try this tip. Apply a liberal amount of petroleum jelly to your hands just before you go to bed. By morning, they'll be soft and smooth.

No more messy manicures During home manicures, it's hard to keep the nail polish from running over on your cuticles. Petroleum jelly can help your manicures look more professional. Dab some along the base of your nails and the sides. If polish seeps off the nail during the manicure, all you do is wipe off the petroleum jelly and the sloppy nail polish is gone.

Smooth wild eyebrow hairs If you have runaway eyebrows—the ones where the hairs won't lie flat but curl up instead, control the wildness with some petroleum jelly. Rub a dab into your brows. They'll calm down and behave.

Stop hair dye runs There's nothing more embarrassing than a home hair color job gone awry. Imagine finishing applying that new auburn shade to your tresses when you notice that you've dyed your hairline and part of your forehead too. Next time, run a bit of petroleum jelly across your hairline. If dye seeps off your hair, the petroleum jelly will catch it.

Heal windburned skin You've just had a glorious hike through the countryside in autumn. And as much as you enjoyed the changing colors of the season, the hike has left you with an unpleasant souvenir: windburn. Grab a jar of petroleum jelly and apply it liberally to your face or wherever you've been chapped. The jelly helps relieve the pain.

Help prevent diaper rash It's so heartbreaking to hear a baby experiencing the pain of diaper rash. Help is just a few moments away. Petroleum jelly sets up a protective coat on the skin so the rash can heal. No more pain.

No more shampoo tears Thinking of buying special no-tears shampoo for your child? Forget about it. If you have some petroleum jelly, you have the solution. Rub a fair amount into your baby's eyebrows. It acts as a protective shield against shampoo running down into his eyes.

✳PETROLEUM JELLY **AROUND THE HOUSE**

Smoother closing shower curtains Stop the water from squirting out onto the bathroom floor. Get that shower curtain into place quickly. Lubricate the curtain rod with petroleum jelly and you'll whip that curtain across the shower in no time.

Take out lipstick stains You set the table at that lovely dinner party with your favorite cloth napkins, but your girlfriends left their mark all over them. Now dotted with lipstick stains, those napkins may be headed for the trash. But try this first. Before you wash them, blot petroleum jelly on the stain. Launder as usual and hopefully you will kiss the stains good-bye.

Eject wax from candlesticks The long red tapers you used at last night's candlelit dinner were a beautiful sight until you saw the candle wax drippings left in the candleholders. Next time apply petroleum jelly to the insides of the holders before you put the candles in. The wax will pop out for easy cleaning.

Remove chewing gum from wood Did you discover bubble gum stuck under the dining room table or behind the headboard of Junior's bed? Trouble yourself about it no further. Squeeze some petroleum jelly on the offending wad, rub it in until the gum starts to disintegrate, then remove.

Make vacuum parts fit together smoothly It's nice that your vacuum cleaner comes with so many accessories and extensions. But it's frustrating when the parts get stuck together and you have to yank them apart. Apply a bit of petroleum jelly to the rims of the tubes and the parts will easily slide together and apart.

Shine patent-leather shoes You've got a great pair of patent-leather shoes and a dynamite bag to match. The luster stays longer if you polish the items with petroleum jelly.

Restore leather jackets You don't need fancy leather moisturizer to take care of your favorite leather jacket. Petroleum jelly does the job just as well. Apply, rub it in, wipe off the excess, and you're ready to go.

Keep ants away from pet food bowls Poor Fido's food bowl has been invaded by ants. Since she prefers her food without them, help her out with this idea. Ring her food bowl with petroleum jelly. The ants will no longer be tempted by the kibble if they have to cross that mountain of petroleum jelly.

Grease a baseball mitt Got a new baseball mitt, but it's as stiff as a dugout bench? Soften it up with petroleum jelly. Apply liberal amounts. Work it into the glove, then tie it up with a baseball inside. Do this in the winter, and by the spring you'll be ready to take the field.

Keep a bottle lid from sticking If you're having a hard time unscrewing that bottle of glue or nail polish, remember this tip for when you finally do get it open. Rub a little petroleum jelly along the rim of the bottle. Next time, the top won't stick.

Soothe sore pet paws Sometimes your cat's or dog's paw pads can get cracked and dry. Give a little tender loving care to your best friend. Squirt a little petroleum jelly on the pads to stop pain. They'll love you for it.

 DID **You** KNOW?

Although there are many generic versions of petroleum jelly, the only real major brand is Vaseline. Because of this, the online American Package Museum has included a jar of Vaseline petroleum jelly in its collection of classic packaging designs—a collection that also includes Alka-Seltzer and Bayer Aspirin. Why did the site include Vaseline? "Vaseline is a well-established brand with a 145-year-old history," says Ian House, who created the site. "It also seems to enjoy popularity as a cultural icon for humorous reasons. Nobody knows quite what to do with it ... but nobody can seem to live without it!"

Mask doorknobs when painting You're about to undertake painting the family room. But do you really want to fiddle with removing all the metal fixtures, including doorknobs? Petroleum jelly rubbed on the metal will prevent paint from sticking. When you're done painting, just wipe off the jelly and the unwanted paint is gone.

Stop battery terminal corrosion It's no coincidence that your car battery always dies on the coldest winter day. Low temperatures increase electrical resistance and thicken engine oil, making the battery work harder. Corrosion on the battery terminals also increases resistance and might just be the last straw that makes the battery give up. Before winter starts, disconnect the terminals and clean them with a wire brush. Reconnect, then smear with petroleum jelly. The jelly will prevent corrosion and help keep the battery cranking all winter long.

Protect stored chrome If you're getting ready to store the kids' bikes for the winter, or stow that stroller until your next baby comes along, stop a moment before you stash. Take some petroleum jelly and apply it to the chrome parts of the equipment. When it's time to take the items out of storage, they'll be rust-free. The same method works for machinery stored in your garage

Keep an outdoor lightbulb from sticking Have you ever unscrewed a lightbulb and found yourself holding the glass while the metal base remains in the socket? It won't happen again if you remember to apply petroleum jelly to the base of the bulb before screwing it into the fixture. This is an especially good idea for lightbulbs used outdoors.

Seal a plumber's plunger Before you reach for that plunger to unclog the bathroom toilet, find some petroleum jelly. Apply it along the rim of the plunger and it will help create a tighter seal. Whoosh, clog's gone.

Lubricate cabinets and windows Can't stand to hear your medicine cabinet door creak along its runners? Or how about that window that you have to force open every time you want a breeze in the house? With a small paintbrush, apply petroleum jelly to the window sash channel and cabinet door runners. Let the sliding begin.

Stop squeaking door hinges It's so annoying when a squeaky door makes an ill-timed noise when you're trying to keep quiet. Put petroleum jelly on the hinge pins of the door. No more squeaks.

Remove watermarks on wood Your most recent party left lots of watermark rings on your wood furniture. To make them disappear, apply petroleum jelly and let it sit overnight. In the morning, wipe the watermark away with the jelly.

Keep squirrels away from bird feeder Feed the birds, not the squirrels. Keep the varmints off the pole of your bird feeder by greasing it with petroleum jelly. Squirrels slide right off, leaving the birds to eat in peace.

Pillowcases

Dust ceiling fan blades Have you ever seen dust bunnies careening off your ceiling fan when you turn it on for the first time in weeks? Grab an old pillowcase and place it over one of the ceiling fan blades. Slowly pull off the pillowcase. The blades get dusted and the dust bunnies stay in the pillowcase, instead of parachuting to the floor.

Clear out cobwebs There's a cobweb way up high in the corner of your dining room. Before you take a broom to it, cover the broom with an old pillowcase. Now you can wipe away the cobweb without scratching the wall paint. It's also easier to remove the cobweb from the pillow than to pull it out of the broom bristles.

Cover a baby's changing table Have you priced those expensive changing-table covers lately? Forget about it! Pick up a few of the cheapest white pillowcases you can find and use those to cover the changing table pad. When one is soiled, just slip it off and replace with a clean one.

Make a set of linen napkins Who needs formal linen napkins that need to be pressed every time you use them? Pillowcases are available in a wide array of colors and designs. Pick a color or design you like, and start cutting. If you're really ambitious, sew a 1/2-inch (1.25-centimeter) hem on each edge. You'll have a new set of colorful napkins for a fraction of the cost of regular cloth napkins.

Prepare travel pillows Road trips can be a lot of fun, but a little dirty too. Your youngsters may want to bring their own pillows along, but they'll stain them with candy, food, and markers. Take their favorite pillows and layer several pillowcases on each. When the outside one gets dirty, remove it for a fresh start.

Use for wrapping paper Trying to wrap a basketball or an odd-shaped piece of art? Is your wrapping paper not doing the trick? Place the gift in a pillowcase and tie closed with a ribbon.

Store your sweaters Stored in plastic, winter sweaters can get musty. But stored just in a closet, they're prey to moths. The solution can be found among your linens. Put the sweaters in a pillowcase for seasonal storage. They will stay free from dust but the pillowcase fabric will allow them to breathe.

Protect clothing hanging in a closet You've just laundered a favorite dress shirt or skirt and you know you won't be wearing it again for a while. To protect the garment, cut a hole in the top of an old pillowcase and slip it over the hanger and clothing.

Stash your leather accessories You reach up to pull a leather purse or suede shoes down from a shelf. Of course, the item is dusty and now you have to clean it. Save yourself the time and hassle next time by storing infrequently used items in a pillowcase. They'll be clean and ready to use when the occasion arises.

Keep matching sheets together Solve this host nightmare. Your recently arrived overnight guests want to go to bed, but it's not made. You run to the linen closet, but you can't find a matched set of sheets. Next time, file away your linens. Place newly laundered and folded sheets in their matching pillowcase before putting them in the closet.

Machine-wash your delicates Sweaters and pantyhose can get pulled out of shape when they twist around in the washer. To protect these garments during washing, toss them into a pillowcase and close with string or rubber band. Set the machine on the delicate setting, add the soap, and worry not about knots.

Machine-wash stuffed animals Your child's Beanie Babies collection is cute but mighty dusty. Time for a bath. Place them in a pillowcase and put them in the washer. The pillowcase will ensure they get a gentle but thorough wash. If any parts fall off the stuffed animals, they'll be caught in the pillowcase so you can reattach them after their washing machine bath.

Kids' Stuff Kids love to personalize their bedrooms. You can help kids as young as 4 or 5 do just that by making a **pillowcase into a wall hanging**. Let the youngster choose a pillowcase color, and then slit a hole about 1 inch long in each side seam. Use **fabric paints** to create a design or scene or let him **rubber-stamp** a picture on the pillowcase. Stick a **dowel** through the seam openings. Cut a length of **yarn** about 30 inches (75 centimeters) long. Tie one end of the yarn to each end of the dowel. Hang on the wall and let the little one collect the compliments.

Use as a traveling laundry bag When you travel, you always want to keep your dirty laundry separate from your clean clothes. Stick a pillowcase in your suitcase and toss in the dirty laundry as it accumulates. When you get home, just empty the pillowcase into the washer and throw in the pillowcase as well.

Wash a lot of lettuce in washing machine Expecting a large crowd for an outdoor salad luncheon? Do you have 20 heads of lettuce to wash? Here's your solution: Place one pillowcase inside another. Pull apart the lettuce heads and fill the inside case with lettuce leaves. Close both pillowcases with string or rubber band, and throw the whole package in the washing machine with another large item, such as a towel, to balance it. Now run the spin cycle a few times. Your leaves come out rinsed and dried. It's better than a salad spinner.

✱ Pipe Cleaners

Decorate a ponytail Need a fresh look for your hair? Tired of using plain old ribbons? Once you have your hair in a ponytail, twist a pipe cleaner around the hair band. Twist a couple together for an even brighter effect.

Use as an emergency shoelace Your shoelace broke and you're about to go out on the court to play that grudge match in basketball. A pipe cleaner is a good stopgap tie-up. Just thread in your shoe as you would a shoelace and twist it up at the top.

Safety pin holder Safety pins come in so many sizes, it's hard to keep them together and organized. Thread safety pins onto a pipe cleaner, through the bottom loop of each pin, for easy access.

Clean gas burners Have you noticed that your stovetop burners are not firing on all their jets? Do you see an interrupted circle of blue when you turn a burner on? Poke a pipe cleaner through the little vents. This cleans the burner and allows it to work more efficiently. This works for pressure cooker safety valves, or pressure cookers' too.

Make napkin rings Colorful pipe cleaners are an easy and fast resource for making napkin rings. Just twist around the napkin and place on the table. If you want to get adventurous, use two, one for the napkin ring, attach the other pipe cleaner to it, shaped into a heart, shamrock, flower, curlicue, or something else.

Use as twist tie You're ready to close up that smelly bag of kitchen garbage when you discover you are out of twist ties. Grab a pipe cleaner instead.

 DID **You** KNOW?

According to reliable sources, pipe cleaners were invented in the late 19th century in Rochester, New York, by J. Harry Stedman, who also came up with the idea of issuing transfers between local streetcars. Although pipe smoking has declined dramatically since then, pipe cleaners have flourished, having been co-opted by the arts-and-crafts community. Technically, the pipe cleaners used in classrooms, summer camps, Scout troops, and so on are called chenille stems. These stems come in various colors and widths and are fuzzier than the real pipe cleaners smokers use.

Use as a travel toy If you're worried about having a bored, wiggly child on your hands during your next long car or plane ride, throw a bunch of pipe cleaners into your bag. Whip them out when the "Are we there yet?" questions start coming your way. Colorful pipe cleaners can be bent and shaped into fun figures, animals, flowers, or whatever. They even make cool temporary bracelets and necklaces.

Use as a mini-scrubber Pipe cleaners are great for cleaning in tight spaces. Use one to remove dirt from the wheel of a can opener or to clean the bobbin area of a sewing machine.

Decorate a gift To give a special touch to a birthday or holiday present, shape a pipe cleaner into a bow or a heart. Poke one end through a hole in the card, and affix it to the package with a dab of glue.

super item 44 uses! Plastic Bags

*PLASTIC BAGS AROUND THE HOUSE

Line a cracked flower vase Grandmother's beautiful flower vase is a sight to behold when it's filled with posies. The problem is the vase leaks from a large crack that runs its length. Line the vase with a plastic bag before you fill it with water and add the bouquet, giving fresh life to a treasured heirloom.

Bulk up curtain valances You've picked out snazzy new curtain balloon valances for your bedroom. The problem is the manufacturer has only sent you enough stuffing to make the valances look a bit better than limp. Recycle some plastic bags by stuffing them in the valances for a resilient pouf.

Stuff crafts or pillows There are a number of ways to stuff a craft project: with beans, rice, fabric filler, plastic beads, pantyhose, and so on. But have you ever tried stuffing a craft item or throw pillow with plastic bags? There are plenty on hand, so you don't have to worry about running out, and you're recycling.

Make party decorations Here is an easy way to create streamers for a party using plastic bags. Cut each bag into strips starting from the open end and stopping short of the bottom. Then attach the bag bottom to the ceiling with tape.

Drain bath toys Don't let Rubber Ducky and all of the rest of your child's bath toys get moldy and create a potential hazard in the tub. Instead, after the bath is done, gather them up in a plastic bag that has been punctured a few times. Hang the bag by its handles on one of the faucets to let the water drain out. Toys are collected in one place, ready for the next time.

Keep kids' mattresses dry There's no need to buy an expensive mattress guard if bed-wetting is a problem. Instead, line the mattress with plastic garbage bags. Big bags are also useful to protect toilet-training toddlers' car seats or car uphol-stery for kids coming home from the swimming pool.

Make a laundry pocket pickin's bag You may think that the laundry's all done, until you open the dryer to find a tissue paper left in someone's pocket has shredded and now is plastered all over the dryer drum. Hang a plastic bag near where you sort laundry. Before you start the wash, go through the pockets and dump any contents in the bag for later sorting.

Treat chapped hands If your hands are cracked and scaly, try this solution. Rub a thick layer of petroleum jelly on your hands. Place them in a plastic bag. The jelly and your body's warmth will help make your hands supple in about 15 minutes.

❋PLASTIC BAGS **FOR STORING STUFF**

Store extra baby wipes Shopping at the warehouse grocer, you picked up a jumbo box of baby wipes at a great price. You've got enough wipes to last for several months, as long as they don't dry out before you can use them. To protect your good investment, keep the opened carton of wipes in a plastic bag sealed with a twist tie.

Collect clothes for thrift shop If you're constantly setting aside clothes to give to charity, but then find them back in your closet or drawers, try this solution: Hang a large garbage bag in your closet. That way, the next time you find something you want to give, you just toss it in the bag. Once it's full, you can take it to the local donation center. Don't forget to hang a new bag in the closet.

Cover clothes for storage You'd like to protect that seersucker suit for next season. Grab a large, unused garbage bag. Slit a hole in the top and push the hanger through for an instant dustcover.

Store your skirts If you find you have an overstuffed closet but plenty of room to spare in your dresser, conduct a clothes transfer. Roll up your skirts and place them

 DID **You** KNOW?

"Paper or plastic?" You hear the question every time you check out at the super-market. Though plastic bags have been around for nearly fifty years, they didn't start getting wide use at super-markets until 1977. Within two decades, plastic had replaced paper bags as the most common grocery bag. Today four out of five bags used at the grocer's are plastic. Thankfully, supermar-kets have imple-mented recycling programs for the proliferating bags.

each in a plastic bag. That will help them stay wrinkle-free until you're ready to wear one.

Keep purses in shape Ever notice that if you've changed purses and leave an empty one in your closet, it deflates and loses its shape? Fill your purse with plastic bags to retain its original shape.

Tip **Storing Plastic Bags**

All those shopping bags are spilling out of the utility drawer in your kitchen. Here are some better ways to store them:
• Stuff them inside an empty tissue box for easy retrieval.
• Poke a bunch down a cardboard tube, such as a paper towel or mailing tube or even a section of a carpet tube.
• Fill a clean, empty gallon (4-liter) plastic jug. Cut a 4-inch (10-centimeter) hole in the bottom. Stuff with bags and hang by its handle on a hook. Pull the bags out of the spout.
• Make a bag "sock." Fold a kitchen towel lengthwise with the wrong side facing out. Stitch the long edges together. Sew 1/2-inch (1.25-centimeter) casings around the top and bottom openings and thread elastic through them, securing the ends. Turn the sock right side out, sew a loop of ribbon or string on the back to hang it up, stuff bags into the top opening, and pull them out from the bottom one.

*PLASTIC BAGS **KEEPING THINGS CLEAN***

Protect hand when cleaning toilet When cleaning your toilets with a long-handled brush or a shorter tool, first wrap your hand in a used plastic bag. You'll be able to do the appropriate scrubbing without your hand getting dirty in the process.

Prevent steel wool from rusting A few days ago you got a new steel wool pad to clean a dirty pot. Now that steel pad is sitting useless in its own pool of rust. Next time, when you're not using the pad, toss it into a plastic bag where it won't rust and you'll be able to use it again.

Make bibs for kids The grandkids just popped in, and they're hungry. But you don't have any bibs to protect their clothes while they eat. Make some by tying a plastic bag loosely around the kids' necks so their clothes stay free of stains. You can make quick aprons this way too.

Create a high-chair drop cloth Baby stores are quite happy to sell you an expensive drop cloth to place under your child's high chair. Why spend the money on a sheet of plastic when you have all those large garbage bags that can do the job? Split the seams of a bag and place it under the high chair to catch all the drips and dribbles. When it gets filthy, take it outside and shake, or just toss it.

Line the litter box Nobody likes to change the cat's litter box. Make the job quick and easy by lining the box with an open plastic bag before pouring in the litter. Use two bags if you think one is flimsy. When it's time to change the litter, just remove the bags, tie, and throw into the trash.

Needle-free Christmas tree removal O Christmas tree, how lovely are thy branches! Until those needles start dropping. When it's time to take down your tree, place a large garbage bag over the top and pull down. If it doesn't fit in one bag, use another from the bottom and pull up. You can quickly remove the tree without needles trailing behind you.

Keep polish off your hand You want to polish up your scruffy white sandals. The problem is, you're going to get more polish on your hands than your shoes. Before you polish, wrap your hand in a plastic bag before inserting it into the sandal. Then when polish runs off the sandal straps, your hand is protected. Leave the bag in the sandal until the polish is dry.

✻PLASTIC BAGS **IN THE KITCHEN**

Cover a cookbook You're trying a new recipe from a borrowed cookbook that you don't want to get splattered during your creation. Cover the book with a clear plastic bag. You'll be able to read the directions, while the book stays clean.

Bag the phone Picture this: You're in the middle of making your famous snickerdoodle cookies. You're up to your elbows in dough. The phone rings. Now what? Wrap your hands in a plastic bag and answer the phone. You won't miss a call or have to clean the phone when you're done.

Scrape dishes Your extended family of 25 has just finished their Sunday dinner. Time to clean the dishes. Here's an easy way to get rid of the table scraps: Line a bowl with a plastic bag and scrape scraps into it. Once it's full, just gather up the

SCIENCE FAIR

It is said that a plastic bag can carry about 20 pounds (9 kilograms) of groceries before you need to double-bag. Find out **how much a bag can hold** without its handles breaking. For this experiment, you will need a **kitchen scale**, a **plastic bag**, and a

bunch of rocks. Place the bag on the scale. Fill it with rocks until the scale reads 10 pounds (4.5 kilograms). Lift the bag. Does it hold? Add more rocks in 2-pound (.9-kilogram) increments, testing the bag's strength after each addition. When the handles start to tear, you'll know the bag's actual strength.

handles and toss. Place the bowl in a prominent place in your kitchen so everyone can scrape their own dishes when bringing them to the sink.

Crush graham crackers Don't spend hard-earned grocery dollars on a box of pre-crushed graham crackers or a ready-to-fill graham cracker crust. It's much cheaper and a real snap to crush graham crackers yourself. Just crumble several graham crackers into a plastic bag. Lay the bag on the kitchen counter and go over it several times with a rolling pin. In no time, you'll have as many graham cracker crumbs as you need, plus the remainder of a box of crackers to snack on as well.

Replace a mixing bowl If you're cooking for a crowd and are short on mixing bowls, try using a plastic bag instead. Place all the dry ingredients to be mixed in the bag, gather it up and gently shake. If the ingredients are wet, use your hands to mix.

Spin dry salad greens The kids will enjoy helping you with this one. Wash lettuce and shake out as much water as you can in the sink. Then place the greens in a plastic grocery bag that has been lined with a paper towel. Grab the handles and spin the bag in large circles in the air. After several whirls, you'll have dry lettuce.

Ripen fruit Some of the fruit from that bushel of peaches you just bought at the local farm stand are hard as rocks. Place the fruit with a few already ripe pieces or some ripe bananas in a plastic bag. The ripe fruit will help soften the others through the release of their natural gas. But don't leave them for more than a day or two or you'll have purple, moldy peaches.

✳ PLASTIC BAGS IN THE YARD

Protect plants from frost When frost threatens your small plants, grab a bunch of plastic bags to protect them. Here's how: Cut a hole in the bottom of each bag. Slip one over each plant and anchor it inside using small rocks. Then pull the bags over the plants, roll them closed, and secure them with clothespins or paper clips. You can open the bags up again if the weather turns warm.

Start poinsettia buds for Xmas You want that Christmas poinsettia to look gorgeous by the time the holidays arrive. You can speed up Mother Nature by placing the poinsettia in a large, dark garbage bag for several weeks to wake up the plant's buds.

Protect fruit on the tree Are there some apples in your orchard you want to protect or some plums that need a little more time on the tree? Slip the fruit into clear plastic bags while still on the trees. You'll keep out critters while the fruit continues to ripen.

Protect your shoes from mud It rained hard last night, and you need to get out in the garden to do your regular weeding. But you're worried about getting mud all over your shoes. Cover them in plastic bags. The mud gets on the bag, not on the shoes, and your feet stay dry so you can stay out longer in the garden.

Clean a grill easily That neighborhood barbecue was a blast, but your grill is a sorry mess now. Take the racks off and place them in a garbage bag. Spray oven cleaner on the grill and close up the bag. The next day, open the bag, making sure to keep your face away from the fumes. All that burned-on gunk should wipe right off.

Cover garage-sale signs If you've gone to the trouble of advertising your upcoming garage sale with yard signs but worry that rain may hurt your publicity campaign before even the early birds show up, protect the signs by covering them with pieces cut from clear plastic bags. Passersby can still see the lettering, which will be protected from smearing by the rain.

Store outdoor equipment manuals Your weed-whacker spindle just gave out and you have to replace it. But how? Stash all your outdoor equipment's warranties and owner's manuals in a plastic bag and hang it in your garage. You'll know exactly where to look for help.

Protect your car mirrors A big snowstorm is due tonight, and you've got a doctor's appointment in the morning. Get a step ahead by covering your car's side mirrors with plastic bags before the storm starts. When you're cleaning off the car the next morning, just remove the bag. No ice to scrape off.

Make a jump rope "I'm bored!" cries your child as you're trying to finish your yard work. Here's a simple solution: Make a jump rope by twisting up several plastic bags and tying them together end to end. Talk about cheap fun.

✳PLASTIC BAGS **ON THE GO**

Pack your shoes Your next cruise requires shoes for all types of occasions, but you worry that packing them in the suitcase will get everything else dirty. Wrap each pair in its own plastic bag. It will keep the dirt off the clothes, and you can rest assured you've packed complete pairs.

DID *You* KNOW?

Worried about the growing number of plastic bags filling landfills, countries across the globe have started putting restrictions on the seemingly indispensable item. Bangladesh has banned plastic bags, blaming them for clogging drainage pipes and causing a flood. Some Australian towns also have banned plastic bags, and the country is pushing stores to halve their use of bags (estimated at 7 billion annually) in a few years. If you want to use a plastic bag in Ireland, you'll be charged about 19 cents a bag. In Taiwan, it's 34 cents a bag.

Protect your hands when pumping gas You've stopped at the gas station for a fill-up while on your way to meet friends for lunch. The last thing you want is to greet them with hands that smell of gasoline. Grab one of those plastic bags you keep in your car and cover your hands with it while you pump.

Stash your wet umbrella When you're out in the rain and running to your next appointment, who wants to deal with a soggy umbrella dripping all over your clothes and car? One of those plastic bags that newspapers are delivered in is the perfect size to cover your umbrella the next time it rains. Just fold the umbrella up and slip it into the bag.

Make an instant poncho Leave a large garbage bag in your car. The next time it rains unexpectedly, cut some arm slits and one for your head. Slip on your impromptu poncho and keep dry.

Scoot in the snow Your neighborhood just got 6 inches (15 centimeters) of snow and the kids are hoping to take advantage of it right now. Grab some garbage bags, tie one around one each of their waists, and let them fanny-slide down the hills.

✳ PLASTIC BAGS FOR THE DO-IT-YOURSELFER

Cover ceiling fans You're painting the sun porch ceiling, and you don't want to remove the ceiling fans for the process. Cover the blades with plastic bags to protect them from paint splatters. Use masking tape to keep the bags shut.

Store paintbrushes You're halfway through painting the living room, and it's time to break for lunch. No need to clean the paintbrush. Just stick it in a plastic bag and it will remain wet and ready to use when you return. Going to finish next weekend, you say? Stick the bag-covered brush in the freezer. Defrost next Saturday and you are ready to go.

Contain paint overspray If you've got a few small items to spray-paint, use a plastic bag to control the overspray. Just place one item at a time in the bag, spray-paint, and remove to a spread-out newspaper to dry. When you're done, toss the bag for a easy cleanup.

✳ Plastic Containers

Trap plant-eating slugs Sock it to those slugs eating your newly planted vegetable plants. Dig a hole the size of a plastic container near the plant. Place the container, flush with the ground, in the hole. Fill the container with beer or salted water and place cut potatoes around the rim to attract the slugs. Slugs crawl in, but they don't crawl out.

Wipe out dangerous wasps Those wasps have been getting a little too close for comfort, threatening to bring your child's outing to the park to a screeching halt. Take a plastic container and fill it with water sweetened with sugar. Cut a hole in the lid. Wasps will be attracted to the water and crawl inside, trapped.

Keep ants away from picnic table You watch helplessly as the ants march up the picnic table leg, onto the tabletop, and into the picnic meal. Here's a foolproof way to stop them in their tracks: Place a plastic container on the bottom of each picnic table leg. Fill with water. The ants won't be able to crawl past.

Use as a portable dog dish The next time you go out for a hike with your dog, pack a portion of its food in a plastic container. Of course, you can pack another container with a snack for yourself. An empty container also makes a great water bowl on the go.

Organize your sewing area You're sitting down at your sewing area to start on your Christmas craft projects. But instead of sewing, you're hunting for that extra bobbin or the right-color thread. Plastic containers can help you bring order to your sewing area. Fill several with thread spools, others with implements such as seam rippers and measuring tapes. Yet another can be filled with pins.

✳ Plastic Lids

Stop a sink or tub If your drain stopper has disappeared, but you need to stop the water in the sink or bathtub, here's a stopgap solution: Place a plastic lid over the drain. The vacuum created keeps the water from slip-sliding away.

Keep the fridge clean Drippy bottles and containers with leaks can create a big mess on your refrigerator shelves. Create coasters from plastic lids to keep things clean. Place the lids under food containers to stop any potential leaks. If they get

DID You KNOW?

The tremendous success of Tupperware plastic bowls is due to one man's inventiveness and one woman's understanding of American society. The man was Earl Tupper of New Hampshire, who in 1942 saw that the durable, flexible new plastic called polyethylene could be molded into plastic bowls with tight-fitting lids. But Tupperware sales were meager until 1948, when Tupper met Brownie Wise, a divorced mother from Detroit. Wise saw that while there was a stigma against women going to work, it was perfectly acceptable for them to have a "party" where Tupperware would be sold.

Tupper wisely put Wise in charge of Tupperware sales, turning the product into what the *Guinness Book of World Records* called "one of the enduring symbols of our era."

dirty, throw them in the dishwasher, while your fridge shelves stay free of a sticky mess.

Use as kids' coasters Entertaining a crowd of kids and want to make sure your tabletops survive? (Or at least give them a fighting chance!) Give kids plastic lids to use as coasters. Write their names on the coasters so they won't get their drinks mixed up.

Use as coasters for plants Plastic lids are the perfect water catcher for small house-plants. One under each plant will help keep watermarks off your furniture.

Scrape nonstick pans We all know that stuff often sticks to so-called nonstick pans. And, of course, using steel wool to get it off is a no-no. Try scraping off the gunk with a plastic lid.

Separate frozen hamburgers The neighborhood block party is next week, but you have the hamburger meat now. Season the meat as desired and shape it into patties. Place each patty on a plastic lid. Then stack them up, place in a plastic bag, and freeze. When the grill is fired up, you'll have no trouble separating your pre-formed hamburgers.

Prevent paintbrush drips Worried about getting messy paint drips all over yourself while you're touching up a repair job on the ceiling? Try this trick. Cut a slot in the middle of a plastic lid. The kind of plastic lid that comes on coffee cans is the perfect size for most paintbrushes. Insert the handle of your paintbrush through the lid so that the lid is on the narrow part of the handle just above your hand. The lid will catch any paint drips. Even with this shield, always be careful not to put too much paint on your brush when you are painting overhead.

Close a bag Out of twist ties? Need to get that smelly garbage bag out of the house? Grab a plastic lid, cut a slit in it, gather the top of the bag, and thread it through. The bag's now completely sealed and ready for disposal.

✳ Plastic Tablecloths

Make a shower curtain A colorful tablecloth can make a great-looking shower curtain to match your bathroom decor. Punch holes about 6 inches (15 centimeters) apart and 1/2 inch (1.25 centimeters) from one edge of a hemmed tablecloth. Insert shower curtain rings or loop strings through the holes and loosely tie to the curtain rod.

Make a high-chair drop cloth Bombs away! It's par for the course for a baby to get more food on the floor than in his or her mouth. Catch the debris and protect your floor by spreading a plastic tablecloth under the high chair.

Collect leaves Save all that bending at leaf-raking time. Don't pick the leaves up to put them in a wheelbarrow to transport them to the curb or leaf pile. Just rake the leaves onto an old plastic tablecloth, gather up the four corners, and drag the tablecloth to the curb or pile.

P

✳ Plastic Wrap

Treat a hangnail Get rid of a hangnail overnight while you sleep. Before going to bed, apply hand cream to the affected area, wrap the fingertip with plastic wrap, and secure in place with transparent tape. The plastic wrap will confine the moisture and soften the cuticle.

Treat psoriasis Here is a method often recommended by dermatologists to treat individual psoriasis lesions. After you apply a topical steroid cream, cover the area with a small piece of plastic wrap and use adhesive tape to affix the wrap to your skin. The wrap will enhance the effect of the steroid, seal in moisture, and inhibit proliferation of the rash.

Enhance liniment effect For pain in your knee or other sore spots, rub in some liniment and wrap the area with plastic wrap. The wrap will increase the heating effect of the liniment. Make sure to test on a small area first to make sure your skin does not burn.

Keep ice cream smooth Ever notice how ice crystals form on ice cream in the freezer once the container has been opened? The ice cream will stay smooth and free of those annoying, yucky crystals if you rewrap the container completely in plastic wrap before you return it to the freezer.

Keep fridge top forever clean Make the next time you clean the top of your refrigerator the last time. After you've gotten it all clean and shiny, cover the top with over-

DID *You* KNOW?

Saran (polyvinylidene chloride) was accidentally discovered in 1933 by Ralph Wiley, a Dow Chemical Company lab worker. One day Ralph came across a vial coated with a smelly, clear green film he couldn't scrub off. He called it eonite, after an indestructible material featured in the "Little Orphan Annie" comic strip. Dow researchers analyzed the substance and dubbed the greasy film Saran. Soon the armed forces were using it to spray fighter planes, and carmakers used it to protect upholstery. Dow later got rid of the green color and unpleasant odor and transformed it into a solid material, which was approved for food packaging after World War II and as a contact food wrap in 1956.

lapping sheets of plastic wrap. Next time it's due for a cleaning, all you need do is remove the old sheets, toss them in the trash, and replace with new layers of wrap.

Protect computer keyboard Hooray! You are off on vacation and won't be tapping that computer keyboard for a couple of weeks. Cover your computer keyboard with plastic wrap during long periods of inactivity to keep out dust and grime.

Repair a kite Flying kites with the kids is a lot of fun, but it can also be frustrating when the kite gets torn by a tree branch or fence. For a temporary fix that will keep the kite airborne for a while, cover the tear with plastic wrap and affix it to the kite with transparent tape.

Keep stored paint fresh Your leftover paint will stay fresh longer if you stretch a sheet of premium plastic wrap over the top of the can before tightly replacing the lid.

> **TAKE CARE** When microwaving foods covered with plastic wrap, always turn back a corner of the wrap or cut a slit in it to let steam escape. Never use plastic wrap when microwaving foods with a high sugar content; they can become extremely hot and melt the wrap.

✳ Plungers

Remove car dents Before forking over big bucks to have an auto body repair shop pull a dent out of your car, try this: Wet a plumber's plunger, push it over the dent, and then pull it out sharply.

Catch chips when drilling ceiling Before you use a star drill to make an overhead hole, remove the handle from a plunger and place the cup over the shank of the drill. The cup will catch falling chunks of plaster, cement, or brick.

Use as an outdoor candleholder Looking for a place to put one of those bug-deterring citronella candles? Plant a plunger handle in the ground and put the candle in the rubber cup.

✳ Popsicle Sticks

Emergency splint for a finger You've got a kid with an apparent broken finger and you're on the way to the emergency room. Use a Popsicle stick as a temporary splint for the finger. Tape it on with adhesive tape to help stabilize the finger until it can be set.

Teach letters to future artists and writers Popsicle sticks are just the thing for spreading finger paint. Or, for a fun way to help youngsters practice their letters, let them use Popsicle sticks to write letters in a pile of shaving cream, whipped cream, or pudding.

Skewer kids' food It's more fun to eat food if you get to play with it first, as the parents of many picky eaters know. Popsicle sticks are good to have in your bag of tricks at mealtime. Skewer bites of hot dog, pineapple, melon, and more. Or give kids a stick and have them spread their own peanut butter and jelly.

Label your plantings Is that parsley, sage, rosemary, or thyme popping up from your garden? Remember what you planted by using Popsicle sticks as plant labels. Just write the type of seeds you planted on the stick with indelible marker.

Keep track of paint colors You're out in the garage searching through the cans of leftover paint. Did you paint the living room with a paint called Whipped Cream or Sand? Don't get mixed up again. After you've painted a room, dip a Popsicle stick in the can. Let it dry. Write the name of the paint and the room where it was used on the stick. Now you'll know what color to use when it's time to paint again. These guides can also help a home decorator pick out fabrics and decorative items.

Kids' Stuff Here's a great little gift to encourage young readers. All you need is a **Popsicle stick**, **paint**, **craft foam**, **glue**, and a **marker**. Paint the Popsicle stick in a bright color, such as red. When it's dry, write on one side a reading slogan such as "I love to read" or "I'll hold the page." Then cut a shape out of the craft foam, such as a heart, flower, a cat, or a dog. Glue the shape to the top of the Popsicle stick, and you have a **homemade bookmark**.

✳ Pots and Pans

Catch draining engine oil No need to run out and buy an oil-collecting pan. When it is time to change the oil in your car engine, just stick an old 5-quart (4.75-liter) or larger pot beneath the drain plug.

Create an instant birdbath You can quickly provide feathered visitors to your backyard with a place to refresh themselves. Just set an old pan atop a flowerpot and keep it filled with water.

Use as a large scoop Leave those 50-pound (20-kilogram) sacks of fertilizer and grass seed in the garden shed and use a pot to carry what you need to the place you're tending. A small pot with a handle also makes a terrific boat bailer or dog-food scoop.

Make an extra grill You've got a big barbecue planned, and your grill is not big enough to handle all those burgers and dogs. Improvise an auxiliary grill by building a fire in an old, large pot. Cook on a cake rack placed over the pot. After you are finished, put the pot's cover on to choke out the fire and save the charcoal for another cookout.

✳ Potatoes

Make a decorative stamp Forget those expensive rubber stamps that go for up to $10 or more apiece. A potato can provide the right medium for making your own stamp for decorating holiday cards and envelopes. Cut a potato in half widthwise. Carve a design on one half. Then start stamping as you would with a wooden version.

Remove stains on hands Your family's favorite carrot soup is simmering on the stove, and you've got the orange hands to show for it. Otherwise hard-to-remove stains on hands from peeling carrots or handling pumpkin come right off if you rub your hands with a potato.

Extract salt for soup Hm, did you go a bit overboard when salting the soup? No problem. Just cut a few potatoes into large chunks. Toss them into the soup pot still on the stove. When they start to soften, in about 10 minutes, remove them and the excess salt they have absorbed. Save them for another use, such as potato salad.

Remove a broken lightbulb You're changing a lightbulb in the nightstand lamp, and it breaks off in your hand. So now the glass is off, but the stem's still inside. Unplug the lamp. Cut a potato widthwise and place it over the broken bulb. Twist, and the rest of the lightbulb should come out easily.

Remove tarnish on silverware High tea is being served at your house later today, and you're out of silver polish. Grab a bunch of potatoes and boil them up. Remove them from the water and save them for another use. Place your silverware in the remaining water and let it sit for an hour. Then remove the silverware and wash. The tarnish should be gone.

Keep ski goggles clear You can't keep a good lookout for trees and other skiers through snow goggles that fog up during your downhill descent. Rub raw potato over the goggles before you get on the ski lift, and the ride down should be crystal clear.

End puffy morning eyes We all hate waking up in the morning and looking at our mug in the mirror. What are those puffy spots on your face? Oh yeah, those are your eyes. A little morning TLC is what you need. Apply slices of raw, cold potatoes to your peepers to make the puffiness go away.

Lure worms in houseplants The worms crawl in and the worms crawl out of the roots of your favorite houseplant. The roots are suffering. What to do? Slice raw potato around the base of the plant to act as a lure for the worms. They'll crawl up to eat, and you can grab them and toss them out.

Feed new geraniums A raw potato can give a fledgling geranium all the nutrients it could desire. Carve a small hole in a potato. Slip a geranium stem into the hole. Plant the whole thing, potato and all.

Hold a floral arrangement in place If you have a small arrangement of flowers that you'd like to stabilize but have none of that green floral foam on hand to stick the flower stems in, try a large baking potato. Cut it in half lengthwise and place it cut side down. Poke holes where you want the flowers and then insert the stems.

Restore old, beat-up shoes Try as you might, your old shoes are just too scuffed to take a shine anymore. They don't have holes, and they are so nice and comfy that you hate to throw them away. Before you give them the brush-off, cut a potato in half and rub those old shoes with the raw potato. After that, polish them; they should come out nice and shiny.

Make a hot or cold compress Potatoes retain heat and cold well. The next time you need a hot compress, boil a potato, wrap it in a towel, and apply to the area. Refrigerate the boiled potato if you need a cold compress.

SCIENCE FAIR

Here's a way to demonstrate the **power of air pressure**. Grasp a **plastic straw** in the middle and try to **plunge it into a potato**. It crumples and bends, unable to penetrate the potato. Now grasp another straw in the middle, but

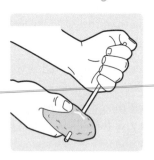

this time, put your **finger** over the top. The straw will plunge right into the tuber. When the air is trapped inside the straw, it presses against the straw's sides, stiffening the straw enough to plunge into the potato. In fact, the deeper the straw plunges, the less space there is for the air and the stiffer the straw gets.

✳ Return Address Labels

Tag your bags Address labels aren't only for sticking on envelopes. They can be an effective, inexpensive way of making sure your lost items stand a chance of finding their way home. Place an address label—covered with a small piece of transparent or clear packing tape to prevent wear—inside your laptop PC bag, designer eyewear case, gym bag, knapsack, and all pieces of luggage—whether they are tagged or not.

Label your stuff Few folks bother to take out insurance on their collection of personal electronics equipment, but replacing a high-end PDA, camera, camcorder, or MP3 player can run into some serious money. Still, a tape-covered address label conspicuously placed on your gear just may facilitate its safe return. Of course, there are no guarantees in these matters, but at least the policy is cheap enough.

Hang on to your umbrella A well-made umbrella can last for years, but that won't help if it's left behind on a bus or train. Minimize the risk of your loss becoming someone else's gain by sticking an address label on the umbrella handle and wrapping it once around with clear packing tape. This protects the label from the elements—and makes it considerably more difficult to remove.

Secure school supplies It's one of the universal truths of parenthood: Kids' pencil cases, folders, markers, and other school supplies are forever disappearing. You may be able to lessen the losses, however, by affixing address labels with a piece of transparent tape to the contents of your child's desk and backpack.

Identify items for repair Do you suffer separation anxiety when you bring your beloved stereo equipment or another precious item into the repair shop? You may feel better if you place an address label on the base or some other unobtrusive, undamaged area. *Note:* This practice is not recommended for all personal treasures—you probably wouldn't want to label paper documents, paintings, photos, and such.

Rubber Bands

Stop sliding spoons Plop! The spoon slipped into the mixing bowl again, and now you have to fish it out of the messy batter. This time, after you rinse off the spoon, wrap a rubber band around the top of the handle to catch the spoon and avoid the mess.

Secure your casserole lids Don't spill it! That's what you say when you hand somebody your lovingly prepared casserole dish to carry in the car on the way to that potluck dinner. You won't have to worry if you secure the top to the base with a couple of wide rubber bands.

Anchor your cutting board Do you find yourself chasing your cutting board around the counter when you're chopping up veggies? Give the board some traction by putting a rubber band around each end.

Get a grip on twist-off tops Ouch! The tops on most beer bottles these days are supposed to be twist-off, but for some reason they still have those sharp little crimps from the bottle-opener days. And those little crimps can really dig into your hand. Wrap the top in a rubber band to save the pain. The same trick works great for smooth, tough-to-grip soda bottle tops too.

Get a grip on drinking glasses Does arthritis make it tough for you to grasp a drinking glass securely, especially when it is wet with condensation? Wrap a couple of rubber bands around the glass to make it easier to grip. Works great for kids, too, whose small hands sometimes have a hard time holding a glass.

Reshape your broom No need to toss out that broom because the bristles have become splayed with use. Wrap a rubber band around the broom a few inches from the bottom. Leave it for a day or so to get the bristles back in line.

DID *You* KNOW?

The first rubber band was patented in 1845 by Stephen Perry, who owned a manufacturing company in London.

A key ingredient in making rubber bands is sulfur. When it is added to the rubber and heated—a process known as vulcanization—it makes the rubber strong and stretchy and prevents it from rotting. The process of making rubber bands is surprisingly similar to making a loaf of bread. First the dry ingredients are mixed with natural rubber. The resulting friction and chemical reaction heats and partially vulcanizes the rubber. The rubber is cooled, then rolled out like bread dough. It's extruded into a long tube, and the tube is heated to finish the vulcanization. Then it's rinsed, cooled, and sliced into bands.

Childproof kitchen and bath cabinets The grandkids are coming! Time to get out the rubber bands and temporarily childproof the bathroom and kitchen cabinets you don't want them to get into. Just wrap the bands tightly around pairs of handles.

Keep thread from tangling Tired of tangled thread in your sewing box? Just wrap a rubber band around the spools to keep the thread from unraveling.

Make a holder for your car visor Snap a couple of rubber bands around the sun visors of your car. Now you have a handy spot to slip toll receipts, directions, maybe even your favorite CD.

Thumb through papers with ease Stop licking your finger. Just wrap a rubber band around your index finger a few times the next time you need to shuffle papers. Not too tight, though! You don't want to cut off circulation to your fingertip.

Extend a button Having trouble breathing? Maybe that top shirt button is a tad too tight. Stick a small rubber band through the buttonhole, then loop the ends over the button. Put on your tie and breathe easy.

Use as a bookmark Paper bookmarks work fine, until they slip out of the book. Instead, wrap a rubber band from top to bottom around the part of the book you've already read. You won't lose your place, even if you drop the book.

Cushion your remote control To protect your fine furniture from scratches and nicks, wrap a wide rubber band around both ends of the television remote control. You'll be protecting the remote too—it will be less likely to slide off a table and be damaged.

Secure bed slats Do the slats under your mattress sometimes slip out? Wrap rubber bands around their ends to make them stay in place.

Tighten furniture casters Furniture leg casters can become loose with wear. To tighten up a caster, wrap a rubber band around the stem and reinsert.

Gauge your liquids Hm, just how much finish is left in that can up on the shelf anyway? Snap a band around the liquid containers in your workshop to indicate how much is left and you'll always know at a glance.

Wipe your paintbrush Every time you dip your paintbrush, you wipe the excess against the side of the can. Before you know it, paint is dripping off the side of the can and the little groove around the rim is so full of paint that it splatters everywhere when you go to hammer the lid back on. Avoiding all this mess is easy. Just wrap a rubber band around the can from top to

bottom, going across the middle of the can opening. Now, when you fill your brush, you can just tap it against the rubber band and the excess paint will fall back into the can.

✳ Rubber Jar Rings

Keep rug from slipping If you have a throw rug that tends to skate across the floor, keep it in place by sewing a rubber jar ring or two on the underside in each corner.

Play indoor quoits What else can you do to keep antsy pre-schoolers happily occupied on a rainy day? Turn a stool or small table upside down and let them try to toss rubber jar rings over the legs.

Protect tabletops Protect your tabletops from scratches and watermarks by placing a rubber jar ring under vases and lamps.

✳ Rubbing Alcohol

Clean bathroom fixtures Just reach into the medicine cabinet the next time you need to clean chrome bathroom fixtures. Pour some rubbing alcohol straight from the bottle onto a soft, absorbent cloth and the fixtures. No need to rinse—the alcohol just evaporates. It does a great job of making chrome sparkle, plus it will kill any germs in its path.

Remove hair spray from mirrors When you are spritzing your head with hair spray, some of it inevitably winds up on the mirror. A quick wipe with rubbing alcohol will whisk away that sticky residue and leave your mirror sparkling clean.

Clean venetian blinds Rubbing alcohol does a terrific job of cleaning the slats of venetian blinds. To make quick work of the job, wrap a flat tool—a spatula or maybe a 6-inch (15-centimeter) drywall knife—in cloth and secure with a rubber band. Dip in alcohol and go to work.

Keep windows sparkling and frost-free Do your windows frost up in the wintertime? Wash them with a solution of 1/2 cup rubbing alcohol to 1 quart (1 liter) water to prevent the frost. Polish the windows with newspaper after you wash them to make them shine.

Dissolve windshield frost Wouldn't you rather be inside savoring your morning coffee a little longer instead of scrape, scrape, scraping frost off your car windows? Fill a spray bottle with rubbing alcohol and spritz the car glass. You'll be able to wipe the frost right off. Ah, good to the last drop!

Prevent ring around the collar To prevent your neck from staining your shirt collar, wipe your neck with rubbing alcohol each morning before you dress. Feels good too.

TAKE CARE Don't confuse denatured alcohol with rubbing alcohol. Denatured alcohol is ethanol (drinking alcohol) to which poisonous and foul-tasting chemicals have been added to render it unfit for drinking. Often, the chemicals used in denatured alcohol are not ones you should put on your skin. Rubbing alcohol is made of chemicals that are safe for skin contact—most often it's 70 percent isopropyl alcohol and 30 percent water.

Clean your phone Is your phone getting a bit grubby? Wipe it down with rubbing alcohol. It'll remove the grime and disinfect the phone at the same time.

Remove ink stains Did you get ink on your favorite shirt or dress? Try soaking the spot in rubbing alcohol for a few minutes before putting the garment in the wash.

Erase permanent markers. Did Junior decide to decorate your countertop with a permanent marker? Don't worry, most countertops are made of a nonpermeable material such as plastic laminate or marble. Rubbing alcohol will dissolve the marker back to a liquid state so you can wipe it right off.

Remove dog ticks Ticks hate the taste of rubbing alcohol as much as they love the taste of your dog. Before you pull a tick off Fido, dab the critter with rubbing alcohol to make it loosen its grip. Then grab the tick as close to the dog's skin as you can and pull it straight out. Dab again with alcohol to disinfect the wound. This works on people too.

Get rid of fruit flies The next time you see fruit flies hovering in the kitchen, get out a fine-misting spray bottle and fill it with rubbing alcohol. Spraying the little flies knocks them out and makes them fall to the floor, where you can sweep them up. The alcohol is less effective than insecticide, but it's a lot safer than spraying poison around your kitchen.

Make a shapeable ice pack The problem with ice packs is they won't conform to the shape of the injured body part. Make a slushy, conformable pack by mixing 1 part rubbing alcohol with 3 parts water in a self-closing plastic bag. The next time that sore knee acts up, wrap the bag of slush in a cloth and apply it to the area. Ahhh!

Stretch tight-fitting new shoes This doesn't always work, but it sure is worth a try: If your new leather shoes are pinching your feet, try swabbing the tight spot with a cotton ball soaked in rubbing alcohol. Walk around in the shoes for a few minutes to see if they stretch enough to be comfortable. If not, the next step is to take them back to the shoe store.

S

super item
65 uses! Salt

Clear flower residue in a vase Once your beautiful bouquet is gone, the souvenir it leaves behind is not the kind of reminder you want: deposits of minerals on the vase interior. Reach inside the vase, rub the offending ring of deposits with salt, then wash with soapy water. If your hand won't fit inside, fill the vase with a strong solution of salt and water, shake it or brush gently with a bottle brush, then wash. This should clear away the residue.

Clean artificial flowers You can quickly freshen up artificial flowers—whether they are authentic silk ones or the more common nylon variety—by placing them in a paper bag with 1/4 cup salt. Give the bag a few gentle shakes, and your flowers will emerge as clean as the day you bought them.

Hold artificial flowers in place Salt is a great medium for keeping artificial flowers in the arrangement you want. Fill a vase or other container with salt, add a little cold water, and arrange your artificial flowers. The salt will solidify, and the flowers will stay put.

Keep wicker looking new Wicker furniture can yellow with age and exposure to the sun and elements. To keep your wicker natural-looking, scrub it with a stiff brush dipped in warm salt water. Let the piece dry in the sun. Repeat this process every year or every other year.

Give brooms a long life A new straw broom will last longer if you soak its bristles in a bucket of hot, salty water. After about 20 minutes, remove the broom and let it dry.

Ease fireplace cleanup When you're ready to turn in for the night but the fire is still glowing in the hearth, douse the flames with salt. The fire will burn out more quickly, so you'll wind up with less soot than if you let it smolder. Cleanup is easier, too, because the salt helps the ashes and residue gather into easy sweepings.

SALT✳

280

Make your own brass and copper polish When exposure to the elements dulls brass or copper items, there's no need to buy expensive cleaning products. To shine your candlesticks or remove green tarnish from copper pots, make a paste by mixing equal parts salt, flour, and vinegar. Use a soft cloth to rub this over the item, then rinse with warm, soapy water and buff back to its original shine.

Remove wine from carpet Argggh! Red wine spilled on a white carpet is the worst. But there's hope. First, while the red wine is still wet, pour some white wine on it to dilute the color. Then clean the spot with a sponge and cold water. Sprinkle the area with salt and wait about 10 minutes. Now vacuum up the whole mess.

Clean grease stains from rugs Did that football-watching couch potato knock his greasy nachos onto your nice white carpet? Before you kill him, mix up 1 part salt to 4 parts rubbing alcohol and rub it hard on the grease stain, being careful to rub in the direction of the rug's natural nap. Or better yet, have him do it. Then you can kill him.

Remove watermarks from wood Watermarks left from glasses or bottles on a wood table really stand out. Make them disappear by mixing 1 teaspoon salt with a few drops of water to form a paste. Gently rub the paste onto the ring with a soft cloth or sponge and work it over the spot until it's gone. Restore the luster of your wood with furniture polish.

?? DID *You* KNOW?

Salt may be the key to life on Mars. Thanks to Mars missions, scientists have confirmed two things about the Red Planet: There's plenty of ice and plenty of salt. Of course, life as we know it requires water. And while temperatures on Mars are either too high or too low for fresh water, the presence of salt makes it possible that there is life-sustaining salt water below the planet's surface.

Restore a sponge Hand sponges and mop sponges usually get grungy beyond use long before they are really worn out. To restore sponges to a pristine state, soak them overnight in a solution of about 1/4 cup salt per quart (liter) of water.

Relieve stings, bites, and poison ivy Salt works well to lessen the pain of bee stings, bug bites, and poison ivy:

- Stung by a bee? Immediately wet the sting and cover with salt. It will lessen the pain and reduce the swelling. Of course, if you are allergic to bee stings, you should get immediate medical attention.

- For relief from the itching of mosquito and chigger bites, soak the area in salt water, then apply a coating of lard or vegetable oil.

When poison ivy erupts, relieve the itching by soaking in hot salt water. If the case is very unfortunate, you might want to immerse yourself in a tub full of salt water.

Keep windows and windshields frost-free As you probably know, salt greatly decreases the temperature at which ice freezes. You can use this fact to keep the windows in your home frost-free by wiping them with a sponge dipped in salt water, then letting them dry. In the winter, keep a small cloth bag of salt in your car. When the windshield and other windows are wet, rub them with the bag. The next time you go out to your car, the windows won't be covered with ice or snow.

Deodorize your sneakers Sneakers and other canvas shoes can get pretty smelly, especially if you wear them without socks in the summertime. Knock down the odor and soak up the moisture by occasionally sprinkling a little salt in your canvas shoes.

Make a scented air freshener Buying fragranced air fresheners can get expensive. Here is a wonderful way to make your room smell like a rose any time of the year: Layer rose petals and salt in a pretty jar with a tight-fitting lid. Remove the lid to freshen the room.

Give goldfish a parasite-killing bath The next time you take your goldfish out of its tank to change the water, put Goldie in an invigorating saltwater bath for 15 minutes while you clean the tank. Make the bath by mixing 1 teaspoon plain (noniodized) salt into 1 quart (1 liter) freshwater. (Just like the tank water, you should let tap water sit overnight first to let the chlorine evaporate.) The salt water kills parasites on the fish's scales and helps the fish absorb electrolytes. Don't add salt to the fish's tank, though. Goldfish are freshwater fish and can't spend a lot of time in salt water.

Clean your fish tank To remove mineral deposits from hard water in your fish tank, rub the inside of the tank with salt, then rinse the tank well before reinstalling the fish. Use only plain, not iodized, salt.

DID *You* KNOW?

The United States is the world leader in salt production. In 2002 the U.S. produced 43.9 million metric tons of salt, according to the Salt Institute. China was second, with 35 million metric tons. Among other nations producing significant amounts of salt were Germany, with 15.7 million metric tons; India, with 14.8 million metric tons; and Canada, with 13 million metric tons.

Repel fleas in pet habitats If Fido enjoys his doghouse, chances are fleas do too. Keep fleas from infesting your pet's home by washing down the interior walls and floor every few weeks with a solution of salt water.

End the ant parade If ants are beating a path to your home, intercept them by sprinkling salt across the door frame or directly on their paths. Ants will be discouraged from crossing this barrier.

*SALT **IN THE KITCHEN**

Freshen your garbage disposal Is an unpleasant odor wafting from your garbage disposal? Freshen it up with salt. Just dump in 1/2 cup salt, run the cold water, and start the disposal. The salt will dislodge stuck waste and neutralize odors.

Remove baked-on food Yes, you can remove food that has been baked onto cooking pans or serving plates. In fact, it's easy. Baked-on food can be "lifted" with a pre-treatment of salt. Before washing, sprinkle the stuck-on food with salt. Dampen the area, let it sit until the salt lifts the baked-on food, then wash it away with soapy water.

Soak stains off enamel pans You can run out of elbow grease trying to scrub burned-on stains off enamel pans. Skip the sweat. Soak the pan overnight in salt water. Then boil salt water in the pan the next day. The stains should lift right off.

Keep oven spills from hardening The next time food bubbles over in your oven, don't give it a chance to bake on and cool. Toss some salt on the stuff while it is still liquid. When the oven cools, you'll be able to wipe up the spill with a cloth. The same technique works for spills on the stovetop. The salt will remove odors too, and if you'd like to add a pleasant scent, mix a little cinnamon in with the salt.

Scrub off burned milk Burned milk is one of the toughest stains to remove, but salt makes it a lot easier. Wet the burned pan and sprinkle it with salt. Wait about 10 minutes, then scrub the pan. The salt absorbs that burned-milk odor too.

Clean greasy iron pans Grease can be tough to remove from iron pans, because it is not water-soluble. Shortcut the problem by sprinkling salt in the pan before you wash it. The pan will absorb most of the grease. Wipe the pan out and then wash as usual.

Clean discolored glass Did your dishwasher fail to remove those stubborn stains from your glassware? Hand-scrubbing failed too? Try this: Mix a handful of salt in a quart of vinegar and soak the glassware overnight. The stains should wipe off in the morning.

Clean your cast-iron wok No matter how thoroughly you dry them, cast-iron woks tend to rust when you wash them in water. Instead, when you're done cooking, but while your wok is still hot, pour in about 1/4 cup salt and scrub it with a stiff wire brush. Wipe it clean, then apply a light coating of sesame or vegetable oil before stowing it. Don't clean a wok with a nonstick coating this way, because it will scratch the coating.

Remove lipstick marks from glassware Lipstick smudges on glassware can be hard to remove, even in the dishwasher. That's because the emollients designed to help lipstick stay on your lips do a good job sticking to glassware too. Before washing your stemware, rocks glasses, or water tumblers, rub the edges with salt to erase lipstick stains.

Brighten up your cutting boards After you wash cutting boards and breadboards with soap and water, rub them with a damp cloth dipped in salt. The boards will be lighter and brighter in color.

Clean the refrigerator We all have to do it sometime, and today it's your turn. You've removed all the food and the racks from the fridge. Now mix up a handful of salt in 1 gallon (3.7 liters) or so of warm water and use it with a sponge to clean the inside of the refrigerator. The mixture isn't abrasive, so it won't scratch surfaces. And you won't be introducing chemical fumes or odors.

Speed cleanup of messy dough Here's a way to make short work of cleanup after you've rolled out dough or kneaded breads. Sprinkle your floury countertop with salt. Now you can neatly wipe away everything with a sponge. No more sticky lumps.

Erase tea and coffee stains Tea and coffee leave stains on cups and in pots. You can easily scrub away these unattractive rings by sprinkling salt onto a sponge and rubbing in little circles across the ring. If the stain persists, mix white vinegar with salt in equal proportions and rub with the sponge.

Shine your teapot spout Teapots with seriously stained spouts can be cleaned with salt. Stuff the spout with salt and let it sit overnight or at least several hours. Then run boiling water through the pot, washing away the salt and revealing the old sparkle. If the stain persists, treat the rim with a cotton swab dipped in salt.

DID *You* KNOW?

Salt was surely the first food seasoning. Prehistoric people got all the salt they needed from the meat that made up a large portion of their diet. When humans began turning to agriculture as a more reliable food source, they discovered that salt—most likely from the sea—gave vegetables that salty taste they craved. As the millennia passed, salt gradually made life more comfortable and certain as people learned to use it to preserve food, cure hides, and heal wounds.

Clean your coffee percolator If your percolated coffee tastes a bit bitter these days, try this: Fill the percolator with water and add 4 tablespoons salt. Then percolate as usual. Rinse the percolator and all of its parts well and the next pot you make should have that delicious flavor we all love.

Revive overcooked coffee You made a pot of coffee and then got distracted for an hour. Meanwhile, the coffee continued to cook in the pot and now it's bitter. Before you throw out the brew, try adding a pinch of salt to a cup.

Kids' Stuff Here's a **craft dough** easily fashioned into detailed **ornaments, miniature foods,** and **dolls.** In a bowl, slowly stir 1 cup **salt** into 1 cup boiling water. After the salt dissolves, stir in 2 cups **white all-purpose flour.** Turn the dough out onto a work surface and knead until smooth. If the dough sticks, add flour by the tablespoon until it is pliant. It should be easy to shape into balls, tubes, wreaths, and other shapes. Air-dry your creations or bake them in a 200°F (95°C) oven for up to two hours; time depends on thickness. Or microwave on High 1-2 minutes. Apply **paint;** protect and shine with **clear nail polish** or varnish.

Prevent grease splatters How many times have you been burned by splattering grease while cooking bacon when all you wanted was a hearty breakfast? Next time, add a few dashes of salt to the pan before beginning to fry foods that can splatter. You'll cook without pain and you won't have to clean grease off your cooktop.

Speed up cooking time In a hurry? Add a pinch or two of salt to the water you are boiling food in. This makes the water boil at a higher temperature so the food you are cooking will require less time on the stovetop. Keep in mind: Salt does not make the water boil faster.

Shell hard-boiled eggs with ease Ever wonder whether there's a secret to peeling hard-boiled eggs without breaking the shell into a million tiny pieces? There is, and now it's out of the box! Add a teaspoon of salt to your water before placing the eggs in it to boil.

Make perfect poached eggs You *know* it's possible to keep the whites intact when you poach eggs—you've had them in a restaurant. But no matter how careful you are, the whites always diffuse into the water when you poach eggs at home. Here's the secret the restaurant chefs know: Sprinkle about 1/2 teaspoon salt into the water just before you put in your eggs. This helps to "set" the whites in a neat package. A dash of vinegar also helps, and improves the taste of the eggs too.

Test an egg's freshness In doubt about whether your eggs are fresh? Add 2 teaspoons salt to 1 cup water and gently place the egg in the cup. A fresh egg will sink. An old one floats.

Shell pecans easier Pecans can be tough nuts to crack. And once you do crack them, it can be tough to dig out the meat. Soak the nuts in salt water for several hours before shelling, and the meat will come cleanly away from the shells.

Wash spinach more easily Fresh spinach leaves are lovely to look at, but their curving, bumpy surface makes it difficult to wash away all the dirt that collects in the crevices. Try this trick: Wash spinach leaves in salted water. Dirt is driven out along with salt in the rinse water, and you can cut the rinses down to just one.

Keep salad crisp Do you need to prepare leafy salad in advance of a dinner party? Lightly salt the salad immediately after you prepare it, and it will remain crisp for several hours.

Revive wrinkled apples Do your apples need a face-lift? Soak them in mildly salted water to make the skin smooth again.

Stop cut fruit from browning You're working ahead, making fruit salad for a party and you want to make sure your fresh-cut fruit looks appetizing when you serve the dish. To ensure that cut apples and pears retain their color, soak them briefly in a bowl of lightly salted water.

Use to whip cream and beat eggs The next time you whip cream or beat eggs, add a pinch of salt first. The cream will whip up lighter. The eggs will beat faster and higher, and they'll firm up better when you cook them.

Keep your milk fresh Add a pinch of salt to a carton of milk to make it stay fresh longer. Works for cream too.

Prevent mold on cheese Cheese is much too expensive to throw away because it has become moldy. Prevent the mold by wrapping the cheese in a napkin soaked in salt water before storing it in the refrigerator.

Extinguish grease fires Store your box of salt next to the stove. Then, should a grease fire erupt, toss the salt on it to extinguish the flames. *Never* pour water on a grease fire—it will cause the grease to splatter and spread the fire. Salt is also the solution when the barbecue flames from meat drippings get too high. Sprinkling salt on the coals will quell the flames without causing a lot of smoke and cooling the coals as water does.

DID *You* KNOW?

The concentration of salt in your body is nearly one-third of the concentration found in seawater. This is why blood, sweat, and tears are so salty. Many scientists believe that humans, as well as all animals, need salt because all life evolved from the oceans. When the first land dwellers crawled out of the sea, they carried the need for salt—and a bit of the supply—with them and passed it on to their descendants.

SALT*

Pick up spilled eggs If you've ever dropped an uncooked egg, you know what a mess it is to clean up. Cover the spill with salt. It will draw the egg together and you can easily wipe it up with a sponge or paper towel.

Clean your iron's metal soleplate It seems to happen on a regular basis. No matter how careful you are while ironing, something melts onto the iron, forming a rough surface that is difficult to remove. Salt crystals are the answer. Turn your iron onto high. Sprinkle table salt onto a section of newspaper on your ironing board. Run the hot iron over the salt, and you'll iron away the bumps.

Make a quick pre-treatment You're out to a restaurant dining with friends and notice that a little salad dressing has spotted your slacks. You know it can't be checked with water, but here's an idea that will stop the stain from ruining your clothing. Drown the spot in salt to absorb the grease. When you get home, wash as usual.

Remove perspiration stains Salt's the secret to getting rid of those stubborn yellow perspiration stains on shirts. Dissolve 4 tablespoons salt in 1 quart (1 liter) hot water. Just sponge the garment with the solution until the stain disappears.

DID *You* KNOW?

One of the several words salt has added to our language is *salary.* It comes from the Latin word *salarium,* which means "salt money" and refers to that part of a Roman soldier's pay that was made in salt or used to buy salt—a life-preserving commodity. This is also the origin of the phrase "worth one's salt."

Set the color in new towels The first two or three times you wash new colored towels, add 1 cup salt to the wash. The salt will set the colors so your towels will remain bright much longer.

Stop weeds in their tracks Those weeds that pop up in the cracks of your walkways can be tough to eradicate. But salt can do the job. Bring a solution of about 1 cup salt in 2 cups water to a boil. Pour directly on the weeds to kill them. Another equally effective method is to spread salt directly onto the weeds or unwanted grass that come up between patio bricks or blocks. Sprinkle with water or just wait until rain does the job for you.

Rid your garden of snails and slugs ~~These little critters are not good for your plants.~~ But there's a simple solution. Take a container of salt into the garden and douse the offenders. They won't survive long.

Clean flowerpots without water Need to clean out a flowerpot so that you can reuse it? Instead of making a muddy mess by washing the pot in water, just sprinkle in a little salt and scrub off the dry dirt with a stiff brush. This method is especially handy if your potting bench is not near a water source.

✳SALT **IN THE BATH**

A pre-shampoo dandruff treatment The abrasiveness of ordinary table salt works great for scrubbing out dandruff before you shampoo. Grab a saltshaker and shake some salt onto your dry scalp. Then work it through your hair, giving your scalp a massage. You'll find you've worked out the dry, flaky skin and are ready for a shampoo.

Condition your skin You've heard of bath salts, of course. Usually this conjures images of scented crystals that bubble up in your tub and may contain coloring and other stuff that leave a dreaded bathtub ring. Now strip that picture to its core, and you've got salt. Dissolve 1 cup table salt in your tub and soak as usual. Your skin will be noticeably softer. Buy sea salt for a real treat. It comes in larger chunks and can be found in health food stores or the gourmet section of a grocery store.

Give yourself a salt rubdown. Try this trick to remove dead skin particles and boost your circulation. Either while still in the tub, or just after stepping out of the tub—while your skin is still damp—give yourself a massage with dry salt. Ordinary salt works well; the larger sea salt crystals also do the job.

Freshen your breath the old-fashioned way Store-bought mouthwash can contain food coloring, alcohol, and sweeteners. Not to mention the cost! Use the recipe Grandma used and your breath will be just as sweet. Mix 1 teaspoon salt and 1 teaspoon baking soda into 1/2 cup water. Rinse and gargle.

Open hair-clogged drains It's tough to keep hair and shampoo residues from collecting in the bathtub drain and clogging it. Dissolve the mess with 1 cup salt, 1 cup baking soda, and 1/2 cup white vinegar. Pour the mixture down the drain. After 10 minutes, follow up with a 1/2 gallon (2 liters) boiling water. Run your hot-water tap until the drain flows freely.

Remove spots on tub enamel Yellow spots on your enamel bathtub or sinks can be lessened by mixing up a solution of salt and turpentine in equal parts. Using rubber gloves, rub away the discoloration and then rinse thoroughly. Don't forget to ventilate the bathroom while performing this cleaning task.

✳ Saltshakers

Cut back on sugar You can cut back on sugar but still keep your sweet tooth happy if you fill a saltshaker with sugar. For sugar-restricted diets, use your sugar shaker as an alternative to dipping into the sugar bowl, and sprinkle lightly over food.

Use as a cinnamon/sugar dispenser Cinnamon toast is a great comfort food, and everyone likes it made a certain way. Mix sugar and cinnamon to your taste in a saltshaker. Once you've found the proportions you like, you can make it easily and consistently every time. Your cinnamon/sugar shaker is also perfect for sprinkling a little flavor on cereal.

Use for flour-dusting Baking is sometimes a messy job, so make at least one part of it tidier by putting flour into a large saltshaker. It's perfect for dusting your cake pans or muffin cups. Keep it neat and keep it handy in the cupboard, especially if you have an aggressively helpful junior chef!

 **Colored Salt**

> Want to bring a little unexpected fun to your dinner table? Try colored salt! Put a few tablespoons of salt into a plastic sandwich bag and add a few drops of food coloring. Work it gently with your fingers to mix, and let dry in the open bag for about a day. Just cut a hole in the corner of the bag to pour the festive salt into your shaker. As a bonus, your colored table or kosher salt is wonderful homemade glitter!

Use to apply dry fertilizer If you use dry fertilizer, try putting it in a saltshaker to use when fertilizing seedlings. It gives you lots of application control so you can prevent fertilizer burn on your tender babies.

✳ Sand

Protect and store garden tools Your gardening tools are meant to last longer than your perennials, so keep them clean and protected from the elements. Fill a 5-gallon (19-liter) bucket with builder's sand (available at masonry supply and home centers) and pour in about 1 quart (1 liter) of clean motor oil. Plunge shovels and other tools into the sand a few times to clean and lubricate them. To prevent rust, you can leave the tool blades in the bucket of sand for storage. A coffee can filled with sand and a little motor oil will give the same protection to your pruners and hand trowels.

Clean a narrow-neck vase You've held on to your bouquet as long as possible, but it's finally time to toss it along with the water it was sitting in. Now the vase needs cleaning, but the opening is too narrow for your hand. Put a little sand and warm, sudsy water in the vase, and swish gently. The sand will do the work of cleaning the residue inside for you!

Hold items while gluing Repairing small items, such as broken china, with glue would be easy if you had three hands—one for each piece along with one to apply the glue. Since you only have two hands, try this: Stick the biggest part of the item in a small container of sand to hold it steady. Position the large piece so that when you set the broken piece in place, the piece will balance. Apply glue to both edges and stick on the broken piece. Leave the mended piece there, and the sand will hold it steady until the glue dries.

Carry in trunk for traction A bag of sand in the trunk of your car is good insurance in icy weather against getting stuck or spinning out from a parking spot. Throw in a clean margarine tub as well, to use as a scoop. For those with rear-wheel-drive vehicles, a bag or two of sand will also give you some extra traction.

❋ Sandpaper

Sharpen sewing needles Think twice before throwing out a used piece of fine-grit sandpaper; the unused edges or corners are perfect for tucking into your sewing box. Poking your sewing needles through sandpaper a few times, or twisting them inside a folded piece of sandpaper, will make them sharper than ever.

Sharpen your scissors Are your scissor cuts less than crisp? Try cutting through a sheet of fine-grit sandpaper to finish off the edge and keep your cuts clean.

Remove fuzzy pills on sweaters If you're fighting a losing battle with the fuzz balls on your sweaters, a little sandpaper will handle them. Use any grit, and rub lightly in one direction.

Remove scorches on wool Take some medium-grit sandpaper to any small scorch spots on your woolen clothing. The mark left by a careless spark will be less noticeable with some light sanding around the edges.

Hold pleats while ironing If you're a pleat perfectionist, keep some fine- or medium-grit sandpaper handy with your iron. Put the sandpaper under the pleat to hold it in place while you iron a nice sharp fold.

Kids' Stuff You or your little Leonardo can make a beautiful **one-of-a-kind T-shirt**. Have the youngster use **crayons** to draw a bold design on the rough side of a sheet of **sandpaper.** Lay the T-shirt on your **ironing board** and slip a sheet of **aluminum foil** inside, between the front and back of the shirt. Place the sandpaper onto the T-shirt, design side down. Using an **iron** on the warm setting, press the back of the sandpaper in one spot for about ten seconds and then move on to the next spot until the entire design has been pressed. Let the shirt cool to set the design, launder on a cool setting, then hang to dry.

Roughen slippery leather soles New shoes with slippery soles can send you flying, so take a little sandpaper and a little time to sand across the width of the soles and roughen up the slick surface. It's thriftier and easier than taking your new shoes to a repair shop to have new rubber soles put on.

Remove ink stains and scuff marks from suede A little fine-grit sandpaper and a gentle touch is great for removing or at least minimizing an ink stain or small scuff mark on suede clothing or shoes. Afterward, bring up the nap with a toothbrush or nailbrush. You might avoid an expensive trip to the dry cleaner!

Use to deter slugs Slugs are truly the unwelcome guests that will never leave, but you can stop them from getting into your potted plants in the first place. Put those used sanding disks to work under the bases of your pots, making sure the sandpaper is wider than the pot base.

Remove stubborn grout stains Sometimes your bathroom abrasive cleaner is just not abrasive enough. Get tough on grout stains with fine-grit sandpaper. Fold the sandpaper and use the folded edge to sand in the grout seam. Be careful not to sand the tile and scratch the finish.

Open a stuck jar Having a tough time opening a jar? Grab a piece of sandpaper and place it grit side down on the lid. The sandpaper should improve your grip enough to do the job.

Make an emery board If you don't have an emery board handy the next time you need to smooth your nails, just raid the sandpaper stash in the garage workshop. Look for a piece marked 120 grit or 150 grit on the back.

Sandwich and Freezer Bags

✳ SANDWICH AND FREEZER BAGS **AROUND THE HOUSE**

Protect your pictures You just picked up a batch of beautiful photos of your newest grandchild. Before you pass them around your bridge party, encase each in a small, clear sandwich bag. Then you can hear the oohs and aahs without smudges on your pictures.

Freeze a washcloth for a cold pack It's hard to predict when someone in your household will next suffer a burn, teething pain, or another bump or scrape. Be ready. Freeze a wet washcloth in a sandwich or freezer bag. Pull it out of the freezer the next time someone needs some cold care.

Protect your padlocks When the weather is cold enough to freeze your padlocks on the outdoor shed or garage, remember that a sandwich bag can help. Slip one over the lock and you'll avoid frozen tumblers.

Make a fabric-softener dispenser Who can ever remember to add the fabric softener to the wash at the right time? You won't have to again. Punch some pinholes in a sealable plastic bag and, holding it over the washer basin, fill it with fabric softener. Seal the bag and toss into the laundry. The softener dispenses slowly through the pinholes during the wash and you won't have to remember that extra step.

Display baby teeth Your daughter has lost her first tooth and wants to show it off. You don't want to lose that precious memento of this important rite of passage. Place it in a sealable plastic bag. She can easily display it, and you won't worry about the tooth getting lost.

Make baby wipes for pennies You could buy the outrageously expensive baby wipes at the store or purchase some in bulk and hope they don't dry out before you use them up. Or you can just take the thrifty parent's way out: Make your own baby wipes by placing soft paper towels in a sealable bag with a mixture of 1 tablespoon gentle antibacterial soap, 1 teaspoon baby oil, and 1/3 cup water. Use enough of the mixture just to get the wipes damp, not drenched.

DID *You* KNOW?

Of course, we haven't always carried our ham-and-cheese sandwiches to work in plastic bags. Sandwich-size plastic bags were first introduced in 1957. Seven years later, Mobil Corp. introduced sandwich bags with tuck-in flaps, also known as Baggies. Just in case you are too young to remember, before plastic bags, we wrapped our sandwiches in paper or wax paper, like they still do in most delis.

Mold soap scraps into a new bar The thrifty among us hate to throw out a sliver of soap. Yet they're impossible to use when they get small. Instead, start collecting them all in a sealable plastic bag. When you have several, place the bag in a pan of warm, not boiling, water. Watch the soap pieces melt. When the mixture cools, you have a new bar of soap.

Starch craft items You've just completed that handmade Christmas stocking for your grandchild. But the last fabric ornaments to attach need to be starched. Throw them in a sealable plastic bag that contains a bit of starch. Shake until covered, remove, and let dry. Save the starch in the bag for your next craft project.

Feed the birds Be kind to the birds in your yard during the lean winter months. Mix some birdseed with peanut butter in a sealable plastic bag. Seal the bag and mix the ingredients by kneading the outside of the bag. Then place the glob in a small net bag or spread on a pinecone. Attach to a tree and await the grateful flock.

✻ SANDWICH AND FREEZER BAGS **IN THE KITCHEN**

Store grated cheese Pasta or pizza is always better with a dash of freshly grated Parmesan cheese. But who wants to bother with getting the grater out every time you want that taste? Instead, take a wedge of Parmesan cheese, grate the whole thing at once, and then double bag it in two self-closing bags to protect the freshness. Or stick the grater in the bag with the cheese wedge and pull it out for a short grate when the pesto gets to the table. That way you won't have to clean the grater after each use.

Make a pastry bag Pastry bags can be cumbersome, expensive, and hard to clean. Stop scrounging around the kitchen drawer for the pastry bag tip. Place the food to be piped, be it deviled-egg mix or decorating frosting, into a sealable bag. Squish out the air and close the top. Snip off a corner of the bag to the size you want—start conservatively—and you are ready to begin squeezing.

Dispose of cooking oil Unless you want the plumber for a best friend, don't clog your kitchen drain with used cooking oil. Instead, wait for it to cool, then dump it in a sealable plastic bag. Toss the bag into the trash.

Color cookie dough without stained hands Experienced bakers know what a mess your hands can be after coloring cookie dough. Here's a clean idea: Place your prepared dough in a bag, add the drops of food coloring, and squish around until the color is uniform. You can use the dough now or stick it in the freezer ready to roll out when the next occasion arises.

Stop ice crystals on ice cream It's truly annoying to open up that container of mint chocolate chip ice cream from the freezer to find unappetizing crystals forming on the frozen dessert. Place your half-full ice-cream container in a sealable bag and no crystals will form.

Store extra ice cubes It's a common experience. You open the freezer to grab some ice cubes from the ice cube maker and they're all stuck together, sometimes clogging the ice cube dispenser on the front of the fridge. When your tray fills up, toss the cubes in a sealable freezer bag. They won't stick together and you'll have easy access to the ice.

Soften hard marshmallows You're about to pull out that bag of marshmallows from your kitchen cabinet to make s'mores around the dying grill when you notice that the once-fluffy puffs have turned hard as rocks. Warm some water in a pan. Place the marshmallows in a sealable plastic bag, seal, and place in the pan. The warmth will soften them up in no time.

Melt chocolate without a mess Melting chocolate in a microwave or double boiler leaves you with a messy bowl or pot to wash. Here's a mess-free method: Warm some water in a pan (do not boil). Place the chocolate you want to melt in a sealable freezer bag. Seal and place the bag in the pan. In a few moments, you have melted chocolate, ready to bake or decorate with. You can even leave the bag sealed and snip off a bottom corner of the bag to pipe the chocolate onto a cake. When you are done, just toss the bag.

Keep soda from going flat You have to run out for a few errands and you don't want to take that soda with you. Leave the opened bottle or can at home zipped up in a large self-closing bag. That should help keep the fizz in until you get back.

Grease your pans If you're never quite sure how to handle shortening and butter when greasing a cake pan or cookie sheet, here's a tip: Place a sandwich bag over your hand, scoop up a small amount of shortening or butter from the tub, and start greasing. You can leave the bag in the canister of shortening for next time.

Kids' Stuff **Dyed dry pasta** in different shapes and sizes is great for getting kids' creative juices flowing. They can use it to make string jewelry on yarn, or to decorate a picture frame or pencil canister, for example. To dye the pasta, put a handful of **pasta** in a **sealable plastic bag**. Add several drops of **food coloring**. Next squirt in a few drops of **rubbing alcohol**. Seal the bag. Shake it up so the coloring dyes the pasta. Spread the pasta out on foil and let dry.

Use as kids' gloves There's nothing more welcome than helping hands in the kitchen. But when they're little hands that tend to get dirty and leave prints all over the place, then something must be done. Before they start "helping" you make those chocolate chip cookies, place small sandwich bags over their hands. These instant gloves are disposable for easy cleanup.

Make a funnel That handiest of kitchen tools, the funnel, can be replicated easily with a small sandwich bag. Fill the bag with the contents you need funneled. Snip off the end and transfer into the needed container. Then just toss the bag when the funneling is done.

✳ SANDWICH AND FREEZER BAGS **FOR STORING THINGS**

Protect your fragile breakables There's a precious family heirloom, a statue, a vase, or a trinket that needs some extra padding when storing. Here's what to do: Place it gently in a self-closing bag, close the bag most of the way, blow it up with air, then seal it. The air forms a protective cushion around the memento.

Save your sweaters You're about to put away that pile of winter sweaters for the season. Don't just throw them in a box without protection. Place each sweater in a sealable plastic bag and seal. They'll be clean and moth-free when the cold weather rolls around again. Save the bags for next spring when the sweaters need to be stored again.

Create a sachet If your drawers are starting to smell musty, a sealable bag can be your dresser's best friend. Fill the bag with potpourri—for example, flower petals along with a few crushed fragrant leaves and a couple of drops of aromatic oil. Punch a bunch of small holes in the bag. Then place in the drawer. Your drawers will smell fresh again soon.

Add cedar to your closet Cedar closets smell great, and, more important, they repel moths. If you aren't lucky enough to have a cedar closet, you can easily create the next best thing. Fill a sealable bag with cedar chips—the kind you buy at a pet store for the hamster cage. Zip it closed, then punch several small holes in it. Hang the bag in your closet (a pants hanger is handy for this) and let the cedar smell do its work.

Make a pencil bag Do the kids have trouble keeping track of their school pencils, pens, and rulers? Puncture three holes along the bottom edge of a sealable freezer bag so it will fit in a three-ring binder. Now the young scholars can zip their supplies in and out of the bag.

DID You KNOW?

The self-sealing plastic bag became a part of our lives in 1969, when Dow Chemical introduced the Ziploc bag. A wide variety of sealable bags has been developed since then, including snack, sandwich, quart (liter), gallon (3.7 liter), and 2-gallon (7.4 liter) sizes, and double-strength freezer bags. There are even ones with flat bottoms to make them easy to pour into. The vegetable bag, with holes in it to help keep veggies fresh, was short-lived, however. You can even get sealable bags in small pouches of 10 and 8 bags, so you can take a bagful of bags with you.

De-clutter the bathroom Here's a quick cleanup solution: Guests are coming over and the bathroom is strewn with Hubby's razor, shave cream, and more. Quickly gather up all the supplies in one clear sealable bag. That way, he will know where his shaving supplies are and you don't have to deal with them. Now, if we could just do something about the whiskers in the sink!

Make a bath pillow Ready for a nice hot bath? Want to luxuriate in the warm water with bubbles and champagne? Well, here's the perfect, and cheap, thing to make your bath experience complete: Blow up a gallon-size (3.7-liter) sealable plastic bag and you'll have a comfortable pillow during your soak.

Clean your dentures No more dentures in a cup by your bedside. Toss your teeth in with their cleaner in a sealable plastic bag. They'll be clean and ready to go in the morning.

Organize your makeup Many of us have scads of makeup. Pats of ill-advised eye shadow and samples of powder and blush from department stores fill our makeup cases. Problem is, there are only a few cosmetics we really use every single day. Stash those favorites in a sealable plastic bag so you don't have to hunt around for them every morning.

❋ SANDWICH AND FREEZER BAGS **OUT AND ABOUT**

Stash dirty clothes Chocolate ice cream is careering down your child's white Sunday-best shirt. If you can keep the stain from drying, it will be a lot easier to get out. Change your child's shirt and spray the stained shirt with stain remover if you have a small bottle handy or just soak in water if you don't. Then seal the shirt in a sealable plastic bag, and it will be ready for the wash when you get home.

Hold spare clothes Toilet training a child? Need to be ready for meal mishaps? Put a change of clothes for your son or daughter in a sealable plastic bag, and keep it in the trunk of your car. You won't have to think twice the next time you have an "accident."

Carry detergent for washing If you're planning a trip to a friend's beach house and think you'll be doing a few loads of laundry while you're there, premeasure some detergent in a bag that you can pour out when the time comes. Beats lugging a big box of detergent down to the shore.

Carry wet washcloth for cooling off Going for a long trip on a hot and sticky day? Use a sealable bag to take along a wet washcloth that has been soaked in water and lemon juice so that everyone can get a refreshing wipe-off. This is a good trick for fast on-the-road face and hand cleanups anytime.

Keep your valuables dry and afloat Whoops! You tipped the canoe and got dunked. No biggie, until that sinking feeling hits—your car keys and cell phone are at the bottom of the lake. Avoid this disaster by putting your valuables in a sealable bag. Blow air into it before you seal the bag so it will float. A sealable bag is perfect for keeping valuables dry at the water park or beach too.

> *Kids' Stuff* This is a great and **yummy activity** if you're outdoors. Pour a small box of instant **pudding mix** in a **sealable plastic bag** and add the amount of **milk** called for on the box. Seal it up and then seal that bag in **another sealable bag**. Now you're ready to **play football**. Toss the bag of pudding around with your friends until it mixes and the pudding forms. Open the first bag and remove the second bag. Pour the pudding into flat-bottomed **ice-cream cones** and chow down.

Create a beach hand cleaner You're sitting on the beach and it's time for lunch. But before you reach into your cooler, you want to get the grit off your hands. Baby powder in a sealable plastic bag is the key. Place your hands in the bag, then remove them and rub them together. The sand is gone.

Apply bug spray to your face It's difficult to cleanly apply bug spray to your face without squirting yourself in the eyes or getting it on your hands. Instead, throw some cotton balls into a plastic bag, squirt in the bug spray, seal, and shake. Now use the cotton balls to apply the bug spray.

Cure car sickness The last thing you need in your car is a child throwing up. Make your child feel better and head off the mess and stench. Place a few cotton balls in a sealable plastic bag. Squirt in 2 drops lavender oil. If motion sickness strikes, the child can open the bag and take a few whiffs of the oil.

Use as a portable water dish Your furry best friend has happily hiked alongside you during your trek in the great outdoors. You take a break, and he gives you one of those longing looks as you draw on your canteen. No problem. You pull a sealable plastic bag full of water from your pack and hold it open while Buddy laps his fill.

✳ Screening

Store pierced earrings Keep your pierced and hook earrings organized and ready at-a-glance with a spare piece of window screen. Cut a square of screen with metal shears or utility scissors and cover the edges of the square with duct or cloth tape. Then push the earrings through the holes in the screen. If you like, you can hang the screen square on the wall by attaching string or floral wire to the top corners.

Get rid of paint lumps You want to do a touch-up paint job, but your used can of paint has some lumps in it. Instead of going through the bother of straining the paint into another container, try this: Cut a circle of screening sized to fit inside the can (use the lid as a guide). Place the screen circle on top of the paint and push it gently down to the bottom with your stir stick. The lumps will now be trapped at the bottom of the can. Stir up the paint and get to work.

Protect newly planted seeds Who knows what is walking around your garden at night, so protect newly planted seeds by covering them with a sheet of screen material. It also might deter the neighborhood felines from using your nice, fluffy soil as a cat box. When the seedlings emerge, you can bend the screening to make cages.

❋ Shampoo

Revitalize leather shoes and purses You don't need expensive mink oil to bring life back to your leather shoes and purses. A little shampoo and a clean rag will do the job. Rub shampoo into worn areas in circles to clean and bring back the color of your accessories. It will protect your shoes from salt stains as well.

Lubricate a zipper If your zipper gets stuck, don't yank on it until it breaks. Put a drop of shampoo on a cotton swab and dab it onto the zipper. The shampoo will help the zipper to slide free, and any residue will come out in the next wash.

Resize a shrunken sweater Oh no, you've shrunk your favorite sweater! Don't panic, you can bring it back to full size again with baby shampoo and warm water. Fill a basin with warm water, squirt in some baby shampoo, and swish once with your hand. Lay the sweater on top of the water and let it sink on its own and soak for 15 minutes. Gently take your sweater out without wringing it and put it in a container, then fill the sink again with clean water. Lay the sweater on top and let it sink again to rinse. Take the sweater out, place it on a towel, and roll the towel to take out most of the moisture. Lay the sweater on a dry towel on a flat surface and gently start to reshape it. Come back to the sweater while it's drying to reshape a little more each time. Your patience will be rewarded!

Wash houseplant leaves Houseplants get dusty too, but unlike furniture they need to breathe. Make a soapy solution with a few drops of shampoo in a pot of water, dunk in a cloth and wring it out, and wipe those dusty leaves clean.

DID *You* KNOW?

In the early 1900s, Martha Matilda Harper invented the reclining chair used when shampooing hair at beauty salons—unfortunately, she never patented it. But Harper was still a success. She emigrated from Canada to the United States as a young girl, bringing her own recipe for a hair "tonic" (shampoo). Eventually she went from making her tonic in a shed to opening her own shop, where she offered the Harper Method. She enticed wealthy women to leave their homes for a health-conscious salon experience where they would be shampooed and pampered by professionals. She was her own best advertisement, with hair that reached down past her feet.

Clean your car The grease-cutting power of shampoo works on the family grease monkey's baby as well. Use about 1/4 cup shampoo to a bucket of water and sponge up the car as usual. Use a dab of shampoo directly on a rag or sponge for hard-to-remove tar spots.

Remove sticky gunk from pet fur Did Rex or Fluffy step on tar or roll in what you hope is gum? Rub a tiny amount of shampoo on the spot and gently draw out the sticky stuff toward the end of the fur. Rinse with a wet cloth.

Lubricate stubborn nuts and bolts Got a nut and bolt that won't come apart? If your spot lubricant isn't handy or you've run out, try a drop of shampoo. Let it seep into the threads and the bolt will be much more cooperative.

Remove bandages painlessly Now you don't have to say "Ready?" when removing a bandage. Rub just a drop of shampoo on and around the bandage to let it seep through the air holes. It will come off with no muss and definitely no fuss.

Revitalize your feet Give your feet a pick-me-up while you sleep. Rub a little shampoo all over your feet and put on a light pair of cotton socks. When you wake up, your feet will feel smooth and silky.

Remove your eye makeup You can't beat no-tears baby shampoo for a thrifty eye makeup remover. Put a drop on a damp cotton pad to gently remove the makeup, then rinse clear. No frills, no tears!

Give yourself a bubble bath Shampoo makes a nice and sudsy bubble bath. It's especially relaxing if you love the scent of your favorite shampoo, and the tub will rinse cleaner.

Substitute for shaving cream You're on the road and discover you forgot to bring your shaving cream. Don't use soap to lather up. With its softening agents, shampoo is a much better alternative.

Clean grimy hands In place of soap, some straight shampoo works wonders for cleaning stubborn or sticky grime from your hands. It even works well to remove water-based paint.

Remove hair spray from walls If you've been using hair spray to kill flies, or you've just noticed hair spray buildup on your bathroom walls, reach for the shampoo. Put some on a wet sponge to clean, and wipe off suds with a clean, wet sponge. Shampoo is tailor-made to handle hair product buildup.

Clean the tub and faucets Need to do a quick tub cleanup before guests arrive? Grab the handiest item—your shampoo! It does a great job on soap scum because it rinses clean. You can use it to buff a shine into your chrome faucets as well.

Use to wash delicates Shampoo makes a great cleanser for your delicates. It suds up well with just a drop, and you get two cleaning products for the price of one!

Clean brushes and combs Skin oils can build up on your combs and brushes faster than you realize. And if you're tucking them into your purse or pocket, they're accumulating dust and dirt as well. Give them a fresh start in a shampoo bath. First comb any loose hair out of the brush, then rub a little shampoo around the bristles or along the teeth of the comb. Put a small squirt of shampoo in a tall glass of water, let the comb and brush sit for a few minutes, swish, and rinse clean.

DID *You* KNOW?

Johnson & Johnson introduced the world's first shampoo made specifically for infants in 1955—containing its now-famous No More Tears formula. The company has promoted its baby shampoo to be "as gentle to the eyes as pure water." But, in fact, like most baby shampoos, Johnson's contains many of the same ingredients found in adult formulations, including citric acid, PEG-80 sorbitan laurate, and sodium trideceth sulfate. The lack of baby tears has less to do with the shampoo's purity than it does with maintaining a relatively neutral pH.

✳ Shaving Cream

Use to clean hands The next time your hands get dirty on a camping trip, save that hard-lugged water for cooking and drinking. Squirt a little shaving cream in your hands and rub as you would liquid soap. Then wipe your hands off with a towel.

Prevent bathroom mirror fog-up Before you shower, wipe some shaving cream onto your bathroom mirror. It will keep it from fogging up so you don't have to wait to get to work with your toiletries or shaving after you get out of the shower.

DID *You* KNOW?

From the late 1920s through the early 1960s, one of the best things about a long, tedious car ride were the signs every hundred yards or so advertising Burma-Shave, a brushless shaving cream. Here are some of the more memorable ones:

Shaving Brushes …
You'll Soon See 'Em …
On The Shelf …
In Some Museum …
Burma-Shave.

Are Your Whiskers …
When You Wake …
Tougher Than …
A Two-Bit Steak? …
Try … Burma-Shave.

Within This Vale …
Of Toil … And Sin …
Your Head Grows Bald …
But Not Your Chin—Use …
Burma-Shave.

Golfers!
If Fewer Strokes …
Are What You Crave …
You're Out Of The Rough …
With … Burma-Shave.

Remove stains from carpeting Junior is very sorry for spilling a little juice on the carpet, so make it "all better" with some shaving cream on the spot. Blot the stain, pat it with a wet sponge, squirt some shaving cream on it, and then wipe clean with a damp sponge. Use the same technique on your clothes for small stains; shaving cream can remove that spot of breakfast you discovered you're wearing during your once-over in the bathroom.

Silence a squeaky door hinge A squeaky door hinge can ruin a peaceful nap-time. With its ability to seep into nooks and crannies, a little shaving cream on the hinge will let you check on the baby undetected.

✳ Sheets

Make a beanbag bull's-eye Are the kids rained out of their ball game? Here's one way to ease their disappointment and let them give their pitching arms a workout anyway. Draw a large bull's-eye on a sheet. Tape the sheet to a wall and let the kids pitch beanbags at it.

Use as a tablecloth It is your turn to host the whole clan for Thanksgiving. You're using every table in the house, but you don't have enough tablecloths. A patterned sheet makes an attractive festive table covering.

Repel deer from your yard Circle the garden with a cord about 3 feet (1 meter) above the ground, then tie strips of white sheets to it every 2 feet (60 centimeters); a tail-height flash of white is a danger sign to a deer.

Scoop up all those fall leaves No reason to strain your back by constantly lifting piles of leaves into a wheelbarrow or bag. Just rake the leaves onto a sheet laid on the ground. Then gather the four corners and drag the leaves to the curb or leaf pile.

Wrap up the old Christmas tree After removing holiday decorations, wrap an old sheet around the tree so that you can carry or pull it out of the house without leaving a trail of pine needles.

✳ Shoe Bags

Organize your utility closet A hanging shoe bag is a great organizer in the utility closet. Use its pockets to store sponges, scrub brushes, and other cleaning utensils—and even some bottles of cleaning products. It's also good for separating your clean, lemon-oil, and lint-free rags so you'll always have the right one for the job.

Organize your office area Free up some valuable drawer space in your office with an over-the-door shoe holder. Its pockets can store lots of supplies that you need to keep handy, like scissors, staples, and markers. You can use the pockets to organize bills and other "to do" items as well.

Organize your bathroom A shoe bag can keep lots of everyday bathroom items handy and neat. Brushes, shampoo, hand towels, hair spray—almost everything can be stored at your fingertips instead of cluttering the shower or counter.

Organize your child's room A shoe bag hung over their bedroom door is a great way to help your kids organize their small toys. Whether your child likes dolls, dinosaurs, or different-colored blocks, a shoe bag puts the toys on display and kids can keep them sorted themselves.

Organize car-trip toys and games Cut a shoe bag to fit the back of your car seat, and let your children make their own choices for back seat entertainment.

Organize your bedroom Instead of lifting a hanger to get a belt, or rummaging through your drawer for a scarf, try organizing your clothing accessories with an over-the-door shoe bag. The pockets can be used in the bedroom for keeping socks, gloves, and much more than shoes handy.

✱ Shoe Boxes

Make a gift ribbon dispenser You will thank yourself each time you look for ribbon to wrap a present, if you use a shoe box to make this handy ribbon dispenser. Take a used broom handle or piece of a bamboo garden stake— anything you can use as a small dowel—and cut it a little longer than the length of the shoe box. Cut two holes for the dowel, one in each short end of the box, at a height where a spool of ribbon slipped onto the dowel would spin freely. Slip your ribbon spools onto the dowel as you poke it from one end of the shoe box through to the other. Once the dowel is in place, you can duct tape it at either short end to keep it from slipping out. You could also cut holes along one long side of the shoe box for each spool of ribbon, and pull a little bit of each ribbon through the hole. Now you're ready to wrap!

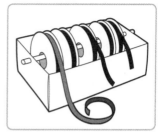

Use for play bricks Kids can get creative using a collection of shoe boxes as building bricks. Tape the lids on for them. You can even let the little ones color the "bricks" with poster paint.

Get your stuff organized There are lots of ways shoe boxes can help you get organized besides collecting old photos and receipts. Label the boxes and use them to store keepsakes, canceled checks, bills to be paid, and other items you want to keep track of. For a neater appearance, cover the boxes with contact paper or any other decorative self-adhesive paper.

Pack yummy gifts Shoe boxes are the perfect size for loaves of homemade bread, but of course, you can also pack cookies in them.

Use as a whelping box Puppies or kittens on the way! To reduce the risk of the mother rolling onto a newborn and smothering it, place one or several puppies or kittens in a towel-lined shoe box while the others are being born.

✱ Shortening

Clean ink stains Next time a leaky pen leaves your hands full of ink, reach for a can of shortening. To remove ink stains from your hands and also from vinyl surfaces, rub on a dollop of shortening and wipe the stains away with a rag or paper towel.

Remove sticky adhesives Don't wear down your fingernails trying to scratch off resistant sticky labels and price tags. Instead use shortening to remove them (and their dried glue and gum residue) from glass, metals, and most plastics. Simply coat the area with shortening, wait 10 minutes, and scrub clean with a gentle scrub-sponge.

Polish galoshes To make dirty galoshes shine like new again, rub on some shortening and wipe with a clean rag or cloth.

Tip Using Shortening

- Keep shortening away from sunlight to keep it from turning rancid.
- Never leave shortening unattended while frying.
- The most efficient temperature for frying with shortening is 325°F-350°F (165°C-180°C). Do not overheat shortening or it will burn. If shortening starts to smoke, turn off the heat and let it cool.
- If shortening catches fire, cover the pan with its lid, turn off the heat, and let it cool. Never put water on burning or hot shortening: It may splatter and burn you.

Soothe and prevent diaper rash Next time the baby is fussing from a painful case of diaper rash, rub some shortening on his bottom for fast relief. It will soothe and moisturize his sensitive skin.

Remove tar from fabric Tar stains on clothing are icky and tough to remove, but you can make the job easier with a little help from some shortening. After scraping off as much of the tar as you can, put a small glob of shortening over the remaining spot. Wait 3 hours, and then launder as usual.

Keep snow from sticking to shovel Before you dig out the car or shovel the driveway after a snowstorm, coat the blade of your snow shovel with shortening or liquid vegetable oil. It will not only keep snow from sticking but also make shoveling less tiring and more efficient.

Remove makeup All out of your regular makeup remover? Don't fret: Just use a dab of shortening instead. Your face won't know the difference.

Moisturize dry skin Why pay for fancy creams and lotions to moisturize your skin when ordinary shortening can do the trick at a fraction of the cost? Some hospitals even use shortening to keep skin soft and moist, and you can too. Next time your hands are feeling dry and scaly, just rub in a little shortening. It's natural and fragrance-free.

Repel squirrels Keep pesky squirrels from getting at a bird feeder. Just grease the pole with a liberal amount of shortening and the rodents won't be able to get a claw hold to climb up.

❋ Shower Curtains

Line cabinet shelves Don't discard your old vinyl shower curtains or tablecloths. Turn them into easy-to-clean shelf liners instead. Simply cut to shelf size and set in place, using some rubber cement to hold them if you prefer. When it's time for cleaning, just wipe with a damp sponge.

Make a protective apron For those extra messy jobs around the house, wear a homemade apron made from an old shower curtain. Make a cobbler's style apron, with a vest as well as a skirt. Use pinking shears to cut the vinyl to size. Poke two holes at the top of the vest for cords or ribbons to tie around your neck, and make two more holes in the sides for tying it around your waist.

Durable painting drop cloth Save an old shower curtain liner and use it as a drop cloth the next time you paint a room. The material is heavier and more durable than that used in commercially sold plastic drop cloths!

Protect floor under high chair Even the best-behaved and cutest babies leave a mess on the floor when they eat. Protect your floor or carpet and make cleanup a breeze. Cut a 36- to 48-inch (about 1-meter) square from an old shower curtain and place it under the baby's high chair. You can use the leftover scraps to make bibs too.

Cover picnic tables and benches Don't let a yucky table or sticky benches spoil your next picnic. Use an old shower curtain as a makeshift tablecloth (or as a tablecloth liner). Bring an extra shower curtain and fold it over a sticky or dirty picnic bench before you sit down to eat.

DID *You* KNOW?

In the early 1920s, Waldo Semon, a rubber scientist, was none too thrilled when he first discovered polyvinyl chloride, commonly known as vinyl. He was trying to develop a new adhesive, and this stuff just didn't stick at all! But Waldo was quick to recognize the material's potential and began experimenting with it, even making golf balls and shoe heels out of it. Soon vinyl products like raincoats and shower curtains reached the consumer. Today vinyl is the second-largest selling plastic in the world, and the vinyl industry employs more than 100,000 people in the United States alone.

Protect table when cutting fabric Next time you're cutting a pattern on your dining room table, put a shower curtain or plastic tablecloth under it before you cut. The scissors will glide more easily across the surface and you'll protect the tabletop from an accidental nick.

Block weeds in mulched beds Those old shower curtains will also come in handy next time you do any landscaping with gravel or bark chips. Just place the shower curtain under the mulching material to prevent annoying weeds from poking through.

* Skateboards

Use as a laundry cart If your home has a laundry chute, keep a basket atop a skateboard directly below the chute. When you're ready to do the laundry, simply roll the load over to the washer.

Make a shelf Is your kid an avid skateboarder? When he or she is ready for a new skateboard, turn the old one into a shelf for his or her room. Support it on a couple of metal shelf brackets. You can remove the wheels or leave them on.

Use as a painter's scooter. Crawling along the floor to paint a baseboard can get real old real fast. Borrow your kid's skateboard and save your knees. Sit cross-legged on the skateboard and roll along with your paintbrush and can.

* Soap

Loosen stuck zippers Zipper stuck? Rub it loose with a bar of soap along the zipper's teeth. The soap's lubrication will get it moving.

Unstick furniture drawers If your cabinet or dresser drawers are sticking, rub the bottom of the drawer and the supports they rest on with a bar of soap.

Lubricate screws and saw blades A little lube with soap makes metal move through wood much more easily. Twist a screw into a bar of soap before driving it and rub some on your handsaw blade.

Remove a broken lightbulb If a bulb breaks while still screwed in, don't chance nicks and cuts trying to remove it. First, turn off the power. Insert the corner of a large, dry bar of soap into the socket. Give it a few turns and that base will unscrew.

Say farewell to fleas Fed up with those doggone fleas? Put a few drops of dish soap and some water on a plate. Place the plate on the floor next to a lamp. Fleas love light—they will jump on the plate and drown.

DID *You* KNOW?

Contrary to popular belief, hanging a perfumed bar of soap won't necessarily keep deer off your property. Stephen Vantassel, who runs Wildlife Damage Control in Springfield, Massachusetts, says that how long or how well soap works depends on a number of factors, including the type of plant you are protecting and the location of the soap. However, studies have shown that soap, especially tallow-based soap, will stop deer from making lunch out of your shrubbery. Local gardening centers can advise you about commercial spray repellents.

Deodorize your car Want your car to smell nice, but tired of those tree-shaped pine deodorizers? Place a little piece of your favorite-smelling soap in a mesh bag and hang it from your rearview mirror.

Mark a hem Forget store-bought marking chalk. A thin sliver of soap, like the ones left when a bar is just about finished, works just as well when you are marking a hem, and the markings wash right out.

Make a pin holder Here's an easy-to-make alternative to a pincushion. Wrap a bar of soap in fabric and tie the fabric in place with a ribbon. Stick in your pins. As a bonus, the soap lubricates the pins, making them easier to insert.

Prevent cast-iron marks Nip cookout cleanup blues in the bud. Rub the bottom of your cast-iron pot with a bar of soap before cooking with it over a sooty open flame. Look, Ma! No black marks!

Tip **Homemade Soap**

> Handcrafted soap makes a great gift and is easy to make. You need a solid bar of glycerin (from a drugstore); soap molds (from a crafts store); a clean, dry can; a double boiler; food coloring; and essential oil. Place the glycerin in the can and put the can in a double boiler, which has water in the top as well as the bottom, and heat until the glycerin melts. For color, mix in food coloring. Spray a mold with nonstick cooking spray and fill it halfway with melted glycerin. Add a few drops of essential oil and fill the rest with glycerin. Let it harden.

Keep stored clothes fresh Pack a bar of your favorite scented soap when you store clothes or luggage. It will keep your clothes smelling fresh till next season and prevent musty odor in your luggage.

Save those soap slivers When your soap slivers get too tiny to handle, don't throw them away. Just make a small slit in a sponge and put the slivers inside. The soap will last for several more washings. Or make a washcloth that's easy for little hands to hold by putting the soap slivers in a sock.

✳ Socks

Protect stored breakables Want to protect Grandma's precious vase or your bobble head collection? Wrap it up! Slip the item into a sock to help protect it from breaking or chipping.

Cover kids' shoes when packing Does Junior insist on bringing along his favorite old sneakers? Before you toss them into the suitcase, cover each one with an adult-size sock to protect the rest of the clothing.

Polish your car A big old soft sock makes a perfect hand mitt for buffing the wax on your car.

Keep hands clean changing tire If you ever get a flat tire on your way to a fancy party or job interview, you'll thank yourself for having the foresight to throw a pair of socks in the trunk. Slip the socks on your hands while handling the tire, and they'll be clean when you arrive.

Protect floor surfaces The next time you need to move a heavy table or sofa across a smooth floor, put socks over the legs and just slide the piece.

Store your work goggles Shop goggles won't fit in an eyeglass case, so just slip them into a sock to protect them from getting scratched. You can even nail or screw the sock to the wall or bench so you will always know where the goggles are.

Wash bag for dainty lingerie Protect your precious delicates in the washing machine. Slip them into a sock and tie the ends.

Use as cleaning mitts Save those old or solo socks to use as cleaning mitts. Slip them on, and they are great for cleaning in tight corners and crevices.

Clean shutter and blind slats Forget wasting money on those expensive gadgets and gizmos for cleaning venetian blind slats. Just slip a sock over your hand and gently rub the dust off. You can use some dusting spray on the sock, if you like.

Clean rough plaster walls Use nylon or Ban-Lon socks, instead of a sponge or cloth, to clean rough plaster walls. No small pieces of material will be left behind.

Wash small stuffed animals Does your child's favorite stuffed fuzzy need a bath? Slip small stuffed animals into a sock and tie the end to prevent buttons, eyes, and other decorative items from coming loose.

Protect a wall from ladder marks To prevent marks on the wall when you're leaning your ladder on it, slip socks over the ladder top ends. For safety reasons, however, make sure someone is holding the ladder.

✳ Soda Pop

Clean car battery terminals Yes, it's true, the acidic properties of soda pop will help to eliminate corrosion from your car battery. Nearly all carbonated soft drinks contain carbonic acid, which helps to remove stains and dissolve rust deposits. Pour some soda pop over the battery terminals and let it sit. Remove the sticky residue with a wet sponge.

Loosen rusted-on nuts and bolts Stop struggling with rusted-on nuts and bolts. Soda pop can help to loosen any rusted-on nuts and bolts. Soak a rag in the soda pop and wrap it around the bolt for several minutes.

Remove rust spots from chrome Are you babying an older car—you know, one of those babies that has real chrome on the outside? If the chrome is developing small rust spots, you can remove them by rubbing the area with a crumpled piece of aluminum foil dipped in cola.

Make cut flowers last longer Don't throw away those last drops of soda pop. Pour about 1/4 cup into the water in a vase full of cut flowers. The sugar in the soda will make the blossoms last longer. *Note:* If you have a clear vase and want the water to remain clear, use a clear soda pop, such as Sprite or 7-Up.

Clean your toilet Eliminate dirt and odor with a simple can of soda. Pour into the toilet, let sit for an hour, then scrub and flush.

DID *You* KNOW?

Ginger has long been a traditional remedy for nausea, and recent scientific research has shown that ginger ale does work better than a placebo. Ginger ale was first marketed about 100 years ago by a Toronto pharmacist named John McLaughlin. McLaughlin kept trying new formulas until he patented what is now known throughout the world as Canada Dry Ginger Ale. Soda pops—carbonated beverages—originally were served only to customers at drugstore soda fountains. McLaughlin was one of the pioneers of the technology of mass bottling, which allowed customers to take soda pop home in bottles.

Keep drains from clogging Slow drain and no drain cleaner in the house? Pour a 2-liter bottle of cola down the drain to help remove the clog.

Get gum out of hair It's inevitable—kids get gum in their hair. Put the gummy hair section in a bowl with some cola. Let soak for a few minutes and rinse.

Make a roast ham moist Want to make your ham juicier? Pour a can of cola over your traditional ham recipe and follow regular baking instructions. Yum!

Clean your coins Who wants dirty money? If coin collecting is your hobby, use cola to clean your stash. Place the coins in a small dish and soak in cola for a shimmering shine. Of course, you don't want to do this with very rare and valuable coins.

Remove oil stains from concrete Here's how to remove oil stains from concrete driveways and garage floors: Gather up a small bag of cat litter, a few cans of cola, a stiff bristle broom, bucket, laundry detergent, bleach, eye protection, and rubber gloves. Cover the stain with a thin layer of cat litter and brush it in. Sweep up the litter and pour cola to cover the area. Work the cola in with a bristle broom, and leave the cola for about twenty minutes. Mix 1/4 cup laundry detergent with 1/4 cup bleach in 1 gallon (3.7 liters) warm water and use it to mop up the mess.

✳ Spices

Make a hair tonic You can spice up your hair care regimen with a homemade tonic that will enhance your natural color and impart shine. For dark hair, use 1 tablespoon crumbled sage or 1 sprig chopped fresh rosemary or a mixture of 1 teaspoon allspice, 1 teaspoon ground cinnamon, and 1/2 teaspoon ground cloves. For blond hair, use 1 tablespoon chamomile. Pour 1 cup boiling water over the herb or spice mix, let it steep for 30 minutes, strain it through a coffee filter, and let it cool. Pour it repeatedly over your hair (use a dishpan to catch the runoff) as a final rinse after shampooing.

Treat minor cuts If you nick your finger while chopping vegetables for dinner, you may not even need to leave the kitchen for first aid. Alum, the old-fashioned pickling salt at the back of your spice cupboard, is an astringent. In a pinch, sprinkle some on a minor cut to stanch the flow of blood.

Keep feet smelling sweet If you use sage only to stuff turkeys, then you've been missing out. Sage is great for preventing foot odor because it kills the odor-causing bacteria that grow on your feet in the warm, moist environment inside your shoes. Just crumble a leaf or two into your shoes before you put them on. At the end of the day, just shake the remains into the trash.

Deodorize bottles for reuse You'd like to reuse those wonderful wide-mouthed pickle jars, but simply washing them with soap and water doesn't get rid of the pickle smell. What to do? Add 1 teaspoon dry mustard to 1 quart (1 liter) water, fill the jar, and let it soak overnight. It'll smell fresh by morning. This solution banishes the odor of tomatoes, garlic, and other foods with strong scents.

Keep your thermos fresh You just uncapped the thermos bottle you haven't used for six months, and the inside smells musty. To keep it from happening the next time, place a whole clove inside the thermos before capping it. A teaspoon of salt works too. Be sure to empty and rinse the thermos before using it.

Scent your home What could be more welcoming than the smell of something good cooking? Instead of using commercial air fresheners, simply toss a handful of

DID *You* KNOW?

What's the difference between a spice and an herb? The basic guideline is this: If it's made from a plant's leaf, it's an herb; if it's made from the bark, fruit, seed, stem, or root, it's a spice. Parsley and basil are typical herbs because we eat their leaves. Cinnamon (the bark of a tree) and pepper (the fruit of a vine) are considered spices. Then what to call salt, perhaps the most essential food enhancer of all but not a plant product at all? *Seasoning* is the word that describes anything used to flavor foods, regardless of its origin.

whole cloves or a cinnamon stick in a pot of water and keep it simmering on the stove for half an hour. Or place a teaspoon or two of the ground spices on a cookie sheet and place it in a 200°F (93°C) oven with the door ajar for 30 minutes. Either way, your house will naturally smell spicy good.

Keep woolens whole Woolen clothing can last a lifetime—if you keep moths away. If you don't have a cedar-lined chest or closet, preserve your cold-weather clothing using clove sachets. Purchase some small drawstring muslin bags at a tea shop or health food store, and fill each one with a handful of whole cloves. To prevent any transfer of oils or color to clothes and to contain any spills, put the sachet in a small plastic bag, but don't seal it. Attach it to a hanger in your closet or tuck one in your sweater chest for woolens without holes.

Keep ants at bay Flour, sugar, and paprika can all fall prey to ants. Keep these cooking essentials safe by slipping a bay leaf inside your storage containers. If you're concerned about the flour or sugar picking up a bay leaf flavor, tape the leaf to the inside of the canister lid. This trick works inside cabinets, too, where sachets of sage, bay, stick cinnamon, or whole cloves will smell pleasant while discouraging ants.

Stamp out silverfish These pesky critters frequent places with lots of moisture, such as kitchens, baths, and laundry rooms. Hang an aromatic sachet containing apple pie spices, sage, or bay leaves on a hook in your bathroom vanity and behind the washer, or keep a few in decorative baskets along baseboards.

Control insects in the garden You don't have to use harsh pesticides to control small-insect infestation outdoors. If ants are swarming on your garden path, add 1 tablespoon ground black pepper (or another strong-smelling ground spice, such as ground cloves or dry mustard) to 1 cup sifted white flour and sprinkle the mixture on and around the pests. They'll vanish within the hour. Sweep the dry mix into the garden or yard instead of trying to hose it off; water will just make it gooey.

Deter plant-eating animals Everyone knows that hot peppers make your mouth burn. So if rodents are attacking your ornamental plants, the solution may be to make them too "hot" for the critters. In fact, hot peppers are the basis for many commercial rodent repellents. Chop up the hottest pepper you can find (habañero is best) and combine it with 1 tablespoon ground cayenne pepper and 1/2 gallon (2 liters) water. Boil the mix for 15-20 minutes, then let it cool. Strain it through cheesecloth, add 1 tablespoon dishwashing liquid, and pour it into a spray bottle. Spray vulnerable plants liberally every five days or so. The spray works best for rabbits, chipmunks, and woodchucks, but may also deter deer, especially if used in combination with commercial products.

Shield your vegetable garden For centuries, gardeners have used companion planting to repel insect pests. Aromatic plants such as basil, tansy, marigolds, and sage are all reputed to send a signal to bugs to go elsewhere, so try planting some near your prized vegetables. Mint, thyme, dill, and sage are old-time favorites near cabbage family plants (cabbage, broccoli, cauliflower, and brussels sprouts) for their supposed ability to fend off cabbage moths. Best of all, you can eat the savory herbs!

Tip **Toothache and Oil of Cloves**

> If you have a toothache, get to a dentist as soon as possible. Meanwhile, oil of cloves may provide temporary relief. Place a drop directly into the aching tooth or apply it with a cotton swab. But don't put it directly on the gums. An active ingredient in the spice oil, eugenol, is a natural pain reliever.

* Sponges

Make flowerpots hold water longer If your potted houseplants dry out too quickly after watering, when you repot them, try this simple trick for keeping the soil moist longer. Tuck a damp sponge in the bottom of the pot before filling it with soil. It'll act as a water reservoir. And it will also help prevent a gusher if you accidentally overwater.

An unwelcome mat for garden Anyone who's ever cleaned a floor with ammonia knows that the smell of this strong, everyday household cleaner is overpowering. Throw browsing animals "off the scent" of ripening vegetables in your garden by soaking old sponges in your floor-cleaning solution and distributing them wherever you expect the next garden raid.

Keep your veggies fresh Moisture that collects at the bottom of your refrigerator bins hastens the demise of healthful vegetables. Extend their life by lining bins with dry sponges. When you notice that they're wet, wring them out and let them dry before putting them back in the fridge. Every now and then, between uses, let them soak in some warm water with a splash of bleach to discourage the growth of mold.

Sop up umbrella overrun It's raining, and the family has been tramping in and out with umbrellas all day. Your umbrella stand has only a shallow receptacle to catch drips. Suddenly there's a waterfall coming out of it! Protect your flooring from umbrella stand overflow with a strategically placed sponge in its base. If you forget to squeeze it out, it'll dry on its own as soon as the weather clears.

Stretch the life of soap A shower is so refreshing in the morning—until you reach for the soap and are treated to the slimy sensation of a bar that's been left to marinate in its own suds. You'll enjoy bathing more and your soap will last longer if you park a sponge on the soap dish. It'll absorb moisture so soap can dry out.

> *Kids' Stuff* Making seeds grow seems magical to young children. For an easy and renewable **play garden** with a minimum of mess, all you need is an **old soap dish**, a **sponge**, and **seeds** of a plant such as lobelia, flax, or chia (yes, the same "chia" as in Chia Pet; look for the seed at health food stores). Cut the sponge to fit the dish, add water until it's moist but not sopping, and sprinkle the seed liberally over the top. Prop an **inverted glass bowl** over it until the seeds begin to grow. A bright window and a daily watering will keep it going for weeks.

Protect fragile items If you're shipping or storing small, fragile valuables that won't be harmed by a little contact with water, sponges are a clever way to cushion them. Dampen a sponge, wrap it around the delicate item, and use a rubber band to secure it. As it dries, the sponge will conform to the contours of your crystal ashtray or porcelain figurine. To unpack it, just dip the item in water again. You'll even get your sponge back!

Lift lint from fabric To quickly remove lint and pet fur from clothes and upholstery, give the fabric a quick wipe with a dampened and wrung-out sponge. Just run your fingers over the sponge and the unwanted fuzz will come off in a ball for easy disposal.

✳ Spray Bottles

Mist your houseplants Keep your houseplants healthy and happy by using an empty trigger-type spray bottle as a plant mister. Clean the bottle by filling it with equal parts water and vinegar—don't use liquid soap, as you may not be able to get it all out—let the solution sit for an hour, and rinse it out thoroughly with cold water. Repeat if necessary. Then, fill the bottle with lukewarm warm water, and use it to frequently give your plants a soothing, misty shower.

Help with the laundry An empty spray bottle can always be put to good use around your laundry room. Use clean, recycled bottles to spray water on your clothes as you're ironing. Or fill a spray bottle with stain remover solution so that you can apply it to your garments without having to blot up drips.

Cool off in summer Whether you're jogging around the park, taking a breather between volleyball matches, or just sitting out in the sun, a recycled spray bottle filled with water can make a great summer companion. Use it to cool off during and after your workouts, or while simmering on the beach (or in beach traffic).

Keep car windows clean Be sure to include a recycled spray bottle filled with windshield cleaner in the trunk of your car as part of your roadside emergency kit. Use it to clean off your car's headlights, mirrors, and of course, windows whenever needed. During winter months, mix in 1/2 teaspoon antifreeze, and you can spray it on to melt the ice on your windshield or mirrors.

Spray away garden pests Keep a few recycled spray bottles on hand to use around the yard. Here are two immediate uses:

● Fill one with undiluted white vinegar to get rid of the weeds and grass poking out of the cracks in your concrete, as well as ants and other insects— but be careful not to spray it on your plants; the high acidity could kill them.

● For an effective homemade insecticide recipe that works on most soft-bodied pests, but won't harm your plants, mix several cloves crushed garlic, 1/4 cup canola oil, 3 tablespoons hot pepper sauce, and 1/2 teaspoon mild liquid soap in 1 gallon (3.7 liters) water. Pour some into your spray bottle, and shake well before using.

✳ Squirt Bottles

Stop cooking oil drips Tired of cleaning up the oil spills around your kitchen? Fill a cleaned, recycled squirt bottle with olive oil or another favorite cooking oil. It's a lot easier to handle than a jar or bottle, and you can pour precisely the right amount of oil over your salads or into your frying pan without having to worry about drips or spills.

Substitute for a baster If you can't find your kitchen baster, or one that's in working condition, a cleaned squeeze bottle makes a dandy substitute. Simply squeeze out some air first, and use it to suck up the fat from your roasts and soups. You can even effectively use it to distribute marinades and drippings over meat.

Put the squeeze on condiments Recycled squirt bottles are great for storing condiments and other foodstuffs that are typically sold in jars—such as mayonnaise, salad dressing, jelly and jams, or honey. In addition to having fewer sticky or messy jars in your refrigerator, you'll also be lightening the load in your dishwasher by eliminating the need for knives or spoons. Make sure you give the bottles a thorough cleaning before using.

Clean out crevices A clean, empty squeeze bottle may be just the cleaning tool you need to get the dust out of the corners of your picture frames and other tight spaces. Use it to give a good blast of air to blow out the dirt you can't other-wise reach.

Let the children play Fill up a few clean squeeze bottles with water, then give them to your kids to squirt each other with in the yard on those hot summer days. It will keep them cool while they burn off some energy.

✳ Steel Wool

Turn nasty sneakers nice If your sneakers are looking so bad that the only thing you'd do in them is, well, *sneak* around, some steel wool may keep them from the trash can. Moisten a steel wool soap pad and gently scrub away at stains and stuck-on goo. Wipe them clean with a damp sponge or send them through the washer, and you may be able to enjoy many more months of wear.

Crayons begone Your toddler just created a work of crayon art on paper. Unfortunately, it's on the *wall*paper. Use a bit of steel wool soap pad to just skim the surface, making strokes in one direction instead of scrubbing in a circle, and your wall will be a fresh "canvas" in no time.

"Shoo" heel marks away Those black marks that rubber soles leave behind just don't come off with a mop, no matter how long you try. To rid a vinyl floor of unsightly smudges, gently rub the surface with a moistened steel wool soap pad. When the heel mark is gone, wipe the floor clean with a damp sponge.

Tip **No Steel Wool on Stainless Steel**

An oft-repeated advice is to clean stainless steel with steel wool. Yet stainless steel manufacturers caution against using any abrasive on stainless steel. Steel wool may make stainless steel look better, but it scratches the surface and ultimately hastens rusting. The safest way to care for stainless steel is to wash with a sponge and mild soap and water.

Sharpen your scissors Sometimes you just want a small piece of a steel wool soap pad for a minor job. Cutting it in half with a pair of scissors will help keep the scissors sharp while giving you the pint-size pad you need for your project.

Rebuff rodents Mice, squirrels, and bats are experts at finding every conceivable entry into a house. When you discover one of their entry points, stuff it full of steel wool. Steel wool is much more effective than foam or newspaper because even dedicated gnawers are unlikely to try to chew through such a sharp blockade.

Keep garden tools in good shape Nothing will extend the life of your gardening tools like a good cleaning at the end of each growing season. Grab a wad of fine steel wool from your woodshop (000, or "three aught," would be a good choice), saturate it with the same ordinary household oil you use on squeaky door hinges, and rub rust off your shears, loppers, shovels, and anything else with metal parts. Wipe them clean with a dry rag, sharpen any blades, and reapply a bit of oil before storing them for the winter.

S

✳ Straws

Keep jewelry chains unknotted You're dressing for dinner out, and you reach into your jewelry box for your best gold chain only to find that it's tangled and kinked. Next time, run it through a straw cut to the proper length and close the clasp before putting it away. It'll always be ready to wear.

Give flowers needed height Your flower arrangement would be just perfect, except a few of the flowers aren't tall enough. You can improve on nature by sticking each of the too-short stems into plastic straws, trimming the straw to get the desired height, and inserting them into the vase.

Get slow ketchup flowing Anticipation is great, but ketchup that comes out of the bottle while your burger and fries are still hot is even better. If your ketchup is recalcitrant, insert a straw all the way into the bottle and stir it around a little to get the flow started.

Improvise some foamy fun To make enough cheap and easy toys for even a large group of children, cut the ends of some plastic straws at a sharp angle and set out a shallow pan of liquid dish soap diluted with a little bit of water. Dip a straw in the soap and blow through the other end. Little kids love the piles of bubbles that result.

Make a pull-toy protector Pull toys are perennial favorites of young children, but you can spend all day untying the knots that a toddler will inevitably put in the pull string. By running the string through a plastic straw (or a series of them), you can keep it untangled.

DID *You* KNOW?

The quest for a perfectly cold mint julep led to the invention of the drinking straw. Mint juleps are served chilled, and their flavor diminishes as they warm up. Holding a glass heats the contents, so the custom was to drink mint juleps through natural straws made from a section of hollow grass stem, usually rye. But the rye imparted an undesirable "grassy" flavor. In 1888 Marvin Stone, a Washington, D.C., manufacturer of paper cigarette holders, fashioned a paper tube through which to sip his favorite libation. When other mint julep aficionados began clamoring for paper straws, he realized he had a hot new product on his hands.

Have seasonings, will travel Maybe you're on a low-sodium diet and need potassium salt that most restaurants don't keep on the table, or perhaps you want salt and pepper to season your brown-bag lunch just before you eat it. Straws provide an easy way to take along small amounts of dry seasonings. Fold one end over and tape it shut, fill it, and fold and tape the other end. If moisture is a concern, use a plastic straw.

Fix loose veneer The veneer from a favorite piece of furniture has lost its grip near the edge of the piece. A bit of yellow carpenter's glue is the obvious solution for re-adhering the veneer, but how do you get the glue under there? Veneer can be very brittle, and you don't want to break off a piece by lifting it up. The solution: Cut a length of plastic drinking straw and press it to flatten it  somewhat. Fold it in half and fill one half with glue, slowly dripping the glue in from the top. Slip the filled half under the veneer and gently blow in the glue. Wipe off any excess, cover the area with wax paper and a wood block, and clamp overnight.

✳ String

Polish silverware more easily Remember Dad or Grandpa taking a photograph of the dining room table beautifully set for holiday meals? The rich shine of polished silverware was part of what made it so beautiful. To get your silverware looking that good, run a length of string through some silver polish and use it to get at those hard-to-reach spots between fork tines.

Make wicks for watering plants Keeping plants watered while you're on a short trip is easier than you think. Fill a large container with water and place it next to your potted plants. Cut pieces of string so they're long enough to hang down to the bottom of the container at one end and be buried a few inches in the soil of the pots at the other. Soak the strings until they're thoroughly  wet and put them in position. As the soil begins to dry, capillary action will draw water from the reservoir to the pots through the strings.

Stop the sound of a dripping faucet If a leaky faucet going "plop … plop … plop" is keeping you awake at night, there's a way to silence it until the plumber arrives. Tie a piece of string to the fixture with one end right where the water is oozing out and the other end hanging down to the bottom of the sink basin. Water droplets will travel down the string silently instead of driving you to distraction.

Use as a straight-line guide Trimming a long hedge straight is a
near-impossible feat unless you use a visual guide.
Drive two stakes into the ground, one at each end
of the hedge. Measure the height you want for
the trimmed hedge, then run the string between
the two stakes, tying it to each one at that exact
height. As you clip away, cut down to the string
line but no farther; the top of your hedge will be
straight as an arrow.

Make a quick package opener Next time you're preparing a box for mailing, take a
second to make it easier for the recipient to open. Place a piece of string along
the center and side seams before you tape, allowing a tiny bit to hang free at
one end. That way, the recipient just needs to pull the strings to sever the tape
without resorting to sharp blades that might damage delicate contents. Do the
same for packing boxes when you move.

Outline garden features When you're making a new garden, lay common bright white
string on the ground to outline paths and beds. From an upstairs window or
other high vantage point, you'll be able to tell at a glance if borders are straight
and whether the layout is pleasing.

Measure irregular objects A cloth tape measure is the ideal tool for measuring odd-
shaped objects, but you may not have one if you don't sew. Wrap a plain
piece of string around the item instead, then hold it up to a ruler to get the
measurement you need.

Plant perfectly straight rows It's harder than it looks to make straight garden rows
freehand. Use string two ways to keep plants in line:

- For planting heavy seeds such as beans, put sticks in the ground at each end
of a row and run a piece of string between to guide you as you plant.

- To plant dozens of lightweight seeds in a snap, cut string to the length of a
row, wet it thoroughly, then sprinkle the seed directly on it. The moisture
will make seeds stick long enough to lay the string in a prepared furrow. Just
cover the string with soil and you're done!

Stop slamming doors Is a slamming door getting on your nerves? Here are two ideas for
using string to control the way a door closes:

- A piece of light twine tied to both sides of a knob and running around the
door edge provides just enough friction to slow it down and prevent a loud
slam when it shuts.

- Use thicker rope the same way to temporarily prop open a door that automatically locks when it closes or to make sure pets don't get trapped in one
room of the house.

❋ Styrofoam

Keep nail polish nice When applying nail polish, a foam pellet or a small chunk cut from a block of foam packaging placed between each finger or toe will help spread them apart and keep the polish unblemished until it can dry.

Make your own shipping pellets You'd like to use foam to ship some fragile things, but all you've got is sheets or blocks of foam, not pellets. No problem. Just break up what you have into pieces small enough to fit in a blender and pulse it on and off to shred the foam into perfect packing material.

Hold treats for freezing and serving To prepare a quantity of snow cones or ice-cream cones in advance, cut a foam block to size so it will fit flat in your freezer. Cut holes just large enough and close enough to hold cones so they won't touch, fall over, or poke through the bottom. Fill the cones and slip them into the waiting holes. Then pop the whole thing into the freezer ready for serving at a moment's notice.

?? DID *You* KNOW?

Ask anyone what kind of material those coffee cups, packing material, picnic coolers, and other white foam products are made from, and they'll reply Styrofoam. But strictly speaking, Styrofoam, a trademark of the Dow Chemical Company, refers only to durable extruded polystyrene, like that used in the blue insulation boards familiar to anyone who's been around a construction site. Those other more commonplace white foam items that you can easily tear or crumble are made of cheaper expanded polystyrene and are better referred to as foam plastic or styrene foam.

Make a buoyant tray for the pool Styrofoam is nearly unsinkable. Use the scraps from a construction project to make a drink holder or tray that will float in your pool:

- To make a soda-can holder, cut two pieces to the size you want the finished holder to be, then cut holes the same size as a soda can in one piece. Glue the piece with holes on top of the other piece, using a glue gun with hot-melt glue.

- To make a tray with a rim, just glue small strips of foam that are at least 1 inch (2.5 centimeters) high around the edge of a larger tray-size section of the material.

Make a kickboard A sharp kitchen knife is all you need to cut a scrap of Styrofoam insulation into a kickboard for your swimming pool.

Help shrubs withstand winter Sometimes shrubs need a little help to survive winter's ravages. Leftover sheets of extruded tongue-and-groove Styrofoam insulation are perfect for the job. They're rigid, waterproof, and block wind and road salt. Here are two ways to use the material:

● To give moderate protection, cut two Styrofoam sheets and lash them together to form a pup tent over the plant. To hold the pieces in place, drive bamboo garden stakes through the bottom of each piece into the ground.

● For something more substantial, fit pieces together to box in the plants on four sides. Put a stake inside each corner and join the pieces with duct or packing tape.

Plants in containers that overwinter outdoors are more likely to survive with Styrofoam protection too.

 **Recycling Foam Pellets**

> Even with lots of creative reuse, sometimes foam packing pellets just come in faster than they go out again. If you've got more than you can handle, remember that packing and shipping businesses often accept clean pellets for reuse. Just call to confirm before you bring them in.

✳ Sugar

Keep cut flowers fresh Make your own preservative to keep cut flowers fresh longer. Dissolve 3 tablespoons sugar and 2 tablespoons white vinegar per quart (liter) of warm water. When you fill the vase, make sure the cut stems are covered by 3-4 inches (7-10 centimeters) of the prepared water. The sugar nourishes the plants, while the vinegar inhibits bacterial growth. You'll be surprised how long the arrangement stays fresh!

Nix nematode worms in garden If your outdoor plants look unhealthy, with ugly knots at the roots, chances are they've been victims of an attack of the nematodes! The nematode worm, nemesis of many an otherwise healthy garden, is a microscopic parasite that pierces the roots of plants and causes knots. You can prevent nematode attacks by using sugar to create an inhospitable environment for the tiny worms. Apply 5 pounds (2 kilograms) sugar for every 250 square feet (25 square meters) of garden. Microorganisms feeding on the sugar will increase the organic matter in the soil, thereby eliminating those nasty little nematodes.

Clean greasy, grimy hands Your work is done for the day, but your hands are still covered with grease, grime, or paint. To clean filthy hands easily and thoroughly, pour equal amounts of olive oil and sugar into the cupped palm of one hand, and then gently rub your hands together for several minutes. Rinse thoroughly and dry. The grit of the sugar acts as an abrasive to help the oil remove grease, paint, and grime. Your hands will look and feel clean, soft, and moisturized.

Make a nontoxic fly trap Keep your kitchen free of flies with a homemade fly trap that uses no toxic chemicals. In a small saucepan, simmer 2 cups milk, 1/4 pound (113 grams) raw sugar, and 2 ounces (56 grams) ground pepper for about 10 minutes, stirring occasionally. Pour into shallow dishes or bowls and set them around the kitchen, patio, or anywhere the flies are a problem. The pesty bugs will flock to the bowls and drown!

Exterminate roaches If you hate smelly, noxious pesticides as much as you loathe cockroaches, don't call an exterminator. Instead, when you have a roach infestation, scatter a mixture of equal parts sugar and baking powder over the infested area. The sugar will attract the roaches, and the baking powder will kill them. Replace it frequently with a fresh mixture to prevent future infestations.

Soothe a burned tongue That slice of piping-hot pizza sure looked great, but ouch! You burned your tongue when you bit into it. To relieve a tongue burned by hot pizza, coffee, tea, or soup, reach for the sugar bowl and sprinkle a pinch or two of sugar over the affected area. The pain will begin to subside immediately.

Keep desserts fresh You used sugar to sweeten the cake batter; now use it to keep the finished cake fresh and moist. Store the cake in an airtight container with a couple of sugar cubes, and it will stay fresh for days longer. Store a few lumps of sugar with cheese the same way to prevent the cheese from molding.

✳ Talcum Powder

Keep ants away For an effective organic ant repellent, scatter talcum powder liberally around house foundations and known points of entry, such as doors and windows. Other effective organic repellents include cream of tartar, borax, powdered sulfur, and oil of cloves. You can also try planting mint around the house foundations.

Fix a squeaky floor Don't let squeaky floorboards drive you crazy. For a quick fix, sprinkle talcum powder or powdered graphite between the boards that squeak. If that doesn't do the trick, squirt in some liquid wax.

Remove bloodstains from fabric To remove fresh bloodstains from clothing or furniture, make a paste of water and talcum powder and apply it to the spot. When it dries, brush away the stain. Substitute cornstarch or cornmeal if you are out of talcum powder.

Get rid of greasy carpet stain A greasy stain can spoil the look of the most luxurious carpeting. You can remove greasy stains from a carpet with a combination of talcum powder and patience. Just cover the affected area with talcum powder and wait at least 6 hours for the talcum to absorb the grease. Then vacuum the stain away. Baking soda, cornmeal, or cornstarch may be substituted for the talcum powder.

> **TAKE CARE** Health care experts warn that scented talcum powder may cause skin allergies and worsen body odors. They recommend only unscented powder, used on dry skin. Women are advised not to use talcum powder in the vaginal or anal areas, where excessive powdering has been linked to an increased risk of ovarian cancer.

Degrease polyester stains Your favorite polyester shirt or blouse may come back in style someday, but you'll have to get rid of that ugly grease stain before you wear it. To get rid of grease stains on polyester, sprinkle some talcum powder directly onto the spot and rub it in with your fingers. Wait 24 hours, and gently brush. Repeat as necessary until the stain is completely gone.

Loosen tangles and knots Don't break a fingernail trying to untie that knot in your shoelace. Sprinkle some talcum powder on shoelaces (or any knotted cords) and the knots will pull apart more easily. Use talcum powder to help untangle chain necklaces too.

super item 30 uses! Tape

Safely pick up glass shards Why risk cutting yourself picking up bits of broken glass from the kitchen floor? Just hold a long piece of transparent tape tightly at each end and use it to blot up all the shards.

Create a no-fly zone Make your own fly and pest strips that are free of polluting toxic chemicals and poisons. Cover empty paper towel or toilet paper rolls with transparent tape, sticky side out, and hang them in the kitchen or wherever else you need them.

Mark start of plastic-wrap roll If you've ever had trouble finding the beginning of a roll of plastic food wrap, you'll appreciate this time-saving trick: Put a piece of transparent tape on your finger, sticky side out, and dab your finger on the roll until you find the edge. Use a short piece of tape to lift the edge and pull gently.

Prevent salt and pepper spills Many salt and pepper shakers, especially ceramic ones, have to be filled through a hole in the bottom. Before you refill one of these shakers, tape over the holes on top. That way you won't have any wasteful spills when you turn the shaker upside down to fill it. Also, remember to tape the tops when moving to a new home, or even when you're just transporting the shakers to and from a picnic.

Keep hands free at grocery Next time you go food shopping, bring some tape with you and use it to affix your shopping list to the handle of your grocery cart. This will free both your hands and you won't keep misplacing or dropping your list.

Make candles fit snugly Don't let loose candles spoil the romantic mood or cause a fire at your next candlelight dinner. If the candles don't fit snugly into the holder, wrap layers of tape around their bottom edges until they fit just right.

❋TAPE **AROUND THE HOUSE**

Keep spare batteries handy You won't be behind the times for long if you remember to tape extra batteries to the back of your wall clock! When the clock stops and it's time to replace the batteries, they'll be readily at hand.

Code your keys Are you always groping around to find the right key when you get home in the dark? Just wrap some tape around the top of your house key, and you'll be able to feel for the right key when it is too dark to see. Or if you have several similar-looking keys that you can't tell apart, color-code them with different-colored tape.

Prevent jewelry tangles To keep fine chains from tangling when you travel, cover both sides of each chain with transparent tape. You can also use tape to keep a pair of earrings from separating.

Mark a phone number for quick reference Use transparent tape to highlight numbers in the phone book that you often look up. The tape will make the page easier to find and you will also be able to find the number easily without having to search the whole page.

Contain grease stains on paper You may never be able to get rid of grease spots on books or important papers, but you can keep them from spreading with a little help from some transparent tape. Affix tape over both sides of the spot to keep the grease from seeping through to other pages or papers.

Keep papers from blowing in the wind If you have to make a speech or accept an award at an outdoor event, bring a roll of transparent tape with you. When it's your turn to talk, place some tape on the lectern, sticky side out, to prevent your papers from blowing away.

Find your favorite photo negative Before framing a favorite photograph, tape the negative to the back of the picture. If you ever want to make copies of the photo, you won't have to go searching through piles of old negatives to find the right one.

Deter cat from scratching Stop naughty cats and kittens from scratching your fine furniture! Sprinkle ground red pepper on a strip of tape and attach it to the areas you don't want them to scratch. They hate the smell, and they'll quickly get the message.

Keep flowers upright in vase To keep cut flowers from sagging in their vase, crisscross several pieces of transparent tape across the mouth of the vase, leaving spaces where you can insert the flowers. The flowers will look perky and fresh for a few extra days.

DID You KNOW?

Scotch tape got its name from an insult hurled at Richard Drew, the 3M company engineer who invented it. In 1925, five years before he invented the world's first and best-known transparent cellophane tape, Drew invented masking tape. He was field-testing his first masking-tape samples to find the right amount of adhesive when a frustrated body-shop painter exclaimed, "Take this tape back to those Scotch bosses of yours and tell them to put more adhesive on it!"

TAPE*

Make sewing easier Let transparent tape simplify your sewing: Use it to hold a zipper in place when you're making a garment. (You can sew through the tape and remove it when you're done.) Keep badges, patches, or name tags in place when sewing them onto shirts, uniforms, or caps. Tape hooks, eyes, and snaps to garments when sewing so they won't slip. Just pull the tape off when you're done. Tape a pattern to the material; when you cut the pattern, you'll have a reinforced edge.

End loose ends on thread spools Put an end to time-wasting frustrating searches for loose ends of thread. Just tape the ends to the top or bottom of the spool when you're done sewing and they'll be at your fingertips and ready to use next time you sew.

Remove lipstick from silk Why pay an expensive dry-cleaning bill to remove a lipstick spot from a silk scarf or dress when you can do it yourself for free? Just place a piece of transparent tape (or masking tape) over the spot and yank it off. If you can still see some of the lipstick color, sprinkle on some talcum powder or chalk and dab until the powder and the remaining lipstick disappear.

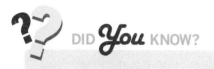 DID *You* KNOW?

Transparent tape is made from an acetate film derived from wood pulp or cotton fibers. It is formed into paper-thin sheets and wound onto giant rolls before being coated with adhesive. Twenty-nine raw materials go into the adhesive used in transparent tape. Even after the film and adhesive have been produced, 10 separate steps remain to be done before a roll of tape is manufactured.

Clean your nail file Clean a nail file easily and effectively. Simply place a piece of transparent tape over it, press, and pull off. The tape will pick up all the dirt embedded in the surface of the file.

*TAPE **FOR THE DO-IT-YOURSELFER**

Keep picture nails from damaging wall Before driving a nail into the wall, put a piece of tape on the wall at the site. This will prevent the paint from peeling off if you have to remove the nail, and it will prevent wallboards from cracking too.

Keep screws handy When doing household repairs, place loose screws, nuts, and bolts directly on a piece of transparent tape so they won't roll around and get lost.

Stick some double-sided tape on your workbench and use it to hold screws and such in place while you're working on a project.

Mend a broken plant stem Use transparent tape to add support to a broken plant stem. Just wrap the stem in tape at the damaged area and leave the tape on until it mends. The taped plant will keep growing as long as moisture can continue to travel up the stem.

Make a seed strip Make your own seed strip to create perfectly straight rows in your garden with almost no effort. Sprinkle some seeds on a piece of wax paper and use your fingers to arrange and align them. After removing the excess, take a strip of transparent tape and place it over the seeds. Then just bury the tape in the garden and you will soon have perfect rows.

Catch cricket invaders If noisy crickets have invaded your basement or garage, try trapping them with packaging tape. Take a strip of the tape and place on the floor, sticky side up. Later, just release your catch into the wild or feed them to a cricket-eating pet.

✴TAPE **FOR SAFETY'S SAKE**

Make safety markers for a car emergency You'll be a lot safer when your car breaks down at night if you have safety markers on hand to warn oncoming drivers. You can make your own safety markers easily at home. Just put strips of brightly colored reflector tape on some old coffee cans. Keep them in the trunk of your car for use in an emergency.

Mark dark stairways Stop stumbling on those poorly lit cellar or outdoor stairways or worrying about guests tripping and falling. Simply apply reflector tape along the edges of the steps and you and your guests will be able to see exactly where you're stepping.

Make pets visible at night Don't let your beloved family pet get hit by a car during the night. Put reflector tape on Rover's collar so drivers will be able to see him immediately in the dark.

✴TAPE **FOR THE KIDS**

Secure baby's bib Stop bits of food from getting under a child's bib by taping the edges of the bib to her clothes.

Makeshift childproofing If you bring a baby or small child with you when visiting a home that isn't childproofed, bring a roll of transparent tape along too. Use it to cover electrical outlets as a temporary safety measure. Although it will not confer a lot of protection, it could give you the extra time you need to remove a child from a potentially hazardous situation.

Make multicolored designs Tape a few different-colored markers or pencils together and give them to the kids to draw multicolored designs. Be careful not to use too many, so the children can maintain control of the drawings.

super item 23 uses! Tea

✱TEA FOR HEALTH AND BEAUTY

Cool sunburned skin What can you do when you forget to use sunscreen and have to pay the price with a painful burn? A few wet tea bags applied to the affected skin will take out the sting. This works well for other types of minor burns (i.e., from a teapot or steam iron) too. If the sunburn is too widespread to treat this way, put some tea bags in your bathwater and soak your whole body in the tub.

Relieve your tired eyes Revitalize tired, achy, or puffy eyes. Soak two tea bags in warm water and place them over your closed eyes for 20 minutes. The tannins in the tea act to reduce puffiness and soothe tired eyes.

Reduce razor burn Ouch! Why didn't you remember to replace that razor blade *before* you started to shave? To soothe razor burn and relieve painful nicks and cuts,

DID *You* KNOW?

Legend has it that tea originated some 5,000 years ago with the Chinese emperor Shen Nung. A wise ruler and creative scientist, the emperor insisted that all drinking water be boiled as a health precaution. One summer day, during a rest stop in a distant region, servants began to boil water for the royal entourage to drink when some dried leaves from a nearby bush fell into the pot. As the water boiled, it turned brown. The emperor's scientific curiosity was aroused, and he insisted on tasting the liquid. It was just his cup of tea.

apply a wet tea bag to the affected area. And don't forget to replace the blade before your next shave.

Get the gray out Turn gray hair dark again without an expensive trip to the salon or the use of chemical hair dyes. Make your own natural dye using brewed tea and herbs: Steep 3 tea bags in 1 cup boiling water. Add 1 tablespoon each of rosemary and sage (either fresh or dried) and let it stand overnight before straining. To use, shampoo as usual, and then pour or spray the mixture on your hair, making sure to saturate it thoroughly. Take care not to stain clothes. Blot with a towel and do not rinse. It may take several treatments to achieve desired results.

Condition dry hair To give a natural shine to dry hair, use a quart (liter) of warm, unsweetened tea (freshly brewed or instant) as a final rinse after your regular shampoo.

Tan your skin with tea Give pale skin a healthy tan appearance without exposure to dangerous ultraviolet rays. Brew 2 cups strong black tea, let it cool, and pour into a plastic spray bottle. Make sure your skin is clean and dry. Then spray the tea directly onto your skin and let it air-dry. Repeat as desired for a healthy-looking glowing tan. This will also work to give a man's face a more natural look after shaving off a beard.

Drain a boil Drain a boil with a boiled tea bag! Cover a boil with a wet tea bag overnight and the boil should drain without pain by the time you wake up next morning.

Soothe nipples sore from nursing When breast-feeding the baby leaves your nipples sore, treat them to an ice-cold bag of tea. Just brew a cup of tea, remove the bag, and place it in a cup of ice for about a minute. Then place the wet tea bag on the sore nipple and cover it with a nursing pad under your bra for several minutes while you enjoy a cup of tea. The tannic acid in the wet tea leaves will soothe and help heal the sore nipple.

Soothe those bleeding gums The child may be all smiles later when the tooth fairy arrives, but right now those bleeding gums are no fun whatsoever. To stop the bleeding and soothe the pain from a lost or recently pulled tooth, wet a tea bag with cool water and press it directly onto the site.

Relieve baby's pain from injection Is the baby *still* crying from that recent inoculation shot? Try wetting a tea bag and placing it over the site of the injection. Hold it gently in place until the crying stops. The tannic acid in the tea will soothe the soreness. You might try it on yourself the next time an injection leaves your arm sore.

Dry poison ivy rash Dry a weepy poison ivy rash with strongly brewed tea. Simply dip a cotton ball into the tea, dab it on the affected area, and let it air-dry. Repeat as needed.

Stop foot odor Put an end to smelly feet by giving them a daily tea bath. Just soak your tootsies in strongly brewed tea for 20 minutes a day and say good-bye to offensive odors.

Make soothing mouthwash To ease toothache or other mouth pain, rinse your mouth with a cup of hot peppermint tea mixed with a pinch or two of salt. Peppermint is an antiseptic and contains menthol, which alleviates pain on contact with skin surfaces. To make peppermint tea, boil 1 tablespoon fresh peppermint leaves in 1 cup water and steep for several minutes.

✳TEA AROUND THE HOUSE

Tenderize tough meat Even the toughest cuts of meat will melt in your mouth after you marinate them in regular black tea. Here's how: Place 4 tablespoons black tea leaves in a pot of warm (not boiling) water and steep for 5 minutes. Strain to remove the leaves and stir in 1/2 cup brown sugar until it dissolves. Set aside. Season up to 3 pounds (1.5 kilograms) meat with salt, pepper, onion, and garlic powder, and place it in a Dutch oven. Pour the liquid over the seasoned meat and cook in a preheated 325°F (165°C) oven until the meat is fork tender, about 90 minutes.

Clean wood furniture and floors Freshly brewed tea is great for cleaning wood furniture and floors. Just boil a couple of tea bags in a quart (liter) of water and let it cool. Dip a soft cloth in the tea, wring out the excess, and use it to wipe away dirt and grime. Buff dry with a clean, soft cloth.

Create "antique" fashions Soak white lace or garments in a tea bath to create an antique beige, ecru, or ivory look. Use 3 tea bags for every 2 cups of boiling water and steep for 20 minutes. Let it cool for a few minutes before soaking the material for 10 minutes or more. The longer you let it soak, the darker the shade you will get.

Tip **Dyeing with Herbal Teas**

> Using regular tea to dye fabrics has been around for a long time and was first used to hide stains on linens. But you can also use herbal teas to dye fabric different colors and subtle hues. Try using hibiscus to achieve red tones and darker herbal teas like licorice for soft brown tints. Always experiment using fabric scraps until you obtain the desired results.

Shine your mirrors To make mirrors sparkle and shine, brew a pot of strong tea, let it cool, and then use it to clean the mirrors. Dampen a soft cloth in the tea and wipe it all over the surface of the mirrors. Then buff with a soft, dry cloth for a sparkly, streak-free shine.

Control dust from fireplace ash Keep dust from rising from the ashes when you clean out your fireplace. Before you begin cleaning, sprinkle wet tea leaves over the area. The tea will keep the ashes from spreading all over as you lift them out.

Perfume a sachet Next time you make a sachet, try perfuming it with the fragrant aroma of your favorite herbal tea. Just open a few used herbal tea bags and spread the wet tea on some old newspaper to dry. Then use the dry tea as stuffing for the sachet.

✳TEA IN THE GARDEN

Give roses a boost Sprinkle new or used tea leaves (loose or in tea bags) around your rosebushes and cover with mulch to give them a midsummer boost. When you water the plants, the nutrients from the tea will be released into the soil, spurring growth. Roses love the tannic acid that occurs naturally in tea.

Feed your ferns Schedule an occasional teatime for your ferns and other acid-loving houseplants. Substitute brewed tea when watering the plants. Or work wet tea leaves into the soil around the plants to give them a lush, luxuriant look.

Prepare planter for potting For healthier potted plants, place a few used tea bags on top of the drainage layer at the bottom of the planter before potting. The tea bags will retain water and leach nutrients to the soil.

Enhance your compost pile To speed up the decomposition process and enrich your compost, pour a few cups of strongly brewed tea into the heap. The liquid tea will hasten decomposition and draw acid-producing bacteria, creating desirable acid-rich compost.

✳ Tennis Balls

Fluff down-filled clothes and comforters Down-filled items like jackets, vests, comforters, and pillows get flat and soggy when you wash them. You can fluff them up again by tossing a couple of tennis balls into the dryer when you put them in.

Sand curves in furniture Wrap a tennis ball in sandpaper and use it to sand curves when you're refinishing furniture. The tennis ball is just the right size and shape to fit comfortably in your hand.

Cover your trailer hitch To protect chrome trailer hitches from scratches and rust, cut a tennis ball and slip it over your hitching ball. The tennis ball will keep moisture out and rust away.

Massage your back Give yourself a relaxing and therapeutic back massage. Simply fill a long tube sock with a few tennis balls, tie the end, and stretch your homemade massager around your back just as you would a towel after a shower or bath.

Keep swimming pool oil-free Float a couple of tennis balls in your swimming pool to absorb body oils from swimmers. Replace the balls every couple of weeks during high-use periods.

Make bike kickstand for soft soil To prevent a bicycle kickstand from sinking into soft grass, sand, or mud, cut a slit in a tennis ball and put it on the end of the kickstand.

Store your valuables at gym Here's a neat way to hide and store valuables when you're working out at the gym. Make a 2-inch (5-centimeter) slit along one seam of a tennis ball and insert the valuables inside. Keep the ball in your gym bag among other sporting gear. Just remember not to use the doctored ball next time you're out on the tennis court!

Park right every time Make parking your car in the garage easier. Hang a tennis ball on a string from the garage ceiling so it will hit the windshield at the spot where you should stop the car. You'll always know exactly where to park.

SCIENCE FAIR

Teach kids about **gravity**. Stand on a chair holding **two tennis balls**, one in each hand, and extend your arms so they're at the same distance from the floor. Ask the kids to observe as you release both balls at once. Did they hit the floor at the same time? Now repeat using a **tennis ball** and a

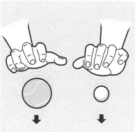

much lighter **Ping-Pong ball**. Again ask which will land first. Most will guess the heavier tennis ball, but they'll **land at the same time** because gravity exerts the same force on all objects regardless of their weight. Of course, if you try this with a ball and a feather, the kids will also learn that less dense objects fall slower due to air resistance.

Massage your sore feet For a simple but amazingly enjoyable and therapeutic foot massage, take your shoes off, place a tennis ball on the floor, and roll it around under your feet.

Get a better grip on bottle caps If your hands are weakened by arthritis or other ailments, you probably have a difficult time removing twist-off bottle caps. An old tennis ball may help. Simply cut a ball in half and use one of the halves to enhance your grip.

✳ Tires

Protect your vegetables Plant your tomatoes, potatoes, eggplants, peppers, or other vegetables inside tires laid on the ground. The tires will protect the plants from harsh winds, and the dark rubber will absorb heat from the sun and warm the surrounding soil.

Make a wading pool for kids To make an impromptu wading pool for toddlers, drape a shower curtain over the center of a large truck tire and fill it with water.

Make a classic tire swing A swing made from an old tire is a timeless source of pleasure for children of all ages. To make one in your backyard, drill a few drainage holes in the bottom of the tire. Drill two holes for bolts in the top, bolt two chains to the tire, and suspend it by the chains from a healthy branch of a hardwood tree. Use 3/16-inch (18-millimeter) playground chain. Put some wood chips or other soft material under and around the swing to cushion falls.

Tip Tire Checkup

Spending five minutes a month to check your tires can protect against avoidable breakdowns and crashes, improve vehicle handling, increase gas mileage, and extend the life of your tires. Here are some guidelines:
● Check tire air pressure at least once a month and before going on a long trip. Don't forget the spare.
● Inspect for uneven wear on tire treads, cracks, foreign objects, or other signs of wear or trauma. Remove bits of glass and other objects wedged in the tread.
● Make sure your tire valves have caps.
● Do not overload your vehicle.

Store plumbing snakes An old bicycle tire is just the right size to store metal snakes used to clean plumbing lines or "fish wires" used to run electrical cables inside walls. Just lay the snake or fish wire inside the tire, where it will expand to the shape of the tire and become encased within it. Then you can hang the tire conveniently on a hook in your workshop, garage, basement, or shed.

✳ Tomato Juice

Deodorize plastic containers To remove foul odors from a plastic container, pour a little tomato juice onto a sponge and wipe it around the inside of the container. Then wash the container and lid in warm, soapy water, dry well, and store them separated in the freezer for a couple of days. The container will be stench-free and ready to use again.

Remove skunk stink from dog Is there a dog alive that hasn't been
sprayed by a skunk at least once? If your dog gets skunked,
douse the affected area thoroughly with undiluted
tomato juice. Make sure to sponge some of the juice
over the pet's face, too, avoiding its eyes. Wait a few
minutes for the acids from the tomatoes to neutralize
the skunk smell and then give the dog a shampoo or
scrub with soap and water. Repeat as necessary over several
days until the smell is completely gone.

Rid fridge of odors Did a power failure cause the food to spoil and become malodorous
in your fridge? Get rid of spoiled-food smells in your refrigerator and freezer
with the help of some tomato juice. After disposing of the bad food that caused
the smell, thoroughly wipe the insides of the fridge and freezer with a sponge
or washcloth doused in undiluted tomato juice. Rinse with warm, soapy water
and wipe dry. If traces of the smell remain, repeat the procedure or substitute
vinegar for the tomato juice.

Restore blond hair color If you're a blonde who has ever gone swimming in a chlorine-
treated pool, you know it can sometimes give your hair an unappealing green
tint. To restore the blond color to your hair, saturate it with undiluted tomato
juice, cover it with a shower cap, and wait 10-15 minutes. Then rinse thoroughly, shampoo, and soon you'll be ready to have more fun.

Relieve a sore throat For temporary relief of sore throat symptoms, gargle with a mixture of 1/2 cup tomato juice and 1/2 cup hot water, plus about 10 drops hot
pepper sauce.

* Toothbrushes

Use as all-purpose cleaners Don't throw out your old toothbrushes. Instead, use them
to clean a host of diverse items and small or hard-to-reach areas and crevices.
Use a toothbrush to clean artificial flowers and plants, costume jewelry, combs,
shower tracks, crevices between tiles, and around faucets. Also clean computer
keyboards, can-opener blades, and around stove burners. And don't forget the
seams on shoes where the leather meets the sole.

Brush your cheese grater Give the teeth of a cheese grater a good brushing with an old
toothbrush before you wash the grater or put it in the dishwasher. This will
make it easier to wash and will prevent clogs in your dishwasher drain by getting rid of bits of cheese or any other item you may have grated.

Remove tough stains Removing a stain can be a pain, especially one that has soaked
deep down into soft fibers. To remove those deep stains, try using a soft-bris-
tled nylon toothbrush, dabbing it gently to work in the stain-removing agent
(bleach or vinegar, for example) until the stain is gone.

Clean silk from ears of corn Before cooking shucked corn, take an old toothbrush and gently rub down the ear to brush away the remaining clingy strands of silk. Then you won't have to brush them out from between your teeth after you eat the corn!

Clean and oil your waffle iron A clean, soft toothbrush is just the right utensil to clean crumbs and burned batter from the nooks and crannies of a waffle iron. Use it to spread oil evenly on the waffle iron surface before the next use too.

Apply hair dye Dyeing your hair at home? Use an old toothbrush as an applicator. It's the perfect size.

Clean gunk from appliances Dip an old toothbrush in soapy water and use it to clean between appliance knobs and buttons, and raised-letter nameplates.

DID **You** KNOW?

The ancient Chinese were apparently the first to use toothbrushes, which they made with bristles from the necks of cold-climate pigs. The first toothbrushes in America were manufactured in the late 19th century, but toothbrushing did not become a two- or three-times-a-day habit for many common folks until after World War II, when returning GIs brought home their army-enforced habits. By then DuPont had invented the nylon bristle, which, unlike the natural bristles used earlier, dried completely between brushings and was resistant to the growth of bacteria. Nylon bristles are still used in most toothbrushes made today.

✳ Toothpaste

Remove scuffs from shoes A little toothpaste does an amazing job of removing scuffs from leather shoes. Just squirt a dab on the scuffed area and rub with a soft cloth. Wipe clean with a damp cloth. The leather will look like new.

Clean your piano keys Has tickling the ivories left them a bit dingy? Clean them up with toothpaste and a toothbrush, then wipe them down with a damp cloth. Makes sense, since ivory is essentially elephant teeth. However, toothpaste will work just as well on modern pianos that usually have keys covered with plastic rather than real ivory.

Spiff up your sneakers Want to clean and whiten the rubber part of your sneakers? Get out the non-gel toothpaste and an old toothbrush. After scrubbing, clean off the toothpaste with a damp cloth.

Clean your clothes iron The mild abrasive in non-gel toothpaste is just the ticket for scrubbing the gunk off the bottom plate of your clothes iron. Apply the toothpaste to the cool iron, scrub with a rag, then rinse clean.

Polish a diamond ring Put a little toothpaste on an old toothbrush and use it to make your diamond ring sparkle instead of your teeth. Clean off the residue with a damp cloth.

Deodorize baby bottles Baby bottles inevitably pick up a sour-milk smell. Toothpaste will remove the odor in a jiffy. Just put some on your bottle brush and scrub away. Be sure to rinse thoroughly.

Prevent fogged goggles Whether you are doing woodworking or going skiing or scuba diving, nothing is more frustrating (and sometimes dangerous) than fogged goggles. Prevent the problem by coating the goggles with toothpaste and then wiping them off.

Prevent bathroom mirrors from fogging Ouch! You cut yourself shaving and it's no wonder—you can't see your face clearly in that fogged-up bathroom mirror. Next time, coat the mirror with non-gel toothpaste and wipe it off before you get in the shower. When you get out, the mirror won't be fogged.

Shine bathroom and kitchen chrome They make commercial cleaners with a very fine abrasive designed to shine up chrome, but if you don't have any handy, the fine abrasive in non-gel toothpaste works just as well. Just smear on the toothpaste and polish with a soft, dry cloth.

Clean the bathroom sink Non-gel toothpaste works as well as anything else to clean the bathroom sink. The tube's sitting right there, so just squirt some in, scrub with a sponge, and rinse it out. Bonus: The toothpaste will kill any odors emanating from the drain trap.

Remove crayon from walls Did crayon-toting kids get creative on your wall? Roll up your sleeves and grab a tube of non-gel toothpaste and a rag or—better yet—a scrub brush. Squirt the toothpaste on the wall and start scrubbing. The fine

 DID You KNOW?

Ancient Egyptians used a mixture of ox-hoof ashes, burned eggshells, myrrh, pumice, and water to clean their teeth. And for most of history, tooth-cleaning concoctions were used mostly by the wealthy. That began to change in 1850, when Dr. Washington Sheffield of New London, Connecticut, developed a formula we would recognize as toothpaste. He called it Dr. Sheffield's Creme Dentifrice. It was his son, Dr. Lucius Tracy Sheffield, who observed collapsible metal tubes of paint and thought, Why not toothpaste? To this day, Sheffield Laboratories, the company Dr. Washington Sheffield founded in 1850, continues to make toothpaste and put it in tubes.

abrasive in the toothpaste will rub away the crayon every time. Rinse the wall with water.

Remove ink or lipstick stains from fabric Oh no, a pen opened up in the pocket of your favorite shirt! This may or may not work, depending on the fabric and the ink, but it is certainly worth a try before consigning the shirt to the scrap bin. Put non-gel toothpaste on the stain and rub the fabric vigorously together. Rinse with water. Did some of the ink come out? Great! Repeat the process a few more times until you get rid of all the ink. The same process works for lipstick.

Remove watermarks from furniture You leave coasters around. But some people just won't use them. To get rid of those telltale watermark rings left by sweating beverages, gently rub some non-gel toothpaste on the wood with a soft cloth. Then wipe it off with a damp cloth and let it dry before applying furniture polish.

Remove beach tar Getting that black beach tar on your feet can put a small crimp in your vacation, but it is easy enough to remove. Just rub it with some non-gel toothpaste and rinse.

Clear up pimples Your teenager is bemoaning a prominent pimple, and the day before the dance too! Tonight, have her or him dab a bit of non-gel, nonwhitening toothpaste on the offending spot, and it should be dried up by morning. The toothpaste dehydrates the pimple and absorbs the oil. This remedy works best on pimples that have come to a head. Caution: This remedy may be irritating to sensitive skin.

> **TAKE CARE** All toothpaste, including gels, contains abrasives. The amount varies, but too much can damage your tooth enamel. People with sensitive teeth in particular should use a low-abrasive toothpaste. Ask your dentist which is the best toothpaste for you.

Clean smells from hands The ingredients in toothpaste that deodorize your mouth will work on your hands as well. If you've gotten into something stinky, wash your hands with toothpaste, and they'll smell great.

✳ Toothpicks

Mark rare, medium, and well done Your guests want their steaks done differently at the family cookout, but how do you keep track of who gets what? Easy. Just use different-colored toothpicks to mark them as rare, medium, and well done and get ready for the accolades.

Stick through garlic clove for marinade If you marinate foods with garlic cloves, stick a toothpick through the clove so you can remove it easily when you are ready to serve the food.

Keep pots from boiling over Oh darn! It seems like all you have to do is turn around for one minute and the pot is boiling over, making a mess on the stovetop. Next time, just stick a toothpick, laid flat, between the lid and pot. The little space will allow enough steam to escape to prevent the pot from boiling over. This also works with a casserole dish that's cooking in the oven.

Microwave potatoes faster The next time you microwave a potato, stick four toothpick "legs" in one side. The suspended potato will cook much faster because the microwaves will reach the bottom as well as the top and sides.

 DID **You** KNOW?

- Buddhist monks used toothpicks as far back as the 700s, and researchers have even found toothpick grooves in the teeth of prehistoric humans.

- Toothpicks were first used in the United States at the Union Oyster House, the oldest restaurant in Boston, which opened in 1826.
- In 1872 Silas Noble and J. P. Cooley patented the first toothpick-manufacturing machine.

- One cord of white birch wood, (also known as the toothpick tree) can make 7.5 million toothpicks.

Control your use of salad dressing Restrict your intake of carbs and calories from salad dressing. Instead of removing the foil seal when you open the bottle, take a toothpick and punch several holes in the foil. This will help prevent overuse of the dressing and make it last longer.

Keep sausages from rolling around When cooking sausages, insert toothpicks between pairs to make turning them over easy and keep them from rolling around in the pan. They'll cook more evenly and only need to be turned over once.

Mark start of tape roll Instead of wasting time trying to find the beginning of a tape roll, just wrap it around a toothpick whenever you are done using the tape, and the start of the roll will always be easy to find. No more frustration, and you can use the time you just saved to attack something else on your to-do list.

Use to light candles When a candle has burned down and the wick is hard to reach, don't burn your fingers trying to use a small match to light it. Light a wooden toothpick instead and use it to light the wick.

Clean cracks and crevices To get rid of dirt, grime, and cobwebs in hard-to-reach cracks or crevices, dip an ordinary toothpick in some alcohol and run it through the affected area. Also try this to clean around the buttons of your phone.

Apply glue to sequins If you're working on a project that calls for gluing on sequins or buttons, squirt a little glue on a piece of paper and dip in a toothpick to apply small dabs of glue. You won't make a mess, and you won't waste glue.

Make sewing easier Make sewing projects easier and complete them faster. Just use a round toothpick to push fabrics, lace, or gatherings under the pressure foot as you sew.

Touch up furniture crevices The secret to a good paint touch-up job is to use as little paint as possible, because even if you do have the right paint, the stuff in the can may not exactly match the sun-faded or dirty paint on the furniture. The solution: Dip the end of a toothpick in the paint and use it to touch up just the crevice. Unlike a brush, the toothpick won't apply more paint than you need, and you won't have a brush to clean.

Repair small holes in wood Did you drive a finish nail or brad into the wrong spot in your pine project? Don't panic. Dip the tip of a toothpick into white or yellow glue. Stick the toothpick in the hole and break it off. Sand the toothpick flush to the surface and you will never notice the repair.

Repair a loose hinge screw You took the door off and removed the hinges before you painted it. Now as you reattach the hinges, a screw just keeps turning without tightening—the hole is stripped. The fix is easy: Put some glue on the end of a toothpick and stick it in the hole. Break it off. Add one or two more tooth-picks with glue until the hole is tightly filled, breaking each one off as you go. Re-drill the hole and you're ready to screw the hinge in place.

Repair a bent plant stem If the stem of your favorite plant has folded over, it by no means dooms the plant. Straighten the stem and support it by placing a tooth-pick against the stem and wrapping the toothpick on with tape. Water the plant. Keep your eye on the plant—depending on how fast it grows, the stem will regain its strength and you'll need to remove the splint so you don't strangle the stem.

TAKE CARE Overuse of toothpicks can damage tooth enamel and lac-erate gums. If you have bonding or veneers, be extra careful to avoid breakage. Toothpicks can also cause wear to tooth roots, especially in the elderly whose gums have pulled away, exposing the roots.

Repair a leaky garden hose If your garden hose springs a leak, don't go out and buy another one; just find the hole and insert a toothpick in it. Cut off the excess part of the toothpick. The water will make the wood swell, plugging up the leak every time.

Foil those cutworms Cutworms kill seedlings by encircling the stem and severing it. To protect your seedlings, stick a toothpick in the soil about 1/4 inch (60 millimeters) from each stem. This prevents a cutworm from encircling it.

✳ Twist Ties

Organize electrical cords Does the top of your computer desk look like wild vines have overtaken it? Is there a thicket of wires behind your entertainment center? Tame the jungle of electrical wires by rolling each one up neatly and securing the extra length with a twist tie.

Make a trellis All you need are some twist ties and some of those plastic rings from soda six-packs to make a terrific trellis for climbing annual vines such as peas or morning glories. Just use the twist ties to join together as many of the six-pack rings as you want. Attach the trellis between two stakes, also using twist ties. You can even add sections to the trellis as the plant grows so that it looks like the plant is climbing on its own. At the end of the season, just roll the trellis up for storage and you can use it again next year.

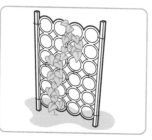

Tie up plant stems Twist ties are handy for securing a drooping plant stem to a stake or holding vines to a trellis. Don't twist the ties too tight, because you might injure the stem and restrict its growth.

Temporarily repair eyeglasses Whoops! Your specs slip off because that tiny screw that holds the earpiece fell out. Secure the earpiece temporarily with a twist tie. Trim the edges off the tie so that you just have the center wire. After you insert and tie it off, snip the excess with scissors.

Use for emergency shoelace Don't have a replacement shoelace handy? Try some twist ties. Use one tie across each opposing pair of eyelets.

Code your keys Got several similar-looking keys on your chain? Quickly identify them with twist ties of different colors secured through the holes in the keys.

Hang Christmas tree ornaments Some of those Christmas tree ornaments have been in the family for generations. As extra insurance against breakage, secure them to the tree with twist ties.

Make an emergency cuff link Oh, brother, you are in trouble! You packed a nice shirt with French cuffs to wear to the wedding, but you forgot your cuff links. Well, it's not so bad. Secure the cuffs with twist ties. Pull the ties through so the twist is discreetly hidden inside the cuff.

Bind loose-leaf paper Hold sheets of loose-leaf paper together by inserting twist ties in the holes.

U

✻ Umbrellas

Use as a drying rack An old umbrella makes a handy drying rack. Just strip off the fabric and hang the frame upside down from your shower bar. Attach wet clothing with clothespins. Plus, your new drying rack easily folds up for storage.

Clean a chandelier The next time you climb up there to clean the chandelier or ceiling fan, bring an old umbrella with you. Open the umbrella and hook its handle on the fixture so that it hangs upside down to catch any drips or dust.

Cover your picnic food To keep flies from feasting on your picnic before you do, open an old umbrella and cut off the handle. Place the umbrella over the dishes. It will shield your repast from the sun too.

Signal in a crowd The next time you and your sweetie go to a crowded event, carry a couple of identical bright-colored umbrellas. If you get separated, you can hold the umbrellas over your head and open them up to find each other in a flash.

Block plant overspray Houseplants love to be misted with water, but your walls don't love to get soaked with overspray. Stick an open umbrella between the plants and the wall and give your plants a shower.

Make plant stakes The wind caught your umbrella, turned it inside out, and ripped the fabric. Before you toss it into the trash, remove the umbrella's ribs. They make excellent supports for top-heavy garden plants, such as peonies.

Make an instant trellis Remove the fabric from an old umbrella and insert the handle into the ground to support climbing vines such as morning glories. The umbrella's shape, covered with flowers, will look terrific in the garden.

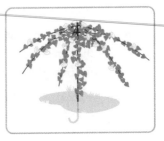

Shield your seedlings You thought you waited long enough before planting your seedlings outside, but now they're predicting a killer frost tonight. Sacrifice an old umbrella to save the seedlings. Open the umbrella, then cut off the handle. Place the umbrella over the seedlings to keep the frost them.

Vanilla Extract

Freshen up the fridge Having trouble getting rid of that bad odor in your refrigerator, even after scrubbing it out? Wipe down the inside of the fridge with vanilla extract. To prolong the fresh vanilla scent, soak a cotton ball or a piece of sponge with vanilla extract and leave it in the refrigerator.

Deodorize your microwave Is the odor of fish, or some other strong smell, lingering in your microwave? Pour a little vanilla extract in a bowl and microwave on High for one minute. Now, that's better.

Neutralize the smell of fresh paint If you would rather not have the unpleasant smell of fresh paint in your house, mix 1 tablespoon vanilla extract into the paint can when you open it. The house will smell delicious!

Sweeten the smell of your home It's an old Realtor's trick. Put a drop or two of vanilla extract on a lightbulb, turn on the light, and your house will be filled with the appealing scent of baked goods in the oven.

Use as perfume Try it! Just put a dab of vanilla extract on each wrist. You'll smell delicious, and many people find the scent of vanilla to be very relaxing.

Repel bugs Everybody likes the smell of vanilla. Everybody but bugs, that is. Dilute 1 tablespoon vanilla extract with 1 cup water and wipe the mixture on your exposed skin to discourage mosquitoes, blackflies, and ticks.

Relieve minor burns Yee-oow! You accidentally grabbed a hot pot or got splattered with grease in the kitchen. Grab the vanilla extract for quick pain relief. The evaporation of the alcohol in the vanilla extract cools the burn.

Vegetable Oil

Help remove a splinter That stubborn splinter just won't come out. Take a break from poking at your finger for a few minutes and soak it in vegetable oil. The oil will soften up your skin, perhaps just enough to ease that splinter out with your tweezers.

Remove labels and stickers Used jars—both plastic and glass—are always handy to have around. But removing the old labels always leaves a stubborn sticky residue. Soak the label with vegetable oil and the label will slide right off. Works great for sticky price tags too.

Separate stuck glasses When stacked drinking glasses get stuck together, it seems like nothing you can do will separate them. But the solution is simple: Just pour a little vegetable oil around the rim of the bottom glass and the glasses will pull apart with ease.

Tip **Oiling Cutting Boards**

> To restore and preserve dried-out wooden kitchen items such as cutting boards and salad bowls and tongs, use salad bowl oil—a food-safe oil that won't get rancid and is designed to protect wood that will come into contact with food. Don't use regular vegetable oil. Vegetable oil will soak into dried-out wood and make it look much better, but it never really dries and can get rancid after soaking into the wood.

Smooth your feet Rub your feet with vegetable oil before you go to bed and put on a pair of socks. When you awaken, your tootsies will be silky-smooth and soft.

Prevent clippings from sticking to your mower The next time you turn over your lawn mower to remove the stuck-on grass clippings, rub some vegetable oil under the housing and on the blade. It will take a lot longer for the clippings to build up next time.

Control mosquitoes in the birdbath It's so satisfying to watch birds enjoying the garden bath you provide. But unfortunately, that still water is a perfect breeding ground for mosquitoes. Floating a few tablespoons of vegetable oil on the surface of the water will help keep mosquitoes from using the water, and it won't bother the birds. But it's still important to change the water twice a week so any larvae don't have time to hatch.

Season cast-iron cookware After washing and thoroughly drying a cast-iron skillet or wok, use a paper towel to wipe it down with vegetable oil. Just leave a very thin layer of oil. It will prevent the pan from rusting and season it for the next time you use it.

✻ Vegetable Peelers

Slice slivers of cheese or chocolate When you need cheese slivers that are thinner than you can cut with a knife, or you want to decorate a cake with fine curlicues of chocolate, reach for the vegetable peeler.

Sharpen your pencils No pencil sharpener handy? A vegetable peeler will do a fine job of bringing your pencil to a point.

Soften hard butter fast You're ready to add the butter to your cake mix when you discover that the only sticks you have are as hard as a rock. When you need to soften cold, hard butter in a hurry, shave off what you need with a vegetable peeler. You'll have soft butter in moments.

Renew scented soaps Ornamental scented soaps are a great addition to the powder room because they make the room smell great as well as adding a decorative touch. But after a while, the surface of exposed ornamental soaps dries out, causing the scent to fade. To renew the scent, use a vegetable peeler to skim off a thin layer, revealing a new moist and fragrant surface.

super item *175 uses! Vinegar

Clear dirt off PCs and peripherals Your computer, printer, fax machine, and other home office gear will work better if you keep them clean and dust-free. Before you start cleaning, make sure that all your equipment is shut off. Now mix equal parts white vinegar and water in a bucket. Dampen a clean cloth in the solution—never use a spray bottle; you don't want to get liquid on the circuits inside—then squeeze it out as hard as you can, and start wiping. Keep a few cotton swabs on hand for getting to the buildups in tight spaces (like around the keys of your PC keyboard).

Clean your computer mouse If you have a mouse with a removable tracking ball, use a 50/50 vinegar-water solution to clean it. First, remove the ball from underneath the mouse by twisting off the cover over it. Use a cloth, dampened with the solution and wrung out, to wipe the ball clean and to remove fingerprints and dirt from the mouse itself. Then use a moistened cotton swab to clean out the gunk and debris from inside the ball chamber (let it dry a couple of hours before reinserting the ball).

Tip Buying Vinegar

Vinegar comes in a surprising number of varieties—including herbal organic blends, Champagne, rice, and wine—not to mention bottle sizes. For household chores, however, plain distilled white vinegar is the best and least expensive choice, and you can buy it by the gallon (3.7 liters) to save even more money. Apple cider vinegar runs a close second in practicality and is also widely used in cooking and home remedies. All other types of vinegar are strictly for ingestion and can be pretty pricey as well.

VINEGAR ✳

Clean your window blinds You can make the job of cleaning mini-blinds or venetians considerably less torturous by giving them "the white glove treatment." Just put on a white cotton glove—the kind sold for gardening is perfect—and moisten the fingers in a solution made of equal parts white vinegar and hot tap water. Now simply slide your fingers across both sides of each slat and prepare to be amazed. Use a container of clean water to periodically wash off the glove.

Unclog and deodorize drains The combination of vinegar and baking soda is one of the most effective ways to unclog and deodorize drains. It's also far gentler on your pipes (and your wallet) than commercial drain cleaners.

- To clear clogs in sink and tub drains, use a funnel to pour in 1/2 cup baking soda followed by 1 cup vinegar. When the foaming subsides, flush with hot tap water. Wait five minutes, and then flush again with cold water. Besides clearing blockages, this technique also washes away odor-causing bacteria.

- To speed up a slow drain, pour in 1/2 cup salt followed by 2 cups boiling vinegar, then flush with hot and cold tap water.

Get rid of smoke odor If you've recently burned a steak—or if your chain-smoking aunt recently paid you a surprise visit—remove the lingering smoky odor by placing a shallow bowl about three-quarters full of white or cider vinegar in the room where the scent is strongest. Use several bowls if the smell permeates your entire home. The odor should be gone in less than a day. You can also quickly dispense of the smell of fresh cigarette smoke inside a room by moistening a cloth with vinegar and waving it around a bit.

Wipe away mildew When you want to remove mildew stains, reach for white vinegar first. It can be safely used without additional ventilation and can be applied to almost any surface—bathroom fixtures and tile, clothing, furniture, painted surfaces, plastic curtains, and more. To eliminate heavy mildew accumulations, use it full strength. For light stains, dilute it with an equal amount of water. You can also prevent mildew from forming on the bottoms of rugs and carpeting by misting the backs with full-strength white vinegar from a spray bottle.

Clean chrome and stainless steel To clean chrome and stainless steel fixtures around your home, apply a light misting of undiluted white vinegar from a recycled spray bottle. Buff with a soft cloth to bring out the brightness.

Shine your silver Make your silverware—as well as your pure silver bracelets, rings, and other jewelry—shine like new by soaking them in a mixture of 1/2 cup white vinegar and 2 tablespoons baking soda for two to three hours. Rinse them under cold water and dry thoroughly with a soft cloth.

Polish brass and copper items Put the shimmer back in your brass, bronze, and copper objects by making a paste of equal parts white vinegar and salt, or vinegar and baking soda (wait for the fizzing to stop before using). Use a clean, soft cloth or paper towel to rub the paste into the item until the tarnish is gone. Then rinse with cool water and polish with a soft towel until dry.

Erase ballpoint-pen marks Has the budding young artist in your home just decorated a painted wall in your home with a ballpoint original? Don't lose your cool. Rather, dab some full-strength white vinegar on the "masterpiece" using a cloth or a sponge. Repeat until the marks are gone. Then go out and buy your child a nice big sketch pad.

Unglue stickers, decals, and price tags To remove a sticker or decal affixed to painted furniture or a painted wall, simply saturate the corners and sides of the sticker with full-strength white vinegar and carefully scrape it off (using an expired credit card or a plastic phone card). Remove any sticky remains by pouring on a bit more vinegar. Let it sit for a minute or two, and then wipe with a clean cloth. This approach is equally effective for removing price tags and other stickers from glass, plastic, and other glossy surfaces.

Burnish your scissors When your scissor blades get sticky or grimy, don't use water to wash them off; you're far more likely to rust the fastener that holds the blades together—or the blades themselves—than get them clean. Instead, wipe down the blades with a cloth dipped in full-strength white vinegar, and then dry it off with a rag or dish towel.

Get the salt off your shoes As if a winter's worth of ice, slush, and snow wasn't rough enough on your shoes and boots, the worst thing, by far, is all the rock salt that's used to melt it. In addition to leaving unsightly white stains, salt can actually cause your footwear to crack and even disintegrate if it's left on indefinitely. To remove it and prevent long-term damage, wipe fresh stains with a cloth dipped in undiluted white vinegar.

Clean your piano keys Here's an easy and efficient way to get those grimy fingerprints and stains off your piano keys. Dip a soft cloth into a solution of 1/2 cup white vinegar mixed in 2 cups water, squeeze it out until there are no drips, then gently wipe off each key. Use a second cloth to dry off the keys as you move along, then leave the keyboard uncovered for 24 hours.

Deodorize lunch boxes, footlockers, and car trunks Does your old footlocker smell like, well, an old footlocker? Or perhaps your child's lunch box has taken on the bouquet of week-old tuna? What about that musty old car trunk? Quit holding your breath every time you open it. Instead, soak a slice of white bread in white vinegar and leave it in the malodorous space overnight. The smell should be gone by morning.

Freshen a musty closet Got a closet that doesn't smell as fresh as you'd like? First, remove the contents, then wash down the walls, ceiling, and floor with a cloth dampened in a solution of 1 cup each of vinegar and ammonia and 1/4 cup baking soda in 1 gallon (3.7 liters) water. Keep the closet door open and let the interior dry before replacing your clothes and other stuff. If the smell persists, place a small pan of cat litter inside. Replenish every few days until the odor is gone.

Brighten up brickwork How's this for an effortless way to clean your brick floors without breaking out the polish? Just go over them with a damp mop dipped in 1 cup white vinegar mixed with 1 gallon (3.7 liters) warm water. Your floors will look so good you'll never think about cleaning them with anything else. You can also use this same solution to brighten up the bricks around your fireplace.

Revitalize wood paneling Does the wood paneling in your den look dull and dreary? Liven it up with this simple homemade remedy: Mix 1 pint warm water, 4 tablespoons white or apple cider vinegar, and 2 tablespoons olive oil in a container, give it a couple of shakes, and apply with a clean cloth. Let the mixture soak into the wood for several minutes, then polish with a dry cloth.

Restore your rugs If your rugs or carpets are looking worn and dingy from too much foot traffic or an excess of kids' building blocks, toy trucks, and such, bring them back to life by brushing them with a clean push broom dipped in a solution of 1 cup white vinegar in 1 gallon (3.7 liters) water. Your faded threads will perk up, and you don't even need to rinse off the solution.

Remove carpet stains You can lift out many stains from your carpet with vinegar:

- Rub light carpet stains with a mixture of 2 tablespoons salt dissolved in 1/2 cup white vinegar. Let the solution dry, then vacuum.

- For larger or darker stains, add 2 tablespoons borax to the mixture and use in the same way.

- For tough, ground-in dirt and other stains, make a paste of 1 tablespoon vinegar with 1 tablespoon cornstarch, and rub it into the stain using a dry cloth. Let it set for two days, then vacuum.

- To make spray-on spot and stain remover, fill a spray bottle with 5 parts water and 1 part vinegar. Fill a second spray bottle with 1 part nonsudsy ammonia and 5 parts water. Saturate a stain with the vinegar solution. Let it settle for a few minutes, then blot thoroughly with a clean, dry cloth. Then spray and blot using the ammonia solution. Repeat until the stain is gone.

Tip **Vinegar and Floor Cleaning**

> Damp-mopping with a mild vinegar solution is widely recommended as a way to clean wood and no-wax vinyl or laminate flooring. But, if possible, check with your flooring manufacturer first. Even when diluted, vinegar's acidity can ruin some floor finishes, and too much water will damage most wooden floors. If you want to try vinegar on your floors, use 1/2 cup white vinegar mixed in 1 gallon (3.7 liters) warm water. Start with a trial application in an inconspicuous area. Before applying the solution, squeeze out the mop thoroughly (or just use a spray bottle to moisten the mop head).

✳ VINEGAR **IN THE GARAGE**

Remove bumper stickers If those tattered old bumper stickers on your car make you feel more nauseated than nostalgic, it's time to break out the vinegar. Saturate the top and sides of the sticker with undiluted distilled vinegar and wait 10-15 minutes for the vinegar to soak through. Then use an expired credit card (or one of those promotional plastic cards that come in the mail) to scrape it off. Use more full-strength vinegar to get rid of any remaining gluey residue. Use the same technique to detach those cute decals your youngster used to decorate the back windshield.

Clean windshield wiper blades When your windshield actually gets blurrier after you turn on your wipers during a rainstorm, it usually means that your wiper blades are dirty. To make them as good as new, dampen a cloth or rag with some full-strength white vinegar and run it down the full length of each blade once or twice.

Keep car windows frost-free If you park your car outdoors during the cold winter months, a smart and simple way to keep frost from forming on your windows is by wiping (or, better yet, spraying) the outsides of the windows with a solution of 3 parts white vinegar to 1 part water. Each coating may last up to several weeks—although, unfortunately, it won't do much in the way of warding off a heavy snowfall.

Care for your car's carpets A good vacuuming will get up the sand and other loose debris from your car's carpeting, but it won't do diddly for stains or ground-in dirt. For that, mix up a solution of equal parts water and white vinegar and sponge it into the carpet. Give the mixture a couple of minutes to settle in; then blot it up with a cloth or paper towel. This technique will also eliminate salt residues left on car carpets during the winter months.

Remove candle wax Candles are great for creating a romantic mood, but the mood can quickly sour if you wind up getting melted candle wax on your fine wood furniture. To remove it, first soften the wax using a blow-dryer on its hottest setting and blot up as much as you can with paper towels. Then remove what's left by rubbing with a cloth soaked in a solution made of equal parts white vinegar and water. Wipe clean with a soft, absorbent cloth.

Give grease stains the slip Eliminate grease stains from your kitchen table or counter by wiping them down with a cloth dampened in a solution of equal parts white vinegar and water. In addition to removing the grease, the vinegar will neutralize any odors on the surface (once its own aroma evaporates, that is).

Conceal scratches in wood furniture Got a scratch on a wooden tabletop that grabs your attention every time you look at it? To make it much less noticeable, mix some distilled or cider vinegar and iodine in a small jar and paint over the scratch with a small artist's brush. Use more iodine for darker woods; more vinegar for lighter shades.

TAKE CARE Don't use vinegar—or alcohol or lemon juice—on marble tabletops, countertops, or floors. Vinegar's acidity can dull or even pit the protective coating—and possibly damage the stone itself. Also, avoid using vinegar on travertine and limestone; the acid eats through the calcium in the stonework.

Get rid of water rings on furniture To remove white rings left by wet glasses on wood furniture, mix equal parts vinegar and olive oil and apply it with a soft cloth while moving with the wood grain. Use another clean, soft cloth to shine it up. To get white water rings off leather furniture, dab them with a sponge soaked in full-strength white vinegar.

Wipe off wax or polish buildup When furniture polish or wax builds up on wood furniture or leather tabletops, get rid of it with diluted white vinegar. To get built-up polish off a piece of wood furniture, dip a cloth in equal parts vinegar and water and squeeze it out well. Then, moving with the grain, clean away the polish. Wipe dry with a soft towel or cloth. Most leather tabletops will come clean simply by wiping them down with a soft cloth dipped in 1/4 cup vinegar and 1/2 cup water. Use a clean towel to dry off any remaining liquid.

Revitalize leather furniture Has your leather sofa or easy chair lost its luster? To restore it to its former glory, mix equal parts white vinegar and boiled linseed oil in a recycled spray bottle, shake it up well, and spray it on. Spread it evenly over your furniture using a soft cloth, give it a couple of minutes to settle in, then rub it off with a clean cloth.

Refresh your refrigerator Did you know that vinegar might be an even more effective safe cleanser for your refrigerator than baking soda? Use equal parts white vinegar and water to wash both the interior and exterior of your fridge, including the door gasket and the fronts of the vegetable and fruit bins. To prevent mildew growth, wash the inside walls and bin interiors with some full-strength vinegar on a cloth. Also use undiluted vinegar to wipe off accumulated dust and grime on top of your refrigerator. Of course, you'll still want to put that box of baking soda inside your refrigerator to keep it smelling clean when you're done.

Steam-clean your microwave To clean your microwave, place a glass bowl filled with a solution of 1/4 cup vinegar in 1 cup water inside, and zap the mixture for five minutes on the highest setting. Once the bowl cools, dip a cloth or sponge into the liquid and use it to wipe away stains and splatters on the interior.

? DID *You* KNOW?

Taken literally, vinegar is nothing more than wine that's gone bad; the word derives from the French *vin* (wine) and *aigre* (sour). But, in fact, anything used to make alcohol can be turned into vinegar, including apples, honey, malted barley, molasses, rice, sugarcane, and even coconuts. Vinegar's acidic, solvent properties were well known even in ancient times. According to one popular legend, Cleopatra is said to have wagered she could dispose of a fortune in the course of a single meal. She won the bet by dissolving a handful of pearls in a cup of vinegar ... and then consuming it.

Disinfect cutting boards To disinfect and clean your wood cutting boards or butcher block countertop, wipe them with full-strength white vinegar after each use. The acetic acid in the vinegar is a good disinfectant, effective against such harmful bugs as *E. coli, Salmonella,* and *Staphylococcus.* Never use water and dishwashing detergent, because it can weaken surface wood fibers. When your wooden cutting surface needs deodorizing as well as disinfecting, spread some baking soda over it and then spray on undiluted white vinegar. Let it foam and bubble for five to ten minutes, then rinse with a cloth dipped in clean cold water.

Deodorize your garbage disposal Here's an incredibly easy way to keep your garbage disposal unit sanitized and smelling clean: Mix equal parts water and vinegar in a bowl, pour the solution into an ice cube tray, and freeze it. Then simply drop a couple of "vinegar cubes" down your disposal every week or so, followed by a cold-water rinse.

Wash out your dishwasher To keep your dishwasher operating at peak performance and remove built-up soap film, pour 1 cup undiluted white vinegar into the bottom of the unit—or in a bowl on the top rack. Then run the machine through a full cycle without any dishes or detergent. Do this once a month, especially if you have hard water. *Note:* If there's no mention of vinegar in your dishwasher owner's manual, check with the manufacturer first.

Clean china, crystal, and glassware Put the sparkle back in your glassware by adding vinegar to your rinse water or dishwater.

- To keep your everyday glassware gleaming, add 1/4 cup vinegar to your dishwasher's rinse cycle.

- To rid drinking glasses of cloudiness or spots caused by hard water, heat up a pot of equal parts white vinegar and water (use full-strength vinegar if your glasses are very cloudy), and let them soak in it for 15-30 minutes. Give them a good scrubbing with a bottle brush, then rinse clean.

- Add 2 tablespoons vinegar to your dishwater when cleaning your good crystal glasses. Then rinse them in a solution of 3 parts warm water to 1 part vinegar and allow them to air-dry. You can also wash delicate crystal and fine china by adding 1 cup vinegar to a basin of warm water. Gently dunk the glasses in the solution and let dry.

- To get coffee stains and other discolorations off china dishes and teacups, try scrubbing them with equal parts vinegar and salt, followed by rinsing them under warm water.

Clean a coffeemaker If your coffee consistently comes out weak or bitter, odds are, your coffeemaker needs cleaning. Fill the decanter with 2 cups white vinegar and 1 cup water. Place a filter in the machine, and pour the solution into the coffeemaker's water chamber. Turn on the coffeemaker and let it run through a full brew cycle. Remove the filter and replace it with a fresh one. Then run clean water through the machine for two full cycles, replacing the filter again for the second brew. If you have soft water, clean your coffeemaker after 80 brew cycles—after 40 cycles if you have hard water.

Clean a teakettle To eliminate lime and mineral deposits in a teakettle, bring 3 cups full-strength white vinegar to a full boil for five minutes and leave the vinegar in the kettle overnight. Rinse out with cold water the next day.

Cut the grease Every professional cook knows that distilled vinegar is one of the best grease cutters around. It even works on seriously greasy surfaces such as the fry vats used in many food outlets. But you don't need to have a deep fryer to find plenty of ways to put vinegar to good use:

- When you're finished frying, clean up grease splatters from your stovetop, walls, range hood, and surrounding countertop by washing them with a sponge dipped in undiluted white vinegar. Use another sponge soaked in cold tap water to rinse, then wipe dry with a soft cloth.

- Pour 3-4 tablespoons white vinegar into your favorite brand (especially bargain brands) of liquid dishwashing detergent and give it a few shakes. The added vinegar will not only increase the detergent's grease-fighting capabilities, but also provide you with more dishwashing liquid for the money, because you'll need less soap to clean your dishes.

- Boiling 2 cups vinegar in your frying pan for 10 minutes will help keep food from sticking to it for several months at a time.

- Remove burned-on grease and food stains from your stainless steel cookware by mixing 1 cup distilled vinegar in enough water to cover the stains (if they're near the top of a large pot, you may need to increase the vinegar). Let it boil for five minutes. The stains should come off with some mild scrubbing when you wash the utensil.

- Get that blackened, cooked-on grease off your broiler pan by softening it up with a solution of 1 cup apple cider vinegar and 2 tablespoons sugar. Apply the mixture while the pan is still hot, and let it sit for an hour or so. Then watch in amazement as the grime slides off with a light scrubbing.

- Got a hot plate that looks more like a grease pan? Whip it back into shape by washing it with a sponge dipped in full-strength white vinegar.

- Fight grease buildups in your oven by wiping down the inside with a rag or sponge soaked in full-strength white vinegar once a week. The same treatment gets grease off the grates on gas stoves.

Tip **Homemade Wine Vinegar**

Contrary to popular belief, old wine rarely turns into vinegar; usually a half-empty bottle just spoils due to oxidation. To create vinegar, you need the presence of *Acetobacter,* a specific type of bacteria. You can make your own wine vinegar, though, by mixing one part leftover red, white, or rosé wine with 2 parts cider vinegar. Pour the mixture into a clean, recycled wine bottle and store it in a dark cabinet. It just might taste as good, if not better, on your salads than some of those fancy wine vinegars sold at upscale food shops.

Brush-clean can opener blades Does that dirty wheel blade of your electric can opener look like it's seen at least one can too many? To clean and sanitize it, dip an old toothbrush in white vinegar, and then position the bristles of the brush around the side and edge of the wheel. Turn on the appliance, and let the blade scrub itself clean.

Remove stains from pots, pans, and ovenware Nothing will do a better job than vinegar when it comes to removing stubborn stains on your cookware. Here's how to put the power of vinegar to use:

● Give those dark stains on your aluminum cookware (caused by cooking acidic foods) the heave-ho by mixing in 1 teaspoon white vinegar for every cup of water needed to cover the stains. Let it boil for a couple of minutes, then rinse with cold water.

● To remove stains from your stainless steel pots and pans, soak them in 2 cups white vinegar for 30 minutes, then rinse them with hot, soapy water followed by a cold-water rinse.

● To get cooked-on food stains off your glass ovenware, fill them with 1 part vinegar and 4 parts water, heat the mixture to a slow boil, and let it boil at a low level for five minutes. The stains should come off with some mild scrubbing once the mixture cools.

● They call it nonstick, but no cookware is stainproof. For mineral stains on your nonstick cookware, rub the utensil with a cloth dipped in undiluted distilled vinegar. To loosen up stubborn stains, mix 2 tablespoons baking soda, 1/2 cup vinegar, and 1 cup water and let it boil for 10 minutes.

Clear the air in your kitchen If the smell of yesterday's cooked cabbage or fish stew is hanging around your kitchen longer than you'd like, mix a pot of 1/2 cup white vinegar in 1 cup water. Let it boil until the liquid is almost gone. You'll be breathing easier in no time.

Refresh your ice trays If your plastic ice trays are covered with hard-water stains—or if it's been a while since you've cleaned them—a few cups of white vinegar can help you in either case. To remove the spots or disinfect your trays, let them soak in undiluted vinegar for four to five hours, then rinse well under cold water and let dry.

Make all-purpose cleaners For fast cleanups around the kitchen, keep two recycled spray bottles filled with these vinegar-based solutions:

● For glass, stainless steel, and plastic laminate surfaces, fill your spray bottle with 2 parts water, 1 part distilled white vinegar, and a couple of drops of dishwashing liquid.

● For cleaning walls and other painted surfaces, mix up 1/2 cup white vinegar, 1 cup ammonia, and 1/4 cup baking soda in 1 gallon (3.7 liters) water and pour some into a spray bottle. Spritz it on spots and stains whenever needed and wipe off with a clean towel.

Make an all-purpose scrub for pots and pans How would you like an effective scouring mix that costs a few pennies, and can be safely used on all of your metal cookware—including expensive copper pots and pans? Want even better news? You probably already have this "miracle mix" in your kitchen. Simply combine equal parts salt and flour and add just enough vinegar to make a paste. Work the paste around the cooking surface and the outside of the utensil, then rinse off with warm water and dry thoroughly with a soft dish towel.

Sanitize jars, containers, and vases Do you cringe at the thought of cleaning out a mayonnaise, peanut butter, or mustard jar to reuse it? Or worse, getting the residue out of a slimy vase, decanter, or container? There is an easy way to handle these jobs. Fill the item with equal parts vinegar and warm, soapy water and let it stand for 10-15 minutes. If you're cleaning a bottle or jar, close it up and give it a few good shakes; otherwise use a bottle brush to scrape off the remains before thoroughly rinsing.

Clean a dirty thermos To get a thermos bottle clean, fill it with warm water and 1/4 cup white vinegar. If you see any residue, add some uncooked rice, which will act as an abrasive to scrape it off. Close and shake well. Then rinse and let it air-dry.

Purge bugs from your pantry Do you have moths or other insects in your cupboard or pantry? Fill a small bowl with 1 1/2 cups apple cider vinegar and add a couple of drops of liquid dish detergent. Leave it in there for a week; it will attract the bugs, which will fall into the bowl and drown. Then empty the shelves, and give the interior a thorough washing with dishwashing detergent or 2 cups baking soda in 1 quart (1 liter) water. Discard all wheat products (breads, pasta, flour, and such), and clean off canned goods before putting them back.

Trap fruit flies Did you bring home fruit flies from the market? You can make traps for them that can be used anywhere around your house by filling an old jar about halfway with apple cider. Punch a few holes in the lid, screw it back on, and you're good to go.

*❋ VINEGAR **FOR THE COOK***

Tenderize and purify meats and seafood Soaking a lean or inexpensive cut of red meat in a couple of cups of vinegar breaks down tough fibers to make it more tender—and in addition, kills off any potentially harmful bacteria. You can also use vinegar to tenderize seafood steaks. Let the meat or fish soak in full-strength vinegar overnight. Experiment with different vinegar varieties for added flavor, or simply use apple cider or distilled vinegar if you intend to rinse it off before cooking.

Keep corned beef from shrinking Ever notice how the corned beef that comes out of the pot is always smaller than the one that went in? Stop your meat from shrinking by adding a couple of tablespoons of apple cider vinegar to the water when boiling your beef.

Make better boiled or poached eggs Vinegar does marvelous things for eggs. Here are the two most useful "egg-samples":

● When you are making hard-boiled eggs, adding 2 tablespoons distilled vinegar for every quart (liter) of water will keep the eggs from cracking and make them easier to shell.

● When you are poaching eggs, adding a couple of tablespoons of vinegar to the water will keep your eggs in tight shape by preventing the egg whites from spreading.

Wash store-bought produce You can't be too careful these days when it comes to handling the foods you eat. Before serving your fruits and vegetables, a great way to eliminate the hidden dirt, pesticides, and even insects, is to rinse them in 4 tablespoons apple cider vinegar dissolved in 1 gallon (3.7 liters) cold water.

DID **You** KNOW?

Authentic balsamic vinegar comes solely from Modena, Italy, and is made from Trebbiano grapes, a particularly sweet white variety grown in the surrounding hills. Italian law mandates that the vinegar be aged in wooden barrels made of chestnut, juniper, mulberry, or oak. There are only two grades of true balsamic vinegar—which typically sells for $100-$200 for a 100-milli-liter bottle: *tradizionale vecchio*, vinegar that is at least 12 years old, and *tradizionale extra vecchio*, vinegar that's aged for at least 25 years (some balsamic vinegars are known to have been aged for more than 100 years).

Remove odors from your hands It's often difficult to get strong onion, garlic, or fish odors off your hands after preparing a meal. But you'll find these scents are a lot easier to wash off if you rub some distilled vinegar on your hands before and after you slice your vegetables or clean your fish.

Get rid of berry stains You can use undiluted white vinegar on your hands to remove stains from berries and other fruits.

Control your dandruff To give your dandruff the brush-off, follow up each shampoo with a rinse of 2 cups apple cider vinegar mixed with 2 cups cold water. You can also fight dandruff by applying 3 tablespoons vinegar onto your hair and massaging into your scalp before you shampoo. Wait a few minutes, then rinse it out and wash as usual.

Condition your hair Want to put the life back into your limp or damaged hair? You can whip up a terrific hair conditioner by combining 1 teaspoon apple cider vinegar with 2 tablespoons olive oil and 3 egg whites. Rub the mixture into your hair, then keep it covered for 30 minutes using plastic wrap or a shower cap. When time's up, shampoo and rinse as usual.

Protect blond hair from chlorine Keep your golden locks from turning green in a chlorinated pool by rubbing 1/4 cup cider vinegar into your hair and letting it set for 15 minutes before diving in.

Apply as antiperspirant Why not put the deodorizing power of vinegar to use where it matters most? That's right, you don't need a roll-on or spray to keep your underarms smelling fresh. Instead, splash a little white vinegar under each arm in the morning, and let it dry. In addition to combating perspiration odor, this method also does away with those deodorant stains on your garments.

Soak away aching muscles Got a sore back, a strained tendon in your shoulder or calf, or maybe you're just feeling generally rundown? Adding 2 cups apple cider vinegar to your bathwater is a great way to soothe away your aches and pains, or to simply to take the edge off a stressful day. Adding a few drops of peppermint oil to your bath can lend an able assist as well.

Freshen your breath After you consume a fair portion of garlic or onions, a quick and easy way to sweeten your breath is to rinse your mouth with a solution made by dissolving 2 tablespoons apple cider vinegar and 1 teaspoon salt in a glass of warm water.

Ease sunburn and itching You can cool a bad sunburn by gently dabbing the area with a cotton ball or soft cloth saturated with white or cider vinegar. (This treatment is especially effective if it's applied before the burn starts to sting.) The same technique works to instantly stop the itch of mosquito and other insect bites, as well as the rashes caused by exposure to poison ivy or poison oak.

Banish bruises If you or someone you care about has a nasty fall, you can speed healing and prevent black-and-blue marks by soaking a piece of cotton gauze in white or apple cider vinegar and leaving it on the injured area for one hour.

Soothe a sore throat Here are three ways that you can make a sore throat feel better:

- If your throat is left raw by a bad cough, or even a speaking or singing engagement, you'll find fast relief by gargling with 1 tablespoon apple cider vinegar and 1 teaspoon salt dissolved in a glass of warm water; use several times a day if needed.

● For sore throats associated with a cold or flu, combine 1/4 cup cider vinegar and 1/4 cup honey and take 1 tablespoon every four hours.

● To soothe both a cough and a sore throat, mix 1/2 cup vinegar, 1/2 cup water, 4 teaspoons honey, and 1 teaspoon hot sauce. Swallow 1 tablespoon four or five times daily, including one before bedtime. *Warning:* Children under one year old should never be given honey.

Breathe easier Adding 1/4 cup white vinegar to the water in your hot-steam vaporizer can help ease congestion caused by a chest cold or sinus infection. It can also be good for your vaporizer: The vinegar will clear away any mineral deposits in the water tubes resulting from the use of hard water. *Note:* Check with the manufacturer before adding vinegar to a cool-mist vaporizer.

Treat an active cold sore The only thing worse than a bad cold is a bad cold sore. Fortunately, you can usually dry up a cold sore in short order by dabbing it with a cotton ball saturated in white vinegar three times a day. The vinegar will quickly soothe the pain and swelling.

Make a poultice for corns and calluses Here's an old-fash-
ioned, time-proven method to treat corns and calluses: Saturate a piece of white or stale bread with 1/4 cup white vinegar. Let the bread soak in the vinegar for 30 minutes, then break off a piece big enough to completely cover the corn. Keep the poultice in place with gauze or adhesive tape, and leave it on overnight. The next morning, the hard, callused skin will be dissolved, and the corn should be easy to remove. Older, thicker calluses may require several treatments.

Get the jump on athlete's foot A bad case of athlete's foot can drive you hopping mad. But you can often quell the infection, and quickly ease the itching, by rinsing your feet three or four times a day for a few days with undiluted apple cider vinegar. As an added precaution, soak your socks or stockings in a mixture of 1 part vinegar and 4 parts water for 30 minutes before laundering them.

Pamper your skin Using vinegar as a skin toner dates back to the time of Helen of Troy. And it's just as effective today. After you wash your face, mix 1 tablespoon apple cider vinegar with 2 cups water as a finishing rinse to cleanse and tighten your skin. You can also make your own facial treatment by mixing 1/4 cup cider vinegar with 1/4 cup water. Gently apply the solution to your face and let it dry.

Say good-bye to age or sun spots Before you take any drastic measures to remove or cover up those brown spots on your skin caused by overexposure to the sun or hormonal changes, give vinegar a try. Simply pour some full-strength apple cider vinegar onto a cotton ball and apply it to the spots for 10 minutes at least twice a day. The spots should fade or disappear within a few weeks.

Soften your cuticles You can soften the cuticles on your fingers and toes before manicuring them by soaking your digits in a bowl of undiluted white vinegar for five minutes.

Make nail polish last longer Your nail polish will have a longer life expectancy if you first dampen your nails with some vinegar on a cotton ball and let it dry before applying your favorite polish.

Clean your eyeglasses When it's more difficult to see with your glasses on than it is with them off, it's a clear indication that they're in need of a good cleaning. Applying a few drops of white vinegar to your glass lenses and wiping them with a soft cloth will easily remove dirt, sweat, and fingerprints, and leave them spotless. Don't use vinegar on plastic lenses, however.

Treat a jellyfish or bee sting A jellyfish can pack a nasty sting. If you have an encounter with one, pouring some undiluted vinegar on the sting will take away the pain in no time, and let you scrape out the stinger with a plastic credit card. The same treatment can also be used to treat bee stings. But using vinegar on stings inflicted by the jellyfish's cousin the Portuguese man-of-war is now discouraged because vinegar may actually increase the amount of toxin released under the skin. *Warning:* If you have difficulty breathing or the sting area becomes inflamed and swollen, get medical attention at once; you could be having an allergic reaction.

✱ VINEGAR **IN THE BATHROOM**

Wash mildew from shower curtains Clean those ugly mildew stains off your plastic shower curtain by putting it and a couple of soiled towels in your washing machine. Add 1/2 cup laundry detergent and 1/2 cup baking soda to the load,

 DID *You* KNOW?

The world's only museum dedicated to vinegar, the International Vinegar Museum, is located in Roslyn, South Dakota. Housed in a building that was the former town hall, the museum is operated by Dr. Lawrence J. Diggs, an international vinegar consultant also known as the Vinegar Man (visit him online at www.vinegarman.com). The museum showcases vinegars from around the world, has displays on the various methods used to make vinegar, and even lets visitors sample different types of vinegars. It's also among the world's least expensive museums: Admission for adults is $2; for those under 18, $1; and "instant scholarships for those too poor to pay."

and wash it in warm water on your machine's regular cycle. Add 1 cup white vinegar to the first rinse. Before the machine goes into the spin cycle, remove the curtain and let it hang-dry.

Shine ceramic tiles If soap scum or water spots have dulled the ceramic tiles around your sink or bath, bring back the brightness by scrubbing them with 1/2 cup white vinegar, 1/2 cup ammonia, and 1/4 cup borax mixed in 1 gallon (3.7 liters) warm water. Rinse well with cool water and let air-dry.

Whiten your grout Has the grout between the tiles of your shower or bathtub enclosure become stained or discolored? Restore it to its original shade of white by using a toothbrush dipped in undiluted white vinegar to scrub away the dinginess.

Clean sinks and bathtubs Put the shine back in your porcelain sinks and bathtubs by giving them a good scrubbing with full-strength white vinegar, followed by a rinse of clean cold water. To remove hard-water stains from your tub, pour in 3 cups white vinegar under running hot tap water. Let the tub fill up over the stains and allow it to soak for four hours. When the water drains out, you should be able to easily scrub off the stains.

Shine up your shower doors To leave your glass shower doors sparkling clean—and to remove all of those annoying water spots—wipe them down with a cloth dipped in a solution of 1/2 cup white vinegar, 1 cup ammonia, and 1/4 cup baking soda mixed in 1 gallon (3.7 liters) warm water.

Disinfect shower door tracks Use vinegar to remove accumulated dirt and grime from the tracks of your shower doors. Fill the tracks with about 2 cups full-strength white vinegar and let it sit for three to five hours. (If the tracks are really dirty, heat the vinegar in a glass container for 30 seconds in your microwave first.) Then pour some hot water over the track to flush away the gunk. You may need to use a small scrub brush, or even a recycled toothbrush, to get up tough stains.

DID You KNOW?

Some researchers believe vinegar will ultimately be adopted as a simple and inexpensive way to diagnose cervical cancer in women—especially those living in impoverished nations. In tests conducted over a two-year period, midwives in Zimbabwe used a vinegar solution to detect more than 75 percent of potential cancers in 10,000 women (the solution turns tissue containing precancerous cells white). Although the test is not as accurate as a Pap smear, doctors believe it will soon be an important screening tool in developing countries, where only 5 percent of women are currently tested for this often fatal disease.

Remove mineral deposits from showerheads Wash away blockages and mineral deposits from removable showerheads by placing them in 1 quart (1 liter) boiling water with 1/2 cup distilled vinegar for 10 minutes (use hot, not boiling, liquid for plastic showerheads). When you remove it from the solution, the obstructions should be gone. If you have a nonremovable showerhead, fill a small plastic bag half full with vinegar and tape it over the fixture. Let it sit for about 1 hour, then remove the bag and wipe off any remaining vinegar from the showerhead.

Wipe down bathroom fixtures Don't stop at the shower when you're cleaning with vinegar! Pour a bit of undiluted white vinegar onto a soft cloth and use it to wipe your chrome faucets, towel racks, bathroom mirrors, doorknobs, and such. It'll leave them gleaming.

> **TAKE CARE** Combining vinegar with bleach—or any other product containing chlorine, such as chlorinated lime (sold as bleaching powder)—may produce chlorine gas. In low concentrations, this toxic, acrid-smelling gas can cause damage to your eyes, skin, or respiratory system. High concentrations are often fatal.

Fight mold and mildew To remove and inhibit bathroom mold and mildew, pour a solution of 3 tablespoons white vinegar, 1 teaspoon borax, and 2 cups hot water into a clean, recycled spray bottle and give it a few good shakes. Then spray the mixture on painted surfaces, tiles, windows, or wherever you see mold or mildew spots. Use a soft scrub brush to work the solution into the stains or just let it soak in.

Disinfect toilet bowls Want an easy way to keep your toilet looking and smelling clean? Pour 2 cups white vinegar into the bowl and let the solution soak overnight before flushing. Including this vinegar soak in your weekly cleaning regimen will also help keep away those ugly water rings that typically appear just above the water level.

Clean your toothbrush holder Get the grime, bacteria, and caked-on toothpaste drippings out of the grooves of your bathroom toothbrush holder by cleaning the openings with cotton swabs moistened with white vinegar.

Wash out your rinse cup If several people in your home use the same rinse cup after brushing their teeth, give it a weekly cleaning by filling it with equal parts water and white vinegar, or just full-strength vinegar, and let it sit overnight. Rinse thoroughly with cold water before using.

✳ VINEGAR **IN THE LAUNDRY**

Soften fabrics, kill bacteria, eliminate static, and more There are so many benefits to be reaped by adding 1 cup white vinegar to your washer's rinse cycle that it's surprising that you don't find it prominently mentioned inside the owner's manual of every washing machine sold. Here are the main ones:

- A single cup of vinegar will kill off any bacteria that may be present in your wash load, especially if it includes cloth diapers and the like.

- A cup of vinegar will keep your clothes coming out of the wash soft and smelling fresh—so you can kiss your fabric-softening liquids and sheets good-bye (unless, of course, you happen to like your clothes smelling of heavy perfumes).

- A cup of vinegar will brighten small loads of white clothes.

- Added to the last rinse, a cup of vinegar will keep your clothes lint- and static-free.

- Adding a cupful of vinegar to the last rinse will set the color of your newly dyed fabrics.

Clean your washing machine An easy way to periodically clean out soap scum and disinfect your clothes washer is to pour in 2 cups vinegar, then run the machine through a full cycle without any clothes or detergent. If your washer is particularly dirty, fill it with very hot water, add 2 gallons (7.5 liters) vinegar, and let the agitator run for 8-10 minutes. Turn off the washer and let the solution stand overnight. In the morning, empty the basin and run your washer through a complete cycle.

Stop reds from running Unless you have a fondness for pink-tinted clothing, take one simple precaution to prevent red—or other brightly dyed—washable clothes from ruining your wash loads. Soak your new garments in a few cups of undiluted white vinegar for 10-15 minutes before their first washing. You'll never have to worry about running colors again!

Brighten your loads Why waste money on that costly all-color bleach when you can get the same results using vinegar? Just add 1/2 cup white vinegar to your machine's wash cycle to brighten up the colors in each load.

Make new clothes ready to wear Get the chemicals, dust, odor, and whatever else out of your brand-new or secondhand clothes by pouring 1 cup white vinegar into the wash cycle the first time you wash them.

Whiten your dingy crew socks If it's getting increasingly difficult to identify the white socks in your sock drawer, here's a simple way to make them so bright you can't miss them. Start by adding 1 cup vinegar to 1 1/2 quarts (1.5 liters) tap water in a large pot. Bring the solution to a boil, then pour it into a bucket and drop in your dingy socks. Let them soak overnight. The next day, wash them as you normally would.

Get the yellow out of clothing To restore yellowed clothing, let the garments soak overnight in a solution of 12 parts warm water to 1 part vinegar. Wash them the following morning.

Soften up your blankets Add 2 cups white vinegar to your washer's rinse water (or a washtub filled with water) to remove soap residue from both cotton and wool blankets before drying. This will also leave them feeling fresh and soft as new.

Spray away wrinkles In a perfect world, laundry would emerge from the dryer freshly pressed. Until that day, you can often get the wrinkles out of clothes after drying by misting them with a solution of 1 part vinegar to 3 parts water. Once you're sure you didn't miss a spot, hang it up and let it air-dry. You may find this approach works better for some clothes than ironing; it's certainly a lot gentler on the material.

Flush your iron's interior To eliminate mineral deposits and prevent corrosion on your steam iron, give it an occasional cleaning by filling the reservoir with undiluted white vinegar. Place the iron in an upright position, switch on the steam setting, and let the vinegar steam through it for 5-10 minutes. Then refill the chamber with clean water and repeat. Finally, give the water chamber a good rinsing with cold, clean water.

Clean your iron's soleplate To remove scorch marks from the soleplate of your iron, scrub it with a paste made by heating up equal parts vinegar and salt in a small pan. Use a rag dipped in clean water to wipe away the remaining residue.

Sharpen your creases You'll find the creases in your freshly ironed clothes coming out a lot neater if you lightly spray them with equal parts water and vinegar before ironing them. For truly sharp creases in slacks and dress shirts, first dampen the garment using a cloth moistened in a solution of 1 part white vinegar and 2 parts water. Then place a brown paper bag over the crease and start ironing.

> **TAKE CARE** Keep cider vinegar out of the laundry. Using it to pretreat clothes or adding it to wash or rinse water may actually create stains rather than remove them. Use only distilled white vinegar for laundering.

Make old hemlines disappear Want to make those needle marks from an old hemline disappear for good? Just moisten the area with a cloth dipped in equal parts vinegar and water, then place it under the garment before you start ironing.

Erase scorch marks Did your iron get too hot under the collar—or perhaps on a sleeve or pant leg? You can often eliminate slight scorch marks by rubbing the spot with a cloth dampened with white vinegar, then blotting it with a clean towel. Repeat if necessary.

Dull the shine in your seat Want to get rid of that shiny
seat on your dark pants or skirt? Just brush
the area lightly with a soft recycled toothbrush dipped in equal parts white vinegar
and water, then pat dry with a soft towel.

Remove cigarette smell from suits If you find yourself in a situation where you wind up heading
home with the lingering smell of cigarette smoke on
your good suit or dress, you can remove the odor without having to take your
clothes to the dry cleaner. Just add 1 cup vinegar to a bathtub filled with the
hottest water your tap can muster. Close the door and hang your garments
above the steam. The smell should be gone after several hours.

Reshape your woolens Shrunken woolen sweaters and other items can usually be
stretched back to their former size or shape after boiling them in a solution of
1 part vinegar to 2 parts water for 25 minutes. Let the garment air-dry after
you've finished stretching it.

❄ **VINEGAR FOR REMOVING STAINS**

Brush off suede stains To eliminate a fresh grease spot on a suede jacket or skirt, gently
brush it with a soft toothbrush dipped in white vinegar. Let the spot air-dry,
then brush with a suede brush. Repeat if necessary. You can also generally tone
up suede items by lightly wiping them with a sponge dipped in vinegar.

Pat away water-soluble stains You can lift out many water-soluble stains—including
beer, orange and other fruit juices, black coffee or tea, and vomit—from your
cotton-blend clothing by patting the spot with a cloth or towel moistened with
undiluted white vinegar just before placing it in the wash. For large stains, you
may want to soak the garment overnight in a solution of 3 parts vinegar to
1 part cold water before washing.

Unset old stains Older, set-in stains will often come out in the wash after being pre-
treated with a solution of 3 tablespoons white vinegar and 2 tablespoons liquid
detergent in 1 quart (1 liter) warm water. Rub the solution into the stain, then
blot it dry before washing.

Sponge out serious stains Cola, hair dye, ketchup, and wine stains on washable cotton
blends should be treated as soon as possible (that is, within 24 hours). Sponge
the area with undiluted vinegar and launder immediately afterward. For severe
stains, add 1-2 cups vinegar to the wash cycle as well.

Get the rust out To remove a rust stain from your cotton work clothes, moisten the spot
with some full-strength vinegar and then rub in a bit of salt. If it's warm outdoors, let it dry in the sunlight (otherwise a sunny window will do), then toss
it in the wash.

Clear away crayon stains Somehow or other, kids often manage to get crayon marks on their clothing. You can easily get these stains off by rubbing them with a recycled toothbrush soaked in undiluted vinegar before washing them.

Remove rings from collars and cuffs Are you tired of seeing those old sweat rings around your shirt collars? What about the annoying discoloration along the edges of your cuffs? Give them the boot by scrubbing the material with a paste made from 2 parts white vinegar to 3 parts baking soda. Let the paste set for half an hour before washing. This approach also works to remove light mildew stains from clothing.

Pretreat perspiration stains Want to see those sweat marks disappear from shirts and other garments? Just pour a bit of vinegar directly onto the stain, and rub it into the fabric before placing the item in the wash. You can also remove deodorant stains from your washable shirts and blouses by gently rubbing the spot with undiluted vinegar before laundering.

Make pen ink disappear Did someone in your house come home with a leaky pen in his pocket? Treat the stain by first wetting it with some white vinegar, then rub in a paste of 2 parts vinegar to 3 parts cornstarch. Let the paste thoroughly dry before washing the item.

> *Kids' Stuff* Making **tie-dyed clothing** is tons of fun for kids of all ages. Start with a few **white T-shirts**, then use as many colors as allowed by your local supermarket's selection of unsweetened Kool-Aid powder mixes. Dissolve each package of **Kool-Aid** into 1 ounce **vinegar** in its own bowl or container. Use **rubber bands** to twist your shirts into unusual shapes, then dip them into the bowls (snap on a pair of rubber gloves beforehand). After drying, set your colors by placing a pillowcase or thin dish towel over each shirt and ironing it with a **medium-hot iron**. Wait at least 24 hours, then wash each shirt separately.

Soak out bloodstains Whether you nick yourself while shaving, or receive an unexpected scratch, it's important to treat the stains on your clothing as soon as possible; bloodstains are relatively easy to remove before they set but can be nearly impossible to wash out after 24 hours. If you can get to the stain before it sets, treat it by pouring full-strength white vinegar on the spot. Let it soak in for 5-10 minutes, then blot well with a cloth or towel. Repeat if necessary, then wash immediately.

✳ VINEGAR **IN THE GREAT OUTDOORS**

Use as insect repellent Planning a camping trip? Here's an old army trick to keep away the ticks and mosquitoes: Approximately three days before you leave, start taking 1 tablespoon apple cider vinegar three times a day. Continue using the vinegar throughout your trek, and you just might return home without a bite. Another time-honored approach to keep gnats and mosquitoes at bay is to moisten a cloth or cotton ball with white vinegar and rub it over your exposed skin.

Maintain fresh water when hiking Keep your water supply fresh and clean tasting when hiking or camping by adding a few drops of apple cider vinegar to your canteen or water bottle. It's also a good idea to use a half-vinegar, half-water rinse to clean out your water container at the end of each trip to kill bacteria and remove residue.

Clean outdoor furniture and decks If you live in a hot, humid climate, you're probably no stranger to seeing mildew on your wooden decks and patio furniture. But before you reach for the bleach, try these milder vinegar-based solutions:

- Keep some full-strength white vinegar in a recycled spray bottle and use it wherever you see any mildew growth. The stain will wipe right off most surfaces, and the vinegar will keep it from coming back for a while.

- Remove mildew from wood decks and wood patio furniture by sponging them off with a solution of 1 cup ammonia, 1/2 cup white vinegar, and 1/4 cup baking soda mixed in 1 gallon (3.7 liters) water. Keep an old toothbrush on hand to work the solution into corners and other tight spaces.

- To deodorize and inhibit mildew growth on outdoor plastic mesh furniture and patio umbrellas, mix 2 cups white vinegar and 2 tablespoons liquid dish soap in a bucket of hot water. Use a soft brush to work it into the grooves of the plastic as well as for scrubbing seat pads and umbrella fabric. Rinse with cold water; then dry in the sun.

Make a trap to lure flying insects Who wants to play host to a bunch of gnats, flies mosquitoes, or other six-legged pests when you're trying to have a cookout in your yard? Keep the flying gate-crashers at bay by giving them their own VIP section. Place a bowl filled with apple cider vinegar near some food, but away from you and guests. By the evening's end, most of your uninvited guests will be floating inside the bowl.

Give ants the boot Serve the ants on your premises with an eviction notice. Pour equal parts water and white vinegar into a spray bottle. Then spray it on anthills and around areas where you see the insects. Ants hate the smell of vinegar. It won't take long for them to move on to better-smelling quarters. Also keep the spray bottle handy for outdoor trips or to keep ants away from picnic or children's play areas. If you have lots of anthills around your property, try pouring full-strength vinegar over them to hasten the bugs' departure.

Clean off bird droppings Have the birds been using your patio or driveway for target practice again? Make those messy droppings disappear in no time by spraying them with full-strength apple cider vinegar. Or pour the vinegar onto a rag and wipe them off.

✱ VINEGAR IN THE GARDEN

Test soil acidity or alkalinity To do a quick test for excess alkalinity in the soil in your yard, place a handful of earth in a container and then pour in 1/2 cup white vinegar. If the soil fizzes or bubbles, it's definitely alkaline. Similarly, to see if your soil has a high acidity, mix the earth with 1/2 cup water and 1/2 cup baking soda. This time, fizzing would indicate acid in the soil. To find the exact pH level of your soil, have it tested or pick up a simple, do-it-yourself kit or meter.

Clean a hummingbird feeder Hummingbirds are innately discriminating creatures, so don't expect to see them flocking around a dirty, sticky, or crusted-over sugar-water feeder. Regularly clean your feeders by thoroughly washing them in equal parts apple cider vinegar and hot water. Rinse well with cold water after washing, and air-dry them outdoors in full sunlight before refilling them with food.

Speed germination of flower seeds You can get woody seeds, such as moonflower, passionflower, morning glory, and gourds, off to a healthier start by scarifying them—that is, lightly rubbing them between a couple of sheets of fine sandpaper—and soaking them overnight in a solution of 1/2 cup apple cider vinegar and 1 pint (half liter) warm water. Next morning, remove the seeds from the solution, rinse them off, and plant them. You can also use the solution (minus the sandpaper treatment) to start many herb and vegetable seeds.

Keep cut flowers fresh Everyone likes to keep cut flowers around as long as possible, and there are several good methods. One way is to mix 2 tablespoons apple cider vinegar and 2 tablespoons sugar with the vase water before adding the flowers. Be sure to change the water (with more vinegar and sugar, of course) every few days to enhance your flowers' longevity.

Tip A Myth About Vinegar

It's a rural legend that you can substantially lower your soil's pH (which is the same as raising its acidity), by simply pouring a vinegar-water solution around your yard. In fact, it takes a lot of hard work to lower the pH of high-alkaline soil. You can, however, use vinegar around the garden to help existing plants (see the tips below for treating plant diseases and encouraging blooms on azaleas and gardenias). But even that takes diligence—and repeated applications. Also, vinegar loses most of its potency after a rainfall. So you'll need to reapply any treatments after those surprise downpours.

Wipe away mealybugs They're among the most insidious and common pests on both houseplants and in the garden. But you can nip a mealybug invasion in the bud by dabbing the insects with a cotton swab dipped in full-strength white vinegar. You may need to use a handful of swabs, but the vinegar will kill the fluffy monsters and any eggs left behind. Be vigilant for missed targets, and break out more vinegar-soaked swabs if you spot bugs.

Eliminate insects around the garden If the bugs are feasting on the fruits and vegetables in your garden, give them the boot with this simple, nonpoisonous trap. Fill a 2-liter soda bottle with 1 cup apple cider vinegar and 1 cup sugar. Next, slice up a banana peel into small pieces, put them in the bottle, add 1 cup cold water, and shake it up. Tie a piece of string around the neck of the bottle and hang it from a low tree branch, or place it on the ground, to trap and kill the six-legged freeloaders. Replace used traps with new ones as needed.

Encourage blooms on azaleas and gardenias A little bit of acid goes a long way toward bringing out the blooms on your azalea and gardenia bushes—especially if you have hard water. Both bushes do best in acidic soils (with pH levels between 4 and 5.5). To keep them healthy and to produce more flowers, water them every week or so with 3 tablespoons white vinegar mixed in 1 gallon (3.7 liters) water. Don't apply the solution while the bush is in bloom, however; it may shorten the life of the flowers or harm the plant.

Stop yellow leaves on plants The sudden appearance of yellow leaves on plants accustomed to acidic soils—such as azaleas, hydrangeas, and gardenias—could signal a drop in the plant's iron intake or a shift in the ground's pH above a comfortable 5.0 level. Either problem can be resolved by watering the soil around the afflicted plants once a week for three weeks with 1 cup of a solution made by mixing 2 tablespoons apple cider vinegar in 1 quart (1 liter) water.

Treat rust and other plant diseases You can use vinegar to treat a host of plant diseases, including rust, black spot, and powdery mildew. Mix 2 tablespoons apple cider vinegar in 2 quarts (2 liters) water, and pour some into a recycled spray bottle. Spray the solution on your affected plants in the morning or early evening (when temperatures are relatively cool and there's no direct light on the plant) until the condition is cured.

Clean your lawn mower blades Grass, especially when it's damp, has a tendency to accumulate on your lawn mower blades after you cut the lawn—sometimes with grubs or other insects hiding inside. Before you park your mower back in the garage or toolshed, wipe down the blades with a cloth dampened with undiluted white vinegar. It will clean off leftover grass on the blades, as well as any pests that may have been planning to hang out awhile.

Keep out four-legged creatures Some animals—including cats, deer, dogs, rabbits, and raccoons—can't stand the scent of vinegar even after it has dried. You can keep these unauthorized visitors out of your garden by soaking several recycled rags in white vinegar, and placing them on stakes around your veggies. Resoak the rags about every 7-10 days.

SCIENCE FAIR

Mix 1/2 cup **vinegar** and 1/4 teaspoon **salt** in a **glass jar**. Add 25 **copper pennies** to the solution, and let them sit for five minutes. While you're waiting, take a large **iron nail** and clean it off with some baking soda applied to a damp sponge. Rinse off the nail, and place it into the solution. After 15 minutes, the **nail will be coated with copper**, while the pennies will shine like new. This is a result of the acetic acid in the vinegar combining with the copper on the pennies to form copper acetate, which then accumulates on the nail.

Exterminate dandelions and unwanted grass Are dandelions sprouting up in the cracks of your driveway or along the fringes of your patio? Make them disappear for good by spraying them with full-strength white or apple cider vinegar. Early in the season, give each plant a single spritz of vinegar in its midsection, or in the middle of the flower before the plants go to seed. Aim another shot near the stem at ground level so the vinegar can soak down to the roots. Keep an eye on the weather, though; if it rains the next day, you'll need to give the weeds another spraying.

✳ VINEGAR **PET CARE**

Keep the kitties away If you want to keep Snowball and Fluffy out of the kids' playroom, or discourage them from using your favorite easy chair as a scratching post, sprinkle some full-strength distilled white vinegar around the area or onto the object itself. Cats don't like the smell of vinegar and will avoid it.

Unmark your pet's spots When housebreaking a puppy or kitten, it'll often wet previously soiled spots. After cleaning up the mess, it's essential to remove the scent from your floor, carpeting, or sofa. And nothing does that better than vinegar:

● On a floor, blot up as much of the stain as possible. Then mop with equal parts white vinegar and warm water. (On a wood or vinyl floor, test a few drops of vinegar in an inconspicuous area to make sure it won't harm the finish.) Dry with a cloth or paper towel.

● For carpets, rugs, and upholstery, thoroughly blot the area with a towel or some rags. Then pour a bit of undiluted vinegar over the spot. Blot it up with a towel, then reapply the vinegar—let it air-dry. Once the vinegar dries, the spot should be completely deodorized

Add to pet's drinking water Adding a teaspoon of apple cider vinegar to your dog or cat's drinking water provides needed nutrients to its diet, gives it a shinier, healthier-looking coat, and acts as a natural deterrent to fleas and ticks.

Directly protect against fleas and ticks To give your dog effective flea and tick protection, fill a spray bottle with equal parts water and vinegar and apply it directly to the dog's coat and rub it in well. You may have more trouble doing this with cats, because they really hate the smell of the stuff.

Clean your pet's ears If you've noticed that Rover has been scratching around his ears a lot more than usual lately, a bit of vinegar could bring him some big relief. Swabbing your pet's ears with a cotton ball or soft cloth dabbed in solution of 2 parts vinegar and 1 part water will keep them clean and help deter ear mites and bacteria. It also soothes minor itches from mosquito bites and such. *Warning*: Do not apply vinegar to open lacerations. If you see a cut in your pet's ears, seek veterinary treatment.

Remove skunk odor If Fido has an unpleasant encounter with an ornery skunk, here are some ways to help him get rid of the smell:

● Bathe your pet in a mixture of 1/2 cup white vinegar, 1/4 cup baking soda, and 1 teaspoon liquid soap in 1 quart (1 liter) 3% hydrogen peroxide. Work the solution deep into his coat, give it a few minutes to soak in, then rinse him thoroughly with clean water.

● Bathe your pet in equal parts water and vinegar (preferably outdoors in a large washtub). Then repeat the procedure using 1 part vinegar to 2 parts water, followed by a good rinsing.

● If you happen to have an unscheduled meeting with skunk, use undiluted vinegar to get the smell out your own clothes. Let the affected clothing soak in the vinegar overnight.

✱ VINEGAR **FOR THE DO-IT-YOURSELFER**

Wash concrete off your skin Even though you wear rubber gloves when working with concrete, some of the stuff inevitably splashes on your skin. Prolonged contact with wet concrete can cause your skin to crack, and may even lead to eczema. Use undiluted white vinegar to wash dried concrete or mortar off your skin, then wash with warm, soapy water.

Remove paint fumes Place a couple of shallow dishes filled with undiluted white vinegar around a freshly painted room to quickly get rid of the strong paint smell.

Degrease grates, fans, and air-conditioner grilles Even in the cleanest of homes, air-conditioner grilles, heating grates, and fan blades eventually develop a layer of dust and grease. To clean them, wipe them with full-strength white vinegar. Use an old toothbrush to work the vinegar into the tight spaces on air-conditioner grilles and exhaust fans.

Disinfect air-conditioner and humidifier filters An air-conditioner or humidifier filter can quickly become inundated with dust, soot, pet dander, and even potentially harmful bacteria. Every 10 days or so, clean your filter in equal parts white vinegar and warm water. Let the filter soak in the solution for an hour, then simply squeeze it dry before using. If your filters are particularly dirty, let them soak overnight.

Keep the paint on your cement floors Painted cement floors have a tendency to peel after a while. But you can keep the paint stuck to the cement longer by giving the floor an initial coat of white vinegar before you paint it. Wait until the

 DID **You** KNOW?

You just came across an old, unopened bottle of vinegar, and you wonder: Is it still any good? The answer is an unqualified yes. In fact, vinegar has a practically limit-less shelf life. Its acid content makes it self-preserving and even negates the need for refrigeration (although many people mistakenly believe in refrigerating their open bottles). You won't see any changes in white vinegar over time, but some other types may change slightly in color or develop a hazy appearance or a bit of sediment. However, these are strictly cos-metic changes; the vinegar itself will be virtually unchanged.

vinegar has dried, then begin painting. This same technique will also help keep paint affixed to galvanized metal.

Get rid of rust If you want to clean up those rusted old tools you recently unearthed in your basement or picked up at a tag sale, soak them in full-strength white vinegar for several days. The same treatment is equally effective at removing the rust from corroded nuts and bolts. And you can pour vinegar on rusted hinges and screws to loosen them up for removal.

Peel off wallpaper Removing old wallpaper can be messy, but you can make it peel off easily by soaking it with a vinegar solution. Spray equal parts white vinegar and water on the wallpaper until it is saturated and wait a few minutes. Then zip the stuff off the wall with a wallpaper scraper. If it is stubborn, try carefully scoring the wallpaper with the scraper before you spritz.

Slow hardening of plaster Want to keep your plaster pliable a bit longer to get it all smoothed out? Just add a couple of tablespoons of white vinegar to your plaster mix. It will slow down the hardening process to give you the extra time you need.

Revive your paintbrushes To remove dried-on paint from a synthetic-bristle paintbrush, soak it in full-strength white vinegar until the paint dissolves and the bristles are soft and pliable, then wash in hot, soapy water. Does a paintbrush seem beyond hope? Before you toss it, try boiling it in 1-2 cups vinegar for 10 minutes, followed by a thorough washing in soapy water.

✳ Vodka

Make your own vanilla extract Here's an unusual homemade treat you can use to spice up a gift basket, and it takes only minutes to make. Get one real dried vanilla bean (available at specialty food stores) and slice it open from top to bottom. Place it in a glass jar and cover it with 3/4 cup vodka. Seal the jar, and let it rest

DID **You** KNOW?

Essential to James Bond's martini—and so intrinsic to Russian culture that its name derives from the Russian word for water (voda)—vodka was first made in the 1400s as an antiseptic and painkiller before it was drunk as a beverage. But what exactly is it? Classically, vodka starts as a soupy mixture of ground wheat or rye that's fermented (sugars in the grain are converted into alcohol by yeast), then distilled (heated until the alcohol evaporates and then condenses). Flavorings such as citrus were originally added to mask the taste of impurities, but are used today for enhancement and brand identification.

in a kitchen cabinet for 4-6 months, shaking it occasionally. Filter your home-made vanilla extract through an unbleached coffee filter or cheesecloth into a decorative bottle and watch the face of your favorite cook light up with pleasure!

Clean glass and jewelry In a pinch, a few drops of vodka will clean any kind of glass or jewelry with crystalline gemstones. So although people might look at you askance, you could dip a napkin into your vodka on the rocks to wipe away the grime on your eyeglasses or dunk your diamond ring for a few minutes to get it sparkling again. But don't try this with contact lenses! Also avoid getting alcohol on any gemstone that's not a crystal. Only diamonds, emeralds, and the like will benefit from a vodka bath.

Use as a hygienic soak Vodka is an alcohol, and like any alcohol, it kills germs. If you don't have ordinary rubbing alcohol on hand, use vodka instead. You can use it to soak razor blades you plan to reuse, as well as to clean hairbrushes, tooth-brushes, and pet brushes, or on anything else that might spread germs from person to person or animal to animal.

Keep cut flowers fresh The secret to keeping cut flowers looking good as long as pos-sible is to minimize the growth of bacteria in the water and to provide nourishment to replace what the flower would have gotten had it not been cut. Add a few drops of vodka (or any clear spirit) to the vase water for antibacterial action along with 1 teaspoon sugar. Change the water every other day, refreshing the vodka and sugar each time.

Kill weeds in the yard For a quick and easy weed killer, mix 1 ounce (30 milliliters) vodka, a few drops liquid dish soap, and 2 cups water in a spray bottle. Spray it on the weed leaves until the mixture runs off. Apply it at midday on a sunny day to weeds growing in direct sunlight, because the alcohol breaks down the waxy cuticle covering on leaves, leaving them susceptible to dehydration in sunlight. It won't work in shade.

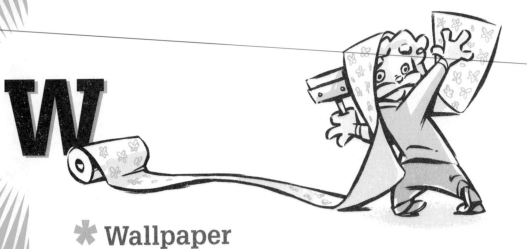

✳ Wallpaper

Line your drawers Wallpaper remnants can be a great substitute for shelf liner paper when used to line dresser drawers or closet shelves—especially designs with raised patterns or fabrics, which may add a bit of friction to prevent things from moving around. Cut the wallpaper into strips sized in both length and width to accommodate the space.

Restore a folding screen If you have an old folding screen that's become torn or stained over the years, give it a new, younger look by covering it with leftover wallpaper. Use masking tape to hold the strips at top and bottom if you don't want to glue it on top of the original material.

Protect schoolbooks If your child goes through book covers on textbooks on a semi-regular basis, get your hands on some old rolls of wallpaper. Book covers made of wallpaper are typically more rugged than even the traditional brown paper bag sleeves; they can hold their own against pens and pencils, and are much better at handling the elements, especially rain and snow.

Make a jigsaw puzzle What to do with your leftover wallpaper? Why not use a piece to make a jigsaw puzzle? Simply cut off a medium-sized rectangular piece and glue it onto a piece of thin cardboard. Once it's dried, cut it up into a bunch of curvy and angular shapes. It'll give you, or the kids, something to do on a rainy or snowbound day.

✳ Wax Paper

Fail-safe cake decorating You made a special birthday cake, and now comes the moment of truth: Can you pipe out the lettering in frosting on the first try? Not many of us can, so try this trick to make it easier. Cut a piece of wax paper the same size as your cake, using the cake pan as a guide. Then pipe the name and the message onto the paper and freeze it. After just half an hour it should be easy to handle. Loosen the frosting and slide it off onto the cake using a spatula. Everyone will think you're a cake-decorating professional!

Funnel spices into jars Filling narrow-mouthed spice jars can make a big mess on your kitchen counter. Roll a piece of wax paper into a funnel shape and pour spices into your jars without spilling a single mustard seed. In a pinch, you can even funnel liquids by using a couple of layers of wax paper offset so the seams in the layers don't line up.

Speed kitchen cleanup Wax paper can help keep all kinds of kitchen surfaces clean.

- Line vegetable and meat bins with a layer of wax paper. When it needs replacement, just wad it up and throw it in the trash or, if it's not stained with meat juices, the compost pile.

- If your kitchen cabinets don't extend to the ceiling, a layer of wax paper on top will catch dust and grease particles. Every month or two, just fold it up, discard it, and put a fresh layer down.

- If you're worried about meat juices getting into the pores of your cutting board, cover it with three layers of wax paper before slicing raw meat and throw the paper out immediately. It beats scrubbing the cutting board with bleach!

Tame the waffle-eating waffle iron Having trouble extricating waffles from your waffle iron? Nonstick surfaces don't last forever. You can't fix the problem permanently, but if you just want to get it to work today, put a layer of wax paper in between the plates of your waffle iron for a few minutes while it heats up. The wax will be transferred to the plates, temporarily helping waffles pop out again.

Uncork bottles with ease If you keep a bottle of cooking wine in your kitchen, you probably uncork it and recork it many times before using it up. Instead of struggling with the cork each time, wrap some wax paper around the cork before reinserting it. It'll be easier to remove the next time, and the paper helps keep little bits of cork from getting into the wine.

 DID *You* KNOW?

Wax paper is an example of how important packaging can be to a product's success. Before 1927, wax paper was sold in pre-cut sheets in envelopes, but housewives and deli owners alike were frustrated by the tendency of the sheets to stick together on warm summer days. Then an enterprising inventor, Nicholas Marcalus, put wax paper on a roll in a box with a built-in cutter, and the product as we know it today came to be. In fact, Reynolds wax paper is called Cut-Rite after this packaging innovation, which was awarded a patent and is used for a multitude of products today.

WAXPAPER*

Keep cast iron rust-free Cast iron devotees agree that this superior cooking material is well worth a little extra effort to keep it in tip-top shape. To prevent rust from forming on cast iron between uses, rub a sheet of wax paper over your skillet or Dutch oven after washing, while it's still warm. Then place the sheet between the pot and the lid to store.

Keep candles from staining table linens Candles in colors that coordinate with your dining room linens make a lovely finishing touch to table settings—and it's helpful to store them all together—but if you store the candles with table linens, the candle color can rub off on the linens. To avoid this, wrap colorful candles in plain wax paper before storage. Avoid paper with holiday patterns, which can also stain linens.

Store delicate fabrics Treasured lace doilies and other linens handed down in your family can decay quickly if not stored with care. A sheet of wax paper between each fabric piece will help block extraneous light and prevent transfer of dyes without trapping moisture.

Stop water spotting Company's coming, and you want every room of the house to look its best. To keep bathroom fixtures temporarily spotless, rub them with a sheet of wax paper after cleaning them. The wax that transfers will deflect water droplets like magic—at least until the next cleaning.

Give your car antenna a smooth ride If you have a newer vehicle, your car antenna probably retracts each time you turn off the ignition, carrying grime with it that can eventually bring your antenna (and your reception) to a grinding halt. Every now and then, rub the antenna with a piece of wax paper to coat the shaft and help it repel dirt.

Make a snow slide go faster Everyone knows, the more slippery the slide, the more fun it is! Keep tots swooshing on their tushes by balling up a large piece of wax paper and rubbing it all over the slide surface.

Kids' Stuff What kid wouldn't like **homemade "stained glass"** art that takes only minutes to make? First, make **crayon shavings** using a **vegetable peeler**. Keep each color separate. Put a paper towel or bag on your counter. Place a sheet of **wax paper** on top, sprinkle it with crayon shavings, and cover with another layer of wax paper and paper towel. Press it for a few minutes using a **warm iron** and remove the paper towel layers. Cut your new see-through art into **sun-catching medallions** or **colorful bookmarks** using craft scissors to create a decorative edge.

Protect surfaces from glue Woodworkers know that there's enough glue in a wood joint if some squeezes out when they clamp the joint. They also know that excess glue will be a real pain to remove if it drips on the workbench or, worse, bonds the clamping blocks to the project. To prevent this, cover the bench with strips of wax paper and put pieces of wax paper between the clamping blocks and the project. The glue won't adhere to, or soak through, the wax.

Make educational place mats One way to make learning fun is with personalized place mats featuring math facts or other lessons your child is trying to memorize. Take several flash cards and sandwich them between layers of wax paper cut to place-mat size. Sandwich that between two layers of paper towels and press it all with a warm iron to "laminate" the flash cards in place. Remove the paper towels before use.

super item
62 *uses!* **WD-40**

* WD-40 **AROUND THE HOUSE**

Treat your shoes Spray WD-40 on new leather shoes before you start wearing them regularly. It will help prevent blisters by softening the leather and making the shoes more comfortable. Keep the shoes waterproof and shiny by spraying them periodically with WD-40 and buffing gently with a soft cloth. To give the old "soft shoo" to squeaky shoes, spray some WD-40 at the spot where the sole and heel join and the squeaks will cease.

Separate stuck glassware What can you do when you reach for a drinking glass and get two locked together, one stuck tightly inside the other? You don't want to risk breaking one or both by trying to pull them apart. Stuck glasses will separate with ease if you squirt some WD-40 on them, wait a few seconds for it to work its way between the glasses, and then gently pull the glasses apart. Remember to wash the glasses thoroughly before you use them.

Free stuck Lego blocks When Junior's construction project hits a snag because some of the plastic blocks are stuck together, let WD-40 help get them unstuck. Spray a little on the blocks where they are locked together, then wiggle them gently and pull them apart. The lubricant in WD-40 will penetrate into the fine seam where the blocks are joined.

Tone down polyurethane shine A new coat of polyurethane can sometimes make a wood floor look a little *too* shiny. To tone down the shine and cut the glare, spray some WD-40 onto a soft cloth and wipe up the floor with it.

Remove strong glue You didn't wear protective gloves when using that super-strong glue and now some of it is super-stuck to your fingers! Don't panic. Just reach for the WD-40, spray some directly on the sticky fingers, and rub your hands together until your fingers are no longer sticky. Use WD-40 to remove the glue from other unwanted surfaces as well.

WD-40*

375

● Do not spray WD-40 near an open flame or other heat source, or near electrical currents or battery terminals. Always disconnect appliances before spraying.

● Do not place a WD-40 can in direct sunlight or on hot surfaces. Never store it in temperatures above 120°F (50°C) or puncture the pressurized can.

● Use WD-40 in well-ventilated areas. Never swallow or inhale it (if swallowed, call a physician immediately).

Get off that stuck ring When pulling and tugging can't get that ring off your finger, reach for the WD-40. A short burst of WD-40 will get the ring to slide right off. Remember to wash your hands after spraying them with WD-40.

Free stuck fingers Use WD-40 to free Junior's finger when he gets it stuck in a bottle. Just spray it on the finger, let it seep in, and pull the finger out. Be sure to wash Junior's hand and the bottle afterward.

Loosen zippers Stubborn zippers on jackets, pants, backpacks, and sleeping bags will become compliant again after you spray them with WD-40. Just spray it on and pull the zipper up and down a few times to distribute the lubricant evenly over all the teeth. If you want to avoid getting the WD-40 on the fabric, spray it on a plastic lid; then pick it up and apply it with an artist's brush.

Exterminate roaches and repel insects Don't let cockroaches, insects, or spiders get the upper hand in your home.

● Keep a can of WD-40 handy, and when you see a roach, spray a small amount directly on it for an instant kill.

● To keep insects and spiders out of your home, spray WD-40 on windowsills and frames, screens, and door frames. Be careful not to inhale the fumes when you spray and do not do this at all if you have babies or small children at home.

Keep puppies from chewing Your new puppy is adorable, but will he *ever* stop chewing up the house? To keep puppies from chewing on telephone and television-cable lines, spray WD-40 on the lines. The pups hate the smell.

Clean and lubricate guitar strings To clean, lubricate, and prevent corrosion on guitar strings, apply a small amount of WD-40 after each playing. Spray the WD-40 on a rag and wipe the rag over the strings rather than spraying directly on the strings—you don't want WD-40 to build up on the guitar neck or body.

Keep wooden tool handles splinter-free No tools can last forever, but you can prolong the life of your wood-handled tools by preventing splintering. To keep wooden handles from splintering, rub a generous amount of WD-40 into the wood. It will shield the wood from moisture and other corrosive elements and keep it smooth and splinter-free for the life of the tool.

Unstick wobbly shopping-cart wheels Attention supermarket shoppers: Keep a can of WD-40 handy whenever you go food shopping. Then when you get stuck with a sticky, wobbly-wheeled shopping cart, you can spray the wheels to reduce friction and wobbling. Less wobbling means faster shopping.

Remove chewing gum from hair It's one of an adult's worst nightmares: chewing gum tangled in a child's hair. You don't have to panic or run for the scissors. Simply spray the gummed-up hair with WD-40, and the gum will comb out with ease. Make sure you are in a well-ventilated area when you spray and take care to avoid contact with the child's eyes.

? ? DID *You* KNOW?

- In 1953 Norm Larsen founded the Rocket Chemical Company in San Diego and, with two employees, set out to develop a rust-preventing solvent and degreaser for the aerospace industry. On the fortieth try, they succeeded in creating a "water displacement" compound. The name WD-40 stands for "Water Displacement—40th Try."

- In 1958, a few years after WD-40's first industrial use, the company put it in aerosol cans and sold it for home use—inspired by employees who snuck cans out of the plant to use at home.

- In 1962, when U.S. astronaut John Glenn circled the Earth in *Friendship VII*, the space capsule was coated with WD-40 and so was the Atlas missile used to boost it into space.

- In 1969 Rocket Chemical renamed itself the WD-40 Company after the product.

Break in a new baseball glove Use WD-40 instead of neat's-foot oil to break in a new baseball glove. Spray the glove with WD-40, put a baseball in the palm, and fold it sideways. Take a rubber band or belt and tie it around the folded glove. The WD-40 will help soften the leather and help it form around the baseball. Keep the glove tied up overnight, and then wear it for a while so it will begin to fit the shape of your hand.

✳ WD-40 **FOR CLEANING THINGS**

Remove tough scuff marks Those tough black scuff marks on your kitchen floor won't be so tough anymore if you spray them with WD-40. Use WD-40 to help remove tar and scuff marks on all your hard-surfaced floors. It won't harm the surface, and you won't have to scrub nearly as much. Remember to open the windows if you are cleaning a lot of marks.

Clean dried glue Clean dried glue from virtually any hard surface with ease: Simply spray WD-40 onto the spot, wait at least 30 seconds, and wipe clean with a damp cloth.

Degrease your hands When you're done working on the car and your hands are greasy and blackened with grime, use WD-40 to help get them clean. Spray a small amount of WD-40 into your hands and rub them together for a few seconds, then wipe with a paper towel and wash with soap and water. The grease and grime will wash right off.

Remove decals You don't need a chisel or even a razor blade to remove old decals, bumper stickers, or cellophane tape. Just spray them with WD-40, wait about 30 seconds, and wipe them away.

Remove stickers from glass What were the manufacturers thinking when they put that sticker on the glass? Don't they know how hard it is to get off? When soap and water doesn't work and you don't want to ruin a fingernail or risk scratching delicate glass with a blade, try a little WD-40. Spray it on the sticker and glass, wait a few minutes, and then use a no-scratch spatula or acrylic scraper to scrape the sticker off. The solvents in WD-40 cause the adhesive to lose its stickiness.

Wipe away tea stains To remove tea stains from countertops, spray a little WD-40 on a sponge or damp cloth and wipe the stain away.

Clean carpet stains Don't let ink or other stains ruin your fine carpet. Spray the stain with WD-40, wait a minute or two, and then use your regular carpet cleaner or gently cleanse with a sponge and warm, soapy water. Continue until the stain is completely gone.

Get tomato stains off clothes That homegrown tomato looked so inviting you couldn't resist. Now your shirt or blouse has a big, hard-to-remove tomato stain! To

WD-40*

remove stains from fresh tomatoes or tomato sauce, spray some WD-40 directly on the spot, wait a couple of minutes, and wash as usual.

Clean toilet bowls You don't need a bald genie or a specialized product to clean ugly gunk and lime stains from your toilet bowl. Use WD-40 instead: Spray it into the bowl for a couple of seconds and swish with a nylon toilet brush. The solvents in the WD-40 will help dissolve the gunk and lime.

Clean your fridge When soap and water can't get rid of old bits of food stuck in and around your refrigerator, it's time to reach for the WD-40. After clearing all foodstuffs from the areas to be treated, spray a small amount of WD-40 on each resistant spot. Then wipe them away with a rag or sponge. Make sure you wash off all the WD-40 before returning food to the fridge.

Condition leather furniture Keep your favorite leather recliner and other leather furniture in tip-top shape by softening and preserving it with WD-40. Just spray it on and buff with a soft cloth. The combination of ingredients in WD-40 will clean, penetrate, lubricate, and protect the leather.

Pretreat blood and other stains Oh no! Your kid fell down and cut himself while playing, and there's blood all over his brand-new shirt. After you tend to the wound, give some first aid to the shirt too. Pretreat the bloodstains with WD-40. Spray some directly on the stains, wait a couple of minutes, and then launder as usual. The WD-40 will help lift the stain so that it will come out easily in the wash. Try to get to the stain while it is still fresh, because once it sets, it will be harder to get rid of. Use WD-40 to pretreat other stubborn stains on clothing, such as lipstick, dirt, grease, and ink stains.

Clean chalkboards When it comes to cleaning and restoring a chalkboard, WD-40 is the teacher's pet. Just spray it on and wipe with a clean cloth. The chalkboard will look as clean and fresh as it did on the first day of school.

Remove marker and crayon marks Did the kids use your wall as if it was a big coloring book? Not to worry! Simply spray some WD-40 onto the marks and wipe with a clean rag. WD-40 will not damage the paint or most wallpaper (test fabric or other fancy wall coverings first). It will also remove marker and crayon marks from furniture and appliances.

✳ WD-40 **IN THE YARD**

Rejuvenate the barbecue grill To make a worn old barbecue grill look like new again, spray it liberally with WD-40, wait a few seconds, and scrub with a wire brush. Remember to use WD-40 only on a grill that is not in use and has cooled off.

Renew faded plastic furniture Bring color and shine back to faded plastic patio furniture. Simply spray WD-40 directly on the surface and wipe with a clean, dry cloth. You'll be surprised at the results.

Prevent snow buildup on windows Does the weather forecast predict a big winter snowstorm? You can't stop the snow from falling, but you can prevent it from building up on your house's windows. Just spray WD-40 over the outside of your windows before the snow starts and the snow won't stick.

Keep shovel or chute snow-free Here is a simple tip to make shoveling snow quicker and less strenuous by keeping the snow from sticking to your shovel and weighing it down. Spray a thin layer of WD-40 on the shovel blade, and the snow will slide right off. If you have a snow thrower, spray WD-40 on the inside of the chute so snow won't stick and clog the chute.

Protect a bird feeder To keep squirrels from taking over a bird feeder, spray a generous amount of WD-40 on top of the feeder. The pesky squirrels will slide right off.

Remove cat's paw marks Your cat may seem like a member of the family most of the time, but that isn't what you are thinking about when you have to clean a slew of paw marks off patio furniture or the hood of your car. To remove the paw marks, spray some WD-40 on them and wipe with a clean rag.

Keep animals from flowerbeds Animals just love to play in your garden, digging up your favorite plants you worked so hard to grow. What animals *don't* love is the smell of WD-40. To keep the animals out and your flowers looking beautiful all season, spray WD-40 evenly over the flowerbeds one or more times over the course of the season.

Tip **The Little Red Straw**

> "I lost the red straw!" has been a common cry among countless users of WD-40 over the years. In response, the company introduced a notched cap, designed to hold the straw in place across the top of the can when not in use. Because the straw exceeds the width of the can by a substantial margin, the notch may be of little use to those with limited storage space. To save space, store the straw by bending it inside the lip of the can or simply tape it to the side as it was when first purchased. A snug rubber band will also work well.

Repel pigeons Are the pigeons using your balcony more than you are? If pigeons and their feathers and droppings are keeping you from enjoying the view from your balcony, spray the entire area, including railings and furniture, with WD-40. The pigeons can't stand the smell and they'll fly the coop.

Keep wasps from building nests Don't let yellow jackets and other wasps ruin your spring and summer fun. Their favorite place to build nests is under eaves. So next spring mist some WD-40 under all the eaves of your house. It will block the wasps from building their nests there.

Remove doggie-doo Uh-oh, now you've stepped in it! Few things in life are more unpleasant than cleaning doggie-doo from the bottom of a sneaker, but the task will be a lot easier if you have a can of WD-40 handy. Spray some on the affected sole and use an old toothbrush to clean the crevices. Rinse with cold water and the sneakers will be ready to hit the pavement again. Now, don't forget to watch where you step!

Kill thistle plants Don't let pesky prickly weeds like bull and Russian thistle ruin your yard or garden. Just spray some WD-40 on them and they'll wither and die.

✳ WD-40 **IN THE GREAT OUTDOORS**

Winterproof boots and shoes Waterproof your winter boots and shoes by giving them a coat of WD-40. It'll act as a barrier so water can't penetrate the material. Also use WD-40 to remove ugly salt stains from boots and shoes during the winter months. Just spray WD-40 onto the stains and wipe with a clean rag. Your boots and shoes will look almost as good as new.

Remove old wax from skis and snowboards To remove old wax and dirt from skis and snowboards, spray the base sparingly with WD-40 before scraping with an acrylic scraper. Use a brass brush to further clean the base and remove any oxidized base material.

Protect your boat from corrosion To protect your boat's outer finish from salt water and corrosion, spray WD-40 on the stern immediately after each use. The short time it takes will save you from having to replace parts, and it will keep your boat looking like it did on the day you bought it for a long time to come.

Remove barnacles on boats Removing barnacles from the bottom of a boat is a difficult and odious task but you can make it easier and less unpleasant with the help of some WD-40. Spray the area generously with WD-40, wait a few seconds, and then use a putty knife to scrape off the barnacles. Spray any remnants with WD-40 and scrape again. If necessary, use sandpaper to get rid of all of the remnants and corrosive glue still left by the barnacles.

Spray on fishing lures Salmon fishermen in the Pacific Northwest spray their lures with WD-40 because it attracts fish and disguises the human odor that can scare them off and keep them from biting. You can increase the catch on your next fishing trip by bringing a can of WD-40 along with you and spraying it on *your* lures or live bait before you cast. But first check local regulations to make sure the use of chemical-laced lures and bait is legal in your state.

Tip **Don't Overdo the WD-40**

> When you need to apply tiny amounts of WD-40 to a specific area, such as the electrical contacts on an electric guitar, an aerosol spray is overkill. Instead, store some WD-40 in a clean nail-varnish bottle (with cap brush) and brush on as needed.

Untangle fishing lines To loosen a tangled fishing line, spray it with WD-40 and use a pin to undo any small knots. Also use WD-40 to extend the life of curled (but not too old) fishing lines. Just take out the first 10 to 20 feet of line and spray it with WD-40 the night before each trip.

Clean and protect golf clubs Whether you're a duffer or a pro, you can protect and clean your clubs by spraying them with WD-40 after each use. Also use WD-40 to help loosen stuck-on spikes.

Remove burrs To remove burrs from a horse's mane or tail without tearing its hair out (or having to cut any of its hair off!) just spray on some WD-40. You'll be able to slide the burrs right out. This will work for dogs and cats, too.

Protect horses' hooves Winter horseback riding can be fun if you are warmly dressed but it can be downright painful to your horse if ice forms on the horseshoes. To keep ice from forming on horseshoes during cold winter rides, spray the bottom of the horse's hooves with WD-40 before you set out.

Keep flies off cows If flies are tormenting your cows, just spray some WD-40 on the cows. Flies hate the smell and they'll stay clear. Take care not to spray any WD-40 in the cows' eyes.

? DID *You* KNOW?

WD-40 is one of the few products with its own fan club. The official WD-40 Fan Club has more than 63,000-members and is growing. Over the years members have contributed thousands of unique and sometimes strange uses for the product. But according to Gary Ridge, president and CEO of the WD-40 Company, the strangest use of all occurred in China. "In Hong Kong some time ago there was a python caught in the suspension of a public bus," he said. "They used WD-40 to get that little slippery guy out of there!"

Clean your hearing aid To give your hearing aid a good cleaning, use a cotton swab dipped in WD-40. Do not use WD-40 to try to loosen up the volume control (it will loosen it too much).

Relieve bee-sting pain For fast relief of pain from a bee, wasp, or hornet sting, reach for the WD-40 can and spray it directly on the bite site. It will take the "ouch" right out.

Remove stuck prostheses If you wear a prosthetic device, you know how difficult it can be to remove at times, especially when no one is around to help. Next time you get stuck with a stuck prosthesis, spray some WD-40 at the junction where it attaches. The chemical solvents and lubricants in WD-40 will help make it easier to remove.

Keep dead bugs off car grille It's bad enough that your car grille and hood have to get splattered with bugs every time you drive down the interstate, but do they have to be so darn tough to scrape off? The answer is no. Just spray some WD-40 on the grille and hood before going for a drive and most of the critters will slide right off. The few bugs that are left will be easy to wipe off later without damaging your car's finish.

Clean and restore license plate To help restore a license plate that is beginning to rust, spray it with WD-40 and wipe with a clean rag. This will remove light surface rust and will also help prevent more rust from forming. It's an easy way to clean up lightly rusted plates and it won't leave a greasy feel.

Remove stuck spark plugs To save time replacing spark plugs, do it the NASCAR way. NASCAR mechanics spray WD-40 on stuck plugs so they can remove them quickly and easily. Perhaps that's one reason why WD-40 has been designated as NASCAR's "official multi-purpose problem-solver."

Coat a truck bed For easy removal of a truck-bed liner, spray the truck bed with WD-40 before you install the liner. When it comes time to remove it, the liner will slide right out.

Remove "paint rub" from another car You return to your parked car to find that while you were gone, another vehicle got a bit too close for comfort. Luckily there's no dent, but now your car has a blotch of "paint rub" from the other car on it. To remove paint-rub stains on your car and restore its original finish, spray the affected area with WD-40, wait a few seconds, and wipe with a clean rag.

Revive spark plugs Can't get your car to start on a rainy or humid day? To get your engine purring, just spray some WD-40 on the spark-plug wires before you try starting it up again. WD-40 displaces water and keeps moisture away from the plugs.

WD-40 ✳

Clean oil spots from driveway Did a leaky oil pan leave a big ugly spot in the middle of your concrete driveway? To get rid of an unsightly oil spot, just spray it with a generous amount of WD-40 and then hose it down with water.

✳ Weather Stripping

Keep appliances in place Affixing small pieces of weather stripping to the bottom of telephones, electric can openers, PC speakers, and similar items will help keep them from sliding off counters or desktops.

Add traction to boots Some rubber boots may be great at keeping out moisture, but don't prevent you from slipping on ice-, snow-, or slush-covered surfaces. But you can usually improve the traction of your waterproof footwear by gluing a few strips of flat weather stripping onto the toe, middle, and heel sections.

Get a grip on tools Wrapping the handles of tools such as hammers, axes, and wrenches with flat weather stripping will not only give you a better and more comfortable grip on them, but it might even prevent wooden handles from getting damaged. Spiral the weather stripping around the handle, overlapping it half a width.

Fix leaky car windows Use small slivers of household weather stripping to patch up the dented weather stripping around car windows to prevent wind and water from getting inside your car. You can also use it to firm up sagging rubber gaskets around your car's trunk or doors.

✳ Window Cleaner

Reduce swelling from bee stings Spritzing some window cleaner on a bee sting is a quick way to reduce the swelling and pain. But first be sure to remove any stinger. Flick it sideways to get it out—don't tweeze it—then spray. Use only spray-on window cleaner that contains ammonia and never use a concentrated product. It is the small amount of ammonia that does the work, and bee-keepers have known for years that a very dilute solution of ammonia helps relieve stings.

Get off that stuck ring That ring felt a little tight going on, and now ... oops!... it's stuck. Spray a little window cleaner on your finger for lubrication and ease the ring off.

Clean your jewelry Use window cleaner to spruce up jewelry that is all metal or has crystalline gemstones, such as diamonds or rubies. Spray on the cleaner, then use an old toothbrush for cleaning. But don't do this if the piece has opaque stones such as opal or turquoise or organic gems such as coral or pearl. The ammonia and detergents in the cleaner can discolor these porous lovelies.

Remove stubborn laundry stains If laundering with detergent isn't enough to get tough stains such as blood, grass, or tomato sauce out of a fabric, try a clear ammonia-based spray-on window cleaner instead. (It's the ammonia in the window cleaner that does the trick, and you want uncolored cleaner to avoid staining the fabric.) Spray the stain with the window cleaner and let it sit for up to 15 minutes. Blot with a clean rag, rinse with cool water, and launder again. A few tips:

- Do a test on a seam or other inconspicuous part of the garment to see if the color runs.

- Use cool water and don't put the garment in the dryer until the stain is completely gone.

- Don't use this on silk, wool, or their blends.

- If the fabric color seems changed after using window cleaner on it, moisten the fabric with white vinegar and rinse it with water. Acidic vinegar will neutralize alkaline ammonia.

DID You KNOW?

Will spraying window cleaner on a pimple really help make it go away? Although the formula varies by brand, window cleaners generally contain ammonia, detergents, solvents, and alcohol. This combination will clean, disinfect, and dry out skin. So as long as you keep it out of your eyes and have no allergies to the ingredients, it probably will help suppress pimples.

✳ Yogurt

Make moss "paint" for the garden Wouldn't it be nice to simply paint some moss between the cracks of your stone walkway, on the sides of flowerpots, or anywhere else you want it to grow? Well, you can. Just dump a cup of plain active-culture yogurt into your blender along with a handful of common lawn moss and about a cup of water. Blend for about 30 seconds. Use a paintbrush to spread the mixture wherever you want moss to grow—as long as the spot is cool and shady. Mist the moss occasionally until it gets established.

Make a facial mask You don't have to go to a spa to give your face a quick assist:

- To cleanse your skin and tighten the pores, slather some plain yogurt on your face and let it sit for about 20 minutes.

- For a revitalizing facial mask, mix 1 teaspoon plain yogurt with the juice from 1/4 slice of orange, some of the orange pulp, and 1 teaspoon aloe. Leave the mixture on your face for at least five minutes before rinsing it off.

Relieve sunburn For quick, temporary relief of mild sunburn, apply cold plain yogurt. The yogurt adds much needed moisture and, at the same time, its coldness soothes. Rinse with cool water.

Make play finger paint Ready for some messy rainy-day fun? Mix food coloring with yogurt to make finger paints and let the little ones go wild. You can even turn it into a lesson about primary and secondary colors. For example, have the kids put a few drops of yellow food coloring and a few drops of blue in the yogurt to make green finger paint. Or mix red and blue to produce purple.

Cure dog or cat flatulence If Bowser has been a bit odoriferous lately, the problem may be a lack of the friendly digestive bacteria that prevent gas and diarrhea. The active culture in plain yogurt can help restore the helpful bacteria. Add 2 teaspoons yogurt to the food for cats or small dogs weighing up to 14 pounds (6 kilograms). Add 1 tablespoon for medium-sized dogs weighing 15-34 pounds (7-15 kilograms). Add 2 tablespoons for large dogs weighing 35-84 pounds (16-38 kilograms). Add 3 tablespoons for dogs larger than that.

✳ Zippers

Secure your valuables Nothing ruins a vacation like reaching into your pocket and discovering it has been picked. To keep your wallet, passport, and other valuables safe, sew a zipper into the inside pocket of your jacket to keep items safely zipped inside.

Make a sock puppet Create a happy sock puppet that will keep kids amused for hours. Just sew on buttons for the nose and eyes and some yarn for hair, and use a small smiling upturned zipper for the mouth.

Create convertible pants Here's a great idea for hikers and bikers who like to travel light. Cut the legs off a pair of jeans or other comfortable pants above the knee. Then reattach the legs with zippers. Zip off the legs when it gets warm, zip them back on for cool mornings and evenings. Besides lightening your load, you won't need to search for a place to change.

✳ Zucchini

Use as a rolling pin A large zucchini works great for rolling out dough for biscuits or piecrust. The zucchini has just the right shape and weight, and the dough won't stick to its smooth skin.

Use as exercise weights Zucchini come in a large range of sizes, so you'll have no trouble finding a couple that are just the right weight for your arm exercises.

Use as Mr. Zucchini Head Got some bored kids on your hands? Dust off that old Mr. Potato Head set and hand the youngsters a couple of large zucchini. The new vegetable is sure to renew their interest in the old toy.

Juggle 'em! Okay, okay, we're impressed. You can juggle three balls. Now let's see how you do with three zucchini!

Index

Note: **Boldface** entries and page numbers refer to main A-Z headings in text.

﹡ Indicates a Super Item.

391

SCIENCE FAIR FEATURES

These simple experiments for kids demonstrate basic science using everyday items.

398